LifePrints

ESL FOR ADULTS

TEACHER'S EDITION

SECOND EDITION 3

Janet Podnecky

with
Allene Guss Grognet

and
JoAnn (Jodi) Crandall

New Readers Press

LifePrints: ESL for Adults 3, Teacher's Edition, 2nd ed.
ISBN 978-1-56420-315-1

Copyright © 2002, 1995 New Readers Press
New Readers Press
Division of ProLiteracy Worldwide
1320 Jamesville Avenue, Syracuse, New York 13210
www.newreaderspress.com

Printed in the United States of America
9   8   7   6   5   4   3

All proceeds from the sale of New Readers Press materials
support literacy programs in the United States and worldwide.

Developmental Editor: Paula L. Schlusberg
Copy Editor: Judi Lauber
Production Director: Heather Witt
Designer: Fran Forstadt
Cover Designer: Kimbrly Koennecke
Cover Illustration: James P. Wallace
Production Specialists: Debbie Christiansen, Carolyn Boehmer

Series Development: Robert Ventre Associates, Inc.
                        Course Crafters, Inc.

Table of Contents

Introduction: Using *LifePrints* 4
    Student Performance Levels 20
    Scope and Sequence 22

Preliminary Lesson 24

Unit 1   **Continuing Education** 26
Unit 2   **What the Community Offers** 42
Unit 3   **Making Ends Meet** 58
Unit 4   **Living with Machines** 74
Unit 5   **Travels in America** 90
Unit 6   **Discovering Patterns** 106
Unit 7   **Problems on the Job** 112
Unit 8   **Saving the Environment** 128
Unit 9   **Real Costs of a Car** 143
Unit 10 **Under the Law** 158
Unit 11 **Can I Buy a House?** 173
Unit 12 **Discovering Patterns** 188

Tapescripts 198

Index of Functions 215
Index of Structures 216

Introduction:
Using *LifePrints*

Welcome to *LifePrints*. This introduction to the Teacher's Edition will help you understand the rationale behind the program and the relationship among its various components. It will also explain the methodology inherent in the units of this Teacher's Edition (TE) and give you a step-by-step guide to conducting the suggested exercises and activities.

There are eight major sections in this introduction:

- I Philosophy/Principles of the Program
- II Principles of Second Language Acquisition
- III Creating a Learner-Centered Environment
- IV The *LifePrints* Program
- V Developing Literacy and Reading Skills at Level 3
- VI Features of Student Book 3 Lessons
- VII Testing and Assessment
- VIII Classroom Management

The core of the introduction is section VI, which describes the activities and exercise types for developing oral/aural language and reading and writing at this level.

I

Philosophy/Principles of the Program

LifePrints begins with the premise that adult language learners bring diverse life experiences that are rich sources of sharing in the ESL class. These experiences, together with the learners' current needs and desires, form the basis for learning the new language. By tapping into familiar roles and experiences, *LifePrints* allows such learners to see their past experiences as valuable in their new environment and helps them sustain their dignity during a time of transition.

LifePrints also assumes that adults enter the ESL classroom with a life-centered or task-centered orientation to learning. Adults perform many different roles in their daily lives. They are worker, spouse, parent, friend, citizen, and more. These roles often become sources of their self-identity. The role of student may be a new and

frightening one to many adult ESL learners. They do not necessarily want to learn *about* the English language; they want to learn to *use* English in performing their various adult roles. For them, English is not an end in itself; it is a tool with which to do something else. Adult ESL students are fully functional, at least orally, in their native language. *LifePrints* gives them the ability to start transferring to a new language and a new culture what they have done and can do as adults.

The organizing principle of *LifePrints* is not language; it is context. Language learning is contextualized in the everyday life experiences of immigrants, their neighbors, their co-workers. The lives of the characters in the book are entry points into the lives of the individual adult learners, and the lessons immerse the learners in situations where they can hear and see and practice language that is relevant to contexts in their own lives. The linguistic and cultural skills presented in the pages of *LifePrints* are transferable to real contexts in the lives of adult ESL students.

Another principle of this series is authenticity. What would a native speaker hear or say or read or write in a given context? What communicative role do English-language speakers play in a given situation? Are they primarily listeners, as when a doctor is giving them medical advice? Or are they speakers, as when giving someone directions to the library? Are they readers, as when looking up a telephone number? Or are they writers, as when completing a work log at the end of their shift? Or do they combine skills, like listening and writing when taking a telephone message, or reading and writing when completing a form? Learners are asked to practice only those linguistic skills that are authentic to the contexts or roles in which they will find themselves using English.

II

Principles of Second Language Acquisition

The acquisition of a second language is a complex process, representing a delicate balance between the learner and the learning situation. There is no single way in which all learners acquire another language. Many factors pertaining to each learner come into play, including age, preferred learning style, previous education, first language and its similarity to English, and motivation. The teacher has little control over these factors. What the teacher can do, however, is shape and reshape the language-learning environment so that all learners have the greatest opportunity to acquire the English language skills they need to function as adults.

Throughout this introduction, we use the terms *acquisition* and *learning* interchangeably, irrespective of the cognitive processes involved. Some researchers and teachers contrast these two terms, assuming that they represent two different psychological processes. They apply *acquisition* to "picking up a language through exposure, using subconscious processes" and *learning* to the "conscious study of a second language." Other researchers and teachers argue that a sharp distinction between *acquisition* and *learning* is theoretical, not real. In both the acquisition and learning modes, basic principles underlie curriculum development.

These are some of the principles that guided the development of *LifePrints:*

- **The goal of language learning is communication in both oral and written form.**
  Learners should emerge from the language-learning classroom better able to understand and make themselves understood, as well as having greater facility in reading and writing English, than when they entered the classroom. Without being fluent in English, they can communicate on various levels, as described in the Student Performance Levels document (pages 20–21).

- **Communication is a process, not a sequence of memorized patterns or drill and practice exercises.**
  Function is more important than form. That is, what the learner *does* with language is more important than what he or she *knows about* language. Errors are therefore a necessary step in language acquisition. What is being communicated should be the focus, not the accuracy of what is said or correctness in the form of language. This is not to say that form—grammar, punctuation, and pronunciation, for example—is of no concern. Teachers need to focus on form, but at the right time in the learning process and in terms of furthering meaning. Too much attention to form too early will inhibit rather than encourage communication.

- **Language is most effectively learned in authentic contexts.**
  Contexts should reflect the world in which learners are expected to communicate in English and, as much as possible, they should come from the learners themselves. A corollary to this principle is that language is best presented not as isolated sentences or words but as meaningful discourse. The learning of grammar should also emerge from authentic contexts and should comprise a process by which learners discover patterns in language they already know and use.

- **Comprehension precedes production.**
  Learners need time to listen to language and to absorb what is happening in a variety of

communicative situations. They need many and varied opportunities in which to be exposed to spoken and written English, using visual clues such as pictures, film and video, and realia (things from the real world that learners can see and touch).

- **Production of language, both oral and written, will most likely emerge in stages.**

  Beginning language learners will respond first nonverbally, then with single words, then with two- or three-word combinations, later with phrases and sentences, and finally, by linking sentences together to form discourse. Although students should be encouraged to progress in their language learning, they should not be forced to produce language beyond their ability.

- **Key to student participation is a low anxiety level in the classroom.**

  For adults, language learning is by its nature an anxiety-laden pursuit. The more the teacher and the textbook focus on "doing something with language"—for example, solving a problem, finding new information, describing a thing or situation, or buying a product—rather than on "learning language," the more likely students will be to engage in the process of "acquiring" language. *LifePrints* will help the teacher establish a learning environment in the classroom where students can actually function in English through task-oriented activities.

- **Linguistic skills should be as integrated as possible.**

  Adults interact with others and with their environment by using all their senses. By integrating listening, speaking, reading, and writing in meaningful, interesting, and interactive activities, *LifePrints* simulates the processes in which adults interact with their environment. In the following pages we present some particularly effective listening, speaking, reading, and writing strategies. We suggest that these strategies be used together whenever it is feasible and authentic to do so.

III

Creating a Learner-Centered Environment

If language learning is to be successful, the learners' needs, not the grammar or functions of language, must form the core of the curriculum. Before discussing the creation of a learner-centered environment, we ought to look at who our learners are. Adult ESL students are a diverse group, ethnically, linguistically, and culturally. Some are immigrants, some are refugees, and some were even born in the United States. Some are newcomers, while others have lived and worked in this country for a long time. Some had strong academic preparation in their native countries but have weak oral skills; some have strong oral skills but weak or nonexistent literacy skills; and some have problems both with oral interaction and with reading and writing in English. Often these students are grouped in the same classroom, so teachers will have to focus on the language needs of each type.

- Learners who have had academic preparation in their native countries must develop the practical oral language skills necessary to function in everyday life in their new cities or towns, to express their ideas in English, and to work in an English-speaking environment. These adults, who are likely to be newcomers to the United States, may even be comfortable with some reading and writing in English. Literacy in their native language is a part of their lifestyle, and they can use that literacy as a tool in learning a second language.

- Learners who have lived and worked in this country for a number of years have some oral English interaction skills, and they may have developed cultural coping strategies for living and working here. They may have limited formal education in their native countries or in the United States. Their literacy skills in any language may be low or nonexistent, and their academic and study skills may be lacking. Many of these learners come to the ESL classroom looking for programs that upgrade their oral English skills, as well as for literacy skills that prepare them to benefit from academic, vocational, or job-training opportunities.

- Learners who are new to the United States, and who lack both oral and literacy skills needed to access information, express ideas, and solve communication problems in English are also likely to lack cultural coping strategies. They need strong developmental programs that help them acquire the language, literacy, and cultural skills necessary for learning and working in this country.

In addition to background, each adult comes with his or her preferred learning style. In general, *learning style* refers to one's preferred patterns of mental functioning. At least 20 different dimensions of learning style have been identified, far too many to detail here. Some people prefer to learn by watching, listening, and reflecting on their observations. Others are more comfortable learning by using abstract conceptualization, analyzing, and then acting on an intellectual understanding of the situation. Others learn best by doing and by active experimentation, while still others learn from feelings and specific interpersonal experiences. What this means for teachers is that a variety of strategies must be built into lessons so that all learners can draw on their preferred learning styles.

Teachers can use *LifePrints* to help learners with varying learning styles to observe, question, infer, and brainstorm—all activities that imaginative learners find useful. Using full-page illustrations with prompt questions ("What's happening here? What do you think will happen next?") and semantic webbing are examples of activities that are effective with visual learners. Analytic learners can find patterns, organize, identify parts, and classify through activities such as using English to create charts and graphs. Common-sense learners can problem-solve, predict, experiment, and tinker with language. Dynamic learners can integrate, evaluate, explain, and reorganize the learning. In short, teachers using *LifePrints* can choose from a variety of activities that are consistent with students' learning styles and with their own. Research has shown that teachers tend to teach from and to their own learning style, so they should be aware not only of learners' needs but also of their own preferences and behaviors.

Creating a learner-centered environment is at the core of *LifePrints*. *Learner-centered* means that learners are in control of their own learning and direct what happens in the classroom. It also means that the curriculum is communication-based rather than grammar-based and that language lessons center on relevant aspects of learners' lives. Finally, a learner-centered classroom calls for a collaborative effort between teacher and learners, with learners always playing an active role in the learning process. It is perhaps easier to describe than to define the learner-centered principles that guided the development of *LifePrints*.

- In an adult learner-centered class, learners and teacher become partners in a cooperative venture. The teacher creates the supportive environment in which learners can take initiative in choosing what they want to learn and how they want to learn it. This does not mean that the teacher has given up control of the classroom. The teacher must structure and order the learning process, guiding and giving feedback to learners in such a way that learners have the right amount of freedom. Too little freedom, as in a traditional teacher-centered curriculum, will stifle learners; too much freedom will make learners feel that the teacher has abandoned them.

- What happens in the language classroom should be a negotiated process between learners and teacher. The content and sequence of *LifePrints* lessons do not preclude the use of the program in a learner-centered curriculum. Indeed, the program is a starting point for classroom interaction and for student generation of adult learning materials. The language presented and practiced in *LifePrints* is based on issues, situations, and contexts that language-minority adults have expressed as crucial in their lives. Many of these same issues and situations will also be important in the lives of the learners in your class. The participatory process means that teachers must know their students and ask them what they think and what they want to learn and do.

- Problem solving occupies a good portion of any adult's life, so it is not surprising that problem-solving activities are a necessary part of learner-centered curricula. Problem-solving exercises are prominent in *LifePrints*. In beginning units, learners are asked what they would say or do in a particular situation, or about their own experiences in similar circumstances. Later on, they are asked to present the pros and cons of a situation, to negotiate, or to persuade. Learners are also asked to generate problem-solving and simulation activities from their own lives. By presenting and solving problems in the classroom, learners become confident of their ability to use language to solve problems and to take action in the larger social sphere.

- The traditional roles of the teacher as planner of content, sole deliverer of instruction, controller of the classroom, and evaluator of achievement change dramatically in a learner-centered curriculum. When the atmosphere in the classroom is a collaborative one, the teacher becomes facilitator, moderator, group leader, coach, manager of processes and procedures, giver of feedback, and partner in learning. *LifePrints* lends itself to these roles, giving suggestions to the teacher for whole-class, small-group, paired, and one-to-one activities.

- In managing communicative situations in a learner-centered environment, teachers set the stage for learners to experiment with language, to negotiate meaning and make mistakes, and to monitor and evaluate their own language-learning progress. Language is essentially a social function acquired through interaction with others in one-to-one and group situations. Learners process meaningful discourse from others, and they produce language in response to other human beings. The teacher is responsible for establishing the supportive environment in which this can happen. This does not mean that the teacher never corrects errors; it means that the teacher knows when and how to deal with error correction and can help learners understand when errors will interfere with communication.

IV

The *LifePrints* Program

Encompassing four levels, *LifePrints* is designed to enable adult learners who have little or no oral and/or written competence in English to handle most everyday survival, social, and job-related situations independently, using oral and written English. The Literacy Level is designed for adults at Student Performance level (SPL) 0; Level 1 is for those at SPLs 0–1; Level 2 for those at SPLs 2–4; and Level 3 for those at SPLs 5–6. A description of the SPLs appears on pages 22–23 of the Teacher's Edition.

The *LifePrints* program is composed of separate but linked components for each level. All four levels provide:

     (1) the Student Book (SB)
     (2) the Audiotape (▪▫▪)
     (3) the Workbook (WB)
     (4) the Teacher's Edition (TE).

Levels 1, 2, and 3 also provide:

     (5) the Teacher's Resource File (TRF)
     (6) Assessment: Tests and Tools for Measuring Achievement.

The Basic English Skills Test (BEST) is an optional feature of the *LifePrints* Program, providing a means for assessing placement and progress of adult ESL learners.

Student Book

Each Student Book follows a set of characters as they live, work, and study in a given community. Their lives and experiences become the stimuli for learners to talk and write about their own lives and experiences. As language proficiency expands from level to level, so does the number of interactions with people from diverse backgrounds.

The Literacy Student Book has six units, focusing on content and basic skills. In Levels 1, 2, and 3, there are 12 units in each Student Book. Ten (Units 1–5 and 7–11) focus on content, for example, housing, health, shopping, and employment; each concludes with a brief focus on selected grammar (structures) from the unit. The other two (Units 6 and 12) focus on key grammar (structures) that learners have used in the preceding units. A full Scope and Sequence for each Student Book, covering functions, structures, culture, and life tasks, is included in the Teacher's Edition for that book.

These are some of the features of all Student Books:

- Authentic language use.
- Adult contexts relevant to the lives of learners, their families, and friends.
- Visual stimuli for language learning, where appropriate, and a progression from visual to text-oriented material. While effective for all language learners, this progression taps into the natural learning strategies of low-literate individuals who often use visual clues in place of literacy skills.
- An emphasis on paired and group work, because learners acquire language through interaction with others on meaningful tasks in meaningful contexts.
- Integration of listening, speaking, reading, and writing, to reflect natural language use.
- Activities that help students transfer what they learn in the classroom to the world they live in.
- Grammar learning as a discovery process, with a focus on understanding the rules for language that students have already used and internalized. The discovery of rules is contextualized and at the discourse level whenever possible.

- An integration of new cultural skills along with new linguistic skills. *LifePrints* recognizes that adults need to understand and acquire a layer of cultural behaviors along with language. The situations presented help learners explore cross-cultural beliefs, attitudes, and values, and to compare and contrast expected behaviors in their native countries with expected behaviors in the United States.

Audiotape

Because *LifePrints* learners are asked to engage in active listening, not to read conversations, there are no written dialogues in the Student Books. Instead, the audiotapes, an integral partner with the Student Books, offer real listening opportunities by providing all conversations on tape. In keeping with authentic language, they offer authentic listening practice, exposing learners to different voices and relevant listening situations in which learners will find themselves. Learners are given the opportunity to listen to a conversation several times, to ask questions about it, and to develop strategies for understanding what they hear. Most important, learners are not forced to produce language they are not yet ready to produce.

Workbook

The *LifePrints* Workbook provides review and reinforcement activities coordinated to the language and content of each Student Book unit. The activities can be done individually or in pairs or small groups and are suitable for independent work outside of class. They provide targeted practice with selected structures, functions, and life tasks from the Student Book. Workbook activities provide additional opportunity for learners to practice reading and writing skills, but they can also be done or reviewed orally and provide additional stimuli for discussion, role play, and other oral practice.

Teacher's Edition

The layout of the *LifePrints* Teacher's Edition allows for a full view of each student page, along with the purpose of the lesson, materials needed, warm-up, presentation, and expansion activities. For each unit, the *learning objectives* are listed and categorized by linguistic functions, life tasks, structures, and culture. Key and related vocabulary are also provided for easy reference. Following is a description of the learning objectives sections in the TE, with suggestions on how to use them.

1. **Functions.** Functions focus on what people want to do with language or what they want to accomplish through oral communication. Functions can be categorized in different ways. The functions in *LifePrints* relate to *personal matters,* such as identifying oneself and one's family, and expressing needs or emotions; *interpersonal matters,* such as expressing greetings and farewells, expressing likes/dislikes and approval/disapproval, persuading, and interrupting; and *giving and seeking information* by, for example, reporting, explaining, describing, asking, clarifying, and directing. An index of functions for this level of *LifePrints* appears on page 215.

2. **Life Tasks.** Life tasks refer to coping skills required to deal with aspects of daily life in U.S. society, such as shelter, employment, food, clothing, transportation, and health care. The life tasks included in *LifePrints* are listed in the Scope and Sequence. It should be noted that when put into the statement "The learner will be able to . . . ," these life tasks become functional life skills or competencies, correlating with adult competency-based curricula such as the California Adult Student Assessment System (CASAS).

3. **Key and Related Vocabulary.** For every subject or topic, some vocabulary is key, or content-obligatory; that is, without those words, one cannot discuss the subject. Other vocabulary is related, or content-compatible; these are words that modify, describe, or complement the key vocabulary. For each *LifePrints* unit, the most important key and related vocabulary is listed. At a minimum, learners should be able to *understand* these words in context. The subject matter and the proficiency level of the class usually determine whether the teacher should expect learners to *use* this vocabulary actively in conversation.

4. **Structures.** Although grammar is not isolated for practice in the core of each lesson, certain structures are primary and appear frequently in the lesson. Many of these structures are highlighted at the end of each content unit and in Units 6 and 12, where learners are asked to discover patterns of grammar and then to practice the structures in new contexts. To help teachers give explanations where necessary, notes in the Teacher's Edition focus on the important features of a particular structure. The

Scope and Sequence lists the primary structures for each unit, indicating whether they are introduced for the first time or are being recycled.

5. **Culture**. Items inherent in the subject matter of the unit that are cross-cultural (for example, family, shopping, medical care, gender roles, and child-rearing) are noted in the Teacher's Edition. There is often a crossover between cultural points and life tasks. We suggest that, whenever possible, learners discuss cultural similarities and differences so they can reflect on ways of doing things in their native culture and of performing the same tasks in U.S. society, without making value judgments in either case.

Besides outlining the objectives for each lesson, the Teacher's Edition gives detailed suggestions for the teaching of each Student Book page. We use the word *suggestions* because the steps presented are meant as guidelines, not as absolutes. After considering the needs and learning styles of the students in your class, as well as your own teaching style, you might blend them with the suggested steps for teaching the lesson. To feel comfortable with each student page, make your own lesson plan; include, along with the approximate timing, a "grab bag" of possible whole-class, small-group, paired, and one-to-one activities. Gather any needed materials well beforehand and, if you have time, practice-teach the page (without learners) to get a feel for the flow of the lesson, for monitoring your own speech, and for noting what you think might be difficult points for the learners. Suggested teaching steps include the following:

1. Teacher Preparation and Materials.

Gathering materials is an important step, so the TE suggests the materials and any special preparation needed for the lesson. Most lessons require a cassette player for the listening activities, but other equipment and supplies may be needed as well. A language course that is contextualized in survival situations must rely on pictures and real objects to convey meaning. Building a *picture file* for the first time will take some work; however, after you have gone through the book with a class once or twice, the file will need only periodic updating. Highly visual magazines, mail-order and other catalogs, and newspaper advertisements and Sunday supplements are good sources of illustrations for survival

situations. Pictures of houses; the insides of clinics/hospitals and various workplaces; items in grocery stores, supermarkets, and department stores; and people interacting in both everyday and problem situations are examples of visuals for your file. Include pictures that can be used for sequencing and strip stories. In some cases you will want to cut and mount the picture before class; in others you will want to have learners look through a magazine or catalog to find items as part of the class lesson. From time to time, the TE also suggests asking learners to provide pictures as out-of-class work.

For some units you will also need realia. An empty milk carton, an aspirin bottle, a soiled piece of clothing, a bus schedule, or a hammer and screwdriver can make the difference between learners really understanding and internalizing language and having only a vague idea of what a word or concept means. Particularly at the beginning and intermediate levels of language learning, the gathering of materials is a crucial step in the teaching process.

2. Warm-up.

The Teacher's Edition gives suggestions for getting the class started and for eliciting concerns, information, and questions from the learners. Casual conversation with the whole group or a few learners, or small talk on a given topic, can be an icebreaker. Movement, chants, dances, and songs can both stimulate and relax learners so they are ready to attend to class business. The most important part of warm-ups for adult learners is tapping into their prior knowledge and experience, and using their backgrounds to prepare for the lesson topic. Brainstorming activities that involve both learners and teacher in generating vocabulary, multiple associations, and illustrations on a specific topic can set the tone for the entire lesson. Warm-ups help learners organize information about a subject, while lowering their anxiety level and getting them to use the English they have already acquired.

3. Presentation.

This section is the heart of the Teacher's Edition in that it gives step-by-step suggestions for each page. It includes:
- Suggested language for asking questions and eliciting information. "Teacher talk" often gets in the way of the learners under-

standing what they are supposed to do. In giving instructions, teachers sometimes use more complex grammatical structures than the learners can handle. Or they may talk too long, causing learners to lose track of what they are supposed to do. The suggested language in the Presentation section helps teachers avoid these pitfalls.

- Suggested activities or exercises. These activities—often introduced by "Have learners work in small groups to . . ." or "Elicit from learners . . ." or the like—will help the flow of a lesson, though others can be substituted or added. You may need to adapt activities to the needs and proficiency level of the class, as well as to the characteristics of the learning site and your teaching style.

- Suggested teacher modeling and demonstration. Remember to model and/or give examples whenever possible. In activities such as completing interview grids, your asking a question first will make learners feel more comfortable approaching their classmates.

4. Expansion/Extension.

By giving suggestions for additional classroom practice, this section answers the common teacher lament, "I've finished the Student Book, so what do I do now?" It functions as an idea bank both for whole-class exercises and for activities specifically geared to certain types of learners. The more advanced learners are challenged to be creative with the language they have acquired and to try out new language; slower learners are given opportunities for more work in problem areas. Some of the expansion exercises draw on the Teacher's Resource File, or TRF (see below). Others are variations of activities already done in class. Still others help move the language lesson from the classroom to the world outside, asking learners to do something new and immediately useful with the language they have acquired.

The Teacher's Edition also gives less experienced teachers insights into what might be going on when a student or a class is faced with learning a certain function or structure. These insights come both from research into second language acquisition and from classroom practice. It helps teachers to know that when learners continually make mistakes with a certain structure, it is not because teachers haven't presented the struc-

ture correctly or given enough practice with it, but because, as research and experience have shown, the structure is acquired late and will remain a problem even for advanced learners. Similarly, it is helpful to know that, according to classroom experience, a particular exercise works better in small groups than with the whole class, or that learners must be at an intermediate language level before they can be expected to be aware of certain features of language, such as register. The *LifePrints* Teacher's Edition is designed to be used effectively by both experienced and less-experienced teachers.

Teacher's Resource File

The Teacher's Resource File (TRF) extends the Student Book by giving teachers a wide variety of reproducible complementary activities. Only so much text can fit in a Student Book, so the TRF for each level offers exercises, simulations, problem-solving activities, and games relevant to the themes of individual units, as well as generic games or game boards that can be used at any time. Because of the match between the Student Book and the TRF at each level, the Expansion/Extension sections in the Teacher's Edition often refer to specific TRF activities. Though an optional feature of *LifePrints,* the TRF is a resource that teachers can use over and over again, saving countless hours of planning and materials preparation. At the Literacy Level, reproducible TRF-style activities are provided in the Teacher's Edition.

Assessment

The Assessment book for Levels 1, 2, and 3 of the *LifePrints* Program provides achievement tests and informal assessment activities. The reproducible achievement tests, designed to be given after completing a level, include a listening skills test, a reading and writing skills test, and an oral skills test. Learners can be given one or all of these tests. Test activities are similar to the types of activities in the Student Book, so they accurately reflect how as well as what learners have studied. This familiarity is also designed to reduce test anxiety so learners can demonstrate with greater confidence what they have learned. There are two versions of each test, along with instructions for administering the tests, answer keys, and guidelines for interpreting results. In addition, there are detailed guidelines and suggestions for performance-based assessment activities and portfolio assessment.

Basic English Skills Test

The Basic English Skills Test (BEST), another optional feature of *LifePrints,* assesses listening, speaking, reading, and writing in life-skills contexts. It contains two distinct parts: a one-to-one structured oral interview, which uses picture stimuli, and an individual or group-administered reading and writing section. The BEST can be used both as a placement tool and as a progress test. Its scores are correlated with the Student Performance Levels (SPLs) of the Mainstream English Language Training (MELT) Project, as are scores on the California Adult Student Assessment System (CASAS). For a description of the SPLs, see pages 20–21.

V

Developing Literacy and Reading Skills at Level 3

Level 3 of *LifePrints* is designed for learners at Student Performance Levels 5–6. At these levels learners are creating language on their own; that is, they are no longer relying mainly on learned phrases to communicate. With some help they can function independently in most survival situations, they can try new combinations of vocabulary and grammar, and they can reword and clarify to get their point across.

In reading, students have moved from "learning to read" to "reading to learn" (or do). They can skim and scan for information; they can read notices and some newspaper articles; they can read forms; and so on, all with help for unknown vocabulary and complex grammatical constructions. Literacy skills are emphasized at Level 3 and are taught and practiced in meaningful contexts from the beginning pages. Learners are exposed to reading material typically found in many everyday situations; they are also asked to deal with maps, charts and forms, and pricing and budgeting data. Throughout the lessons, stories about the characters and their experiences stimulate learners to discuss and write about their own lives.

In every lesson, learners are asked to write: to complete forms, take notes and messages, write directions for a place or a process, transfer oral information to written form, describe or explain something, or report on an experience. They write letters to community agencies, newspapers, American friends, and government leaders. Most important, they write about themselves, putting their personal, family, and ethnic histories on paper to share with others. Learners and teachers are also asked to keep a journal in which they write to each other. These Dialogue Journals are an important part of the instruction at this level, enabling the teacher to focus on written communication with learners on an individualized basis.

LifePrints draws on a model of literacy in which reading, writing, and oral language are mutually supportive components of a communications system that focuses on meaning. At Level 3, some attention should also be given to form: grammar, spelling, punctuation, and conventions for certain types of writing, such as letters and memoranda. However, the form of writing should not detract from the emphasis on function. The important point to remember is that all skills must be a part of, not separate from, meaningful communication. The following section describes in more detail *LifePrints* activities that develop reading and writing, as well as listening and speaking, through a focus on meaning.

VI

Features of Student Book 3 Lessons

1. The Setting and the Characters

The units in *LifePrints* reflect the lives of real adults doing real tasks in a community. Level 3 is set in the Washington, D.C., metropolitan area, specifically, in the northern Virginia suburbs. In the first unit we meet some of the students in the computer lab of an adult education center. Diep Tran is a medical laboratory technician from Vietnam. Yolette Jamison came to the United States from Haiti. She is the assistant manager of a shoe store. Stan Wolanski, from Poland, works part-time as a gardener. Roberto Silva, a waiter, came to Washington from Puerto Rico. We also meet the spouses, children, other family members, friends, and co-workers of these characters as they go about their daily lives and then come back together to study computer skills, which they each hope will lead to career advancement.

2. First and Last Pages

The first page of every lesson is a full-page visual that introduces a main theme. It also taps into previous knowledge and experience, and into the vocabulary learners might already possess. By considering questions such as "What do you see?" "Where are these people?" "What do you think they're saying?" "What's going on?" "Was it like that in your native country?" and "What's the problem?" learners can explore both the content and the language of what they already know. Other questions on the first page, such as "How would you . . . ?" "Have you ever . . . ?" and "What do you think about . . . ?" help students cope with the language of such skills as inferencing and hypothesizing, and "hook" learners into the lesson. At this point, you will want to write on the board the vocabulary you elicit or provide. You may also want to categorize the words or have learners do so. At Level 3, learners may have a lot of or little vocabulary about a given subject, and the first page of the lesson gives you clues as to how to approach the rest of the lesson. You may want to prepare a set of word and picture cards that can be used throughout the lesson, or you may decide that learners can use their notes and vocabulary categorization without extra cues.

The last page of every lesson gives learners a chance to make the connection between new information and language they have learned in a given unit, what they already knew, and their life beyond the classroom. They are asked to use and stretch their reading and writing skills by doing something authentic with language: completing a form, writing a letter, writing a company newsletter article, putting an opinion in writing, relating their own experiences, and so on. The last page also gives learners a chance to review vocabulary, connect it with what they have learned, and extend it to new situations in their lives outside of class.

Between the first and last pages, a variety of language presentations and exercises introduce and give practice in listening, speaking, reading, and writing holistically, that is, as interacting parts of a complete system. There is no set pattern. Authentic language situations often call for one skill more than another. For instance, Unit 2, "What the Community Offers," elicits listening and speaking practice primarily, while Unit 9, "Real Costs of a Car," requires more reading. The flow of Level 3 follows a situation and the language needed to cope in that situation. In general, though, learners are asked to reflect on their individual experiences and to express their opinions. They are also asked to use critical thinking skills to analyze, compare, classify, predict, hypothesize, justify their viewpoints, and even persuade others. In Level 3, learners are also faced with the language and processes of mathematics. In Units 3 and 11, for instance, they read and compute bills, and figure out costs and eligibility requirements. Learning and practicing the language related to critical thinking skills and applied mathematics is a major focus of Level 3.

3. Activity and Exercise Types

The Student Book contains various exercise and activity types, including question-answer, matching, charts and graphs, identification, interview, fill-in, labeling, listing, and writing directions. Other activities or exercises are suggested in the Teacher's Edition for each page—for example, using graphic organizers such as semantic webs and Venn diagrams; doing a Total Physical Response (TPR) activity; using a substitution drill; playing games; and writing a story or creating a Dialogue Journal. The following are short step-by-step instructions for many of the exercises and activities that appear either in the Student Book or in the Teacher's Edition.

Listening/Speaking Activities

Until recently, listening was considered the passive skill and speaking the active skill in aural/oral communication. We now see that good language learners are active participants in the listening process, not just passive recipients. Besides helping learners develop their own strategies for active listening, Level 3 listening activities are effective lead-ins to the Level 3 speaking activities.

- **Venn Diagrams**

  The Venn Diagram is a graphic organizer that can help learners store and categorize new information. Venn diagrams are good for comparing and contrasting.

  Steps for Using Venn Diagrams

  1. Tell the class that you are going to put the information you are discussing into three categories: one for each of two different topics and one for both (where the topics overlap). You designate the topic headings, such as jobs that can be performed only during the day (e.g., gardener); jobs that can be done only at night (e.g., night watchman); and jobs that can be done at any time (e.g., factory worker). See below for another example using a different topic.

2. Elicit learners' contributions to each of the categories. As they give you the information, write their answers for the first topic on the left side of the board, their answers for the second topic on the right side, and their answers for both in the middle.

3. Draw two intersecting circles around the lists so that the *both* column appears in the intersection. Have learners copy the diagram in their notebooks. Keep a copy for class use.

4. Refer to the diagram during the unit, adding to it when appropriate.

Venn Diagram

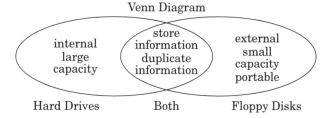

Hard Drives   Both   Floppy Disks

Variation
Venn diagrams can also be used with parts of speech, for example, words that are verbs, nouns, or both.

- ### Time Lines
Time lines are graphic organizers that allow learners to sequence and display events chronologically. They give meaningful practice with tenses, most commonly in the past and present, but also can be used to extend events into the future. Time lines are good devices to use with such functions as sequencing, hypothesizing, and cause and effect.

Steps for Using Time Lines
1. Draw either a horizontal or a vertical line on the board. Write time markers appropriate to the topic at each end of the line, e.g., year, time of day, last week, yesterday.

2. Elicit information from learners, such as "When did you leave on your trip?" "When did you arrive in X?" and "How many days did you spend in Y?" As learners respond, mark points on the time line, writing information on one side of the line and the date, time, etc., on the other side. Information can be of a personal, historical, or hypothetical nature.

3. Have learners copy the time line in their notebooks. Keep a copy for class use during the unit.

Variations
Make a time line from information collected through a guided interview about a learner's work history or an oral report on a diet and exercise plan that learners give to the class. Have learners make individual time lines from listening activities, e.g., stories you read them or directions or information. A flowchart is another variation of a time line. Instead of events in time, it shows progression, sequencing, and cause and effect related to an event or process.

- ### Information Gaps
These are pair or small-group task activities in which each learner or group has some crucial information that the partner or other group members do not, and together they must complete a task. For instance, Unit 4 contains an information-gap activity on using information from the manual to fix a problem with the computer. These are excellent communicative activities, because the task cannot be accomplished without asking and answering questions. The emphasis here should be on task completion, or the acquisition of information that learners can use in some way, not just on exchange of information for the sake of random question-and-answer practice.

Steps for Using Information Gaps
1. Inform the pairs or groups about the task or objective. For instance, they have to gather information from a number of manuals.

2. Give each pair or group different, incomplete information for the task. For the task above, give each learner a different, incomplete set of troubleshooting instructions.

3. Tell learners that they cannot show their information to anyone, but must ask and answer questions, e.g., "Which manual covers connections with printers?" When their partner or a group member responds, they fill in their worksheets with the missing information.

4. When learners think they have all the information, they compare their products with each other. If they have asked the right questions, and have understood and recorded the answers correctly, their completed versions should be identical.

Variations
Give one learner a simple picture and have him or her describe it to a partner or small group. The other learners must re-create the

picture. The closer the re-creation is to the original, the better the language task was performed and received. This is a good activity for mixed pairs or groups in which one learner has more productive language than the other(s). For another variation, give paired learners partial and different information on a chart and ask them to complete their charts by asking and answering questions without looking at their partner's paper.

- **Problem Posing**

  This technique, which has been associated with the Brazilian educator Paulo Freire, has been used in community action to challenge adults to take control of their lives and environment. In ESL, problem posing presents opportunities for learners to learn and use language in different ways. Throughout Level 3, there are stimuli for asking questions that help learners process problems by using the language of description, explanation, analysis, hypothesis, synthesis, and solution. Keep in mind that when you are dealing with critical issues, it is important not to overwhelm the learners.

  ### Steps for Using Problem Posing

  1. Present a problem in a picture, dialogue, or paragraph. The first page of each unit is useful here. The problem should be one that learners can identify with, such as making choices about education, health problems, financial needs, unfair treatment or punishment, or preserving the natural environment. No solution is provided.

  2. Present five sets of questions designed to move learners from simple description to a solution of the problem. Learners need to:

     - Describe the problem. ("What do you see?" "What does it say?")

     - Identify the problem. ("Explain it to me." "Tell me what's wrong.")

     - Relate the problem to learners' experience. ("Are you familiar with the situation?" "Has this or something similar happened to you?")

     - Analyze the underlying reasons for the problem. ("Why is there a problem?" "What are the causes?")

     - Seek change. ("How would you solve the problem?" "What would you do first?")

  3. Ask two volunteers to come to the front of the room to role-play a conversation about the problem. Encourage them to take on behaviors (impatient, helpful, patronizing, angry, etc.) as they act out their roles.

  4. Using this role play as the basis, challenge the class to discuss the problem. Allow learners to generate their own ideas. Encourage them to respond to one another's questions and statements. "Do you agree with that idea?" and "Would anyone like to answer that question?" are questions that encourage participation. However, don't lead learners too much. Allow them to explore possible solutions for themselves.

  5. Record the solution(s) either orally or in writing. First have learners state the problem clearly and concisely; then record the solution(s). By the end of Level 3 you will have a book or tape of real-life problems posed and solved by the class.

  ### Variations

  Oral or written dilemma stories pose problems that require consideration of options and their consequences. There is no "right" answer. Have the class read or listen to a dilemma story. Next have them propose three or four possible solutions, giving the advantages and disadvantages of each. Learners can align themselves in groups according to the solution they think best. Each group then tries to persuade the class that its solution is right. In the process the group must explain the reasoning behind its choice. It can also challenge the other groups' ideas by asking pointed questions.

  Instructions for other listening/speaking exercises useful at Level 3 can be found in the Introduction to the Teacher's Editions for Levels 1 and 2. These include Total Physical Response (TPR), Listen and Do, Chain Drills, Substitution Drills, Paired Exercises, Structured Interviews, and Role Play (in TE 1), Semantic Webbing (in TE 1 and 2), and Continuous Stories (in TE 2).

Reading/Writing Activities

Learners at Level 3 are reading to learn and/or to do. They are also learning to write, and the writing in turn helps them read better. As literate persons they will read for information, meaning, directions, and/or pleasure. The following activities will help Level 3 learners incorporate English literacy as part of their lives.

- **Process Writing**

  Anyone learning how to write, and along the way becoming a better reader, must be given the opportunity to write freely. As with oral language, the focus needs to be on communication and on the development of ideas, but in this case by means of the written word. Good writers produce many drafts before they consider their work final. Learners need to have the same opportunity and to have feedback from both their peers and their teacher. At Level 3 learners are beginning to generate new language, both orally and in writing. So they do not get discouraged by the struggle to put their thoughts on paper, it is important for learners at this level to realize that writing is a process, even for native speakers of English, and that while the final product is important, so is the process.

Steps for Using Process Writing

1. Use the Student Book writing exercises or choose another topic. Group discussions are helpful in identifying potential topics.

2. Write ideas related to the topic on the board, perhaps using a semantic web. This *pre-writing* activity helps learners to focus and recall vocabulary.

3. Have learners write freely for a few minutes. This is the *drafting* part of the process. Learners may also find it useful to draw pictures at this stage.

4. In pairs or small groups, have learners *share, read,* and *discuss* their drafts. At this time, circulate among the groups. You may provide other questions for learners to consider in their writing and help them expand or elaborate on what they have written. For learners who are new to literacy, you (or a peer) can help them put pictures into words or form their letters more precisely. However, at this stage the focus should be on content.

5. Have learners *redraft* and *revise,* focusing specifically on the purpose of their writing and on their audience.

6. Have learners *edit* their work for a final version, paying attention to form or whatever portions of the mechanics of writing they are capable of handling. At this writing proficiency level, it is acceptable for the teacher to function as editor. You can change spelling and punctuation for and/or with the learners.

7. Have those learners who wish to do so read their work to the entire class, display it prominently where other learners can read it, or publish a class anthology. This final *publishing* step is important, because it establishes each learner as an author.

• **Dialogue Journals**

These journals are written "conversations" between learners and teacher. Though not necessarily tied to any specific unit, they will help your students become literate, getting reading as well as writing practice. The teacher is a participant in an ongoing conversation, not an instructor or evaluator. Traditionally, the learner initiates the topic and the teacher responds. Sometimes ESL learners are reluctant to write, so you might prompt them by suggesting that they write about the topic of the lesson. Over time, both the quantity and the quality of learners' writing will increase. Learners will write more about themselves, their families, and their personal experiences and/or problems, or about their native countries. At Level 3 you can expect descriptions, narratives, explanations, complaints, and even arguments.

Steps for Using Dialogue Journals

1. Make sure learners have wide-ruled notebooks or loose-leaf paper for their journals.

2. Introduce the concept of the Dialogue Journal. Tell learners they can write to you and you will write back to them. Learners can write whatever they want; the information will be kept confidential. Even a few sentences are good.

3. Set aside class time (10–15 minutes) for learners to write in their journals.

4. Let learners write (and/or draw) whatever they want, providing prompts if necessary.

5. Respond soon afterward, on the same or a similar topic and with the same amount of writing at the same language level. Do not correct form. You want your students to feel that they can write freely. Your response in the journal will serve as a model of correct English usage. If you do not understand what the learner is trying to communicate, ask for clarification. (For example: "Are you telling me . . . ?" "Did you say . . . ?")

6. Return the journal to the learner for the next entry.

Variations

You may want to start the ball rolling by choosing the first few topics and writing a few sentences in the learners' books. For instance you might write, "I've been told that in (learner's native country) there is a rainy season. Can you tell me about the rainy season in (country)?"

4. Structures

In *LifePrints,* grammar is a discovery process in which learners are exposed to and use structures in context in the thematic units. Then, at the end of each unit and in Units 6 and 12, they focus specifically on a portion of the grammar they have used in the preceding pages and units. Not all the structures presented in the thematic units are emphasized and practiced in these pages. Those that are selected are structures that learners should be able to use actively. If you feel that your learners need or want practice with other structures, you can of course add exercises. At Level 3, learners should be ready for some overt grammar practice. Of course, they will be practicing structures throughout the text, and you may want to point to some patterns as you go through the units. The Index of Structures on page 216 indicates where structures are recycled through the thematic units. While the emphasis in *LifePrints* is on communication over accuracy, on function over form, Level 3 learners have enough language for looking at, comparing, and analyzing form. This becomes an active process in such exercises as "Building a Verb List" in Unit 12.

The exercises on the structure pages and in Units 6 and 12 of Level 3 are contextualized in the characters and content of the previous lessons. You can extend and vary these exercises with transformation drills, that is, by asking learners to change utterances from one grammatical form to another. For instance, you can ask learners to change statements from the active voice to the passive voice, or to change direct speech into reported speech. The Teacher's Resource File also includes activities that focus on grammar. Do not expect all learners to have the same control over grammar. We can look at grammatical control as a continuum, from no control at one end to the control of a native speaker at the other end. Learners at Level 3 will have control of basic grammar but will vary considerably in their control of more advanced grammar. Even those learners further along on the grammatical control continuum will still tend to be inconsistent in their control of more complex structures.

5. Vocabulary

Vocabulary is best taught in context, as part of communicative listening, speaking, reading, and writing activities. Isolated lists of vocabulary items that learners memorize do not lead to meaningful use. New words and phrases become internalized to the point where learners will use them in new situations after multiple opportunities for use. Vocabulary-building and internalizing activities include semantic webbing, matching words to pictures, labeling, TPR, and other types of exercises that require following directions. To elicit known vocabulary at the beginning of a unit, use illustrations and realia, with such prompt questions as "What is this called?" "What are they doing?" "Where are they?" "Do you know another word for that?" and "Give me a word (words) which describes the action." Categorization is a good technique, especially at Level 3, where learners come with known vocabulary and tend to pick up new words very quicky if they are associated with words they already use. It is also very practical, because learners are introduced to far too many words in a given situation through the book, their own research, and their peers. Vocabulary for parts of a car, words associated with insurance, or adjectives describing natural phenomena are more easily remembered and used in new situations if learners have gone through the exercise of categorizing them.

As learners progress through the units, recycle vocabulary from previous lessons and help them recognize synonyms and antonyms. Learners may want to build synonym and antonym lists in their notebooks. Keep on display in the room semantic webs and lists that learners have generated, and see if they can use the vocabulary in new contexts. This gives beginning learners a powerful tool for seeing how much they have learned. Prompt learners to use new vocabulary in LEA stories and to read those stories several times as you go through the units. As learners gain more and more vocabulary, have them see what familiar words they can identify within new words. There are many ways to exploit each activity for its potential to reinforce vocabulary.

6. Culture

Language and culture are integrally bound, so learning a new language means understanding a new culture. Culture is the institutions and shared behavior patterns of a society. But it is also the values, attitudes, and beliefs that underlie the institutions and behaviors. How we think about family is culture-bound. So is our attitude toward education, work, gender roles, authority, competition, technology, and the environment. All these factors are touched upon in Level 3. From the beginning units, learners are asked to reflect upon their experiences in the United States in terms of what things were like or how they did things in their native countries. You as the teacher are the guide in helping learners understand cross-cultural situations. Start from learners' native cultures to help them explore their new one. At Level 3, they have enough language to talk about intercultural issues. If they hesitate, you and other class members may need to help them find the right vocabulary to describe and explain. Ask them, for example, "Is X the word you're looking for?" or "Can you give me an example of what you're telling us?" Both you and the other learners in the class can learn much about culture at this level.

7. Pronunciation

There are few overt pronunciation exercises at Level 3 of *LifePrints*. Like grammar, pronunciation deals with form, not function. Teachers can devise listening/speaking activities (using minimal pairs *[pat / bat]*, for example) to practice sound discrimination or production for situations where pronunciation gets in the way of meaning or where students appear to be having trouble. The following are examples of meaningful pronunciation practice for Level 3.

- You may want to point out intonation patterns and have learners practice them, particularly when it comes to the difference between questions and statements.

- You may want learners to recognize two- versus three-syllable words, particularly in sentences or longer discourse. You can also have them mark the stressed syllables.

- You may want to have learners identify and write the contracted forms they hear in a given conversation or reading. Sometimes you may want them to write a full form that they hear as the contracted form, and sometimes you may want them to convert a contracted form they hear to the full form.

- You may want learners to listen for and identify the plurals of regular nouns they hear in a given conversation or reading.

- Similarly, you may want learners to listen for and identify the past tense forms of regular verbs (/d/, /t/, or /id/) as heard in context.

In providing examples of natural speech, the audiotapes are good models of pronunciation. You might want to use the tapes to point out pronunciation features. However, attention is better devoted to fostering communication than to working on pronunciation. Yet, at Level 3, your students may be aware of their own pronunciation problems and ask for help. The key is to be responsive to their needs without spending a lot of class time on pronunciation in general.

VII

Testing and Assessment

Testing is a part of teaching and provides valuable feedback to learners and teachers as well as program administrators and funders. While no formal end-of-unit tests are included in *LifePrints,* you should use performance-based techniques to see that learners are progressing in the outlined objectives. *LifePrints* Assessment provides guidelines and suggestions of level-appropriate activities for ongoing evaluation. Checklists are an easy way of showing progress over time. The summary pages for each unit in the Teacher's Edition can be used as checklists. The Assessment book has reproducible checklists for oral language and for reading and writing skills at each level. The last page of each unit, Dialogue Journals, and writing assignments suggested in this TE can all become part of a learner's portfolio. At Level 3 you and learners can set writing goals periodically. Then, with learners, look back at these goals, review their portfolios, and assess progress.

In addition to checklists, learner-generated learning logs can be a form of self-assessment. Learners can keep separate pages in their notebooks labeled: Things I Learned This Month; Things I Now Find Easy in English; Things I Still Find Hard in English; Things I Would Like to Be Able to Do in English. Learners should make an entry on one or more pages every week. Every three months or so, go over the logs with learners, showing them how much they have learned and noting their ambitions so that, whenever possible, you can individualize instruction.

VIII

Classroom Management

LifePrints assumes that there are many different class situations. Some of you will teach in open entry/open exit situations. Others will have impossibly large classes with learners both below and above Level 3. *LifePrints* strongly emphasizes pair and small-group work. While pairings and groupings will not solve all classroom management problems, they offer many advantages. When the entire class is actively engaged in pair or small-group work, everyone is communicating. For a learner who is uncomfortable speaking in front of the entire class, for instance, pair work offers an audience of one. Small-group work allows that same learner to contribute what he or she can, relying on others to both add and stimulate.

Pairings are of three types: random, voluntary, and assigned. It is a good idea to vary pairings so learners get to work with different members of the class. *Random pairs* are generally formed by asking two learners who are sitting next to each other to work together. Random pairs can work together for active listening practice, conversation, completing various exercises, cooperative writing, and reviewing each other's work. When learners form *voluntary pairs*, they are likely to gravitate toward a classmate with whom they feel comfortable. Often this is someone who speaks their native language, so expect to hear some non-English conversation in the classroom. You should use voluntary pairs when the task is such that English must be produced, as in the preparation of dialogues to present to the class, the creation and ordering of strip stories, and interviews outside of class that require interaction with native speakers of English. *Assigned pairs* are usually based on proficiency levels. If you pair learners with similar abilities, they can work together at the same pace on various activities or they can correct each other's exercises. At other times, assigning partners of different levels is helpful, because the more advanced learners who are also in the process of language learning can quietly help the less advanced. Both learners benefit. The less advanced are generally not threatened, and the more advanced gain valuable practice and self-esteem. It should be noted that this type of informal peer tutoring is the normal practice in many educational situations around the world. It is part of many cultures for one learner to help another.

In moving from pair work to small-group work, you will be much more involved in forming the groups. Heterogeneous assigned groups usually stay together to complete a task, and if they are working well together, they may remain together for the entire unit. Groups of four to eight work well for cooperative learning tasks. With the groups, specify roles that are required. There needs to be a leader to organize the group, to keep it on track, and to see that everyone participates; a recorder to write down the results of the group; and a reporter to report to the class. These roles can be assigned by you or self-assigned by the group. For a group to be heterogeneous, literacy level comes into play, especially for the role of recorder.

In managing a pair or group activity, you will find that your role changes. First, in your lesson planning you will need to create reasons for the two or more learners to cooperate. Much of that has already been done for you in *LifePrints*. Second, you will need to move around the classroom, paying attention to what each pair or group is doing, rather than orchestrating from up front. Third, for assessment purposes, you will need to focus on what each learner in the pair or group is doing so you can provide appropriate feedback and evaluation.

Most of the exercises and activities geared to pairs and small groups can easily be converted into *one-to-one situations*. Wherever the ▮ icon appears in this Teacher's Edition, you will find a suggestion for adapting group and pair work to a one-to-one exercise. In working with one learner, the tutor plays several roles: those of teacher, facilitator, *and* fellow learner. Classroom management per se is not a problem, but varying the learning situation is. The burden for performing must be shared by the tutor and the learner. If learners feel they must be talking all the time, their affective filters will be high. If teachers feel they must be in charge all the time, they will tire quickly. By doing exercises and conversation activities together—provided that learners have their own listening, reading, and writing time during the tutoring session—learners and tutors will set a comfortable learning/teaching pace.

In going through this Teacher's Edition as you teach the units, note on the TE pages or in a notebook what worked and what didn't work, and why. This will help you in teaching with *LifePrints* later on. Good luck to you and your learners.

Allene Guss Grognet
JoAnn (Jodi) Crandall

Note: *In the following pages, italicized sentences generally indicate suggested questions and other language for the teacher to use. Sentences in regular type (usually in parentheses) generally indicate responses and other language that learners can be expected to produce.*

Student Performance Levels

Level	CASAS SCORE	BEST SCORE	ORAL COMMUNICATION	LISTENING COMPREHENSION	GENERAL LANGUAGE ABILITY
0	150–170	0–8	No ability whatsoever.	No ability whatsoever.	**LITERACY LEVEL/LEVEL ONE** No ability whatsoever.
I	171–180	9–15	• Vocabulary limited to a few **isolated words**. • **No control** of grammar.	• Understands only a few **isolated words**, and **extremely simple learned** phrases (What's your name?).	**LEVEL ONE** • Functions **minimally, if at all**, in English. • Can handle only **very routine entry-level** jobs that do not require oral communication, and in which all tasks can be easily **demonstrated**.
II	181–190	16–28	• Expresses **a limited number** of **immediate** survival needs using **very simple learned** phrases. • Asks and responds to very simple learned questions.	• Understands a **limited number** of **very simple learned** phrases, spoken slowly with frequent repetitions.	**LEVEL TWO** • Functions in a **very limited way** in situations related to **immediate needs**. • Can handle only **routine entry-level** jobs that do not require oral communication, and in which all tasks can be easily **demonstrated**.
III	191–200	29–41	• Expresses **immediate survival** needs using **simple learned** phrases. • Asks and responds to simple learned questions. • **Some control** of **very basic grammar**.	• Understands **simple learned** phrases, spoken **slowly** with **frequent repetitions**.	• Functions **with some difficulty** in situations related to **immediate needs**. • Can handle **routine entry-level** jobs that involve only the **most basic** oral **communication**, and in which all tasks can be demonstrated.
IV	201–210	42–50	• Expresses **basic survival** needs, including asking and responding to related questions, using both **learned** and **a few new phrases**. • Participates in basic conversations in **very routine social** situations (e.g., greeting, inviting). • Speaks with **hesitation** and frequent pauses. • **Some control** of **basic grammar**.	• Understands **simple learned** phrases easily, and **some** simple **new** phrases containing familiar vocabulary, spoken **slowly** with **frequent repetitions**.	• Can satisfy **basic survival** needs and a few **very routine social** demands. • Can handle **entry-level** jobs that involve **some simple oral** communication, but in which tasks can also be **demonstrated**.

	GENERAL LANGUAGE ABILITY	LISTENING COMPREHENSION	ORAL COMMUNICATION	BEST SCORE	CASAS SCORE
V	**LEVEL THREE** • Can satisfy **basic survival** needs and **some limited social** demands. • Can handle **jobs and job training** that involve following **simple oral** and **very basic written** instructions but in which most tasks can also be **demonstrated.**	• Understands **learned** phrases easily and **short new** phrases containing familiar vocabulary spoken slowly with **repetition.** • Has **limited** ability to understand on the telephone.	• Functions independently in most **face-to-face basic survival** situations but needs **some help.** • Asks and responds to direct questions on familiar and some unfamiliar subjects. • Still relies on **learned** phrases but also uses **new** phrases (i.e., speaks with **some creativity**) but with **hesitation** and pauses. • Communicates on the phone to express a **limited** number of **survival** needs, but with **some difficulty.** • Participates in basic conversations in a **limited number** of **social** situations. • Can occasionally clarify general meaning by simple rewording. • Increasing, but inconsistent, control of **basic grammar.**	51–57	211–220
VI	• Can satisfy **most survival needs** and limited social demands. • Can handle **jobs and job training** that involve following **simple oral** and written instructions and diagrams.	• Understands **conversations** containing **some unfamiliar** vocabulary on many **everyday** subjects, with a need for **repetition, rewording, or slower speech.** • Has **some** ability to understand **without face-to-face** contact (e.g., on the telephone, TV).	• Functions **independently** in most survival situations, but needs **some help.** • Relies less on learned phrases; speaks with **creativity,** but with **hesitation.** • Communicates on the **phone** on **familiar** subjects, but with **some difficulty.** • Participates with **some confidence** in **social** situations when addressed **directly.** • Can sometimes **clarify** general meaning by **rewording.** • **Control** of **basic** grammar evident, but **inconsistent;** may attempt to use more difficult grammar but with almost no control.	58–64	221–235

Scope and Sequence

NOTE: Items with a bullet (•) are *introduced* in Level 3. It is assumed that learners are familiar with all other functions and structures listed in this Scope and Sequence. All functions and structures may be recycled throughout the book.

UNIT	FUNCTIONS (• introduce)	STRUCTURES (• introduce)	CULTURE	LIFE TASKS
Preliminary Lesson	Introducing oneself/others; giving/getting personal information; asking for clarification	*Wh-* questions; present tense; past tense; prepositions of time/place	Greetings and introductions in the U.S.; self-assessment and goal setting; expectations	Writing personal information; interviewing others; using a table of contents
1. Continuing Education	Interrupting; •taking turns; making small talk; asking for clarification; requesting assistance	Future tense; imperatives; *if/then* statements (*if* + present tense + modal); *should* vs. *must/have to*	Concept of adult education; concept of work + study	Reading newspaper articles and course catalogs; listening to lectures; taking notes; filling out school registration forms; identifying/classifying educational programs
2. What the Community Offers	Giving reasons; reporting; expressing needs; requesting information over the phone	*Where* questions + modal: *can; looking for* + service/place; reported speech with *that; can/can't* (possibility); *if/then* statements	Private vs. public services	Reading brochures, newspaper articles, and listings of community services in the telephone directory; accessing community services; listening to recorded messages; filling out forms; writing to community leaders; identifying/classifying information
3. Making Ends Meet	•Complaining; •correcting; describing a problem; requesting information; •speaking emphatically; dealing with numbers	Adverbs of indefinite frequency; *if/then* statements; modals: *can/should*; past tense of irregular verbs	Use of credit in the U.S.; U.S. as a consumer society; comparison of consumerism in the U.S. and in native countries; levels of politeness	Preparing a monthly budget; reading articles about money management; reading bills (utility, credit card, phone, etc.); keeping a checking account register; reading credit card policies; reporting an error on a bill; writing to a friend or relative
4. Living with Machines	Following directions; reporting events; describing a process	•Passive voice; imperatives; modal: *must*; adjectives; •reflexive pronouns	U.S. as a technological society	Reading automated teller machine instructions; reading directions; reading a warranty; filling out an accident report form; writing directions
5. Travels in America	Making inquiries; reporting findings; following directions (reading maps); describing events; comparing/contrasting; clarifying; verifying; expressing preferences	Prepositions of place; •prepositional phrases; *while* clauses; descriptive adjectives; superlatives; *would* + *like*; •*how* + *many/much/far*	Distances within the U.S.; climate; accessing travel information; no need for travel documents; automobile clubs; toll-free numbers	Reading a map; reading a weather map; reading vacation ads and travel brochures; reading map keys and distance charts; writing letters and postcards
6. Discovering Patterns		Verbs: past tense in time clauses; questions: *How far? How long? How often?*; two-word verbs: separable; two-word verbs: inseparable; dependent clauses: *who, that, which*		

UNIT	FUNCTIONS (• introduce)	STRUCTURES (• introduce)	CULTURE	LIFE TASKS
7. Problems on the Job	•Giving/accepting apologies; expressing emotions; expressing uncertainty and confusion; •expressing embarrassment; reporting and describing; •predicting	If/then statements (if + past tense + modal); •what + if; •should have + past participle	Responses and reactions to embarrassing situations; apologies; polite language	Reading job evaluations; explaining company policies and rules; preparing for a meeting with a work supervisor; reading magazine advice articles; reading advice columns; writing an advice letter
8. Saving the Environment	Describing; giving directions; persuading; expressing agreement/disagreement; •stating a position; •expressing opinions	•Present perfect tense; reported speech with that; wh- questions: why; should vs. must/have to; dependent clauses	Individual rights vs. the common good; making of local laws	Reading and following recycling instructions/information; classifying recyclable materials; making charts; preparing a report; reading newspaper editorials; considering the impact of industrial development; disposing of hazardous waste
9. Real Costs of a Car	Explaining/describing (problems, events); dealing with numbers	Should; dependent clauses of reason; dependent clauses of time; wh- questions; past continuous tense	Reasons for buying insurance; consumer protection	Questioning a repair bill; checking a procedure in a maintenance manual; reading an insurance policy; using consumer reports to get information; reading classified ads; comparing bank loan information; asking for an estimate; figuring costs; understanding abbreviations
10. Under the Law	Reporting events; expressing surprise; expressing emotions; giving advice	•Wh- questions; prepositions of time and place; intensifiers; when clauses; passive voice; present perfect tense; yes / no questions	Changing sex roles; legal aid/legal services; cross-cultural views of discipline	Reporting a crime; reading a newspaper article; filing a complaint; reading and understanding legal rights; recognizing deceptive advertising; writing an article for a newsletter
11. Can I Buy a House?	Comparing/contrasting; computing costs; expressing preferences; •hypothesizing; giving/getting advice	Comparative adjectives; •ask + infinitive; descriptive adjectives; •What about...? questions; What if...? questions	Owning property; housing grants; remodeling and improving housing; living with roommates	Reading real estate listings; calculating mortgage costs; reading house inspection reports; calculating home improvement costs; reading housing grant information; using eligibility scales; interpreting newspaper apartment ads
12. Discovering Patterns		Verbs: past and present participles; verbs: present perfect tense; verbs: passive voice; verbs: present perfect continuous tense; conditional sentences; modals: should, can, must; wh- questions		

Preliminary Lesson

Summary

The Preliminary Lesson is designed to welcome learners to the classroom environment and to assess learners' familiarity with the basic English skills taught in Levels 1 and 2. Some of the activities in the Preliminary Lesson are similar to those in Level 2. This lesson gives the teacher the opportunity to evaluate learners' strengths and weaknesses in verbal expression, vocabulary, structures, and written skills. Much of the vocabulary used and practiced in the lesson will be determined by what the learners suggest. If they have a great deal of difficulty with the Preliminary Lesson, it may indicate that learners have been inappropriately placed at Level 3 in this series. On the other hand, if learners have some difficulty only in certain areas, it may indicate a weakness in those areas but does not necessarily reflect inappropriate placement. The lesson can be adapted for one or two class periods.

Objectives

Functions
- Introducing oneself and others
- Giving and getting personal information
- Asking for clarification

Life Tasks
- Interviewing others
- Writing personal information
- Using a table of contents

Structures
- *Wh-* questions
- Present tense
- Past tense
- Prepositions of time and place

Culture
- Greetings and introductions in the United States
- Self-assessment and goal-setting expectations

Vocabulary

Key word categories:
- Education
- Languages
- Names
- Native countries
- People
- Places
- Work

Specific vocabulary within each category will be supplied by learners.

Preliminary Lesson

Purpose: To give practice in giving and getting personal information; to assess listening, speaking, reading, and writing skills; to introduce textbook organization and using a table of contents; to introduce self-evaluation of language needs

Teacher Preparation and Materials

1. Maps of the world and the United States (or use map of the United States on Student Book page 150)
2. Prepare copies of an interview form (see *Presentation* #2 for suggested items to include) or use TRF Handout G.1, *Interview Form*.
3. Blank index cards *(Expansion/Extension)*

Presentation

1. Introduce yourself to the group. Write your name on the board and say *My name is . . . , but you can call me . . . . I'm from* (name of country or state). *I live in* (name of city/town). *I came here in* (year). Point to appropriate places on the map. Then have learners write their names on the board, introduce themselves, and point out their native countries on the world map.
2. Give learners copies of TRF Handout G.1 or prepare an interview form. (**Note:** The form should include questions about name, native country, languages, work and/or education in native country and/or in the United States, length of time in the United States, reasons for coming to the United States, reasons for studying English, and favorite leisure-time activities.) Arrange learners in pairs. Have learners interview each other and fill in the form about their partners. Encourage learners to ask for clarification. If necessary, model interviewing a volunteer. As learners are interviewing each other, walk around and listen. Then have learners use the information on the forms to introduce their partners to the entire group. As learners are introducing each other, note learners' use of tenses and other structures, vocabulary, and pronunciation.
   ■ In a one-to-one situation, have the learner interview you and then you interview the learner.
3. Ask learners where and with whom they speak English. List the names of the places and people on the board. Places/people to include might be job/co-workers, school/teacher, clinic/doctor, store/clerk, post office, bank, immigration, welfare, or other government offices. For each of the places/people listed on the board ask *What do you talk about? Is it easy or difficult to talk to people here? What do you need to read or write here?* Write learners' comments on the board.
4. Ask learners to open their books to the table of contents and have them read over the unit titles. Then ask *Which units do you think are about money issues? Which unit will have maps? What places or people from the list on the board will be in Unit 2? Which unit do you think will be the most interesting? Why?* Give learners time to look through the book.
5. Ask learners about their goals for studying English. *Why do you want to study English? What do you want to be able to read or write? What do you want to be able to talk about in English? What is easy for you? What is difficult for you?* Learners can use the lists on the board and the table of contents to help formulate their goals. Have each learner write his or her goals on the inside cover of the student book or in a writing journal. Throughout the course, encourage learners to look at their goals periodically to assess their progress orally or in writing.

Expansion/Extension

- Ask learners to make a time line about themselves. Learners can include important events and experiences, such as date of birth, schooling in native country, work experience, travel, occurrences related to immigration, and family occasions. In pairs or small groups, ask learners to describe their time lines. Learners can write autobiographies based on their time lines. (**Note:** Learners may want to refer to or add to their time lines or autobiographies throughout the level.)
- Learners can play Twenty Questions. Write on index cards the people, places, and things that were listed on the board in *Presentation* #3. Ask a volunteer to choose a card. Have other learners ask *Yes/No* questions to determine what word is on the card. FOR EXAMPLE: *clinic—* Is it a person? (No.) Is it a place? (Yes.) Can you buy food at this place? (No.) Do nurses work there? (Yes.)

Continuing Education

Objectives

Functions
- Interrupting
- Taking turns
- Making small talk
- Asking for clarification
- Requesting assistance

Life Tasks
- Reading newspaper articles
- Reading course catalogs
- Listening to academic lectures
- Taking notes on lectures
- Filling out school registration forms
- Identifying and classifying educational programs

Structures
- Future tense
- Imperatives
- *If/then* statements
  (*If* + present tense + modal)
- *Should* vs. *must/have to*

Culture
- Concept of adult education
- Concept of combining work + study

Vocabulary

Key words:

academic advisor	loan
associate degree program	major
career	prerequisite
college degree	private
college graduate	public
community college	registration
computer lab	required
course catalog	schedule
credit	scholarship
department	semester
financial aid office	tuition
high school equivalency program	vocational school
	work-study grant

Key abbreviation:

GED–General Educational Development

Related words:

aviation science	floppy
bookkeeping	grammar
business sequence	hard disk
data	internal
database	liberal arts
degree	literature
delete	master's degree
disk	memory
doctorate	printer
early childhood education	science
eject	social studies
external	word processing

In the Computer Lab

Purpose: To introduce characters in the book; to introduce vocabulary about education and computers

Teacher Preparation and Materials

1. Pictures from adult education or community college catalogs: classroom, computer lab, computer, college lecture class, vocational program class (such as auto mechanics, electronics, culinary arts), informal discussion group, person studying alone with a book

2. Adult education catalogs *(Expansion/Extension)*

3. Arrange a field trip to a school computer lab. *(Expansion/Extension)*

4. Computer magazines, manuals, computer store fliers *(Expansion/Extension)*

Warm-up

1. Use pictures to review/introduce types of schools, educational programs, and computers. Elicit/introduce vocabulary. Be sure to include *computer, computer lab, adult education, college,* and *vocational school.*

2. For each of the educational programs pictured, have learners suggest courses, subjects, or skills that might be taught. Ask *What can people study in this type of class? Why do you think people want to study . . . ?* List the types of classes, programs, and courses of study on the board.

Presentation

1. Ask learners to turn to page 5 and look at the picture.

2. To review the present continuous tense, ask questions about what the people in the picture are doing. FOR EXAMPLE: *What is the man at the computer on the right doing?*

3. Have learners guess why the people are in the lab, how old they are, what they are talking about, and why they might want to learn about computers. Write learners'

1 2 3 4 5 6 7 8 9 10 11 12
Continuing Education ■ ■ ■ ■ ■ ■

In the Computer Lab
Where are these people?
What do you think they are studying?
How do you feel about using a computer?

Answers will vary.

comments on the board. Introduce the names of the characters by pointing to them and saying their names.

4. Have learners answer the first two questions at the bottom of the page.

5. Ask learners about their experiences with using computers and being in school. FOR EXAMPLE: *What types of schools have you attended? What were the classrooms like? What did you study? Did you ever use a computer?*

6. Have learners discuss the last question at the bottom of the page.

Expansion/Extension

- Learners can make up conversations based on the picture and role-play them for the group.

- Bring in adult education catalogs. Learners can look through them for names of schools and types of course offerings. Learners can discuss which ones sound interesting and explain why.

More *Expansion/Extension* on page 40

Who's in the Lab Today?

Purpose: To give practice in getting information from written sources; to introduce job- and school-related vocabulary

Teacher Preparation and Materials

1. Pictures of workplaces and jobs: hospital, shoe store, restaurant, landscaping business, laboratory assistant, gardener, assistant manager, waiter
2. Copies of TRF Handout 1.1, *Find a Person Who . . . (Expansion/Extension)*
3. Tape recorder *(Expansion/Extension)*

Warm-up

Use pictures to introduce/review the names of workplaces and jobs. Then practice questions and answers about the learners' jobs and computers. Ask *Do you work? What do you do? Are computers used at your workplace? If so, do you use a computer there? Where else can you see people working with computers?* If the group is large, learners can interview each other and then share the information with the group.

Presentation

1. Ask learners to turn to page 6 and look at the pictures. Have learners make predictions about the characters, their jobs, and their interest in computers.
2. Have learners read the biographical information and circle words they do not know. Elicit/explain the meanings of new words, such as *business course, science, athletic, inventory,* and *keep track of.*
3. Ask literal and inferential questions about the biographical pieces, such as *Who studied science? Who wants to have his or her own business? Why would computers be necessary in a hospital? Why do you think Stan wants to study computers? Do you think Roberto uses a computer at work?*

---

6 **Who's in the Lab Today?**

Four friends are working in the computer lab today.
Underline the sentence in each story that tells why each person is in the lab.

Diep Tran is a single parent with two young children. She studied science in Vietnam. Now she is working part-time as a laboratory assistant in a hospital. The hospital is getting a new computer system. Diep is taking a computer course so that she'll be prepared to use the new system.

Yolette Jamison is married. She came to the United States from Haiti. She's the assistant manager of an athletic shoe store. She uses a computer to keep track of inventory. She wants to learn more about computers so that she can get an office job.

Stan Wolanski is single and lives with his parents. He and his family came from Poland. Stan works as a gardener. He wants to be his own boss. He's taking business courses so that he can have his own landscaping business someday.

Roberto Silva is married with two children. He and his family came from Puerto Rico. He's a waiter at a hotel restaurant. He works until midnight and only sees his family on weekends. He's studying computers so that he can get a different kind of job.

---

4. Have learners read the biographies again and underline the reason why each person is in the computer lab.
5. As a group, go over the responses. Have learners explain their responses.
6. Have learners discuss their own reasons for being in class. Ask *Why do you want to study more English? What are your goals for studying English?* Learners can each write a short autobiographical piece in their writing journals. Learners can keep a copy of their writing in their portfolio.

Expansion/Extension

See **TRF HANDOUT 1.1,** *Find a Person Who . . .*

- If tape recorders are available, learners might want to start making personal recordings of their oral production by reading their autobiographical pieces. Learners could add to their recordings throughout the course as part of their portfolios.

Adult Education Options

Purpose: To give practice in reading newspaper articles; to introduce information about adult education programs

Teacher Preparation and Materials

1. Pictures from adult education or community college catalogs, used for page 5
2. Pictures or books about subjects/skills: math, grammar, science, business skills, auto mechanics, early childhood education, health care
3. Copies of TRF Handout 1.4, *Test Is a Four-Letter Word (Expansion/Extension)*
4. Adult education, community college, and vocational school catalogs and/or local telephone books *(Expansion/Extension)*
5. Invite an academic counselor or school administrator to speak to the class. *(Expansion/Extension)*
6. College and university catalogs *(Expansion/Extension)*

Warm-up

1. Use pictures to review names of classrooms and educational programs, including *vocational, adult education,* and *college.*
2. Show pictures or books about skills/subjects. Elicit/introduce the names of skills/subjects. Ask *What types of skills and subjects do you think would be taught in vocational schools? in colleges? in adult education programs? What do you think the differences between these types of schools and programs are?*

Presentation

1. Have learners turn to page 7. Have a volunteer read the title and introductory paragraph. Ask *What do you think the article will tell you? Why do you think these people are interested in learning about adult education programs?*

Adult Education Options   7

Yolette brought in a newspaper article about different kinds of adult education programs in the area. Her friends in the computer lab wanted to know more about their different choices.

Adult Education: *What's Available?*

Planning for college and careers can be an exciting time. But it can also be a time of stress and indecision. According to Ronald Briggs, academic advisor at Tri-County Community College, "Many students think that a four-year college is their only choice. They are intimidated by the requirements they think they have to meet. The first thing I do is make sure that adults know what's out there. I always give them a rundown of the main kinds of educational programs available to them."

- **General Educational Development (GED)** is a national high school equivalency program for adults who do not have a high school diploma. Many local adult education programs, school districts, community colleges, and universities offer classes to prepare adults for the GED exam. Classes include work in grammar, writing, math, science, social studies, and literature.

- **Vocational Programs** offer training to prepare students for many kinds of jobs. The subjects include business skills, hairstyling, drafting, air conditioning and refrigeration repair, and auto mechanics.

Vocational training programs are offered by vocational schools, business schools, and many adult education programs.

- **Associate Degree Programs** are two-year programs offered by community colleges, junior colleges, and some business schools. They are useful for adults who need career skills quickly or who are not ready or able to attend four-year colleges. Associate degree credits can be transferred to four-year college programs. Associate degrees are awarded in a wide variety of subjects, including liberal arts, early childhood education, computer technology, health care, and business administration.

Answer the questions.   Answers will vary.
1. Have you attended any programs like these?
2. What educational programs are you interested in? Why?
3. What programs or subjects might be useful for your goals? Why?

---

2. Have learners skim the article for specific information. Ask *How many programs does the academic advisor talk about? Where can people study for the GED exam? Which programs offer career skills? How long does it take to get an associate degree?*

3. Have learners read the article and underline words they do not know. Elicit/explain the meanings of new words: *careers, academic advisor, intimidated, GED, indecision, rundown, equivalency, school district, junior, credits, transferred,* and *variety.*

4. On the board, list the three programs discussed: *GED, Vocational School,* and *Community College.* Ask why adults study at the three programs. Elicit/provide examples of subjects and skills taught at each. Elicit/introduce degrees offered and write them on the board: *high school equivalency diploma* and *associate degree.*

5. Have learners discuss the questions at the bottom of the page. (**Note:** Not all learners need additional education to achieve their goals.)

Expansion/Extension **on page 40**

What Classes Should I Take?

Purpose: To introduce reading course catalogs; to give practice in interrupting/taking turns and in asking for clarification; to give practice with the modals *should, must, have to*

Teacher Preparation and Materials

1. Community college or adult education course catalogs and schedules
2. Index cards with names of courses: *Basic Mathematics, Beginning Business Math, Advanced Business Math, Beginning Word Processing, Advanced Word Processing, Introduction to Computers*
3. ▄▄▄ Audiotape for Level 3

Warm-up

1. Have learners look through community college or adult education course catalogs and schedules. Ask *What are these? What is listed in the catalogs? Can people take any course they want?*
2. Have learners categorize (by department) the index cards with course names. Then have learners arrange the courses in the order that they should be taken.
3. Elicit/introduce new vocabulary (*department, required,* and *prerequisite*), using the courses on the index cards. Say *Introduction to Computers and Beginning Word Processing are in the Computer Department. You need to take Introduction to Computers before Beginning Word Processing. It's required. It is a prerequisite to Beginning Word Processing.*
4. Use information about Stan and the courses to practice the modals *should* and *must/have to.* FOR EXAMPLE: *Stan works in the afternoon. When do you think he should study?*

Presentation

1. Have learners turn to page 8. Ask *What do you know about Stan? Who do you think the other man is? What do you think*

8

What Classes Should I Take?

▄▄▄ **A. Complete the story.**

Stan needs help deciding which <u>classes</u> [1] to take next semester. He has taken Introduction to <u>Computers</u> [2] and Beginning <u>Word</u> [3] Processing. His counselor, Mr. Briggs, said that Basic <u>Math</u> [4] is a prerequisite for all other <u>business</u> [5] courses. Prerequisites must be taken <u>before</u> [6] other courses. Mr. Briggs also suggested that Stan take a Business <u>Writing</u> [7] class.

> **Basic Mathematics** reviews math for business. It covers addition, subtraction, multiplication, and division of whole numbers; fractions; percents; ratios; and decimals. It uses real business problems. Prerequisite for the business sequence.
>
> | | | |
> |---|---|---|
> | Dept.: **Math** | Cr.: **3** | Rm.: **202** |
> | Title: **Basic Mathematics** | Instr.: **Moy** | Time: **8:30–11:30 a.m.** |
> | Course No./Sec.: **85/01** | Day: **Mon.** | |

B. Find the abbreviation.
Which abbreviation tells you . . .

		Abbreviation	Meaning
1.	the name of the overall subject?	Dept.	Department
2.	the name of the teacher?	Instr.	Instructor
3.	the location of the class?	Rm.	Room
4.	the units toward graduation that the class fulfills?	Cr.	Credit(s)

---

they are talking about? What classes do you think Stan might take?*

2. Ask learners to make a chart:

Stan has taken . . .	Stan will take . . .

▄▄▄ Play the audiotape. Have learners listen for the names of courses and fill them in on the chart.

3. ▄▄▄ Have learners listen again to find out why Stan should take the courses that are suggested.
4. Have learners complete the paragraph in exercise A. ▄▄▄ If necessary, play the audiotape again. Learners can compare responses with a partner or in groups.
5. Have learners look at the course description for Basic Math and circle the abbreviations. Have them guess the meanings of the abbreviations and complete exercise B. Have learners explain what clues or information they used to make their guesses. Explain the concept of credits in degree programs.

Expansion/Extension **on page 40**

Schedule and Registration

Purpose: To give practice in reading course catalogs and in filling out school registration forms

Teacher Preparation and Materials

1. Community college or adult education course schedules, used for page 8
2. Index cards with words and abbreviations: *Dept., Sec., No., Course Title, Cr.*
3. School registration forms
4. Copies of TRF Handout 1.5, *Sign Me Up! (Expansion/Extension)*
5. Copies of TRF Handout 1.2, *English Is a Race Car (Expansion/Extension)*
6. Copies of TRF Handout 1.7, *Setting a Language Goal (Expansion/Extension)*
7. Community college or adult education course catalogs *(Expansion/Extension)*

Warm-up

1. Have learners look through course schedules for courses in mathematics, computers, English, and so on.
2. Tape the index cards on the board as column headings. Ask for the name of a course. Write it under the appropriate heading. Elicit the other information about the course and write it on the board under the correct heading. Repeat with other courses. Review the meaning of *credits.*
3. Show samples of school registration forms. Ask *What do you think these forms are? What are they used for? Why do you need to register for classes? Have you ever filled out forms like these? Did you fill one out for this class? What information is needed about classes when you register?*

Presentation

1. Have learners turn to page 9. Together read the title and introductory paragraph.

Schedule and Registration

9

Stan wants to take three classes next term. He works from noon to 6 p.m. every day. Help Stan choose his courses and complete his registration form.

Dept.	No.	Sec.	Course Title	Cr.	Days	Time	Rm.	INSTR.
Math	85	01	Basic Mathematics	3	M	8:30–11:30 a.m.	202	Moy
		02			M W	9:30–11:00 a.m.	317	Rogers
		03			T Th	6:00–7:30 p.m.	212	Randall
Engl	125	01	Business Writing	3	T Th	2:30–4:00 p.m.	110	Black
		02			M W F	8:00–9:00 a.m.	328	Ross
		03			T	5:00–8:00 p.m.	110	Black
Comp	215	01	Adv. Word Processing	2	T	9:30–11:30 a.m.	5	Jordan
		02			F	9:30–11:30 a.m.	5	Jordan

Complete the Registration Form.

ADULT AND CONTINUING EDUCATION

Have you taken an adult education class before? ☑ Yes ☐ No

If yes, last course and enrollment date: _Intro. to Computers and Beginning Word Processing – Fall '04_

SECTION IV

Dept.	No.	Sec.	Course Title	Credits	Office Use Only
M A T H	8 5	0 2		3	
			Basic Math		
E n g l	1 2 5	0 2	Business Writing	3	
C o m p	2 1 5	0 1	Adv. Word Processing	2	

(or 0 2) Total number of credits: __8__

$80.00 per credit

Amount: __$640__

Method of Payment:
☐ Cash   ☑ Check or Money Order   ☐ Credit Card

---

2. Have learners prepare and ask each other questions about the schedule. (FOR EXAMPLE: Who teaches Business Math on Monday morning? When is Business Writing offered by Instructor Ross? Is there a Word Processing class in the evening?)
3. Have learners look at the registration form. Ask literal and inferential questions about the form, such as *What courses has Stan taken? What math course does he want to take now? Why doesn't he sign up for section 01? Which Business Writing section do you think he should sign up for? Why?*
4. Have learners complete the form, making sure that there are no schedule conflicts with Stan's work. Have learners explain their choices.

Expansion/Extension

***See* TRF HANDOUT 1.5,** *Sign Me Up!*
TRF HANDOUT 1.2, *English Is a Race Car*
TRF HANDOUT 1.7, *Setting a Language Goal*

More *Expansion/Extension* on page 40

Getting Help from a Friend

Purpose: To give practice in requesting assistance and in making small talk; to give practice with *If/then*

Teacher Preparation and Materials

1. Audiotape for Level 3
2. Community college or adult education course catalogs *(Expansion/Extension)*
3. Financial aid application forms *(Expansion/Extension)*

Warm-up

1. Have learners discuss costs for education. Elicit/explain *tuition, financial aid office, scholarship, loan, work-study grant.* Ask *How much money did Stan need to pay for his courses on page 9? How much tuition did he have to pay? How can people get money for education?*

2. Review *If/then* statements. Ask questions about education costs and have learners respond. FOR EXAMPLE: *If Stan takes four courses, how much will it cost? If you need help paying for school, where can you ask for help?*

Presentation

1. Have learners turn to page 10. Ask *Who do you see? What do you think Yolette is thinking about? What are things that make it difficult for adults who go to school?* List responses on the board.

2. Play the first conversation on the audiotape. Ask literal and inferential questions, such as *What happens when Ms. Arno keeps the class late? Do Yolette and Diep like the teacher? Where does Diep go after class? Where does Yolette have to go after class? What happens if they are late? What can they do about the problem?* Have learners suggest what Yolette or Diep might say to Ms. Arno. Have learners role-play the situation.

3. Have learners fill in the answers in exercise A. Then discuss the questions

in exercise B. Ask if learners have ever had to tell (or should have told) a boss or teacher about conflicting schedules or responsibilities. Ask *Did you talk about the problems? What did you say (or could you have said)? How did you feel after asserting yourself (or not asserting yourself)?*

4. Play the second conversation. Ask literal and inferential questions, such as *Why is Diep thinking of taking just one course next term? How can the Financial Aid Office help students like Diep? What else did Diep learn from Yolette that may help her?*

5. Have learners discuss the questions in exercise C. With large classes, have learners work in pairs or small groups. One learner in each group should act as the reporter, asking questions and clarifying responses, and another learner should act as the recorder, writing the responses. Have the reporter in each group share the group's conclusions with the class.

---

10 | **Getting Help from a Friend**

A. Complete the sentences.

1. If Ms. Arno keeps the class late, the students <u>are late for other activities.</u>

2. If Yolette leaves class more than five minutes late, she _____ <u>misses her bus.</u>

3. If Yolette misses her bus, she <u>is late for work.</u>

4. If Diep is late picking up her son, Hai, from day care, she _____ <u>gets charged extra.</u>

5. If Ms. Arno is still talking, the students <u>don't like to get up and leave.</u>

Answers will vary.

B. Think and talk about the questions.

1. How do you think the students feel when Ms. Arno keeps the class late?
2. Why is it hard for them to leave when class is over but the instructor is still talking?
3. What would you do if you had an instructor like Ms. Arno and you had to leave?

C. Think and talk about the questions. Answers will vary.

1. Why is Diep planning to take only one course next term?
2. Why do you think she didn't know about the day care center at her school?
3. Why do you think Yolette's work-study grant ended?
4. Is financial aid available at your school? If so, what kind?
5. How do you feel about taking out a loan to pay for your education?

***Expansion/Extension* on page 41**

Ways People Learn

Purpose: To give practice in discussing learning strategies and experiences; to give practice with the past tense

Teacher Preparation and Materials

Copies of TRF Handout 1.3, *A Successful Learner (Expansion/Extension)*

Warm-up

1. Ask a volunteer *What did you learn when you were a child? What did you learn in school? at home?* (to walk, to ride a bicycle, to do math, to sew, and so on) *What things have you learned as an adult?*

2. On the board, make a chart:

	What	**How**
Children learn . . .		
Adults learn . . .		

Have learners suggest and write different subjects and skills for the two age groups on the chart. Ask how the skills and subjects are learned. FOR EXAMPLE: *How did you learn to cook?* (by watching my parents or helping them) *How did you learn to speak English?* (by listening and reading) Have learners suggest and write different learning strategies on the chart.

Presentation

1. Have learners turn to page 11. Have a volunteer read the title and introduction. Ask *What can you learn by listening? What can you listen to? What types of things can you learn alone?*

2. Have learners identify the way(s) that they feel most comfortable learning. Have learners name something they have learned in the past year. (I learned to use a computer, to play volleyball, to drive, etc.) Ask *How did you learn? Did someone show you what to do? Did you use books, audiotapes, a video, or a machine? How did you feel at first? Was it easy or difficult? Why? Did anyone help you? Did you practice a lot? How did you feel afterward?* Have several learners describe

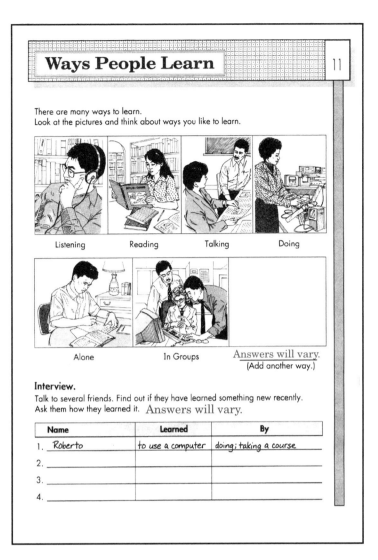

their learning experiences, using the past tense. If necessary, write irregular past tense verbs on the board.

3. Have learners interview three or four classmates, friends, or neighbors about learning experiences and record the responses in their books. If necessary, model interviewing a learner and record the responses on the board. Afterward, have learners report any interesting learning experiences they heard about in their interviews.

Expansion/Extension

See **TRF HANDOUT 1.3,** *A Successful Learner*

- Ask learners to list adjectives to describe how they feel in learning situations. If necessary, give some examples: *eager, attentive, curious, frustrated, afraid, careful.* As a group, compile a list of the most common adjectives mentioned. Learners can suggest ways that teachers can help learners who are frustrated or afraid. Encourage learners to tell instructors how they feel about learning situations.

More *Expansion/Extension* on page 41

Understanding Computers

Purpose: To introduce academic lectures (instructional talk); to give practice in taking lecture notes

Teacher Preparation and Materials

1. Pictures of computers, hard disks, and diskettes
2. 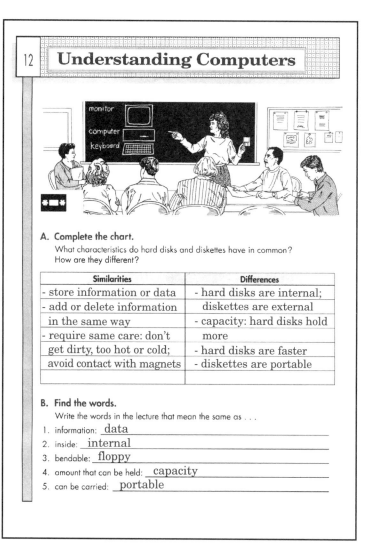 Audiotape for Level 3
3. Copies of TRF Handout 1.6, *Computers for You (Expansion/Extension)*
4. Computer magazines, manuals, or advertisements *(Expansion/Extension)*

Warm-up

1. Show pictures of computers, hard disks, and diskettes, or have learners look at an actual computer. Have learners identify components they know. Elicit/explain *hard disks* and *diskettes* (or *floppy disks*).
2. Ask learners what they think some of the similarities and differences between hard disks and diskettes might be. On the board make a chart of learners' responses.

Presentation

1. Have learners turn to page 12. Ask questions about the picture, such as *What class do you think this is? What do you think the instructor is talking about? Do you think this class would be easy or difficult to understand? Why?*
2. Have learners look at the chart in exercise A to guide their listening. Play the audiotape and ask learners to listen for the similarities and differences and to fill in the information on the chart. Before they check their work, ask learners if they have any questions.
3. Have learners report the information that they heard as you fill in or correct the chart on the board. Replay the audiotape so learners can verify the information on the chart.
4. Have learners look at the vocabulary in exercise B. Explain that Ms. Arno uses technical words in her lecture but she also

explains them. Learners should listen for the words and her explanation and then write the words next to their meanings. Replay the audiotape so learners can complete exercise B.

5. Ask learners if they have any more questions about the lecture. On the board, review the answers to the exercise.
6. Have learners describe how they felt during the lecture. Ask *Was it easy or difficult to understand the information? Why? Was it easy or difficult to take notes? Why?* Have learners share successful strategies they used to accomplish the activities.

Expansion/Extension

See **TRF HANDOUT 1.6,** *Computers for You*

* Learners can look through computer manuals, magazines, or advertisements for information on computer components. Learners can find out types of computer disks used in the computers at their school or workplace.

More *Expansion/Extension* on page 41

Computers at Work

Purpose: To give practice in reading for information; to introduce analyzing tasks

Teacher Preparation and Materials

1. Pictures or index cards with words: *accountant, police officer, secretary, manager, laboratory assistant, shoe store, hospital, landscaping company*

2. Arrange a field trip to a library or another place where learners can observe computers in use. *(Expansion/Extension)*

Warm-up

1. Use pictures to review/introduce names of jobs and workplaces. Be sure to include *accountant, police officer, secretary, manager, laboratory assistant, shoe store, hospital,* and *landscaping company.*

2. Ask learners how computers might be used in each of the workplaces or in each of the jobs. List learners' responses on the board.

Presentation

1. Have learners turn to page 13 and read the title. Ask *What do you think this reading passage is going to tell you?*

2. Have learners read the article and underline words they do not know. Elicit/explain the meanings of new words: *bookkeeping, efficiently, inventory, memories, in stock, analyze lab samples.*

3. Have learners speculate about the various uses of computers. Ask *What other kinds of work do computers do (which we can add to the list on the board)? Do all computers do the same jobs? Why? Do you think computers are replacing too many jobs?*

4. Have learners complete exercise A. As you go over the answers, have learners give reasons for their responses by referring back to the article.

5. Discuss the questions in exercise B. In larger classes, have learners work in small groups, with one learner acting as the reporter and another acting as the recorder. ■ In a one-to-one situation, have the learner answer the questions and then discuss his or her responses with you.

6. Have reporters share their group's responses.

Expansion/Extension

- If possible, have learners observe a computer performing different tasks. Many libraries have computers for researching books and other materials. School offices have computers for word processing, keeping address lists, and attendance/academic records. Learners can take notes on their observations. If learners work, have them find out about the equipment used at their workplaces and then tell others in the class about their findings.

Computers at Work — 13

People all over the world use computers at work. Secretaries use computers to prepare letters. Accountants use computers to do bookkeeping. Even police officers use computers to keep track of crimes in their cities.

Yolette works at The Sport Shoe. She already knows how to keep the store's shoe inventory on the computer. Since computers have large memories, Yolette simply presses a button to see if she has a particular shoe in stock. She doesn't have to waste time searching for the shoes in the back room. The computer even tells her what shelf the shoes are on. Now she is learning additional computer skills so that she can help run the store more efficiently.

Diep works at City Hospital. She is learning more about computers for a similar reason. She has to analyze many lab samples every day. Her supervisor expects her to do the tests as quickly as possible. The hospital is putting in a new computer system so that laboratory workers like Diep can complete their work more efficiently.

Stan works for Manny's Landscaping Company, and he often sees his boss using various computer programs. The programs keep track of who the customers are and where they live. They also keep track of how many full-time and part-time employees are needed at different times of the year. Now Stan is learning how to use these programs too.

All of these people know one major thing: Computers can help make everyone's life much easier.

A. Check (✔) Yes or No. Would these people use a computer at their workplace to do the following things?

	Yes	No
1. Yolette needs to know if she has a pair of red, size 8 sneakers in stock.	✔	
2. Stan's boss wants to know how many employees he needs in August.	✔	
3. Stan has to check a customer's address.	✔	
4. Diep needs to order some sterilized test tubes.		✔
5. Yolette wants to know the names of all the shoe stores in New York City.		✔
6. Diep needs to analyze five blood samples.	✔	

B. Think and talk about the questions. Answers may vary.
1. What other ways can people use computers at work?
2. What ways can people use computers at home?

More *Expansion/Extension* on page 41

Using a Computer

Purpose: To give practice in interrupting, taking turns, and asking for clarification; to give practice with *If/then* statements

Teacher Preparation and Materials

1. Pictures of computers and computer components
2. ▄▄▄ Audiotape for Level 3

Warm-up

1. Show pictures of computers and various components. Have learners identify components that they know. Elicit/explain *hard disk, data, memory,* and *program.* Learners can check back on pages 12 and 13 for some of the vocabulary.
2. Write several *If* phrases on the board. Have learners suggest appropriate *then* phrases using the information about the computer. FOR EXAMPLE: *If Yolette needs to find some sneakers in the store,* ([then] she can check the inventory list on the computer). *If Stan has to check a customer's address,* ([then] he can look it up on the computer). Have learners create other *If/then* sentences.

14 **Using a Computer**

One day when Yolette was working in the shoe store, Lou, the store manager, complained that too many sale fliers had been returned in the mail.

▄▄▄

A. Write the answers.
1. What is Lou's problem? A lot of fliers got returned.
2. What is Yolette's solution? a database of the mailing list
3. What are Yolette's reasons for suggesting the database? target customers; save money and time

B. Think and talk about the questions. Answers may vary.
1. What kind of employee is Yolette?
2. What kind of boss do you think Lou is?
3. How can a computerized mailing list help the business?

Presentation

1. Ask learners to turn to page 14 and look at the picture. Have a volunteer read the introductory paragraph. Ask *Why do you think the store manager is upset about the fliers? What do you know about Yolette? How do you think she will react to this problem?* (Learners can look back at pages 6 and 10 for information on Yolette.)
2. ▄▄▄ Play the audiotape. Ask literal and inferential questions, such as *Why were the fliers returned to the store? What does Yolette suggest doing? What information does she think the list should include? Do you think it will solve the problem of wrong addresses? Why do you think Lou doesn't know much about computers?* Have learners complete exercise A. If necessary, have learners listen again to the conversation.
3. Discuss the questions in exercise B. In larger classes, have learners work

in small groups, with one learner acting as the reporter and another learner acting as the recorder. Have learners support the inferences they make about the characters.
■ In a one-to-one situation, the learner can answer the questions and then discuss his or her responses.
4. Have reporters share their group's conclusions. Allow time for further discussion.

Expansion/Extension

- If possible, learners can prepare a database about their class on an available computer. They may want to include names, addresses, jobs, native languages, ages, and so on.
- Have learners discuss Lou's reaction to Yolette's suggestion. Ask *Was Lou pleased with the suggestion? Who is going to do the work? Do you think Yolette should get something for the extra work she will do, or should she set up the customer mailing list database for free?*

More *Expansion/Extension* on page 41

Practicing Your Skills

Purpose: To give practice in sequencing and in stating/writing goals; to give practice with imperatives and with the future tense

Teacher Preparation and Materials

Small Business Association materials on starting a business *(Expansion/Extension)*

Warm-up

1. Make a chart on the board with the headings *Name* and *Goal*. Have learners review information about the characters in the unit and fill in the chart. Ask *Who are they? What do they do? Why are they studying computers? What are their personal goals?* Learners can look back at other pages in the unit for information.

2. Ask learners about their personal goals. Fill in their names and goals on the chart.

Presentation

1. Have learners turn to page 15, read the story, and underline words they do not know. Elicit/explain the meanings of new words, such as *energy, successful, goal, business sequence,* and *graduate.*

2. Ask *What is Stan's goal? How long does he expect it to take before he will have his own business? How will each of the steps listed help him achieve his goal?*

3. Review the chart on the board. Have learners break their goals into steps: now, soon, and later. (FOR EXAMPLE: Now I want to find out about health-related careers. Soon I'll be able to . . . . Later I'll . . . .) (**Note:** Some long-term goals may have more than three or four steps.)

4. In pairs or small groups, have learners share their goals, the steps, and how they plan to achieve them, using the future tense and sequence words.

5. Have learners individually write about one of their long-term goals on page 15. Encourage learners to review their goals periodically to assess their progress and to determine if they need to change anything.

Practicing Your Skills

15

Stan wants to start his own landscaping company. He believes that he has the skills and energy to be a successful businessman. He wants to be his own boss within the next five years. He's even planned the name of his company—Stan Wolanski: Landscape Designs. He'll take the following steps to help him reach his goal:

1. Complete computer class this term.
2. Continue working and save $300 per month.
3. Take three courses next term.
4. Start the business sequence at the community college next year.

Stan plans to keep working and saving money while he studies. He hopes to start his business right after he graduates.

What long-term goals do you have?
Write about one of your long-term goals. Answers will vary.

My long-term goal is to _____
_____.

To reach my goal I have to . . .

1. _____.
2. _____.
3. _____.
4. _____.

Expansion/Extension

- Have learners create a time line for their goals.

- Learners may want to expand their ideas on their goals in their writing journals.

- Individually or in small groups learners can create a "business." Learners can decide on a type of business, name for the business, trademark, slogan, description of services offered, number of employees, building design (interior and/or exterior), and so on. Learners can share their businesses with the class.

- Bring in information from the Small Business Administration about starting businesses. Learners can explore different options for having their own business, such as self-employment, sole ownership, partnership, and corporation. If learners are interested, bring in information about legal and financial requirements for each type of business.

More *Expansion/Extension* on page 41

Verbs: Future Tense with *Will*/Imperatives

Purpose: To give practice in using the future tense with *will* and in using imperatives

Teacher Preparation and Materials
None

Warm-up

1. Elicit statements about learners' current and future activities. Ask questions about what learners are doing now, today, this week. Then contrast with questions about their plans for the immediate future, asking what they will do tomorrow, in the next few days, or next week. Ask specific questions about work, school, family, leisure, travel, and so on. Include questions to elicit who will do the activities, how much time they will take, and so on. Model use of questions with *won't* to indicate surprise or to ask for clarification. FOR EXAMPLE: *Won't you be at home tomorrow evening?*

2. Review formation and use of imperatives. Say to the class, *I want José to write today's date on the board.* Then turn to José and say, *José, write today's date on the board.* Model with similar statements to other learners. FOR EXAMPLE: *Close the window, please, Leo.* Write the imperative sentences on the board, and focus attention on the base verb forms.

Presentation

1. Have learners turn to page 16. Review the forms of future tense with *will* in sentences and questions. Focus attention on the form of the contractions.

2. Have learners complete the first exercise. Review answers by having one or more pairs of learners say the conversation between Yolette and Lou.

3. Ask questions to check comprehension and reinforce use of the future tense. FOR EXAMPLE: *When will Yolette start the new database? How long will it take?*

4. Look at the examples of imperatives. Make sure learners understand formation of a negative command.

16 | **Verbs: Future Tense with *Will*/Imperatives**

I He She It You We They	will 'll will not won't	write	a new program.

Will Won't	I he she it you we they	write	a new program?

Complete the conversation. Use the future tense.

Example: Yolette: ___I'll start___ the new database next week.
             I/start
       Lou: Will it take long?

1. Yolette: I'm not sure. ___You'll have___ to help.
                   you/have

2. Lou: ___Will Peter help___ ?
           Peter/help

3. Yolette: ___He won't be___ back until Friday.
           he/not be

4. Lou: ___Won't we finish___ before then?
          we/not finish

5. Yolette: I don't think so. ___This will take___ quite a while.
                  this/take

Take Don't take	Mr. Brown's math class next term. the statistics class this year.

Read the situation. Then tell Diep what to do. Use an imperative. Answers will vary.

Example: Diep often wants to ask questions during class, but she doesn't know how.
    ___Raise your hand when you have a question, Diep.___

1. Diep wants to tell her teacher that she has a problem when class runs late.
    _____

2. Diep would like to talk to other students, but she has no time right after class.
    _____

5. Have learners look at the example in the second exercise. Explain that they are going to give advice to Diep. Read the first situation and the suggested answer. Ask learners if this is good advice and if they have anything else to tell Diep. Write additional suggestions on the board, and note use of an imperative verb form.

6. Learners can work in pairs to complete the exercise. Have them share their suggestions. Make sure all are expressed with an imperative form. Discuss the suggestions, and decide which are the best advice.

7. For additional practice, pose another problem for Diep, and have learners tell her what to do. FOR EXAMPLE: *If Diep is late picking up her child from day care, she has to pay extra charges. She can't afford the extra money.*

Expansion/Extension

- Learners can ask each other about future plans for various work, home, or leisure activities. Then have volunteers tell about their own or a classmate's plans. Elicit sentences with *won't* as well as with *will*.

More *Expansion/Extension* on page 41

Modals: *Should, Must/Have to*

Purpose: To give practice in distinguishing and using the modals *should* and *must* or *have to*

Teacher Preparation and Materials

1. Community college or adult education course schedules, used for page 8 *(Warm-up, Expansion/Extension)*

2. Help wanted ads from a local newspaper *(Expansion/Extension)*

Warm-up

1. Have learners focus on a limited part of a course schedule, such as the listing for a multisection course. Use information about various learners to model and elicit the modals *should* and *must / have to*. FOR EXAMPLE: *Ilona works every morning. Which section of this class should she take?* If there is a prerequisite, ask, *What course must learners take before this one?*

2. Elicit suggestions for class rules and rec-ommendations, including what learners have to do or should do in order to succeed in school and what they mustn't do or shouldn't do. (FOR EXAMPLE: Learners have to call in if they are going to be absent. They should always do their homework. Learners shouldn't be late for class.)

Presentation

1. Have learners turn to page 17 and read the example. Then read the course de-scription. Review vocabulary, and make sure learners understand the details of the class schedule (time, instructor, and so on). If necessary, refer learners to the exercise they did on page 8.

2. Have learners look at the example. Say, *Yolette wants to review percents and ra-tios. Has she ever studied those subjects before? Does this class cover them? Is this class a good idea for Yolette or not?*

3. Learners can work in pairs or small groups to complete the exercise. Review answers, and have volunteers explain why their choice is correct.

Modals: *Should, Must/Have to*　　17

Advice	You **should** take a math class.	Diep **shouldn't** miss class.
Requirement	I **have to** take math this term. Roberto **has to** take it, too.	I **don't have to** take a computer class. Diep **doesn't have to** take one, either.
	We **must** take the prerequisite.	They **mustn't** take this class yet.

Read the course description. Check (✔) the correct answer.

Basic Mathematics reviews math for business. It covers addition, subtraction, multiplication, and division of whole numbers; fractions; percents; ratios; and decimals. It uses real business problems. Prerequisite for the business sequence.

Dept.: **Math**	Cr.: **3**	Rm.: **202**
Title: **Basic Mathematics**	Instr.: **Moy**	Time: **8:30–11:30 a.m.**
Course No./Sec.: **85/01**	Day: **Mon.**	

Example: Yolette wants to review percents and ratios.
　　　　　　 ＿＿ a. She must take Basic Mathematics.
　　　　　　 ✔ b. She should take Basic Mathematics.

1. Stan wants to take Small Business Practices.
　　　　 ＿＿ a. He doesn't have to take Basic Mathematics.
　　　　 ✔ b. He has to take Basic Mathematics.

2. Yolette wants to improve her writing skills.
　　　　 ＿＿ a. She shouldn't take Basic Mathematics.
　　　　 ✔ b. She doesn't have to take Basic Mathematics.

3. Roberto wants to understand practical business math.
　　　　 ✔ a. He should take Basic Mathematics.
　　　　 ＿＿ b. He has to take Basic Mathematics.

4. He doesn't want to study with Professor Moy.
　　　　 ＿＿ a. He mustn't take this course.
　　　　 ✔ b. He shouldn't take this course.

5. Roberto and Diep want to take a math class on Tuesday morning.
　　　　 ＿＿ a. They don't have to register for this course.
　　　　 ✔ b. They shouldn't register for this course.

Expansion/Extension

- Have learners look through the course schedules and find courses that interest them. Have them explain why a certain course or section of a course is something they should/have to or should not/must not take, based on their interests, goals, work schedules, and family re-sponsibilities. (FOR EXAMPLE: I want to become a computer programmer. I must start with the Introduction to Com-puters class. It's a prerequisite for other classes. I work on Mondays, Wednesdays, and Fridays. I have to take Section 4 of the class, because it meets on Tuesdays and Thursdays.)

- Have learners look at help wanted ads and decide, based on their current skills and interests, what job or jobs they should apply for. They can also indicate which jobs they shouldn't apply for. Have them share their choices with the class and explain reasons for those choices.

- Learners can pick a job they would like to have but don't currently qualify for. Have them explain what they must do in order to meet the qualifications for the job they want.

More *Expansion/Extension* on page 41

UNIT 1: Continuing Education
Expansion/Extension

In the Computer Lab
More *Expansion/Extension* for SB page 5

- If there is a computer lab in your school or area, arrange a visit to the lab. Learners can find out what courses and programs are available as well as any requirements and costs for using the computer lab.
- Learners can start a writing journal. As the first entry, they can write about their present and past educational experiences.
- Learners can list machines, materials, and objects used in classrooms. Learners can explain how they are used, why they are helpful, and which they enjoy using. Include things like audiotapes, tape recorders, overhead projectors, chalkboards, VCRs, books, dictionaries, encyclopedias, and atlases.
- Learners can look through computer magazines, store ads on computers, and computer manuals for information about computers. Ask *How do computers help people? What can people do with the help of computers? Where are computers used? Can you use a computer if you do not know how to type?*

Adult Education Options
Expansion/Extension for SB page 7

See TRF HANDOUT 1.4, *Test Is a Four-Letter Word*

- Learners can make a list of local school names and programs offered, using program catalogs and/or local phone books.
- Learners can compare educational systems in the United States and in their native countries. Learners can discuss the number of years studied at each level, the types of courses/skills taught, the types of degrees offered, the cost of educational programs, the entrance requirements for different programs, and the educational standards.
- Arrange for a guest speaker, such as an academic counselor or school administrator to visit the class. Learners can prepare questions beforehand and take notes on the talk. Later, learners can write a report about the speech.
- Introduce other types of degrees such as *bachelor's, master's,* and *doctorate.* If appropriate, learners can look at college and university catalogs for information about programs offered.

What Classes Should I Take?
Expansion/Extension for SB page 8

- Have learners look through community college or adult education course catalogs for courses similar to those mentioned in the conversation. Learners can choose possible courses for Stan from the catalogs.
- Learners can choose a major or department that is of interest to them. Then learners can role-play an advisor and student discussing courses appropriate for study.
- Ask learners to write a course description for their English class and other classes offered in their school or program.
- Ask learners to write about things they should do and must/have to do in class or at work. (FOR EXAMPLE: In class, I should listen when others are speaking. At work, I have to wear gloves. I should study every day, but I don't always. The boss has to give me time for lunch.)

Schedule and Registration
More *Expansion/Extension* for SB page 9

- Learners can look through adult education course catalogs and find out which ones give college credits for courses. Learners can find out the number of credits needed for college degrees. Ask *Why do some courses give credits while others don't? What is the difference in cost for credit courses and noncredit courses?*
- Learners can discuss options and suggest solutions for people with work and schedule conflicts. (FOR EXAMPLE: Yolette wants to take a course in accounting. She works from 10 a.m. to 5 p.m. Monday through Friday. Courses are offered from 10 to 11:30 a.m. on Monday, Wednesday, and Friday and 4:30 to 8:30 p.m. on Thursday. What can she do?)

Getting Help from a Friend

Expansion/Extension for SB page 10

- Learners can look through financial aid application forms, list types of information that is asked, and discuss why the information is asked.
- Learners can look through local college or adult education catalogs or call programs to find out the cost of local programs. Ask *Which programs are public? Which ones are private? Which schools offer financial aid? Why do different programs have different prices?*
- Have learners discuss the role of teachers in the United States and in their native countries. Ask *How well respected are teachers? Do students ask a lot of questions? Is it all right to disagree with a teacher? Do teachers ever make mistakes? Are teachers called by first name or by title?*

Ways People Learn

More Expansion/Extension for SB page 11

- Learners can use pictures and/or words to create a story about a learning experience they had. These can be recorded in the learners' writing journals or with a tape recorder.
- Learners can expand the interview charts with additional questions, such as *When did you learn this? How long did it take to learn it? Do you find it useful or not?*
- Have learners compare teaching methods used in their native countries with those used in the United States. Ask *How are classes taught in your native country? Are they similar to or different from those in the United States? What are the advantages and disadvantages of the different methods?*
- Learners can compare a learning experience from their childhood with a recent learning experience. Ask *Have you changed as a learner? What is different now?*

Understanding Computers

More Expansion/Extension for SB page 12

- Ask learners to prepare short lectures on topics of their own choosing. Encourage them to prepare visual aids and use the board to present new or technical terminology. The other learners can take notes on the lectures and ask for clarification.

Computers at Work

More Expansion/Extension for SB page 13

- Have learners make charts of jobs that use computers. Use the following chart as a model:

Job	How Computers Are Used
shoe store manager	keep inventory
laboratory assistant	analyze data on lab samples
secretary	type letters, keep books

Using a Computer

More Expansion/Extension for SB page 14

- Have learners role-play making suggestions at the workplace. One learner can make a suggestion. Another learner can be a co-worker or supervisor and ask for more information about the idea.
- Learners can discuss how they feel when people interrupt them or do not let them finish what they are saying. As a group, make a list of things to say when people interrupt you. Also make a list of polite ways to interrupt others. Learners can create their own role plays of interruptions.

Practicing Your Skills

More Expansion/Extension for SB page 15

- Ask learners to compile a vocabulary list for the unit. Learners can create categories and categorize the new words. Some categories might be Adult Education and Computers.

What the Community Offers

Objectives

Functions
- Giving reasons
- Reporting
- Expressing needs
- Requesting information over the telephone

Life Tasks
- Reading brochures
- Reading newspaper articles
- Reading listings of community services in the telephone directory
- Accessing community services
- Listening to recorded messages
- Filling out forms
- Writing letters to community leaders
- Identifying and classifying information

Structures
- *Where* questions + modal: *can*
- *Looking for* + service/place
- Reported speech with *that*
- *Can/can't* (possibility)
- *If/then* statements

Culture
- Private vs. public services

Vocabulary

Key words:

abuse	eviction
after-school program	facility
	food stamps
child protection	legal services
community	overdue
consumer affairs	recreation center
court	reference (section)
domestic violence	resident
eligibility scale	town meeting
eligible	

Key abbreviation:
WIC–Women, Infants, and Children

Related words:

brochure	lawyer
classroom aide	magazine
cons	neglect
counsel	newspaper
criminal case	pros
crisis	public meeting
dictionary	renovation
encyclopedia	rent subsidy
extended-day program	school board
	town council

Getting Out in the Community

Purpose: To introduce vocabulary about community services

Teacher Preparation and Materials

1. Pictures of community resources: recreation center, library, town or city hall, public school, church or religious meeting place, employment and training office
2. Blank index cards
3. Local newspaper listing of events *(Expansion/Extension)*

Warm-up

1. Use pictures to review/introduce names of community resources. Hold up pictures and have learners identify places they know. Introduce the names of new places. Be sure to include *recreation center* and *library.*
2. For each of the places, have learners give an activity associated with it or a reason for going there. Ask *What can you do there? Why do people go there?* List the places and activities on the board.
3. On blank index cards, write the activities that correspond to the places. Model choosing a card, reading it, and then asking a *Where* question. Have learners respond with the corresponding name of the place. FOR EXAMPLE: *get a book— Where can I go to get a book?* (library) Have learners choose cards and ask each other questions.

Presentation

1. Have learners turn to page 18. Give learners time to look at the picture and share comments among themselves.
2. Ask questions about the picture, such as *What do you see? Where are they? Which places in the community are they talking about? What are they talking about doing?* List words and comments on the board. Be sure to include *recreation center, library, basketball,* and *overdue rent notice.*

Getting Out in the Community

What are Stan's and Roberto's plans?   Answers may vary.
What do you think they are saying?
What is Diep's problem? What do you think she can do?

3. To review the future tense, ask what the people in the picture are going to do or will do. FOR EXAMPLE: Ask *Where's Roberto going to go? Why's he going to go there?*
4. Ask the questions at the bottom of the page. Learners can discuss their answers.
5. Ask learners what places they go to in the community and why they go there. Ask *Which places (in our community) do you go to? Why? Which places don't you go to? Why not? Do you go to the library often? What do you do there? How can you learn about other places like these in our community?*

Expansion/Extension

- Bring in local listings of places of interest and events, such as museums, parks, clubs, workshops, meetings, lectures, and other local programs. Learners can look through them for names of places/organizations and types of activities. Learners can discuss which ones sound interesting to them and explain why.

More *Expansion/Extension* on page 56

The Recreation Center

Purpose: To give practice in reading brochures for information

Teacher Preparation and Materials

1. Pictures of sports, exercise equipment, and facilities: recreation center, basketball, volleyball, dance, football, soccer, baseball, tennis, track, field, weights, stationary bicycles
2. Copies of TRF Handout 2.6, *Community Events Page (Expansion/Extension)*
3. Maps and telephone books for the local area *(Expansion/Extension)*
4. Samples of recreational activity brochures *(Expansion/Extension)*
5. Sports section of newspaper or sports magazines *(Expansion/Extension)*
6. Arrange a field trip to a sporting event or a recreation center. *(Expansion/Extension)*

Warm-up

1. Using the pictures, elicit/introduce names of sports, exercise equipment, and facilities.
2. Practice questions and answers about sports and exercise. Ask *Do you enjoy exercising? Do you like to play soccer? Where can you play? Which sports are played indoors?* and so on.

Presentation

1. Have learners turn to page 19. Ask general questions about the brochure, such as *What kind of place does this brochure tell about? What is the name of the recreation center? What are the people in the pictures doing? What other types of activities do people do at recreation centers?*
2. Have learners read the brochure and underline words they do not know. Elicit/explain new words, including *community, facilities, beginner, advanced, residents,* and *guests*.

The Recreation Center — 19

Herndon Family Recreation Center
5200 Lemon Road
Herndon, VA 22071

Herndon High School opens its doors to the community for sports and exercise programs for the entire family. The facilities are free for town residents and $3.00 a visit for out-of-town guests.

INDOOR ACTIVITIES:
• Play basketball and volleyball.
• Take exercise and dance classes, beginner through advanced. All ages welcome.
• Exercise with weights and stationary bicycle.

OUTDOOR ACTIVITIES:
• Play football, soccer, and baseball.
• Play basketball and tennis, day or night, on lighted courts.
• Run or jog on dirt track.

Open Monday through Friday 7 p.m.–10 p.m.
(except on nights of school events)
Saturdays, Sundays, and holidays 8 a.m.–10 p.m.
Call *471-9155* for additional information.

A. Check (✔) True, False, or No Information (NI).

	True	False	NI
1. The recreation center is free for everyone.		✔	
2. Children can use the recreation center.	✔		
3. Exercise classes are for adults only.		✔	
4. The soccer field has lights for night games.			✔
5. The recreation center is closed during the school day.	✔		
6. There is an indoor track for joggers.			✔

B. Think and talk about the questions. Answers will vary.
1. Is there a recreation center or club that you can use in your community?
2. What kind of recreational activities do you like to do?
3. Where can you do them?

3. Ask literal and inferential questions, such as *What's the address of the recreation center? What's the phone number? Is it open every day? Does the brochure tell you what time the exercise classes start? How can you find out who is teaching the dance class? What other information would you like to know about the recreation center?*
4. Say statements about the recreation center and have learners decide if the statements are true or false or if there is no information in the brochure about the statement. FOR EXAMPLE: *The recreation center is at the high school.* (true) *It is open at 10:00 a.m. on Mondays.* (false) *The dance classes are only on Saturdays.* (no information)
5. Have learners complete exercise A and then explain their answers.
6. Have learners discuss the questions in exercise B.

Expansion/Extension

See TRF HANDOUT 2.6, *Community Events Page*

More *Expansion/Extension* on page 56

44 • UNIT 2

At the Public Library

Purpose: To give practice in stating needs; to introduce *looking for* + service/place, *can/can't* (possibility), and *Where* questions with the modal *can*

Teacher Preparation and Materials

1. Magazines, newspapers, reference materials (dictionary, atlas, encyclopedia, and so on), books (fiction and nonfiction)
2. Index cards with words: *magazines/ newspapers, fiction, nonfiction, reference*
3. ▣ Audiotape for Level 3
4. Arrange a field trip to the local library. *(Expansion/Extension)*

Warm-up

1. Elicit/introduce names of library materials and library sections by holding up books, magazines, and reference materials and having learners identify the ones they know. Be sure to include *fiction, nonfiction, reference materials, magazines,* and *newspapers*.
2. Tape the word cards on the board. Have learners identify the correct categories for books and materials that you hold up.
3. Place books and magazines in various sections of the room. Label the sections with the word cards. Model asking for and giving assistance. FOR EXAMPLE: *Where can I find a dictionary?* (on the table with the reference materials) *Where is the nonfiction?* (by the window) Have learners practice asking and answering questions.

Presentation

1. Have learners turn to page 20. Ask *Where are they? What do you think they are looking for?* On the board list the various items. Be sure to include *magazines, newspapers, reference, fiction, nonfiction.*
2. Ask learners about their local public libraries. Ask *What is the name of the library? Have you been there? Do you*

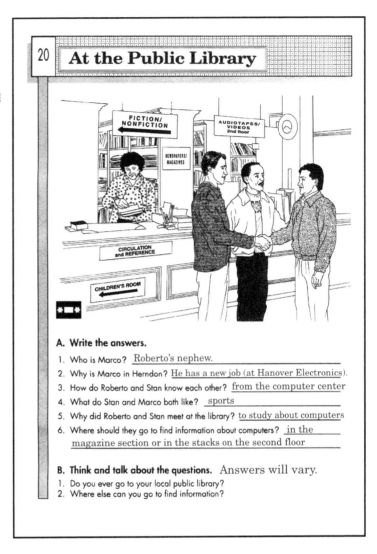

think it is easy or difficult to find information there? How can people find what they need?

3. ▣ Play the audiotape. Have learners identify the speakers. (Stan, Roberto, Marco, and the reference librarian) Ask *What do Roberto and Stan talk about first? Who is Marco? Where is Stan going to take Marco on Friday? What is Roberto looking for? Who does he ask for help? Where are two places he can look?*
4. Have learners answer the questions in exercise A individually or in pairs and then discuss their responses with the entire group.
5. Have learners discuss the questions in exercise B.

Expansion/Extension

- Learners can make a floor plan of a local public or school library and label the sections. Learners can practice asking for materials and giving directions based on the floor plan.

More *Expansion/Extension* on page 56

Using the Library

Purpose: To introduce classifying library materials; to give practice in filling out forms; to give practice with *Where* questions + modal *can* and with *can/can't* (possibility)

Teacher Preparation and Materials

1. Sample library card
2. Library card application forms *(Expansion/Extension)*
3. Books to start class library *(Expansion/Extension)*

Warm-up

1. Show a library card. Ask *What is this? What is it used for? Where can you get one? Do you have one? How can you get a library card?* If necessary, review personal information questions.
2. Write the names of library sections on the board: *newspapers/magazines, reference, fiction, nonfiction.* Ask questions about locations of different library materials and have learners identify the proper section. FOR EXAMPLE: *Where can I find a book about computers?* (in the nonfiction section)

Presentation

1. Have learners turn to page 21. Ask questions about the form. FOR EXAMPLE: *What is this for? Where do you get it? Who needs to fill this out?*
2. Have learners individually fill in the sample library card application.
3. On the board, make a chart of library sections similar to the one on page 21. Show the class several books and magazines. Ask the group where each can be found. FOR EXAMPLE: *What kind of book/magazine is this? Where can I find it?* Write the titles in the appropriate columns.
4. Have learners read the titles in exercise B. Ask learners to classify them on the chart in their books. Have learners add the name of another book, magazine, or library material to the list and classify it on the chart.

5. In pairs or small groups, have learners answer the questions in exercise C. One learner should be the reporter and another the recorder. Have the reporter in each group share the group's conclusions with the class. ■ In a one-to-one situation, discuss the questions together. If appropriate, have the learner write about a personal experience at the library.

Expansion/Extension

- Check on local library card policies. Many libraries are now online, so they can prepare a card on the computer as you wait. If applications are still used in your community, bring copies of an application form to class for learners to fill out.
- Have learners go to the local library and add one or two more titles to each category on the chart.
- Learners can use the card catalog or online search system of the local library to find information and/or book titles on topics of interest.

More *Expansion/Extension* on page 56

Using the Library — Student Page 21

A. Complete the application form. Answers will vary.

Fairfax County Public Library

To get a library card, present this application form, picture identification, and proof of address at the circulation desk.

Please print.
Name: (last) _ _ _ _ _ _ _ _ _ (first) _ _ _ _ _ _ _ (m.i.) _
Address: (no.) _ _ _ _ _ (street) _ _ _ _ _ _ _ _ _ _ _ _
(city) _____ (state) _ _ (zip) _ _ _ _ _
Telephone (_ _ _) _ _ _ - _ _ _ _ Sex: M _ F _
Soc. Sec. No. _ _ _ - _ _ - _ _ _ _ Birthdate: _ _/_ _/_ _

Signature: _____ Date: _____

B. Complete the chart.
Where can you find these materials in the library?

Herald News   Webster's Dictionary   African Tales
History of the United States   People magazine   Encyclopedia
Computers Made Easy   Short Stories of the Caribbean

(Add your own.)

Newspapers/ Magazines	Reference	Fiction	Nonfiction
Herald News People magazine	Webster's Dictionary Encyclopedia	African Tales Short Stories of the Caribbean	History of the United States Computers Made Easy

C. Think and talk about the questions. Answers will vary.
1. Have you ever used the reference section? What for?
2. What other materials can you find in the reference section?

Getting Help

Purpose: To give practice in stating needs and in requesting information over the telephone; to give practice with *If/then* statements

Teacher Preparation and Materials

1. Pictures of community resources, used for page 18
2. [cassette icon] Audiotape for Level 3
3. Local telephone book *(Expansion/Extension)*
4. Blank index cards *(Expansion/Extension)*

Warm-up

1. On the board, tape the pictures of community resources. Model *If/then* statements, such as *If I need a book, (then) I will go to the library. If we want to play volleyball, (then) we will go to the recreation center.* Then have learners create their own sentences about the pictures.
2. Review housing vocabulary. Ask *Do you own or rent your apartment/house? When do you pay the rent/mortgage? How do you pay it? Do you get a receipt when you pay?*
3. Elicit/introduce legal vocabulary and issues related to housing. Ask *What happens if people pay their rent/mortgage one week late? one month late? three months late? What can the landlord/bank do if this happens? What can the people do if the landlord/bank has made a mistake? Who can help if there is a problem?* On the board write new words, including *eviction, final notice, lawyer,* and *legal services.*

Presentation

1. Have learners turn to page 22. Ask *What is Diep looking at? Why do you think she is worried?* (Learners can look back at the picture on page 18.)
2. Have learners read the letter and underline words they do not know. Elicit/explain the meanings of new words: *past due, business days, eviction, initiated, proceedings.*
3. Have learners answer the questions in exercise A. If the class is large, learners can

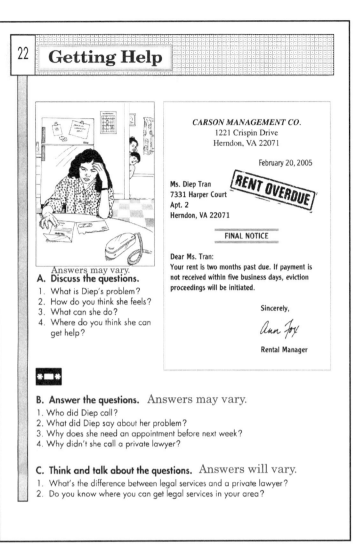

work in small groups. You may want to list the responses on the board.

4. Ask learners if they know of anyone who has received a letter like this one and, if so, what the person did.
5. [cassette icon] Play the first half of the audiotape. Stop after the line: "That's the problem. I don't have them." Have learners predict the rest of the conversation. Ask *Do you think Legal Services will be able to help Diep? What information will they need from her? Do you think Diep needs help right away or next week?* [cassette icon] Continue playing the audiotape. Have learners summarize the conversation.
6. Have learners answer the questions in exercises B and C. In large classes, have learners break into small groups to answer the questions. One learner in each group should be the reporter and another the recorder. Have the reporter in each group share some of the group's answers with the class.

Expansion/Extension on page 56

Legal Services

Purpose: To give practice in reading for information; to give practice with *can/can't* (possibility) and with *If/then* statements

Teacher Preparation and Materials

1. Calculators (optional)
2. Copies of TRF Handout 2.5, *Application for Legal Assistance (Expansion/Extension)*
3. Sample eligibility scales for various community services *(Expansion/Extension)*
4. Invite a legal service lawyer or a representative of legal services to speak to the class. *(Expansion/Extension)*

Warm-up

1. Ask *If/then* questions about community resources. FOR EXAMPLE: *If you want to exercise, where can you go? If you need legal help, who can you call?*
2. On the board, make a sample eligibility scale:

Health-care Assistance	
Number in Family	**Yearly Income**
1	$0–$ 9,000
2	$0–$12,000
3	$0–$15,000
4	$0–$18,000

Give examples to illustrate the meaning of *eligible.* FOR EXAMPLE: *Jerome has a wife and one child. Jerome's wife is not working now. His yearly income is $14,420. How many are in his family? (Circle the appropriate line on the chart.) Is his income more or less than $15,000? Jerome's family is eligible for assistance. They can get help if they want it.* (Write *eligible.*) *Daphne lives alone. She works part time. Her yearly income is $13,100. How many are in her family? (Circle the appropriate line on the chart.) Is her income more or less than $9,000? Daphne is not eligible for assistance. She cannot get help.* (Write *not eligible.*)
3. Write *Eligibility Scale* on top of the chart and explain its use.

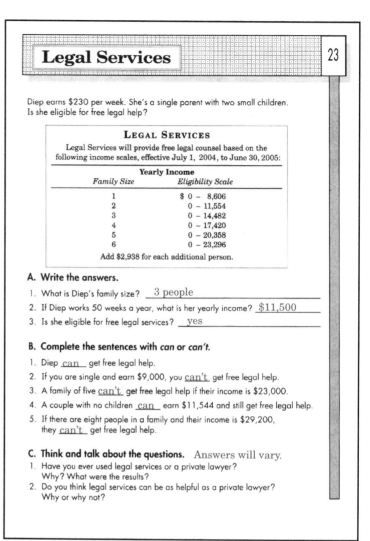

Presentation

1. Have learners turn to page 23 and read the description and questions at the top. Ask *Where does Diep work? How many people are in her family? What is her salary per week? How many weeks are in a year? How much money could she earn in a year? ($11,960 a year)*
2. Have learners look at the chart. Ask questions, such as *There are three people in Diep's family. Can she get free legal help? If there were two people in her family, could she get free help? If there were one person in her family, could she get free help?*
3. Have learners answer the questions in exercise A and complete the sentences for exercise B. Learners can work together and/or use calculators.
4. Have learners discuss the questions in exercise C.

Expansion/Extension

See TRF HANDOUT 2.5, *Application for Legal Assistance*

More *Expansion/Extension* on page 57

Taking Sides

Purpose: To give practice in reading newspaper articles and in expressing opinions; to give practice with reported speech with *that*

Teacher Preparation and Materials

1. Pictures of sports and exercise equipment, used for page 19
2. Copies of TRF Handout 2.7, *Community Meeting (Expansion/Extension)*
3. Arrange a field trip to a community meeting. *(Expansion/Extension)*
4. Local newspapers *(Expansion/Extension)*

Warm-up

1. Review names of sports and exercise equipment by having learners identify pictures. Ask learners about activities they like to do in their free time. Record responses on the board.
2. Model an example of reported speech, using the information on the chart. FOR EXAMPLE: *Juan says that he likes to play basketball.* Have learners report other information from the chart, using the structure.

Presentation

1. Have learners turn to page 24 and look at the picture and newspaper article title. Have learners predict what the article is about. Ask *What do you think "growing pains" are? Do you think everyone is happy about the recreation center?*
2. Have learners read the article and underline words they do not know. Elicit/explain the meanings of new words: *town council, expansion, renovations, civic responsibility, oppose, unsupervised, hangout, critics, public meeting.*
3. Ask literal and inferential questions, such as *Who is the leader of the expansion group? What are the good points about the expansion? Why does Anna Billman oppose the project? Do you think many people will go to the public meeting? Why or why not?*

---

24 **Taking Sides**

Herndon Family Recreation Center: Growing Pains

Residents for and against the expansion of the Herndon Family Recreation Center met with the town council to present their views.

Roberto Silva, a leader of the expansion group, claims that pool renovations and a larger gym will help families spend more time together and will provide more activities for teens and young adults. "It is our civic responsibility to meet the community's needs," asserts Silva. "These changes will help the high school, too," he adds.

Anna Billman, a local store owner, opposes the expansion. She fears that too many "unsupervised young people will use the place as a hangout." The high cost of the project is another worry. "Three million dollars is too much money for recreation when fire and police protection and street repairs are being cut back," says Billman.

Backers of the expansion suggest that an additional five-percent tax on alcohol and cigarettes will raise the $3 million. Critics say that raising taxes is out of the question.

A public meeting to discuss the issue will be held next Wednesday at 7:30 p.m. in the Herndon High School gym.

Should the Herndon Town Council approve the expansion of the recreation center?

Write a list of pros and cons.

Pros	Cons
- will help families spend more time together	- too many unsupervised young people will "hang out"
- more activities for teens and young adults	- too expensive - money is needed for fire/police and street repairs
- 5% tax on alcohol and cigarettes will pay for expansion	- don't want to raise taxes to pay for expansion
- will help the high school	

---

4. Elicit/explain the meanings of *pros* and *cons*. Ask *Which people are for the expansion of the recreation center? Which people are not? What words are used to describe the people who are for the expansion? What words are used to describe the people who are against it?*
5. Have learners scan the article, find arguments used by each side, and list them as the pros and cons in their books.
6. As a group, discuss and prioritize the ideas. Have learners choose which side they feel has the better arguments and explain why. As a group, take a vote on the issue.

Expansion/Extension

See TRF HANDOUT 2.7, *Community Meeting*

- Learners can design an ideal community center. They can work cooperatively, deciding on types of activities, schedules, floor plans, and so on.

More *Expansion/Extension* on page 57

Community Service Agencies: Forms A and B

Purpose: To give practice in accessing information; to give practice with question formation

Teacher Preparation and Materials

1. Local telephone books or copies of the community services guide
2. Copies of TRF Handout 2.1, *I'd Like Some Information Please (Expansion/Extension)*
3. Copies of TRF Handout 2.2, *Go Find Out (Expansion/Extension)*
4. Large sheets of paper, markers, tape *(Expansion/Extension)*
5. Blank index cards *(Expansion/Extension)*

Warm-up

1. Have learners look back at page 18 and discuss the plans of each of the characters: what they plan to do, where they plan to go or call, and so on. Have them make a list of places and reasons for going to or contacting each of the places.
2. Elicit/introduce other categories or general issues for which community services provide assistance. Write the categories on the board. Be sure to include Housing, Food, Shopping/Consumer Issues, Crime, Health, and Employment.
3. Ask learners how the characters knew or found out about the different places and service providers. FOR EXAMPLE: *Where do you think Diep got information about Legal Services? How do you think Stan found out about the Recreation Center?* Ask learners if they know the names of local agencies that provide assistance for the categories listed on the board.
4. Bring in and show the group local phone books or copies of the community services guide (which is usually found in the front of the phone book). Show learners the listing of government offices and agencies (blue pages).

Community Service Agencies: Form A   25

Work with a partner. One person uses Form A. The other uses Form B.
Ask your partner questions to find the missing information.

Examples: What is the phone number for Consumer Affairs?
What kinds of questions does Consumer Affairs answer?

Community Service Phone List

Consumer Affairs .... <u>246-8749</u>
answers questions about consumer rights and responsibilities

Domestic Violence/Child Protection Services 471-9125
examines reports of abuse or neglect of adults and children; provides assistance in <u>crisis situations</u>

Food Stamps and WIC (Women, Infants, and Children) .... <u>471-9147</u>
decides on <u>eligibility</u> and provides food coupons

Housing Assistance
Rent Subsidy Office 713-2134
decides on eligibility and finds help for rent payment
Tenant-Landlord Commission .... <u>713-2155</u>
answers questions about disputes between tenants and landlords

Job Assistance Network 481-9133
provides job training and help in getting jobs; offers workshops on <u>resume writing</u> and <u>interviewing</u>

Legal Services 246-8144
decides on eligibility and offers legal services (except for <u>criminal</u> cases)

<u>Recreation Department</u> 713-9150
coordinates community programs; provides recorded message giving dates, times, places, and fees

---

Presentation

1. Divide the group in half. Have one half of the learners turn to Form A on page 25 and the other half turn to Form B on page 26. Give learners time to look over their forms. If necessary, help learners find various services on the forms. ◼ In a one-to-one situation, have the learner take Form A and you take Form B.
2. Ask a learner with Form A *What is the phone number for Consumer Affairs?* (I don't know. The information is missing.) Then ask a learner with Form B *What's the phone number for Consumer Affairs?* (246-8749) Ask the Form B learner *What kinds of questions does Consumer Affairs answer?* (I don't know. It's blank.) Then ask the Form A learner the same question and let him or her give the answer.
3. Together read the instructions at the top of the page. Assign pairs or have learners with Form A choose a partner with Form B. Instruct learners not to look at each other's forms. If possible, have the pairs sit back-to-back or with a barrier between them. Have pairs ask and answer questions to fill in the gaps on their forms.

(**Note:** New vocabulary items will be studied later in the lesson.) ▣ In a one-to-one situation, have the learner ask questions and fill in the information on Form A. Then you ask questions about Form B and have the learner supply the answers from Form A.

4. Have learners check their answers by comparing forms.

5. Have learners circle or underline words they do not know. Encourage learners to guess the meanings from the context, before you explain the words or have learners check in a dictionary.

6. Have learners share additional information they know about the various service agencies.

Expansion/Extension

See TRF HANDOUT 2.1, *I'd Like Some Information Please*
TRF HANDOUT 2.2, *Go Find Out*

- Give small groups of learners large sheets of paper, markers, and tape. Have each group take a category, such as Housing, Jobs, Legal, Consumer, Welfare, or Crisis Prevention/Protection. Have learners write the names of the community agencies and service providers that deal with their categories and types of problems or issues handled by the agencies. (FOR EXAMPLE: Housing Authority/Court—landlord and lease problems, no heat, unsafe housing) Learners can look in the local telephone book. Have the groups present their charts to the class. Learners can suggest other issues to be added to the charts.

- Have learners practice questions and answers based on the charts. Ask *What kinds of problems does . . . help with? Which office can help with . . . problems?*

- Learners can make their own local directory of agencies and service providers. Learners can look in local phone books or ask for information in city halls and service agencies. In a multilevel group, less advanced learners can find phone numbers and more advanced learners can write descriptions of services offered in your area.

- Ask learners to imagine that they are the governor or president. Their government has some extra money. They would like to create an agency to help people in their

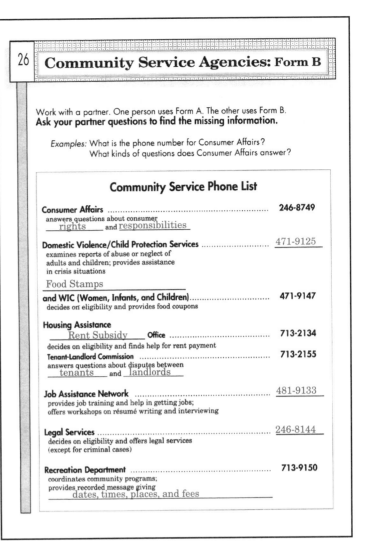

state or country. Have learners create an agency, describe problems that the agency would handle, tell what types of people the agency would help, describe how the agency would help the people, and choose a name for the agency.

- Have learners practice the present real conditional tense by writing *If/then* statements for the community service agencies or other community resources. (FOR EXAMPLE: If Marco wants to check out books, he can apply for a library card. If a family has no money for food, they can ask for food stamps.) Learners can write *if* clauses on one set of index cards and *then* clauses on another set. Learners can match the sets.

- Have learners prepare specific questions on types of information they would like to research about local community service agencies. Learners can call/visit the agencies, ask for information, and report their findings to the group.

More *Expansion/Extension* on page 57

Recorded Messages

Purpose: To introduce listening to recorded messages; to give practice in taking notes

Teacher Preparation and Materials

1. Pictures of community resources, used for page 22
2. ▄▄▄ Audiotape for Level 3
3. Copies of TRF Handout 2.3, *Phone Conversation (Expansion/Extension)*
4. Copies of TRF Handout 2.4, *Can I Take a Message? (Expansion/Extension)*

Warm-up

1. Review names of community resources by having learners identify pictures. List the names on the left-hand side of the board. Label the list *Community Resources.*
2. Add three columns: *Days, Times, Events.* Dictate a sentence about a community resource that learners listed. Have a volunteer fill in information from the sentence in the appropriate columns. FOR EXAMPLE: *The Paterson Public Library is open Monday through Friday from 10 a.m. to 6 p.m.* (Volunteer finds *Library* and writes "Mon.–Fri., 10–6.") *The Job Office will have a new computer-training program on Wednesdays at 11:00.* (Volunteer finds *Job Office* and writes "Wed., 11, computer training.")
3. Ask about services offered by each of the places. FOR EXAMPLE: *What types of things can children do at the library? What can adults do? What kind of help can you get at the job office?* Be sure to include job- and skill-training programs.

Presentation

1. Have learners turn to page 27. Ask questions about the picture and the two information cards for community services. FOR EXAMPLE: *What do you think Marco is doing? Why? What types of information will he find out about the library? What information will he find out about the job assistance network?*
2. Have learners read the instructions. Remind learners to focus on the most

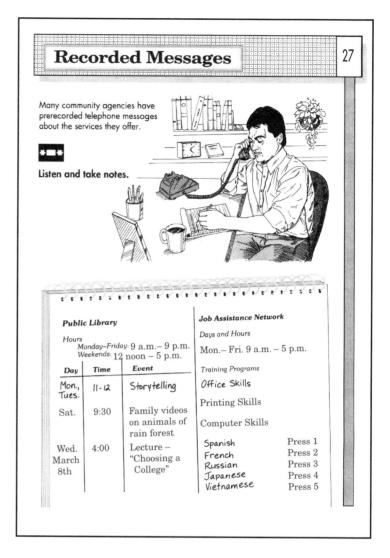

important words and numbers and to use abbreviations. ▄▄▄ Play the audiotape and have learners fill in information. ▄▄▄ Replay the messages so learners can check their work and fill in the missing information.
3. Have learners check their answers in pairs or in groups. Ask questions and have learners supply the answers based on their notes.

Expansion/Extension

See TRF HANDOUT 2.3, *Phone Conversation*
    TRF HANDOUT 2.4, *Can I Take a Message?*

- Find out if there are any local agencies or businesses, such as libraries, banks, or movie theaters, that use prerecorded messages. Learners can call for information, take notes, and share the information with the rest of the group. Learners can talk about difficulties they may have encountered. Ask *What type of information is easy to understand? What information is more difficult to understand? Were you able to get the information the first time you listened?*

More *Expansion/Extension* on page 57

Practicing Your Skills

Purpose: To give practice in stating needs and in giving reasons

Teacher Preparation and Materials

Writing paper, envelopes, and stamps (optional)

Warm-up

Have learners brainstorm and list ideas for community improvements on the board. Have learners suggest what can be done to tell others about their ideas or what people or organizations are responsible for the concerns. Also list possible actions or agencies and people to contact about the ideas.

Presentation

1. Have learners turn to page 28, read Diep's letter, and underline words they do not know. Elicit/explain the meanings of new words: *request, after-school program, private, extended-day program.*

2. Ask questions about the letter, such as *Who did Diep write to? What is her idea? Why does she think an after-school program is important? Do you agree? Why or why not?*

3. Repeat the procedure for Roberto's letter. Elicit/explain the meanings of new words: *classroom aides, immigrant, school board, bilingual, to whom it may concern.*

4. Ask questions about Roberto's letter, such as *What is his idea? Why does he think the bilingual classroom aides are important? Do you think they are important in schools? Why or why not?*

5. Have learners discuss the letters. Ask *Why does Roberto use "To Whom It May Concern" to start his letter? Do you think Diep should go to the town meeting to support her idea? Why or why not? Which letter do you think is more effective? Why?*

6. Have learners read and think about the questions in exercise A. Have them choose an idea of their own or one from the list on the board. Learners can work individually or in pairs to complete exercise B.

---

28 **Practicing Your Skills**

Diep and Roberto have good ideas for their community. They have both written letters to request services.

Dear Town Council Members:
    I am writing to request an after-school program at the Lemon Road School. We need a program now because there are many working parents. Private after-school child care is too expensive for many parents. I think the Lemon Road School is the perfect place for an extended-day program because the school has classrooms and a playground that the children can use between 3 and 6 p.m.
    I hope you will consider this request at your next town meeting.
        Yours truly,
        Diep Tran

To Whom It May Concern:
    As a parent of two children in the schools, I believe we need more bilingual classroom aides. As you know, classes are much larger now, and the teachers do not have time for every child. Our children need extra help learning, especially English. Many immigrant parents only speak a little English, so they also need someone in the school who speaks their language.
    I will present this request at the next school board meeting.
        Sincerely,
        Roberto Silva

A. Do you have any ideas for your community? Prepare one of your ideas for a letter.

Before you write, think about these questions.

• Who should I write to?
• What is my request or idea?
• What reasons can I give to support my request?

B. Write about your idea.   Answers will vary.

To: _____

Request/Idea: _____

Supporting Reasons:

a. _____

b. _____

c. _____

---

7. Use the process writing approach to prepare letters based on the answers in exercise B. Learners can send their letters to the appropriate person or office and keep a copy in their portfolio.

Expansion/Extension

• Learners can find out the names of local officials and school board members. Learners can match the names of the people with the community improvement ideas they listed in the *Warm-up.*

• Learners can suggest ways to make their concerns public. Some ideas might be to have people sign a letter, have people attend town or school board meetings, make posters about the idea, and write letters to the editor or to elected officials.

• Ask learners to compile a vocabulary list for the unit. Learners can create categories and categorize the new words. Some categories might be Community Services and Legal Services.

Modal: *Can*

Purpose: To give practice in using *can* and *can't* to express possibility

Teacher Preparation and Materials

1. Samples of brochures or schedules for local community centers *(Expansion/Extension)*

2. Floor plan of a supermarket (or a sample floor plan drawn on the board) *(Expansion/Extension)*

Warm-up

1. Ask learners when they work or have other regularly scheduled responsibilities (other classes, child care requirements, club meetings, and so on). Create a chart on the board. Then pose questions about what learners can or cannot do at various times. FOR EXAMPLE: *Alain works on the weekends. Can he go shopping with us on Saturday? This class meets from seven to nine Mondays and Wednesdays. Can you go to a movie with your friend next Tuesday evening?* Keep or copy the chart to use in an *(Expansion/Extension)* activity.

2. Learners can make their own statements about activities they can or cannot participate in, based on their schedules.

Presentation

1. Have learners turn to page 29 and read the example sentences.

2. Have learners turn to page 19 and read the flyer from the Herndon Family Recreation Center. Ask questions to review details. FOR EXAMPLE: *How much do town residents pay to use the center? What evenings is the center open? What indoor activities are available?*

3. Learners can work individually or in pairs to complete the first exercise. Review answers, and have learners identify the information in the flyer on which each answer is based.

4. Have learners turn to page 21 and review the chart of where materials are located in the library. Then have them complete the second exercise. Review answers by having one learner ask the question and

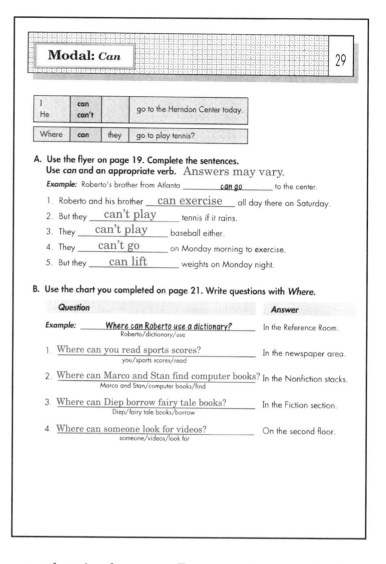

another give the answer. Focus attention on word order in the questions.

Expansion/Extension

- Have learners look at brochures or schedules from local community centers. Using the chart from the *Warm-up*, have them identify activities that they can or can't participate in at the centers and tell why.

- Have learners create a shopping list of food items. They can use the supermarket floor plan to ask and answer questions about where in the store they can find each item. Depending on their experience with local supermarkets, they may be able to identify certain items that can't be found in the supermarket (and may be able to name other stores in the area where those items can be bought).

- Learners can work in small groups to ask for and give advice about where to find various products, activities, or services. (FOR EXAMPLE: My child wants to play soccer after school. Where can she go?) The questions and recommendations can be collated in a booklet of community resources.

Reported Speech with *That*

Purpose: To give practice in recognizing and using reported speech

Teacher Preparation and Materials
None

Warm-up

1. Ask learners questions about recent activities. FOR EXAMPLE: *What did you do last night? Where did you go over the weekend?* Write learners' responses on the board in direct speech. Indicate the speaker.

2. Model turning the responses into reported speech. FOR EXAMPLE: *Ilona said that she went shopping last night. Alfred told me that he studied and watched a movie on Saturday.* Have learners change the rest of the responses into reported speech. Write some examples on the board, and compare the changes.

3. Brainstorm a list of verbs that can be used in reported speech (*say, tell, add, think, state, explain,* and so on).

4. Ask learners their opinions or expectations about places or events in the community. FOR EXAMPLE: *What do you think about the new mall that's being built? What do you think about afterschool activities at your child's school?* Write responses on the board in direct speech, indicating the speaker. Again, model turning responses into reported speech. Then have learners change the rest of the items.

Presentation

1. Have learners turn to page 30 and work individually or in pairs to complete the first exercise. Review answers, and have learners identify the words that signal reported speech.

2. Look together at the example in the second exercise. Note the differences between direct and reported speech.

3. Have learners complete the exercise. Encourage them to use a variety of verbs to introduce the reported speech. Review answers.

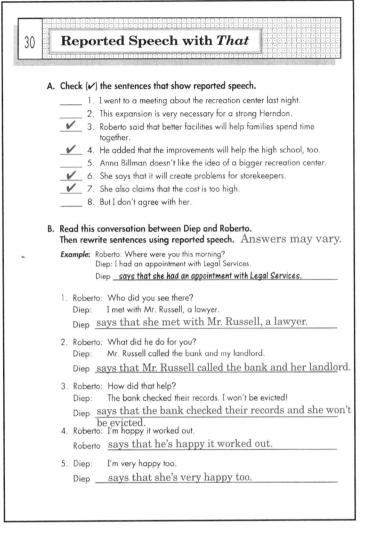

4. Discuss when or why people are likely to use reported speech (FOR EXAMPLE: when talking about other people, in telling a friend about a family activity). Discuss likely uses of reported speech on the job (FOR EXAMPLE: in sharing instructions with a co-worker, in clarifying what someone else said).

Expansion/Extension

• Look at the sentences in the first exercise again. Turn the reported speech back into direct speech.

• Have learners reread the article on page 24 describing the meeting about the Herndon Recreation Center and identify instances of reported speech. Then have them turn the direct quotes in the article into reported speech.

• Learners can create role plays of the meeting about the Herndon Recreation Center. Some can take the role of participants mentioned in the article. They can express opinions based on direct quotes and reported speech from the article on page 24 and the exercise on page 30. Others can express their own opinions on the issue.

UNIT 2: What the Community Offers

Expansion/Extension

Getting Out in the Community

More *Expansion/Extension* for SB page 18

- Learners can make up conversations based on the picture and role-play them for the group.
- Learners can categorize the list of community resources by age of client and purpose. Some categories might be Places for Children, Places for Adults, Places for Teens, Places for Fun, and Places for Help and Information.
- Have learners share experiences they have had at places in the community. Ask *Have you ever been to the library? When did you go there? Why did you go there? Did you go alone?* In their writing journals, learners can write about an interesting experience they have had.

The Recreation Center

More *Expansion/Extension* for SB page 19

- Elicit examples of other types of recreational facilities. (public pools, ice skating rinks, and so on) Have learners look on local maps for recreation centers and playing fields. Learners can check telephone books for names and addresses of facilities.
- Learners can interview each other about sports and exercise preferences and then share the information with the group.
- Learners can call local recreation centers for information or go to different places and ask for brochures. Compare the types of activities, hours, and costs.
- Have learners look in the sports sections of newspapers for articles about their favorite sports. Learners can circle words related to the sport and then summarize the article.
- Learners can look in newspapers and sports magazines for names of local professional teams, players, stadiums, or arenas. Learners may want to follow a particular team throughout the playing season, using the standings charts and game reports in newspapers.

- Take a field trip to a sports event at a local recreation center or high school.

At the Public Library

More *Expansion/Extension* for SB page 20

- Take a field trip to the local library. Some libraries will provide a tour, but an appointment might be necessary. Some libraries may allow you to conduct the tour yourself. Point out the children's room, young adult section, audio-visual resources, career and college sections, and foreign language sections.
- Learners can compare and contrast U.S. library systems to those in their native countries. Ask *Are U.S. libraries similar to or different from libraries in your native country? How are they similar? How are they different?* Learners can make a chart of similarities and differences.

Using the Library

More *Expansion/Extension* for SB page 21

- Make a class library with donated books or books that learners would like to share. Learners can catalog and classify the books.

Getting Help

Expansion/Extension for SB page 22

- Learners can check the local telephone book for phone numbers and descriptions of legal services offered in the area.
- Learners can suggest other solutions for Diep. Make a list of advice for handling purchases and payments. Include getting and keeping receipts, recording check numbers and dates of payment, and keeping carbons or photocopies of money orders.
- Have learners role-play calling for appointments at agencies. One learner plays the role of the receptionist, asking how to spell the name, giving a date and time, and requesting that the person bring something appropriate to the appointment. The other learner asks for an appointment, spells his or her name, asks for a different time or date, and asks for clarification. Some useful phrases and expressions to practice before the role play are *Can I come at a later/earlier date or time? Do you have any openings on*

Tuesday? Are there any other times available?
My last name is Patel. P as in Peter, A as in
apple, T as in Tom, E as in Ed, L as in Larry.
I don't understand. What is a . . . ? My what?
Could you repeat that (more slowly)?

- Write phrases in legal jargon on one set of index cards. Write a simplified version on another set. Have learners match the sets. (FOR EXAMPLE: Eviction proceedings will be initiated. = We will start legal work to get you out of your apartment. I need to verify your income. = I need to see your pay stub.)

- Learners can practice reported speech, using the letter and conversation. FOR EXAMPLE: "Diep paid with a money order." (Diep said [that] she paid with a money order.) "Her rent is past due." (The letter said [that] her rent was past due.) "She can come tomorrow." (The receptionist said [that] she could come tomorrow.)

Legal Services

More *Expansion/Extension* for SB page 23

- Learners can discuss other aspects of Diep's case. Ask *What do you think a lab assistant does? Do you think she had special training? What are the advantages and disadvantages of Diep's part-time job? If Diep had a full-time job, do you think she would be eligible for free services? Why or why not?*

- Learners can discuss which (if any) extended family members can be counted for determining eligibility. Then have them research the exact regulations for their city, county, or state.

- Have a legal service lawyer or a representative of legal services visit the class. Learners can prepare questions beforehand.

- Bring in local eligibility scales for different service agencies. If appropriate, discuss sliding fee scales.

- Learners can write a letter to Diep's landlord or management company, explaining her situation or a similar legal problem. Discuss the need for immediate action.

- Have learners practice changing adjectives to nouns and noting the change in stress patterns. FOR EXAMPLE: Learners can compare the words *eligible* and *eligibility*. Point out the base word and the ending (suffix). Model how the pronunci-

ation changes with the ending (el´-i-gi-ble/ el-i-gi-bil´-i-ty; pos´-si-ble/pos-si-bil´-i-ty; re-spon´-si-ble/re-spon-si-bil´-i-ty). Then have learners use the different forms in sentences about legal issues. Some other words: *active, sensitive, similar, creative, popular, major, personal, equal, legal.*

- Ask learners to make up *If/then* situations based on the eligibility chart. FOR EXAMPLE: *If there are four people in the family with a weekly income of $400, can they get free legal help?*

Taking Sides

More *Expansion/Extension* for SB page 24

- Learners can find out when and where local meetings are held. If possible, have them attend a meeting and take notes on the issues discussed. Learners can report their observations to the class.

- Learners can follow a topic of concern in local newspapers. Learners can keep a scrapbook of articles on a particular issue or post the articles on a bulletin board. Learners can write letters to editors or legislators on the issues.

Community Service Agencies:
Forms A and B

More *Expansion/Extension* for SB pages 25, 26

- Learners can discuss where and how people get help for similar problems and situations in their native countries. Learners can compare service providers, eligibility, funding for services, and so on.

Recorded Messages

More *Expansion/Extension* for SB page 27

- Learners can practice following directions of interactive phone systems. (FOR EXAMPLE: *If you'd like to hear more about savings accounts, press 2 now. Please enter your account number.*)

Making Ends Meet

Objectives

Functions
- Complaining
- Correcting
- Describing a problem
- Requesting information
- Speaking emphatically
- Dealing with numbers

Life Tasks
- Preparing a monthly budget
- Reading articles about money management
- Reading bills (utility, credit card, phone, etc.)
- Keeping a checking account register
- Reading credit card policies
- Reporting an error on a bill
- Writing a letter to a friend or relative

Structures
- Adverbs of indefinite frequency
- *If/then* statements
- Modals: *can/should*
- Past tense of irregular verbs

Culture
- Use of credit in the United States
- United States as a consumer society
- Comparison of consumerism in the United States and in native countries
- Levels of politeness

Vocabulary

Key words:

annual	itemized account
available credit	life insurance
bargain	living expenses
budget payment	membership fee
budget worksheet	minimum
credit card	amount due
discounted calling	overdue notice
times	retailer
down payment	standard
economy	take-home pay
expenses	transaction
finance charge	utility

Key abbreviation:
APR–annual percentage rate

Related words:

balance	invoice
collect call	long-distance
commuting	call
credit	occasionally
credit card terms	predictable
credit limit	quantity
deposit	regularly
energy	secondhand
estimate	statement
evaluate	to the limit
exceed	trade-in
fluctuation	unnecessary
frequently	wisely
inquiry	withdrawal

Bills, Bills, and More Bills

Purpose: To give practice in discussing bills and finances

Teacher Preparation and Materials

1. Index cards with names of utilities and common expenses: *gas, electric, rent/mortgage, telephone, food, clothing, car loan, insurance, college/school, credit card*
2. Large sheet of paper, marker

Warm-up

1. Use word cards to review/introduce names of utilities and common expenses. Hold up cards for learners to identify. Introduce the names of new items. Be sure to include *insurance* and *car loan*.
2. On a large sheet of paper, make four columns. Label the first column *Expenses*. Have learners list expenses from the word cards and brainstorm other expenses to add to the list. Have learners explain which items they think are the most important. (**Note:** This chart will be used again with pages 32, 35, and 41.)

Presentation

1. Have learners turn to page 31. Ask *What do you see? Where are they? What do you think they are talking about? What does "Making Ends Meet" mean?* List learners' comments on the board.
2. Have learners answer the questions at the bottom of the page. In large classes, have learners discuss the questions in small groups, with one learner acting as the reporter and another as the recorder. Have the reporter in each group share the group's conclusions with the class. ▪ In a one-to-one situation, discuss the questions together.
3. Ask learners about types of bills they get in the mail. FOR EXAMPLE: *What types of bills do you get? How often do you pay these bills? How do you feel when you get bills?*

1 2 3 4 5 6 7 8 9 10 11 12
Making Ends Meet ▪ ▪ ▪ ▪ ▪ ▪ ▪

Bills, Bills, and More Bills

How do you think Yolette and Al feel?   Answers may vary.
Why do you think they have so many bills?
What can they do?

Expansion/Extension

- Learners can make up conversations based on the picture and role-play them for the group.
- Discuss family roles in budgetary and financial matters. Ask *Who holds/controls the money in the family? Does everyone have a say in how money is spent? Does one person decide? Is it easy or difficult to talk about finances with family members? Does everyone usually agree?*
- Learners can discuss how and why some people have trouble paying bills. Ask *Why do you think some people have problems paying bills? Is it always because people spend too much? When do people spend too much? Which expenses can people control?*

Monthly Expenses

Purpose: To introduce preparing a monthly budget

Teacher Preparation and Materials

1. List of expenses, used for page 31
2. 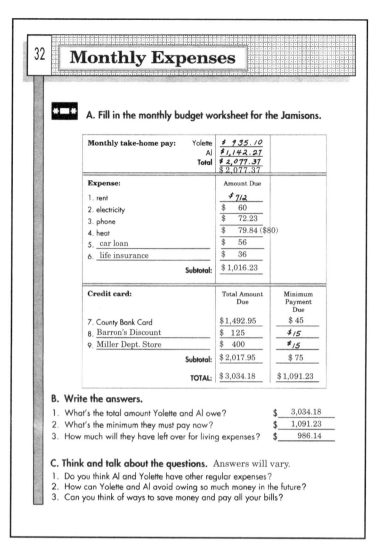 Audiotape for Level 3
3. Copies of TRF Handout 3.2, *How Much Do You Spend? (Expansion/Extension)*
4. Calculator (optional)

Warm-up

1. Use the list of expenses to review the names of budget items.
2. Label the second column *Monthly Amount.* Ask learners what their monthly bills and payments usually are for the various expenses and write in the amounts. If learners are hesitant about discussing their payments, ask for amounts that learners think are appropriate for the local area. For items that learners do not normally pay, leave the space blank. (**Note:** This chart will be used again for pages 35 and 41.)

Presentation

1. Have learners look at the monthly budget worksheet on page 32. Ask questions about the chart and about which items and amounts are missing. Elicit/explain the difference between *Total Amount Due* and *Minimum Payment Due.*
2. Have a volunteer read the direction line for exercise A. Play the audiotape (several times, if necessary) and have learners fill in the missing information.
3. Replay the audiotape for learners to verify responses.
4. Ask inferential questions. FOR EXAMPLE: *How do Al and Yolette sound in the conversation? Do they enjoy talking about their expenses? How do you know?*
5. Have learners calculate the answers for exercise B and explain how they got their answers.
6. In large classes, have learners discuss the questions in exercise C in small groups,

32 Monthly Expenses

A. Fill in the monthly budget worksheet for the Jamisons.

Monthly take-home pay:		Amount
	Yolette	$ 935.10
	Al	$ 1,142.27
	Total	$ 2,077.37
		$ 2,077.37

Expense:		Amount Due
1. rent		$ 712
2. electricity		$ 60
3. phone		$ 72.23
4. heat		$ 79.84 ($80)
5. car loan		$ 56
6. life insurance		$ 36
	Subtotal:	$ 1,016.23

Credit card:	Total Amount Due	Minimum Payment Due
7. County Bank Card	$ 1,492.95	$ 45
8. Barron's Discount	$ 125	$ 15
9. Miller Dept. Store	$ 400	$ 15
Subtotal:	$ 2,017.95	$ 75
TOTAL:	$ 3,034.18	$ 1,091.23

B. Write the answers.

1. What's the total amount Yolette and Al owe? $ 3,034.18
2. What's the minimum they must pay now? $ 1,091.23
3. How much will they have left over for living expenses? $ 986.14

C. Think and talk about the questions. Answers will vary.

1. Do you think Al and Yolette have other regular expenses?
2. How can Yolette and Al avoid owing so much money in the future?
3. Can you think of ways to save money and pay all your bills?

with one learner acting as the reporter and another as the recorder. Have the reporter in each group share the group's conclusions with the class. In a one-to-one teaching situation, discuss the questions together.

Expansion/Extension

See TRF HANDOUT 3.2, *How Much Do You Spend?*

- Ask learners to make a bar graph for the Jamisons' expenses. Learners can make statements comparing the expenses. (FOR EXAMPLE: The Jamisons' largest expense is . . . . They pay the most for . . . .)
- Learners can create their own budget worksheet and make a graph of their expenses.
- Ask learners to suggest ways for the Jamisons to economize. Learners can contact Consumer Credit Counseling Service (a community service available in many areas) for budgeting ideas and information.

More *Expansion/Extension* on page 72

Managing Money

Purpose: To give practice in reading articles about money management; to introduce adverbs of indefinite frequency

Teacher Preparation and Materials

1. Large blank monthly calendar
2. Large sheet of paper, marker
3. Various store fliers and catalogs
4. Copies of TRF Handout 3.1, *Personal Finances Quiz (Expansion/Extension)*

Warm-up

1. Have learners brainstorm household chores. (doing laundry, going shopping, etc.) Create an imaginary schedule for the Jamisons' chores. On the blank calendar have learners fill in the chores. (FOR EXAMPLE: On Wednesdays and Fridays, Al cooks dinner.)

2. On the board, list adverbs of indefinite frequency: *always, usually, often, sometimes, seldom, never.* Model sentences about the chores on the calendar, using the adverbs. Have learners create sentences, using the adverbs.

3. Introduce other adverbs: *regularly, generally, frequently, occasionally, rarely.* Have learners use them in sentences describing the Jamisons' calendar.

4. On a large sheet of paper, write the headings *Necessary* and *Unnecessary.* Elicit/explain the meanings of the headings. Ask *Which expenses on the Jamisons' budget on page 32 do you think are necessary? Which expenses may be unnecessary?* Have learners suggest additional items for the two columns. Have learners explain their choices.

Presentation

1. Have learners turn to page 33. Have one or more volunteers read the introductory paragraphs. Ask *What does "managing money" mean? What ideas do you think will be in the article? How does this tie in with the lists we made of necessary and unnecessary items?*

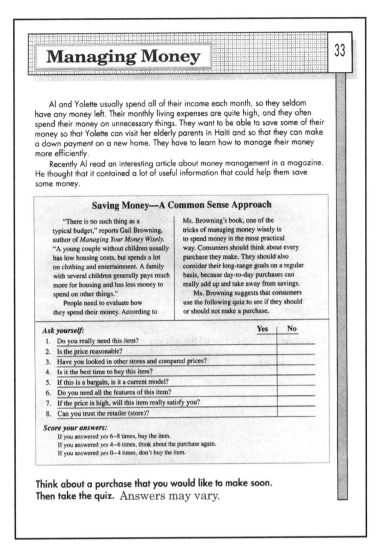

2. Have learners read the article and underline words they do not know. Elicit/explain the meanings of new words: *evaluate, consumers, purchase, reasonable, bargain, current model, satisfy, features,* and *retailer.*

3. Ask literal and inferential questions. FOR EXAMPLE: *What does the author say about a typical budget? Do you agree or disagree that there is no typical budget? Why?*

4. Have learners choose an item they would like to buy. Learners can look through store fliers or catalogs for information about the item and then take the quiz. Learners can report their scores and explain why they would or would not buy the item from that particular store.

Expansion/Extension

See** TRF HANDOUT 3.1, **Personal Finances Quiz

- Ask learners what stores they trust in the local area. Then ask learners why they trust them.

More *Expansion/Extension* on page 72

When to Pay Bills

Purpose: To give practice in reading bills and in keeping a record of payments; to introduce keeping a checking account register

Teacher Preparation and Materials

1. Utility, insurance, and retail store bills
2. Check register
3. Calculators (optional)
4. Copies of TRF Handout 3.3, *Paying the Bills (Expansion/Extension)*
5. Blank checks and deposit slips *(Expansion/Extension)*
6. Bank statements *(Expansion/Extension)*

Warm-up

1. Have learners examine some sample bills. Ask *What's the name of the company? What's the account number? How much is the balance? Is the total amount or balance the same as the minimum amount due on the bill? When is the due date?* Have learners arrange the bills according to the due dates.
2. Ask learners how they pay their bills. *Do you pay in cash? Do you use money orders? Do you use checks? Do you mail payments or pay in person?* Show a sample check register. Elicit/explain the meanings of the column headings. Ask *Do you have a checking account? If so, do you keep a register of transactions? Why is this information important to keep if you have a checking account?*
3. On the board, make a sample check register. Fill in a starting balance of $824.85. Demonstrate filling in a transaction, using one of the sample bills. Elicit/explain how to calculate the new balance. Have volunteers fill in other transactions.

Presentation

1. Have a volunteer read the title and introduction on page 34. Ask *What date is it? How many bills does Diep have? Why doesn't she pay them all now?*

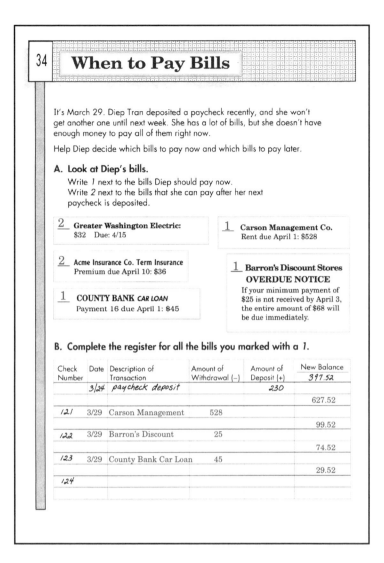

2. Have learners prioritize Diep's bills and explain their answers. Ask learners to complete the register for all the bills marked with the number 1. Learners can use calculators if they are available.
3. Ask learners what Diep should have done if she had only had $147.99 as a starting balance. Ask *Which of the bills would you have paid? What would you do about the other bills? What might happen if she wrote checks for more money than she had in her account?*

Expansion/Extension

***See** TRF HANDOUT 3.3, Paying the Bills*

- Bring in copies of bank statements. Ask learners to find various parts of the statement, such as the list of checks, deposits, withdrawals, and daily balances. Learners can read the instructions on reconciling bank statements with check registers. Discuss why people reconcile their accounts and what to do about an error on a bank statement.

More *Expansion/Extension* on page 72

Reading a Utility Bill

Purpose: To give practice in reading bills; to introduce reading budget payment plans

Teacher Preparation and Materials

1. List of expenses, used for page 32
2. Heating or fuel bills
3. Calculators (optional)
4. Information on fuel assistance programs from energy/fuel companies or social service agencies (*Expansion/Extension*)

Warm-up

1. Tape the chart of expenses on the board. Have learners identify payments that are constant (rent/mortgage, loans, insurance) and payments that vary from month to month (telephone, electricity, food).
2. Label the third column *Yearly Amount*. Have learners calculate and fill in the yearly amounts for payments that are constant.
3. Give an example of a person's expenses throughout a year. FOR EXAMPLE: *For electricity, Pierre paid $97 in January. In February, the bill was $93. In March, it was $90. In April, it was $62. In May, he paid $65. In June, $63. In July, ...* Have a volunteer write the amounts on the board and have the group calculate the annual cost.
4. Label the fourth column *Budget Plan*. Have learners calculate and fill in the average monthly payments. If necessary, demonstrate dividing the yearly amounts by 12. Elicit/explain the meaning of a budget payment plan. Ask *Why might some people want to use a budget plan for paying bills? For which of the items on the chart do you think a budget plan might be useful?*

Presentation

1. Have learners look at the utility bill on page 35. Ask *What kind of bill is this? How much fuel did Roberto get? What's the price per gallon?* Have learners

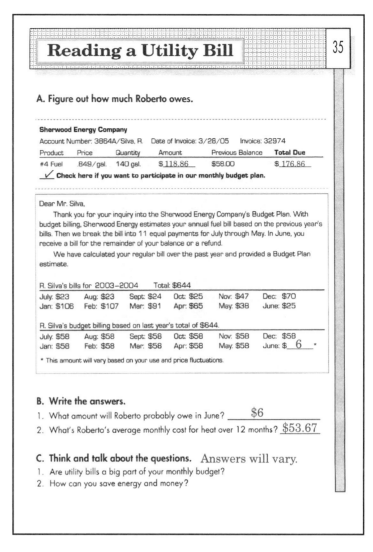

calculate the current amount due and the total amount due. Ask literal and inferential questions. FOR EXAMPLE: *Do you think Roberto will be able to pay the entire amount? What does the company offer to help avoid large bills like this?*

2. Have learners read the letter and underline words they do not know. Elicit/explain the meanings of new words: *estimates, annual, previous, refund, calculate, fluctuations.*
3. Ask *Why did the energy company send the letter to Roberto? Do you think this year's heating bills will be the same as last year's? Why do you think the company uses June as the month to balance the bills?*
4. Learners can do the calculations for exercise B and explain how they got their answers.
5. Have learners discuss their answers to the questions in exercise C.

***Expansion/Extension* on page 72**

Reading a Credit Card Bill

Purpose: To introduce reading a credit card bill; to give practice with the past tense

Teacher Preparation and Materials

1. Credit cards
2. Calculators (optional)
3. Copies of TRF Handout 3.4, *Charge It!* (Expansion/Extension)
4. Credit card bills (Expansion/Extension)

Warm-up

1. Show a credit card. Ask *What is this? What can you use it for? How do you get one? How do you use the cards to buy things? Do all stores accept credit cards?*
2. Give examples of possible credit card purchases and have learners decide if cash or a credit card should be used. FOR EXAMPLE: *I just got a new credit card. Should I to go Tire Town today and buy new tires for my car with it? Should I take all my friends out to dinner at TipTop Restaurant tomorrow? Should I use it next Monday to pay for this term's tuition at Community College? Should I use it every few days at Center Street Gas Station to buy gas for the car?* Have learners suggest possible purchases.
3. On the board, make a chart:

Date	Description	Charges

On the chart, have learners list the items they selected as credit card purchases and fill in the dates and approximate prices. Have learners total the amounts charged and summarize the "bill."

Presentation

1. Have learners look at the bill on page 36. Ask *Whose bill is this? What types of things did they buy?* (Focus on correct usage of the past tense.) *Why is the payment listed as "–100.00"? Do you think they used the credit card too much or too little? Why?*

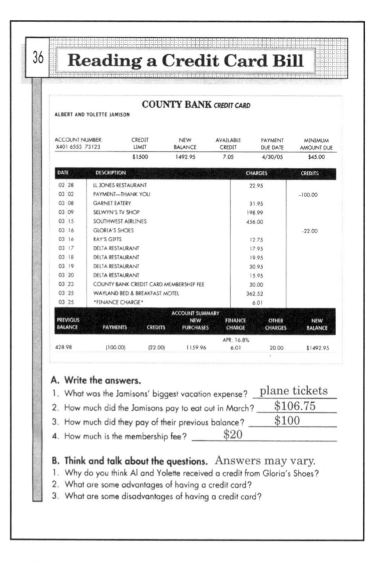

2. Have learners find parts of the bill. Ask *What words tell you the amount to be paid? Where does it tell you what the balance was before February 28?* Have learners check the account summary for possible errors.
3. Elicit/introduce the meanings of new terminology: *credits, membership fee, finance charge, APR.*
4. Have learners answer the questions in exercise A. Learners can use calculators if necessary.
5. Learners can discuss the questions in exercise B. Have learners interview several people outside the class about their use of credit cards and types of purchases charged. Learners can report their findings to the group.
6. If learners have credit cards, they can write about why they use the cards. If learners do not have credit cards, they can write about why they would or would not like to have one.

Expansion/Extension

See TRF HANDOUT 3.4, *Charge It!*

More *Expansion/Extension* on page 73

Understanding Credit Terms

Purpose: To introduce reading credit card policies and information on credit card interest; to give practice with *If/then* statements

Teacher Preparation and Materials

1. Sample credit card policies (on back of bills)
2. Copies of TRF Handout 3.5, *Credit Card Billing (Expansion/Extension)*
3. Sample store credit card policies and bank credit card policies *(Expansion/Extension)*

Warm-up

Have learners look back at page 36 and point out important information on the credit card bill. FOR EXAMPLE: *Find the membership fee. Why do you have to pay that? Find the minimum payment allowed. Find the letters* APR. *What's the annual percentage rate for the Jamisons' credit card? How much is the finance charge?*

Presentation

1. Have learners look at the sample credit card policies on page 37. Have learners find the key words: *membership fee, minimum monthly payment, finance charge, APR.*
2. Have learners read the section on the annual membership fee and underline words they do not know. Elicit/explain the meanings of new words: *terms, anniversary date, renewed, statement.* Have learners look back on page 36 for the amount of the membership fee and anniversary date.
3. Repeat the procedure for the other sections of the policies. Elicit/explain the meanings of new words: *assessed, avoid, Annual Percentage Rate, inquiries, error.*
4. Have learners use the information to calculate payment amounts and length of payment schedule. FOR EXAMPLE: *If Al has a balance of $90, how much will his*

minimum payment be? ($15) *If his balance is $575, how much will the minimum payment be?* ($17.25) *If Al pays $15 a month, about how long will it take for him to pay off $150?* (10 months) Have learners give their answers in complete sentences.

5. Have learners answer the questions in exercise A. Ask *What are the disadvantages of paying just the minimum monthly payment? What are the advantages of paying the entire balance?*
6. Learners can discuss the questions in exercise B in small groups, with one learner acting as the reporter and another as the recorder. Have the reporter in each group share the group's conclusions with the class. ■ In a one-to-one situation, discuss the questions together.

Expansion/Extension

See TRF HANDOUT 3.5, *Credit Card Billing*

Understanding Credit Terms   37

COUNTY BANK *Credit Card*

CREDIT CARD TERMS AND INFORMATION SUMMARY

Annual Membership Fee: This fee will be charged to your account. It will appear on your statement on your anniversary date, one year from the date your account was opened or renewed.

Monthly Payments You Must Agree to Pay:

Balance	Minimum Monthly Payment
$0–$14.99	amount of balance
$15–$500*	$15
over $500*	3% of your balance, rounded up to the nearest dollar

*You may pay all or part of your balance at any time, as long as you pay your minimum monthly payment.

Finance Charge: You will be assessed an ANNUAL PERCENTAGE RATE (APR) of 16.8% (1.4% per month) on all unpaid balances. You can avoid additional finance charges by paying off your New Balance before the Payment Due Date.

Problems or questions about your bill? Send inquiries to:
CBCC
Box 8221
Hanover, PA 17333-8221, or call 1-800-712-0009.
Be sure to include the following information:
1. Your name and account number
2. The item in error and an explanation of the problem
****

A. Complete the sentences.
1. If the Jamisons owed $130, the minimum payment would be __$15__.
2. To avoid a finance charge now, they will have to pay the entire bill by __4/30/05__.
3. Because the Jamisons' bill is over $500, what percentage of the balance do they have to pay? __3%__

B. Think and talk about the questions.   Answers will vary.
1. Why do you think banks make you pay finance charges?
2. What are the risks of using a credit card too often or for expensive purchases?

More *Expansion/Extension* on page 73

The Phone Bill

Purpose: To give practice in reading bills

Teacher Preparation and Materials

1. Sample local and long-distance telephone bills
2. Local telephone books
3. Information on various long-distance telephone companies (*Expansion/Extension*)
4. Sample calling cards (*Expansion/Extension*)

Warm-up

1. Have learners brainstorm and list types of phone calls on the board: *direct, local, operator-assisted, calling card, collect, overseas.* Ask learners about types of calls they have made and those that they usually make.
2. Ask questions about what time of day they make phone calls and why they call at certain times. FOR EXAMPLE: *Do you ever make long-distance calls? When do you call people? What time of day do you make most of your calls? Why? Does it make a difference what time you call? Why?* Introduce different calling times and add them to the list on the board: *Day, Evening, Night/Weekend, Standard, Economy, Discount.*

Presentation

1. Have learners turn to page 38. Have a volunteer read the title and introduction. Ask *What types of information will Al and Yolette look for on the bill? Are there other reasons why the Jamisons might check their phone bill?*
2. Have learners look at the bill and summarize the types of calls listed. Ask questions, such as *How many calls were international? How many were made at night? in the evening? Why do you think the call to Miami was less expensive than the call to the Bronx on April 3?*
3. Ask learners to complete exercise A and to point out the parts of the bill that contain the answers.

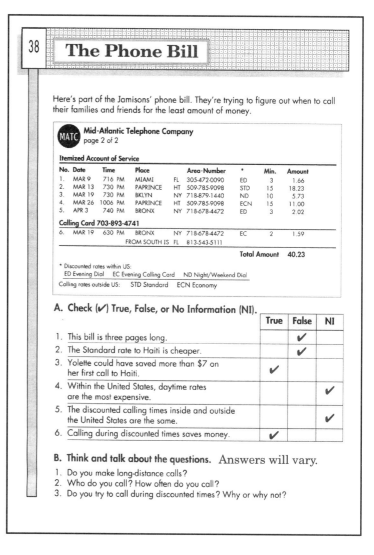

4. In small groups, have learners discuss the questions in exercise B. ◧ In a one-to-one situation, discuss the questions together. Learners can check the front pages of local phone books for information on rates for different types of calls and calling times. Learners can also bring in copies of their long-distance phone bills and compare rates for different calls. Be sure learners understand or can find out when the lower or lowest rates for long-distance calling are in effect. (**Note:** International calls are not all discounted at the same times.)

Expansion/Extension

- Ask learners to make a list of ways to save on both local and long-distance phone bills. Local phone books often have a section on money-saving tips.
- Learners can discuss the difference in cost between dialing a long-distance call direct and getting operator assistance. Learners can check the front pages of local phone books for information on the rate differences.

More *Expansion/Extension* on page 73

A Mistake on the Phone Bill

Purpose: To introduce complaining and correcting; to introduce describing a problem

Teacher Preparation and Materials

1. 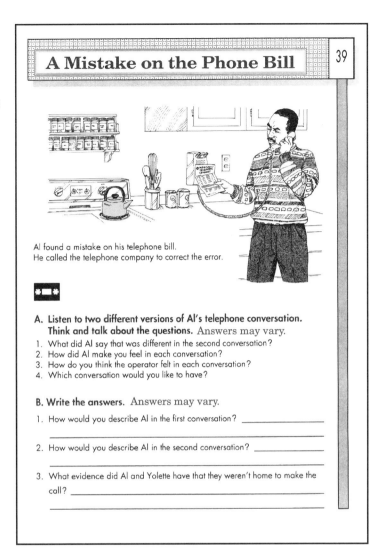 Audiotape for Level 3
2. Index cards with selected pairs of sentences from audiotape (see *Presentation #5*)
3. Copies of TRF Handout 3.6, *Returning Merchandise (Expansion/Extension)*
4. Copies of TRF Handout 3.7, *There Seems to Be a Problem (Expansion/Extension)*

Warm-up

Have learners look at the phone bill on page 38. Ask if there is anything strange about the calls made on March 19. *How many calls were made? Where were they made from?* Have learners discuss which call they think the Jamisons made and why. Have learners suggest things that could be done about the other call. List learners' ideas on the board.

Presentation

1. Have learners turn to page 39. Have a volunteer read the title and introduction. Learners can check to see if calling the phone company was one of their suggestions in the *Warm-up*. Erase the other ideas and then have learners brainstorm what Al might say to the telephone company about the error. Write the ideas on the board.

2. Have learners read the questions in exercise A to focus their listening. Play the audiotape.

3. Ask questions about the similarities and differences between the two conversations. Have learners discuss which conversation they thought was more effective and why.

4. Have learners write the answers to the questions in exercise B. In large classes, this can be done in small groups, with one learner acting as the reporter and another as the recorder. Have the reporter in each group share the group's answers with the class.

A Mistake on the Phone Bill 39

Al found a mistake on his telephone bill.
He called the telephone company to correct the error.

A. Listen to two different versions of Al's telephone conversation. Think and talk about the questions. Answers may vary.

1. What did Al say that was different in the second conversation?
2. How did Al make you feel in each conversation?
3. How do you think the operator felt in each conversation?
4. Which conversation would you like to have?

B. Write the answers. Answers may vary.

1. How would you describe Al in the first conversation? _____

2. How would you describe Al in the second conversation? _____

3. What evidence did Al and Yolette have that they weren't home to make the call? _____

5. On index cards, write pairs of statements from the two conversations that are similar in meaning but use different levels of politeness. Have learners categorize the statements as polite or impolite (rude).

Polite	Impolite
There seems to be an error on my bill.	You made a mistake on my bill!
There's a phone call on my account to Brooklyn. I'm sure it's a mistake.	I never call Brooklyn!
No, I don't know any Ragans.	I never heard of any Ragans!

Model the proper intonation for the statements and have learners repeat after you. Have learners suggest situations in which each of the levels of politeness might be appropriate/effective.

Expansion/Extension

See TRF HANDOUT 3.6, *Returning Merchandise*
TRF HANDOUT 3.7, *There Seems to Be a Problem*

More *Expansion/Extension* on page 73

Why People Save

Purpose: To give practice with adverbs of indefinite frequency

Teacher Preparation and Materials

1. Large sheets of paper, markers, and tape for all
2. Bank information on various savings accounts *(Expansion/Extension)*

Warm-up

1. Have learners brainstorm and list things for which people save money. Have learners explain why these things might be important and estimate a cost for the various items.
2. Ask how often people make these types of purchases and how they might pay for them. If necessary, point out that before people can get loans and credit cards, they need to have some money saved.

Presentation

1. Have learners turn to page 40. Ask questions about the title and pictures, such as *What do you know about these people? What things might they want to save money for?* Learners can look through this and previous units for information about the characters and their families.
2. Have learners read the two paragraphs and underline words they do not know. Elicit/explain the meanings of new words: *secondhand, emergency, put money away, nest egg.*
3. Ask literal and inferential questions. FOR EXAMPLE: *What are the savings goals of these people? What types of emergencies is Diep thinking of? Do you think their savings goals are reasonable? Do you think they will have an easy or difficult time saving? Why or why not?* (Learners can look back at the Jamisons' budget and credit card bill.)
4. Have learners complete the exercise at the bottom of the page. To check the work, have learners use the words or phrases in new sentences.

---

40 **Why People Save**

People save for different reasons. Diep wants to take more courses at school. She also has to buy clothes for her two children frequently because they grow so fast. Even though she only buys secondhand or discount clothes, she often has to buy on credit. She worries that occasionally she will need money for an emergency. She puts $30 each week in a savings account. Having a savings account that grows regularly makes Diep feel much better.

Yolette and Al think about the future too. They'd like to have a little nest egg so that they can own their own home someday. Yolette also wants to visit her parents in Haiti. Al and Yolette know that sometimes they spend money on things they don't need or don't use. They've decided to use their credit cards for emergencies only. After they pay off their credit card bills, they are going to put money away from each paycheck. They've set a goal for themselves to pay off their credit card bills in five months. Then they intend to save $1,000 within a year.

Find the words.

Write the word or phrase in the story that means . . .

1. used or worn by someone else first: _____ secondhand
2. very often: _____ frequently
3. once in a while: _____ occasionally
4. an unexpected problem or crisis: _____ emergency
5. at equal times: _____ regularly
6. money saved for the future: _____ nest egg

---

5. Review the list of savings goals on the board. Give each learner a large sheet of paper, tape, and a marker. On the top of the paper, have learners write the category headings *Necessities, Real Goals, Future Dreams.* Have learners categorize the list from the board. Have learners explain their placement of items.

Expansion/Extension

- Learners can discuss which of the following statements they feel is a better way to save and why:
    1. I pay all my bills first and then save whatever is left over.
    2. I put $30 in my savings account first and then pay my bills.
- Ask learners to write about something they are saving money for or something they would like to save for in the future. Learners can include the amount to be saved and length of time needed to save the amount.
- Bring in information about different savings accounts. Ask learners to find and compare account features.

Practicing Your Skills

Purpose: To give practice in writing a letter describing a savings plan

Teacher Preparation and Materials

1. List of expenses, used for page 35
2. Lists of savings goals, from page 40
3. Store catalogs, fliers, advertisements for various items from the list
4. Classified ads from local newspapers *(Expansion/Extension)*

Warm-up

Tape the lists of expenses and savings goals to the wall or board. Have learners review the items and suggest methods of payment. (cash, check, credit, layaway, loan, mortgage)

Presentation

1. Have learners turn to page 41, read Al's letter, and underline words they do not know. Elicit/explain the meanings of new words: *trade-in, credit union, commuting, down payment, great deal, campaign, sedan.*

2. Ask literal and inferential questions. FOR EXAMPLE: *Does Al usually write letters to Jack and Marta? Why is he doing it now? How much money do you think he can save in a year if he writes instead of calling? How else are Al and Yolette saving money? Are there other ways they can save?*

3. Ask learners to name an item that they recently purchased or would like to purchase. Have them describe the item and its features. Ask *What did you buy? Where did you buy it? How did you pay for it?* Learners can look through store catalogs, fliers, or advertisements for specific vocabulary related to their item.

4. Together, read the instructions for exercise B. If necessary, ask a volunteer questions about his or her savings plans, and write a sample letter on the board. Then have learners individually write a draft of their own letter to a friend or relative about some ways they are saving (or would like to save) money.

5. In pairs, have learners exchange letters. Learners should read, ask questions about, and comment on the drafts. Then, have learners rewrite their own letters in their student book.

Expansion/Extension

- Ask learners to compile a vocabulary list for the unit. Learners can then create categories and categorize the new words. Some categories might be Budgeting, Expenses, Banking, Bills, Shopping, and Miscellaneous.

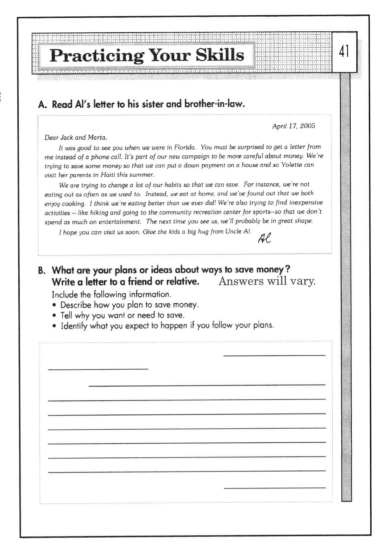

Adverbs of Frequency

Purpose: To give practice in distinguishing and using adverbs of frequency

Teacher Preparation and Materials

Pieces of paper or cardstock ($8\frac{1}{2}$" x 11") with adverbs of frequency written on them (Be sure to include *always* and *never* and at least one from each of the other categories on page 42.) *(Warm-up)*

Warm-up

1. Give out the cards with the adverbs of frequency written on them, one card to a learner. Have the learners with the cards that contain *always* and *never* stand on opposite sides of the room. Have the others line up according to how close their adverbs are to *always* or *never*. Learners who feel the adverbs on their cards express the same degree of frequency can stand as a group or line up one behind the other. In a one-to-one situation, have the learner line up and group the cards on a table.

2. Once the class has agreed on appropriate positions for all adverbs, write the words on the board in that order. Have learners turn to page 42 and compare the chart to the class's ordering. Discuss any differences.

3. Ask questions about how often learners do various activities. FOR EXAMPLE: *How often do you go to the movies?* (I hardly ever go to the movies. I generally go to a movie on Sundays.) *Do you call home rarely or frequently?* (I call home frequently because I miss my family.)

Presentation

1. Have learners look at the picture on page 42 and identify who they see. Ask what they think Diep and her children are doing.

2. Ask learners who have children how often they buy clothes for their children, and why.

3. Review or elicit explanations of difficult vocabulary from the exercise (e.g., *outgrow, secondhand store, double discount*).

---

42 — Adverbs of Frequency

0% ←					→ 100%
never at no time not once	rarely seldom hardly ever	sometimes occasionally now and then	often frequently many times	usually generally regularly	always every time constantly

Complete the sentences with an appropriate adverb from the chart. Answers may vary.

Example: Diep's children are __constantly__ (99%) growing.

1. They ___sometimes___ (55%) outgrow their clothes.
2. They ___seldom___ (10%) wear clothes for a whole year.
3. They ___usually___ (85%) need clothes every few months.
4. She ___occasionally___ (45%) shops at Your Turn, a secondhand store near the hospital.
5. Your Turn ___often___ (75%) has good school clothes.
6. But it ___never___ (0%) carries winter coats.
7. For winter coats, Diep ___always___ (100%) goes to Barron's Discount.
8. She shops at the end of the season and ___generally___ (80%) gets a double discount.
9. The children ___frequently___ (65%) need new shoes twice a year.
10. Diep ___hardly ever___ (5%) buys expensive shoes for them.
11. They ___always___ (100%) outgrow shoes so fast!

---

4. Learners can work individually or in pairs to complete the exercise. Review answers, and discuss any differences in the adverbs chosen for each sentence.

Expansion/Extension

• Discuss why people shop at secondhand stores. Make a chart of some advantages and disadvantages. Ask learners about their experiences with such stores. They should consider issues of quality, selection, and service as well as price.

• Ask learners with children where they buy children's clothes and how their experiences compare to Diep's.

• Learners can use adverbs of frequency to write about shopping for clothes for themselves or their children. They can use the sentences about Diep as a model for their own story.

• Learners can talk or write about other things they do with varying degrees of regularity (FOR EXAMPLE: household chores; family, community, or work activities).

Modals: *Can, Should*/Past Tense of Irregular Verbs

Purpose: To give practice in using *can* and *should* and in recognizing and using the past tense of irregular verbs

Teacher Preparation and Materials

1. ▄▄ Audiotape for Level 3
2. Advertisements for new and used cars *(Expansion/Extension)*

Warm-up

1. Review the meaning and use of *can* and *should*. Have learners turn to page 34 and review the exercise. Discuss why Diep should pay some bills now and why she can wait to pay others.

2. Ask learners to imagine they are planning a vacation. Have them list several possible destinations. Discuss the costs of each, what they can do there, how they can get there, and so on. Then have learners decide which vacation they should choose.

Presentation

1. Have learners turn to page 43 and read the example sentences.

2. Learners can work individually or in pairs to complete the first exercise. Review answers by having three learners role-play the conversation.

3. Discuss why Adela and Roberto should check the features of a car before deciding to buy it. Have learners list features that they should check. Learners can also list options, such as color, in which a buyer has choices.

4. Review past tense forms of irregular verbs used in this unit. Have learners turn to page 39. ▄▄ Play the audiotape, and listen again to the two versions of Al's conversation with the phone company. Have learners identify irregular past tense forms from the conversations, text, and exercise, including answers *(made, heard, found, were, said, did).*

| Advice | What bills **should** Diep **pay** today? | **Should** she **pay** these bills today? |
| Ability | What bills **can** I **pay** next week? | **Can** I **pay** those bills next week? |

Roberto and Adela are looking at new cars. Write questions with *can* or *should*.

Example: Adela: _____What model should we get_____ ? Answers
model/get   may vary.

Roberto: Let's check the features before we decide.

1. Adela: _____Should we look at one_____ with better mileage?
look at/one

Roberto: That's a good idea. Let's talk to a salesperson.

2. Adela: We like this model. But _can we choose a different color_ ?
choose/a different color

Salesperson: Oh yes, it comes in six different colors.

3. Roberto: How much _can you offer for a trade-in_ for our old car?
trade-in/offer

Salesperson: Let me check that out for you.

Underline the irregular verbs. Then write the base form of each verb.

Example: Al and Yolette <u>said</u> they are changing their spending habits. _say_

1. They <u>began</u> to pay off their credit card bills. _begin_
2. They <u>took</u> a cooking course at the adult education center. _take_
3. They <u>found</u> out about free entertainment in their area. _find_
4. Al didn't <u>make</u> a lot of long-distance calls. _make_
5. Instead, he <u>wrote</u> letters to his friends and relatives. _write_
6. They <u>thought</u> their budgeting worked well. _think_
7. They soon <u>paid</u> off their credit cards and started to save. _pay_

---

5. Have learners look at the example in the second exercise to clarify directions. Review answers.

Expansion/Extension

- Learners can extend the conversation between Adela, Roberto, and the salesperson, with questions about other features and about payment options. They can then role-play the extended conversation.

- Have learners look at and compare ads for new and used cars. In pairs or small groups, they can write questions to ask a salesperson about the cars.

- Learners can brainstorm other things that Al and Yolette probably did to save money. Or they can create a list of things that a couple can do to save, then evaluate the possibilities and make recommendations.

- Ask learners if they have ever tried to change their behavior (e.g., to save money, to lose weight). Learners can write about what they did to move towards their goal. Have them exchange papers, read what their partner has written, and circle any irregular verbs the partner used.

UNIT 3: Making Ends Meet
Expansion/Extension

Monthly Expenses
More *Expansion/Extension* for SB page 32

- Have learners compare the Jamisons' expenses to the cost of living expenses in their area. Ask *What things are more expensive? What bills are lower in your area? Why?*
- Have learners list advantages and disadvantages of paying for a purchase with cash, credit, a check, a loan, or by layaway.

Managing Money
More *Expansion/Extension* for SB page 33

- Learners can discuss different types of discount stores, including factory outlets, consignment shops, and discount chain stores. Learners can make a list of advantages and disadvantages of each. FOR EXAMPLE: *Can items be returned? Are items new or repaired? Do items come with guarantees and warranties? Are items damaged or irregulars?*
- Ask learners to compare expenses for different family groups. FOR EXAMPLE: *What might be expenses for families with young children? for families without children? for families with elderly people?*
- On the board, write *I am a careful buyer. I spend my money wisely.* Have learners add the adverb *usually* to the two sentences. (I am usually a careful buyer. I usually spend my money wisely.) Ask learners to give examples of sentences with other adverbs of indefinite frequency and then to create rules for placement.

When to Pay Bills
More *Expansion/Extension* for SB page 34

- Bring in copies of blank checks and deposit slips. Learners can practice filling in checks for the bills on page 34 and a deposit slip for Diep's paycheck.
- Learners can collect brochures on checking accounts at local banks to compare fees, charges, minimum balances, direct deposit policies for paychecks, and other banking requirements. Learners can find out the number of banking days needed for checks and deposits to clear.
- Ask learners if they think Diep's car loan payment will be received by April 1. *Do you think Diep will mail or take the check to the bank? What are the advantages of taking the check to the bank? What are the advantages of mailing the check? What are the disadvantages of both methods of payment?* Learners can find out about grace periods (time after the actual due date when payments will be accepted without adding a finance charge or late fee).

Reading a Utility Bill
Expansion/Extension for SB page 35

- Learners can call energy/fuel companies to find out which ones offer budget plans.
- Learners can make a list of ways to reduce energy costs.
- Ask learners to write questions about the budget plan described on page 35. Learners can role-play calling for budget plan information, with one learner asking questions and another learner supplying information.
- Ask learners to list advantages and disadvantages of using budget plans. Ask learners if budget plans would be useful or appropriate for some of their expense items.
- Bring in information about local fuel assistance programs. These can usually be obtained from local fuel companies and the Department of Social Services. Learners can find out about requirements, application forms, and where to get more information about the programs.
- Ask learners to find electric and/or gas meters in their buildings and to record the readings periodically. Learners can look at corresponding utility bills to see where meter information is reported. Introduce vocabulary, such as *kilowatt hours, volts, watts, meter,* and *gauge.*

Reading a Credit Card Bill

More *Expansion/Extension* for SB page 36

- Learners can find out the names of different credit cards and compare rates and finance charges offered by different companies. Learners can look for application forms in banks, restaurants, and stores.
- Have learners list suggestions to the Jamisons on the use of their credit card. Ask *What advice would you give them about payments? What types of purchases should the card be used for?*

Understanding Credit Terms

More *Expansion/Extension* for SB page 37

- Ask learners to write *If/then* problem situations related to the Jamisons' statement and credit card policies. FOR EXAMPLE: *If their balance is $150, how much will the finance charge be on the next statement?* ($2.10) Learners can present their problem situations for the other learners to solve.
- Bring in sample store credit card policies and bank credit card policies found on the back of credit card bills, applications, and brochures. Have learners find key words and information. Explain that each company sets some of its own policies. Have learners compare membership fees, finance charges, and payments. Many stores do not charge membership fees but do assess finance charges.
- Learners can brainstorm errors that may show up on a credit card statement. (charged twice for the same item, charged the wrong price for an item, not credited for a returned item, charged for an item never purchased, charged for items bought when the card was stolen, etc.) Learners can choose a situation and write a letter or role-play a call to report the error.
- Have learners list ways to protect credit cards. (keep a list of account numbers and telephone numbers in case the cards are lost or stolen, do not give account numbers to people who call on the phone, etc.)
- Discuss options and consequences of not being able to pay credit card bills. Some companies offer hardship plans (with lower minimum payments) for people with temporary problems due to layoffs or medical problems. Consumer Credit Counseling Service offers advice and programs to assist people in paying off accounts.

The Phone Bill

More *Expansion/Extension* for SB page 38

- Ask learners to look at calls and charges on their phone bills and make a list of abbreviations used.
- Bring in information and ads about long-distance companies. Ask learners which long-distance companies they use. Learners can compare the different offerings. Point out the small print on some offerings. Explain that people often shop around to find the long-distance company that saves them the most money.
- Bring in a calling card. Elicit/explain how they are used. Allow learners to share experiences they may have had using calling cards. Point out that calling card procedures vary with different companies. Discuss the advantages and disadvantages/risks of using calling cards.

A Mistake on the Phone Bill

More *Expansion/Extension* for SB page 39

- Learners can role-play the two conversations, using the sentences on the index cards. Then learners can role-play reporting other types of billing problems. (There seems to be a mistake on my credit card statement/gas bill/checking account statement, etc.)
- Introduce descriptive adjectives about the role plays: *angry, pleasant, sarcastic, abrupt, upset, embarrassed, polite, rude.* ▆▆ Learners can listen to the conversations on the audiotape and describe the tones and verbal expressions of the speakers.
- Ask learners how they feel and react when someone is angry or rude to them. Have learners suggest ways of handling hostile situations and role-play some strategies.

Living with Machines

Objectives

Functions
- Following directions
- Reporting events
- Describing a process

Life Tasks
- Reading automated teller machine instructions
- Reading directions
- Reading a warranty
- Filling out an accident report form
- Writing directions

Structures
- Passive voice
- Imperatives
- Modal: *must*
- Reflexive pronouns
- Adjectives

Culture
- United States as a technological society

Vocabulary

Key words:

accident report	manual
computer screen	password
damage	plug
defective	repair
diagram	replacement
electric hedge	solution
trimmer	troubleshooting
limited warranty	warranty
machine	registration card

Key abbreviations:

ATM–automated teller machine
VCR–videocassette recorder

Related words:

annoyed	microwave
cable	patient
cable box	pleased
cancel	proof of purchase
channel	remedy
covered	satisfied
freight prepaid	shipping charges
frustrated	socket
grounded outlet	stubborn
guaranteed	tangled
handling	transaction
(to) hook up	transfer
insure	wire
manufacturer	workmanship
material	

What's the Problem?

Purpose: To introduce vocabulary about machines

Teacher Preparation and Materials

1. Pictures of a personal computer and printer, a vending machine, and other machines
2. Blank index cards
3. Large sheets of paper, marker
4. Hardware, appliance, and department store catalogs or fliers with different types of machines *(Expansion/Extension)*

Warm-up

1. Hold up pictures of different machines and elicit/introduce the names of them. Be sure to include *computer printer* and *vending machine.*
2. For each of the machines, have learners give a function or reason for using the machine. List the machines and functions on the board.
3. Write the functions of the machines on blank index cards. Model choosing a card, reading it, and then asking a *Wh-* question. Have learners respond with the appropriate machine. FOR EXAMPLE: *cut grass—What can I use to cut the grass?* (lawn mower) Have learners choose cards and ask and answer questions.

Presentation

1. Have learners look at the picture on page 44. Ask *Where are they? Which machines are they trying to use? What do you think Roberto and Yolette are saying about the machines?* List words and comments on the board.
2. Have learners discuss the questions at the bottom of the page. Have learners predict what advice Roberto's friends are giving him. Learners can make suggestions for Yolette and her problem.
3. On a large sheet of paper, write two column headings: *Machines Are Friendly* and *Machines Are Frustrating.* Have learners think of ways machines help

1 2 3 4 5 6 7 8 9 10 11 12

Living with Machines ■ ■ ■ ■ ■ ■ ■

What's the Problem?

How do Roberto and Yolette feel?   Answers will vary.
What can they do?
Have you ever had a problem with a machine?

us and problems that machines can cause for us. Learners can write their ideas in the appropriate column. Depending on the size of the class, learners may work in small groups or pairs.

Expansion/Extension

- Learners can make up conversations based on the picture and role-play them for the group.
- Bring in hardware, appliance, and department store catalogs or fliers for learners to look through. Ask learners to find pictures and ads for machines and appliances that they use. Learners can make lists of machines and then categorize the machines by use, location, power source, and so on.
- Introduce meanings of prefixes commonly used with machines. FOR EXAMPLE: *auto-* (working by itself), *tele-* (distance), *audio-* (sound), *trans-* (across). Have learners give examples of words with these prefixes.

More *Expansion/Extension* on page 88

Trouble with Machines

Purpose: To introduce describing mechanical problems; to give practice in giving advice

Teacher Preparation and Materials
1. Pictures of machines, used for page 44
2. Large sheet of paper, marker
3. ▰▰▰ Audiotape for Level 3
4. Copies of TRF Handout 4.7, *The Human Machine (Expansion/Extension)*

Warm-up
1. Review pictures of machines and have learners identify them by name and function.
2. On a large sheet of paper, make a chart:

Name	Problem	Solution

Have learners look back at page 44. Ask *What kind of machine is Roberto using? What is the problem with it? What do you think he can/should do about it?* Encourage learners to be specific about the problems. (FOR EXAMPLE: The machine didn't give him a drink or his money back. The machine gave him the wrong change. The money is stuck inside the machine.) Fill in the ideas on the chart. Repeat the procedure for Yolette's machine problem.

3. Have learners suggest what to do about the problems. Learners may have more than one idea for each problem. List them in the *Solution* column. (**Note:** This chart will be used with page 46 also.)
4. Ask learners about problems they have had with machines.

Presentation
1. Have learners turn to page 45 and look at the picture. Have learners predict what the conversation will be about. Ask *What will Roberto's friends talk about? Will all the solutions/advice be good? How do you think Yolette feels about machines?*

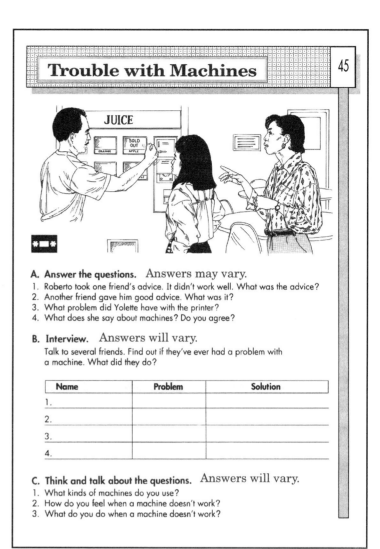

Trouble with Machines 45

A. Answer the questions.   Answers may vary.
1. Roberto took one friend's advice. It didn't work well. What was the advice?
2. Another friend gave him good advice. What was it?
3. What problem did Yolette have with the printer?
4. What does she say about machines? Do you agree?

B. Interview.   Answers will vary.
Talk to several friends. Find out if they've ever had a problem with a machine. What did they do?

Name	Problem	Solution
1.		
2.		
3.		
4.		

C. Think and talk about the questions.   Answers will vary.
1. What kinds of machines do you use?
2. How do you feel when a machine doesn't work?
3. What do you do when a machine doesn't work?

2. Have learners read the questions in exercise A to focus their listening. ▰▰▰ Play the audiotape. Have learners answer the questions in exercise A. You may want to write Yolette's comment about machines on the board before asking learners if they agree or disagree.
3. Have learners read the instructions for exercise B. If necessary, model interviewing a learner and filling in the information on the chart on the board.
4. Have learners interview four friends about problems they have experienced with machines. Learners can share the results of their interviews. ▰▪ In a one-to-one situation, have the learner interview you and then complete the exercise outside the class.
5. In large classes, have learners discuss the questions in exercise C in small groups, with one learner acting as the reporter and another as the recorder. Have the reporter in each group share the group's conclusions with the class. ▰▪ In a one-to-one situation, discuss the questions together.

Expansion/Extension on page 88

Connecting
the New VCR

Purpose: To introduce ways to solve
problems; to give practice with adjectives

Teacher Preparation and Materials

1. A VCR with wires and cables or a picture
   or diagram of one
2. VCR manual
3. Index cards with words: *angry, annoyed,*
   frustrated, pleased, careful, stubborn,
   satisfied, patient
4. Chart of machine problems and solutions,
   used for page 45
5. Copies of TRF Handout 4.2, *Installing*
   Your Smoke Detector (Expansion/Extension)

Warm-up

1. Show learners a VCR or a picture of one.
   Elicit/explain the meanings of *VCR, cable,*
   and *wire.* Ask learners about experiences
   they have had with VCRs.
2. Show a manual for a VCR. Ask *What is*
   this? Where and when do you get it? What
   information is in it? Have you ever used a
   manual? Did it help you? Have learners
   look through the manual for diagrams.
3. Tape the word cards to the board. Elicit/
   explain the meanings of new words. Have
   learners give examples of when a person
   might have these feelings.

Presentation

1. Have learners look at page 46. Ask *Do you*
   think Roberto and Eddy are cooperating
   with each other? When you get a new
   machine do you examine the machine first
   or read the manual first? What do you
   think the story will be about?
2. Have learners read the story and underline words they do not know. Elicit/explain
   the meanings of new words, including
   untangled, equipment, and *expected.*
3. Ask literal and inferential questions, such
   as *Why do you think Roberto didn't study*
   the manual? How did Roberto feel when he
   couldn't connect the VCR correctly? How

Connecting the New VCR

Roberto bought a VCR.
His son, Eddy, read the manual
while Roberto tried to connect the
equipment. Roberto had repaired
many TVs and radios in his shop
in Puerto Rico, so he felt that he
understood that kind of mechanical
equipment. He thought that
he didn't need the manual. The
VCR was more complicated than
Roberto expected. Two hours later he was feeling angry and frustrated
because the VCR still didn't work. He wanted to return it to the store.

Eddy finished reading the manual. He untangled the cables and wires,
following the directions and diagrams in the manual. Soon the VCR was
connected, and Eddy was recording a movie for his little sister, Cruz.

Roberto was frustrated that he couldn't connect the VCR, but he was
very pleased that Eddy had helped him. Now the entire family can watch
or record shows anytime they want.

A. Read these words that can describe Eddy and Roberto. Answers
Check (✔) if a word describes Eddy, his father, or both. may vary.
Add two more words that describe one or both of them.

	Eddy	Roberto	Both
1. careful			
2. stubborn			
3. satisfied			
4. annoyed			
5. patient			
6.			
7.			

B. Think and talk about the questions. Answers will vary.
Do you like people to give you advice when you are working
on a difficult problem? Why or why not?

---

did Eddy help? Do you think it was easy or difficult for
Roberto to accept help from his son?

4. Have a volunteer read the instructions for exercise A.
   Have learners complete the exercise and then give
   reasons for their choices.
5. Have learners discuss the questions in exercise B. Ask
   learners about experiences they have had with giving
   or getting advice. Ask *Did the person (or you) take the*
   advice that was given? Why or why not? Elicit expressions for accepting or politely refusing advice and list
   them on the board. (FOR EXAMPLE: *That's a good idea. I*
   hadn't thought of that. I'll have to try that. I see what
   you mean, but . . . . I really don't think so, because . . . .)
   Have learners practice giving, accepting, and refusing
   advice for the machine problems listed on the chart
   used for page 45.

Expansion/Extension

See TRF HANDOUT 4.2, *Installing Your Smoke Detector*

More *Expansion/Extension* on page 88

Watching and Recording

Purpose: To give practice in giving *how-to* instructions, following directions, describing a process, and taking notes; to give practice with *must* and with imperatives

Teacher Preparation and Materials

1. Videotape, VCR or picture of a VCR
2. 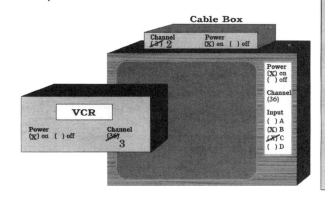 Audiotape for Level 3
3. VCR manual and/or copies of a diagram of a VCR control panel *(Expansion/Extension)*
4. Copies of TRF Handout 4.1, *Buttons, Levers, and Knobs (Expansion/Extension)*
5. Local TV and program schedules *(Expansion/Extension)*

Warm-up

1. Bring in a videotape and a VCR or a picture of a VCR that clearly shows the control panel. Elicit/introduce new vocabulary: *tape, dial, channel, insert.* Practice following simple directions related to the panel, such as *turn on the VCR; put a tape in the VCR; set it to channel 3.* Write new words on the board.
2. Dictate commands and have learners repeat the most important part of the commands. FOR EXAMPLE: *Before you can do anything, you need to plug the VCR into a nearby outlet.* (Plug it in.)

Presentation

1. Have learners turn to page 47. Have a volunteer read the title and introductory paragraph. Ask questions, such as *Who will be giving the directions? Have you ever used a VCR to record a movie? If so, how did you do it? What is a cable movie?*
2. Have learners listen as you play the first two lines of the audiotape. Have learners look at exercise A. Point out how item #1 condenses the information from the conversation.
3. Play the rest of the conversation and have learners take their own notes. If necessary, pause the audiotape after each step.

The right side panel (page 47 reproduction):

Watching and Recording — 47

Roberto wants to watch the basketball game on channel 2. Adela, his wife, wants to see a cable TV movie that's playing at the same time on channel 36. They've decided to watch the game and record the movie for later. Roberto and Eddy are figuring out how to watch one show and record another one at the same time.

A. Listen to Eddy's directions and take notes.

1. Turn on the VCR and insert a new tape.
2. Set the VCR to channel 3.
3. Turn on the cable.
4. Turn on the TV.
5. Set the TV to channel 36.
6. Turn the input dial to B.
7. Set the cable box to channel 2.

B. Use your notes to correct the mistakes.

---

4. Replay the audiotape for learners to check their work. Have learners compare their notes in pairs. Ask *Why does Roberto repeat the instructions? How does saying the instructions again help both Roberto and Eddy? Do you repeat instructions that are given to you? What do you say if you don't understand the instructions?*
5. Have learners look at the diagram in exercise B and identify the components and settings. Ask *Where's the cable box? Where do you turn it on and off? What channel is the TV set to? Is the VCR turned on or off right now?*
6. Have learners read their notes from exercise A and reset the equipment correctly in exercise B. Learners can role-play giving and receiving directions, using the notes from exercise A and the diagram in exercise B.

Expansion/Extension

See TRF HANDOUT 4.1, *Buttons, Levers, and Knobs*

More *Expansion/Extension* on page 88

Limited One-Year Warranty

Purpose: To give practice in reporting events; to introduce reading a warranty

Teacher Preparation and Materials
Sample warranty cards

Warm-up

1. Bring in sample warranty cards. Elicit/ explain information about warranty cards. Ask *What do you do if you buy something like a washing machine and a part in it breaks six months later? What is a warranty? How do you get one? What is it used for? What types of products have warranties? How can it help you if there is a problem with the item you bought? Does it cover all types of problems or just some? Have you ever used one? If so, what did you do? What did the manufacturer do?*

2. Elicit/introduce general problems with machines and appliances. (FOR EXAMPLE: A dial is broken. A wire is missing. A screw is loose. A part inside doesn't work. A fuse blew out.) List learners' responses on the board and label the list *Problems*.

3. Make two more columns on the board. Label them *Material/Workmanship* and *Repair/Replace*. Explain the column headings. For each of the problems listed, have learners decide if the problem is with the material or workmanship, and if the entire machine should be repaired or replaced.

Presentation

1. Have learners turn to page 48. Elicit/ explain the meaning of *Limited One-Year Warranty*.

2. Have learners read the warranty and underline words they do not know. Elicit/ explain the meanings of new words, including *defective, damage, unreasonable, abusive, commercial use, guaranteed, freight prepaid, handling,* and *insure*.

3. Ask literal and inferential questions, such as *How long is the warranty good for?*

---

48 Limited One-Year Warranty

Holmes Electronics Corporation
Keep this portion of the warranty for your records.

1. Fill out and return the Warranty Registration Card (the perforated bottom half of this card) **within 10 days of your purchase.**
2. This warranty applies only to repair or replacement of the VCR if it is defective in material or workmanship. Damage from unreasonable or abusive use or commercial use is not covered by this warranty.
3. All parts of this VCR are guaranteed for a period of one year, as follows:
   a. Holmes will repair or replace this VCR if you return it to our factory, freight prepaid, with a proof of purchase (a dated receipt) and $22.50 for handling and return shipping charges.
   b. When returning the VCR, pack the item carefully, in its original carton if possible. Be sure to attach a tag to the item with your name, address, and phone number. We recommend that you insure the package. Mark the outside of your package **"Attention Repair Dept."** and ship to:
   Holmes Electronics Corp., 78 Broad Street, Dunhill, NC 28334.

Complete this story. Use the information on the warranty card.

Roberto completed the __warranty__ card and __returned__ it within
$\quad\quad\quad\quad\quad\quad\quad\quad\quad$ 1 $\quad\quad\quad\quad\quad$ 2

three days. Six months later, the VCR stopped recording TV programs. Sometimes

it would switch channels on its own. Roberto had kept the warranty __card__
$\quad\quad\quad\quad\quad\quad\quad\quad\quad\quad\quad\quad\quad\quad\quad\quad\quad\quad\quad\quad\quad\quad$ 3

with his important papers. He read it again and decided to __return__ the
$\quad\quad\quad\quad\quad\quad\quad\quad\quad\quad\quad\quad\quad\quad\quad\quad\quad\quad\quad\quad\quad\quad$ 4

VCR to the manufacturer for repairs.

He didn't have the __original__ carton, but he found a sturdy one that
$\quad\quad\quad\quad\quad\quad\quad\quad\quad\quad$ 5

was the right size. He packed it __carefully__ and __attached__
$\quad\quad\quad\quad\quad\quad\quad\quad\quad\quad\quad\quad\quad\quad$ 6 $\quad\quad\quad\quad$ 7

a tag labeled according to the directions. He also sent a check for __$22.50__
$\quad\quad\quad\quad\quad\quad\quad\quad\quad\quad\quad\quad\quad\quad\quad\quad\quad\quad\quad\quad\quad\quad\quad\quad\quad$ 8

and the proof of __purchase__, which was his __receipt__ from
$\quad\quad\quad\quad\quad\quad\quad$ 9 $\quad\quad\quad\quad\quad\quad\quad\quad\quad\quad$ 10

the store.

How does the company know when you bought the item? How much does it cost to use the warranty? Could you use the warranty if someone spilled juice all over the machine? Would the warranty apply if some of the buttons on the control panel didn't work?

4. Introduce the story. Say *Roberto started to have problems with the VCR, so he followed the instructions on the warranty.* Have learners complete the cloze exercise individually or in pairs. To check answers, have volunteers point to the information on the warranty.

Expansion/Extension

- Learners can look through different company warranties for similarities and differences. Learners can check lengths of warranty periods, procedures for using them, and restrictions on use of the warranties.

- Learners can write a letter to the Holmes Electronics Corporation, explaining the problem with the VCR. Elicit/explain business letter conventions.

More *Expansion/Extension* on page 89

Troubleshooting:
Forms A and B

Purpose: To give practice in giving *how-to* instructions, in reading directions, and in asking for advice about machines; to give practice with imperatives and with question formation

Teacher Preparation and Materials

1. Picture of a personal computer with mouse and printer
2. Copies of TRF Handout 4.3, *Troubleshooting (Expansion/Extension)*
3. Blank index cards *(Expansion/Extension)*
4. Manuals for computers, appliances, and other mechanical equipment *(Expansion/Extension)*

Warm-up

1. Tape a picture of a personal computer and printer to the wall. Elicit/introduce names of parts. Be sure to include *printer, mouse, screen, paper tray,* and *switch.*
2. On the board, make three columns and label them *Parts, Problems,* and *Remedies.* Have learners list the computer parts in the first column.
3. Have learners look back at the picture on page 44 and talk about Yolette's problem with the printer. Encourage learners to describe possible problems. List the problems in the second column.
4. Have learners guess names of computer parts that are linked to the printer and may cause some problems.

Presentation

1. On top of the chart of computer problems, write *Troubleshooting.* Elicit/explain the meaning.
2. Divide learners into two groups. Have one group look at page 49 (Form A) and the other group look at page 50 (Form B). ◼ In a one-to-one situation, have the

---

Troubleshooting: Form A   49

Work with a partner.
One person uses Form A.
The other uses Form B.

Yolette and Roberto are both having computer problems. They're helping each other in the computer lab.

You are Yolette. Your partner is Roberto.
Yolette can't get the printer to work correctly. Roberto is checking the User's Guide and giving Yolette some suggestions.

A. Tell your partner about your computer problems and ask for advice.
1. The printer won't work. Ask what button to press.
2. Ask how to reset the printer.
3. You want to print in a vertical page format and the printer is printing horizontally.
4. Now the print is too light. Ask what to adjust.
5. The print is still too light. Ask what to do next.

Now Roberto is trying to clean the mouse for his computer. Yolette is reading about the procedure in the User's Guide.

B. Find the information for your partner in the steps below.
(**Note: The steps are not in the correct order.**)   Answers: d, f, a, e, c.
a. Gently shake the mouse until the ball drops out of its socket.
b. Point to an object on the screen by moving the mouse.
c. Use a cotton swab dipped in alcohol to loosen the lint on the rollers.
d. Turn off the computer when you clean the mouse.
e. Use adhesive tape to pick up the dust and lint on the ball. Wipe out the dirt inside the socket.
f. Turn the mouse over so that the ball is face up and remove the cover.

---

learner look at only Form A. Have a volunteer read the introductory paragraphs. Ask *What's Yolette looking at? What do you think she is trying to do? What is Roberto doing? What is a "User's Guide"? Do you think there is a problem?*

3. Have learners look over the instructions and sentences in exercise A for their role in the information gap exercise. Learners with Form A should try to guess the meaning of new words from the context, before checking in a dictionary or manual. Some new words might be *reset, vertical page format, horizontally,* and *adjust.* Learners can prepare questions orally or in writing. Be sure that learners with Form B understand the vocabulary. Some new words might be *page format, page-orientation switch, contrast, cartridge, reset.* ◼ In a one-to-one situation, explain any new vocabulary and have the learner prepare questions individually.

4. Have learners work in pairs. One learner uses Form A while the other uses Form B. Learners with Form A should ask questions and record the answers for exercise A. Learners with Form B should choose the appropriate answers for the questions.
   ■ In a one-to-one situation, have the learner use Form A and you use Form B.

5. Check the work together by asking questions about computer problems. Learners with Form A should respond with the information that they obtained in the pair work. Learners with Form B can verify the responses.

6. Have learners complete exercise B, following the same procedure, but switching roles. Learners who asked questions should now provide instructions and vice versa. Some new vocabulary might be *socket, cotton swab, lint, adhesive tape,* and *rollers.*

7. Have learners discuss what was easy or difficult about the activity. Ask *Was it easier to ask or answer the questions? Was it difficult to understand the procedures? Why or why not? Do you think you would be able to perform these tasks on a computer? Why or why not? Can you think of other ways that would make it easier to learn about common computer problems?*

Expansion/Extension

See **TRF HANDOUT 4.3,** *Troubleshooting*

- Learners can look for troubleshooting sections in instruction manuals for computers, appliances, or other mechanical equipment. If learners have had problems with the machines, have them describe the problems and find possible remedies in the manuals.

- Ask learners to create their own troubleshooting chart for machines and appliances that they use. The charts can later be used in information gap exercises by copying them and blocking out parts of them.

---

50 | **Troubleshooting: Form B**

Work with a partner.
One person uses Form A.
The other uses Form B.

Yolette and Roberto are both having computer problems. They're helping each other in the computer lab.

You are Roberto. Your partner is Yolette.
Yolette can't get the printer to work correctly. Roberto is checking the User's Guide and giving Yolette some suggestions.

A. Find the information for your partner in the steps below.
(Note: The steps are not in the correct order.)   Answers: e, c, a, b, d.
a. To change the page format, press the page-orientation switch.
b. Adjust the darkness control.
c. Hold the Start/Stop button, and then press and release the Print/Check button to reset the printer.
d. Replace the toner cartridge.
e. Press the Print/Check button if the printer doesn't work. The printer may have to be reset.
f. Change paper trays.

Now Roberto is trying to clean the mouse for his computer. Yolette is reading about the procedure in the User's Guide.

B. Tell your partner about your computer problems and ask for advice.
1. Ask if the computer needs to be on or off when you clean the mouse.
2. Ask how to hold the mouse when taking off the cover.
3. Ask how to get the ball out.
4. Ask how to clean the mouse.
5. Ask what to do about the lint that is on the rollers.

- Learners can write problems and solutions from their troubleshooting charts on separate sets of index cards. Learners can exchange their sets of cards and then try to recreate the charts by matching the problem and solution cards.

- Ask learners to write *If/then* statements based on the troubleshooting information on pages 49 and 50. (FOR EXAMPLE: *If the printer does not work, then you should press the Print/Check button.*)

- Introduce the prefix *re-.* Learners can look through the book for examples, such as *recheck, reset, replace, reread, rewrite.*

At the Automated Teller

Purpose: To introduce reading automated teller machine (ATM) instructions; to give practice in following directions; to give practice with imperatives

Teacher Preparation and Materials

1. Picture of an ATM
2. Sample ATM card
3. Arrange a field trip to a bank that has an ATM. *(Expansion/Extension)*
4. Blank index cards *(Expansion/Extension)*

Warm-up

1. Ask questions to review banking vocabulary, including *teller, deposit, withdrawal, balance,* and *cash.* Ask *Who works at the bank? What types of accounts can you have at banks? Why do people go to the bank?*

2. On the board, write *Automated Teller Machine = ATM.* Bring in a picture of the machine and a sample ATM card. Ask learners if they have ever seen or used an ATM. Let learners talk about their experiences. Point out the magnetic strip on the back of the card. Elicit/explain the general procedure for using ATMs, including the use of a password.

3. On the board, draw a keypad similar to the one on page 51. Have learners practice translating words into numbers, using the keypad. FOR EXAMPLE: *My password is BLUE (because that's my favorite color). What numbers would I enter on the keypad?* (2583) Have learners create their own passwords and translate them into numbers.

Presentation

1. Have learners turn to page 51. Have a volunteer read the title and introductory paragraph. Ask literal and inferential questions. FOR EXAMPLE: *Do you think the bank is open? Why doesn't Stan go into the bank? Why does he want to check his balance?*

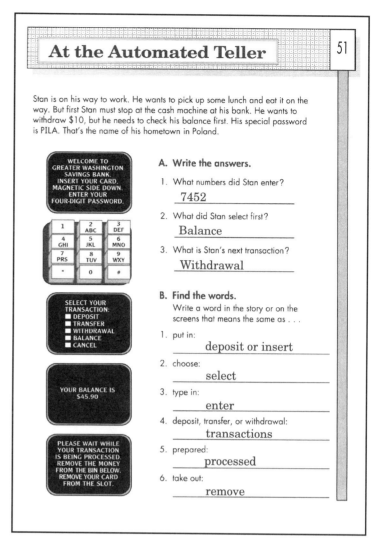

2. Have learners read the first ATM screen and underline words they do not know. Elicit/explain the meanings of new words, including *magnetic side down, enter,* and *four-digit.*

3. Have learners complete exercise A, using the information on the ATM screens.

4. Have learners look back in the story for vocabulary words. Ask *What's another way to say "take money out of the bank"?*

5. Have learners complete exercise B and then use the words in their own sentences.

Expansion/Extension

- Learners can discuss the advantages and disadvantages of using ATMs. Ask *Why are they useful? Why doesn't everyone use them? What happens if your card is lost? What are the risks?*

More *Expansion/Extension* on page 89

Accidents Happen

Purpose: To give practice in reporting a sequence of events; to give practice with the passive voice and with reflexive pronouns

Teacher Preparation and Materials

1. Pictures of workers with common injuries, such as a cut, sprain, broken bone, and burn
2. Picture of an electric hedge trimmer
3. Strips of paper with one line of the story in exercise A written on each
4. Copies of TRF Handout 4.4, *Important Safeguards (Expansion/Extension)*
5. Blank strips of paper *(Expansion/Extension)*

Warm-up

1. Use pictures to review common work-related injuries. Ask *What happened?* (He cut himself. She burned herself.) For each of the injuries, have learners suggest appropriate first aid or medical treatment. Be sure learners include *emergency room, shot, stitches,* and *bandage* in their answers.
2. Show a picture of an electric hedge trimmer. Elicit/explain the machine and its function. Ask learners if they have ever used one. Ask which character in the book might use a hedge trimmer. Learners can look back through the book for clues. Have learners think of accidents that might occur when using such a machine.

Presentation

1. Have learners look at the picture on page 52 and predict what might happen to Stan.
2. Have learners scan the sentences and underline words they do not know. Elicit/explain the meanings of new words: *tangled, foreman, tetanus shot.*
3. Give learners strips of paper with the lines of the story on them. Have learners put the strips in order. Have learners compare versions. Then have them number the sentences in the book correctly.

A. Stan isn't in class today.
Put this story in order to find out what happened to him.

 _3_ While Stan was pulling it free, he cut himself on the sharp blade.

 _4_ He showed his bloody arm to the foreman, who almost passed out.

 _5_ Stan had to drive himself to the emergency room.

 _1_ Stan was trimming some thick hedges with an electric hedge trimmer.

 _8_ Stan went back to work to fill out an accident report, but the foreman had gone home earlier.

 _7_ He was also given a tetanus shot.

 _2_ The trimmer got caught in some tangled branches.

 _6_ It took 10 stitches to close the cut.

 _9_ After the foreman left, the crew gave themselves the afternoon off.

B. Create a new ending to the story. Answers will vary.
Start with the sentence that reads, "He was also given a tetanus shot," and make up a new ending to this story.

C. Think and talk about the questions. Answers will vary.
1. Why did Stan have to fill out an accident report?
2. Have you ever had an accident? What happened?

4. Reread the story up to line 7. Have learners make up a new ending. Ask *Do you think Stan was able to fill out a report form? Do you think he went back to work? What did the other workers say or do? Where did Stan go after that? What do you think the foreman did or said about the accident?*
5. Learners can work individually or in pairs writing new endings to the story. Have learners share their stories aloud. Learners can keep a copy of their writing in their portfolio.
6. In large classes, have learners discuss the questions in exercise C in small groups, with one learner acting as the reporter and another as the recorder. If no one in the class has ever had an accident, have learners talk about people they know who may have had work-related accidents or accidents in the home. ◼ In a one-to-one situation, discuss the questions together.

Expansion/Extension

See **TRF HANDOUT 4.4,** *Important Safeguards*

More *Expansion/Extension* on page 89

An Accident Report

Purpose: To give practice in filling out accident report forms

Teacher Preparation and Materials

1. Pictures of injuries, used for page 52
2. Sample workplace accident report forms
3. ▣▣▣ Audiotape for Level 3
4. Large sheets of paper, marker
5. Copies of TRF Handout 4.5, *An Accident on the Job (Expansion/Extension)*
6. Copies of TRF Handout 4.6, *Injury Investigation Report (Expansion/Extension)*
7. Local worker's compensation law information *(Expansion/Extension)*
8. Occupational Safety and Health Administration (OSHA) information *(Expansion/Extension)*

Warm-up

1. Use pictures to review common injuries. Have learners brainstorm a list of places for injury treatment. (clinic, hospital, emergency room, rehabilitation center) Have learners suggest where to go for treatment of different injuries.
2. Have learners summarize Stan's accident from page 52.
3. Ask learners about paperwork required for work-related accidents. Distribute sample accident report forms. Have learners look for sections that describe the accident, that the supervisor fills out, and that the employee fills out. Ask why it is important for both the supervisor and employee to report information.

Presentation

1. Have learners turn to page 53, read the introductory paragraph, and scan the accident report form. Ask literal and inferential questions about the form.
2. Have learners underline words they do not know. Elicit/explain the meanings of new words: *source, treatment, medication, required, lacerations, embedded foreign bodies, fracture, witness.*

An Accident Report 53

Stan and his supervisor, Bert Daley, had to fill out an accident report after Stan cut himself while trimming a hedge. This is part of their report.

Manny's Landscaping Company
Injury Report

EMPLOYEE: Complete this section.
Job Title: _landscape assistant_   Date of Injury: _5/19/05_   Time: _10:30 a.m._
Place of Accident: _52 Crosby Road, Reston, VA_
Source of injury: _Machine. Cut by hedge trimmer blade._
Treatment by: ☐ screening clinic ☑ emergency room ☐ rehabilitation
☐ other _____

SUPERVISOR: Complete if the employee accident involved one or more of the following:
☑ injuries involving one day or more of lost time   ☑ medication required
☐ burns of second or third degree   ☐ embedded foreign bodies
☑ lacerations requiring stitches   ☐ back strains
Nature of injury (burn, fracture, etc.) and body parts involved: _cut on left arm_
_____

Name(s) of witness(es) to injury: _Pete Ditter, Frank Ward_

▣▣▣ **Listen to the two descriptions of the accident.** Answers may vary.

1. Choose the important facts that Stan mentions. Write a statement that he might write.

   EMPLOYEE'S STATEMENT: _____
   _____
   _____
   _____

2. Choose the important facts that Bert mentions. Write a statement that he might write.

   SUPERVISOR'S STATEMENT: _____
   _____
   _____
   _____

---

3. ▣▣▣ Play the audiotape and have learners listen to the two accounts. Have learners discuss what each person said and why and how they said it. Ask *What is the most important information from each description of the accident? What information did Bert and Stan agree on? What information did they give that was different?*
4. Write questions on the board to guide the notetaking. FOR EXAMPLE: *What happened? Why did it happen? Where was treatment given?*
5. ▣▣▣ Replay the audiotape and have learners take notes on a separate sheet of paper. Ask learners what information may be biased and could be deleted. Discuss how to summarize the notes. In large classes, have learners work in small groups, taking notes on large sheets of paper and discussing a summary of the accounts.
6. Have learners write summary statements for Stan and for Bert in their books.

Expansion/Extension on page 89

Practicing Your Skills

Purpose: To give practice in following and writing directions; to give practice with imperatives

Teacher Preparation and Materials

Microwave and cup of coffee, or picture of or manual for a microwave

Warm-up

If there is a microwave in the building, let learners look at it. Show a picture of or manual for a microwave. Ask learners if they have ever used a microwave. Elicit/ explain the functions of a microwave. Have learners find different controls on the microwave. Be sure to include *defrost, time, high, low,* and *start.* If possible, warm up a cup of coffee in a microwave.

Presentation

1. Have learners turn to page 54. Have a volunteer read the introductory paragraph.
2. Ask learners to brainstorm and to list on the board possible instruction phrases that will be used with the microwave.
3. Have learners read the directions and underline words they do not know. Elicit/ explain the meanings of new words including *fillets, halfway, squeeze,* and *plastic wrap.* Have learners make check marks on the board next to the instruction phrases that were also used on page 54.
4. Ask learners to summarize or restate the microwave directions.
5. Ask learners about appliances and machines that they commonly use. Then have learners individually write instructions on how to operate a machine. Assist learners with vocabulary needed to describe parts of machines and procedures. Learners can consult appliance manuals and dictionaries if necessary.
6. Have volunteers read their instructions to the group without naming the machine. Have the others in the group guess the type of machine from the directions given.

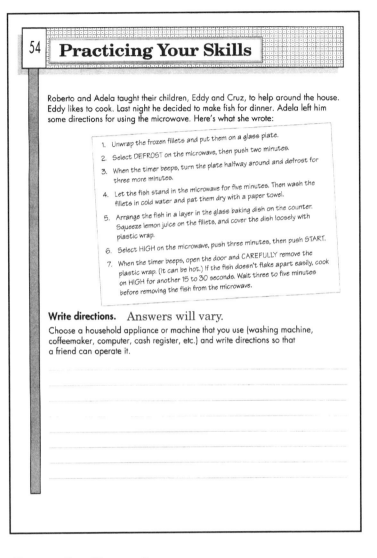

54 Practicing Your Skills

Roberto and Adela taught their children, Eddy and Cruz, to help around the house. Eddy likes to cook. Last night he decided to make fish for dinner. Adela left him some directions for using the microwave. Here's what she wrote:

1. Unwrap the frozen fillets and put them on a glass plate.
2. Select DEFROST on the microwave, then push two minutes.
3. When the timer beeps, turn the plate halfway around and defrost for three more minutes.
4. Let the fish stand in the microwave for five minutes. Then wash the fillets in cold water and pat them dry with a paper towel.
5. Arrange the fish in a layer in the glass baking dish on the counter. Squeeze lemon juice on the fillets, and cover the dish loosely with plastic wrap.
6. Select HIGH on the microwave, push three minutes, then push START.
7. When the timer beeps, open the door and CAREFULLY remove the plastic wrap. (It can be hot.) If the fish doesn't flake apart easily, cook on HIGH for another 15 to 30 seconds. Wait three to five minutes before removing the fish from the microwave.

Write directions. Answers will vary.

Choose a household appliance or machine that you use (washing machine, coffeemaker, computer, cash register, etc.) and write directions so that a friend can operate it.

Expansion/Extension

- Learners can make diagrams of the machines or control panels to go along with their sets of directions.
- Learners can write about a machine that needs to be invented. Ask *What would it do? What would it look like? What types of dials, buttons, and components would it need?*
- Learners can look through a microwave manual for more information. Ask *What is a microwave? How does it work? How safe is it? Why can't you put metal in microwaves?*
- Ask learners to compile a vocabulary list for the unit. Learners can create categories and categorize the new words. Some categories might be Machines, Machine Parts, Machine Problems, Warranties, Workplace Accidents, and Miscellaneous.

Verbs: Passive Voice/ Descriptive Adjectives

Purpose: To give practice in distinguishing active and passive voice and in using selected adjectives

Teacher Preparation and Materials
None

Warm-up

1. Ask learners to look around the classroom and identify things that are different from the end of the previous class session. Ask, *What happened here at school while we were gone?* (Someone moved the chairs. There's no trash now in the trash can. Someone swept the floor.) Write the sentences on the board.

2. Point out that if we don't know who did something, or if it's not important who did it, we often use passive sentences. Provide or elicit passive forms of the sentences on the board. Draw attention to differences in verb form and word order.

Presentation

1. Have learners turn to page 55 and read the example sentences. Review the differences between the active and passive forms.

2. Tell learners that they are going to read about what happened at the ATM when Stan went to the bank, but they are going to focus on what Stan did. Look at the example in the first exercise, and make sure learners understand how to change the passive sentence to active voice.

3. Have learners complete the exercise, and review answers. Stress the active voice by asking, *What did Stan do at the bank? What did he do next? Then what did he do?*

4. Have learners look at the picture of Roberto and Yolette at the bottom of the page. Ask questions to elicit descriptions of the picture. FOR EXAMPLE: *What do you see? Where are Roberto and Yolette? What is the problem? How do they feel?*

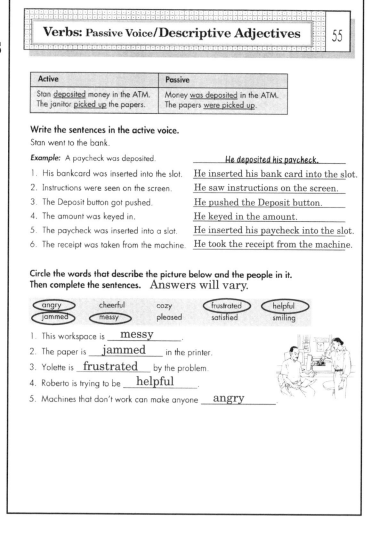

5. Review the vocabulary in the box. Clarify or elicit explanations of any unfamiliar words.

6. Have learners complete the exercise and review answers.

Expansion/Extension

- Have learners use active voice to write the steps in a common process or activity from home, school, the community, or work. Then have them exchange papers with a partner and, wherever possible, rewrite the steps in passive voice.

- Elicit a description of the classroom. Have learners use as many descriptive adjectives as possible. Using LEA techniques, write it on the board. When learners are satisfied with their description, they can copy it in their notebooks.

- Alternatively, learners can write a list or paragraph, using very few or no adjectives to describe what they see in the classroom. They can then exchange papers and rewrite their partner's description using appropriate descriptive adjectives.

Reflexive Pronouns/ Verbs: Past Tense

Purpose: To give practice in using reflexive pronouns; to review use of past tense verbs

Teacher Preparation and Materials

1. A simple puzzle *(Warm-up)*
2. A piece of classroom equipment such as an overhead projector, tape player, or CD player *(Warm-up)*

Warm-up

1. With learners watching, follow the steps to operate a piece of classroom equipment. FOR EXAMPLE: Plug in a tape player (or put in batteries), put in a tape, turn the player on, and adjust the volume. Tell learners, *I got the tape player working by myself. I started it myself.*

2. Have a volunteer start and adjust another piece of classroom equipment or solve the puzzle. Tell learners, *José started the overhead projector himself. Mei Lin solved the puzzle by herself.*

3. With another volunteer, give commands for a simple task or activity. You may wish to use the same piece of classroom equipment. FOR EXAMPLE: *Plug in the overhead projector. Push the red On button. Put a transparency on the glass. Adjust the lens to get a sharp image.* Then ask learners to say what the volunteer did. (He plugged in the overhead, he pushed the On button, and so on.)

Presentation

1. Have learners turn to page 56 and look at the chart of reflexive pronouns. Point out the difference in spelling between singular and plural forms.

2. Have learners complete the first exercise, and review answers. Discuss the use of reflexive pronouns to indicate that a person or group of people has done something alone.

3. Look at the example in the second exercise. Point out that learners will be

---

Reflexive Pronouns/Verbs: Past Tense

Singular	myself	yourself	himself, herself, itself
Plural	ourselves	yourselves	themselves

Complete the sentences with a reflexive pronoun.

1. I tried to connect our new VCR by ___myself___
2. You'll have trouble if you try to do it by ___yourself___.
3. We often think we can do everything ___ourselves___
4. Eddy read the manual ___himself___
5. Cruz is learning to operate the VCR by ___herself___.
6. Soon my wife and kids will be using the VCR all by ___themselves___.

Rewrite the directions in the past tense.

Example: Push the Open button and insert a CD.
Eddy ___pushed the Open button and inserted a CD.___

1. Close the lid and push On.
He ___closed the lid and pushed On.___

2. Push Search to find the song you want to hear.
He ___pushed Search to find the song he wanted to hear.___

3. Hit the Play button to listen.
Then he ___hit the Play button to listen.___

4. Don't leave your compact disks in the player.
Eddy ___didn't leave his compact disks in the player.___

5. Store CDs in their boxes.
He always ___stored CDs in their boxes.___

---

writing about what Eddy did when he followed the directions for using his CD player.

4. Have learners complete the exercise. Review answers by having learners tell Eddy's story in round-robin fashion. Make sure learners have used the correct form of the verb in each sentence.

Expansion/Extension

- Learners can write a short composition on the first time they did some activity by themselves (preparing a meal, driving a car, flying in a plane, carrying out a work assignment, etc.).

- Have learners discuss what age children should be before doing certain things by themselves, such as walking to school, staying home in the evening, getting a job, or riding a bicycle. Learners may wish to write recommendations based on their discussion.

- Have learners describe or write about a process or activity they did in the recent past. If possible, have one or more learners demonstrate an activity while other learners write what the demonstrator did.

UNIT 4: Living with Machines
Expansion/Extension

What's the Problem?
More *Expansion/Extension* for SB page 44

- Review ways of describing things that are broken. FOR EXAMPLE: It isn't working. It's broken. It needs to be fixed/repaired. It doesn't/won't . . . .

Trouble with Machines
Expansion/Extension for SB page 45

See **TRF HANDOUT 4.7,** *The Human Machine*

- Ask learners what causes mechanical problems. (Machine parts break. Machines are misused or overused. People don't take care of or maintain machines properly. Machines are not made to last and so on.) Have learners suggest ways to avoid problems.

- Introduce vocabulary about machine parts: *gears, heating units, tubes, chips, transformers, belts, power supplies,* and so on. If appropriate, learners can talk about experiences with taking machines apart. Ask questions such as *How handy are you with machines?*

- Say *Machines are trouble.* Write the word *TROUBLE* vertically on the board. Have learners think of words to describe machines or words associated with machines that begin with the letters *T, R, O, U, B, L, E.*

- Elicit/introduce different ways of offering advice. List expressions on the board and have learners decide if they should be used in familiar or formal situations. Some expressions might be *You should/ought to/must . . . . Why don't you . . . ? How about . . . -ing? If I were you, I'd . . . . You could always . . . . Have you thought about . . . -ing? I think it might be a good idea to . . . . Can I offer you some advice/a piece of advice/a suggestion?*

Connecting the New VCR
More *Expansion/Extension* for SB page 46

- Learners can role-play conversations between Eddy and Roberto or between Roberto and Adela about the VCR.

- Learners can discuss giving advice within the family. Ask *Do you give advice to your parents? When is it appropriate? How can you give advice and still show respect for an older person? Do your children give you advice? Why or why not? How can you ask for advice without losing face? How could Roberto have used Eddy's ability to read the manual to help connect the VCR? What types of questions could Eddy have asked to assist Roberto?*

- Discuss the differences between Eddy's and Roberto's problem-solving methods. Ask *Is Eddy smarter than his father, or do they just have different ways of attacking problems? Do you think Eddy knows more about how machines work than his father, or does he just know how to operate this one machine? Are you better at following step-by-step instructions or analyzing a mechanical process and developing your own set of instructions?*

- Learners can discuss their experiences with giving advice to Americans. Ask *Have you ever tried to give advice to an American? How do they react to your advice and suggestions? Why do you think they react/feel that way?*

Watching and Recording
More *Expansion/Extension* for SB page 47

- Bring in local TV and cable program schedules. Learners can look for information about their favorite programs, including days, times, and channels.

- Bring in pictures of other types of VCRs and cable equipment. Have learners compare the components and settings used in various models.

- Ask learners how they decide which programs or movies are appropriate for children. Discuss the ratings that are put on videos and used in program schedules. Ask learners how much time children should spend watching TV or movies.

- Bring in information on local cable companies. Learners can look for information on installation or hook-up costs, monthly fees, and rental fees for the cable box. Learners can list advantages and disadvantages of having cable TV.
- Learners can look through VCR manuals for instructions on how to play a video or how to program the VCR to record by itself. Learners can practice using imperatives and the modal *must* to give instructions. Give learners copies of a diagram of a VCR control panel and have them find the buttons and settings mentioned in the instructions.

Limited One-Year Warranty

More *Expansion/Extension* for SB page 48

- Learners can speculate about the company's response to Roberto's warranty claim. Ask *What do you think the company will do: repair or replace the item? How long will it take?*

At the Automated Teller

More *Expansion/Extension* for SB page 51

- Take a field trip to an ATM located in a bank. Learners can ask for information on obtaining an ATM card. Learners can read instructions on the ATM and envelopes used in ATM transactions.
- Ask learners to list suggestions for using ATMs. (FOR EXAMPLE: Do not let others see your password. Do not let others use your card. Do not bend the card. Do not keep a copy of your password in your wallet or with your card.)
- Elicit/explain why names, addresses, and birth-days are not suggested for use as passwords.
- Learners can find out if local banks charge fees for ATM transactions. Ask *Is there a charge for withdrawing money from an ATM? If there is, would it be worth the fee to withdraw $10 from the ATM?*

Accidents Happen

More *Expansion/Extension* for SB page 52

- Ask learners which jobs and machines they think are the most dangerous and why.
- Ask learners to list safety hazards found in their workplaces or homes and then to suggest possible preventive measures.
- Learners can write a description of a workplace accident or home injury discussed in exercise C.
- On strips of paper, write a sequenced accident story of not more than 10 lines that a learner discussed or wrote about for exercise C. Arrange learners in groups according to the number of lines in the story. Give each learner one strip or line of the story to memorize. Collect the story strips and have learners arrange themselves in logical order, after each learner supplies one part of the story orally. Learners should not use any writing to complete the activity.
- Ask learners to find out about emergency procedures to be followed in case of an accident or injury on the job. They should find out if there is a first aid kit at their workplace and, if there is one, where it is and what is in it.

An Accident Report

***Expansion/Extension* for SB page 53**

See **TRF HANDOUT 4.5, *An Accident on the Job***
TRF HANDOUT 4.6, *Injury Investigation Report*

- Bring in forms and information about worker's compensation in your state. Learners can find out about injuries and illnesses that are covered and procedures for applying for compensation.
- Learners can discuss if Stan was right in doing work that was unsafe or if he should have refused to do it. Learners can list the possible consequences of each action.
- Bring in information on OSHA (Occupational Safety and Health Administration). Have learners find out ways that OSHA helps protect the safety of workers.
- Ask learners where accident reports go and who looks at them. Ask *Why is it important to report accidents right away?*

Travels in America

Objectives

Functions
- Making inquiries
- Reporting findings
- Following directions (reading maps)
- Describing events
- Comparing and contrasting
- Clarifying
- Verifying
- Expressing preferences

Life Tasks
- Reading a map
- Reading map keys and distance charts
- Reading a weather map
- Reading vacation ads and travel brochures
- Writing letters and postcards

Structures
- Prepositions of place
- Prepositional phrases
- *While* clauses
- Descriptive adjectives
- Superlatives
- *Would* + *like*
- *How* + *many/much/far*

Culture
- Distances within the United States
- Climate
- Accessing travel information
- No need for travel documents
- Automobile clubs
- Toll-free numbers

Vocabulary

Key words:

admission	one-way
auto club	reservation
coach	round-trip
coast	route
east	scenic
fare	south
forecast	southeast
interstate	southwest
lodging	student discount
mileage	temperature
national park	tour information
north	weather
northeast	west
northwest	

Related words:

air quality	museum
atlas	necessities
bus terminal	North Carolina
cabin	overcast
campground	performance
cloudy	rain
comedy	region
country	scenery
craft shop	side trip
forest	snow
geography	summit
Georgia	sunshine
Great Smoky Mountains	Tennessee
half-price	theme park
history	toiletries
humidity	tourist season
layover	thunderstorms
motel	Virginia

Planning a Trip

Purpose: To introduce travel-related vocabulary, comparing and contrasting, and stating preferences

Teacher Preparation and Materials

1. Pictures of forms of transportation: plane, train, bus, car
2. Large sheets of paper, markers
3. Copies of TRF Handout 5.7, *You Win a Vacation! (Expansion/Extension)*
4. Map of the United States and/or map of the world *(Expansion/Extension)*
5. Arrange a field trip to a local tourist information center. *(Expansion/Extension)*

Warm-up

Use pictures to review types of transportation. Ask learners where people might go using the different types of transportation and why people might choose these forms. Ask learners what their favorite way to travel is. Ask learners about travel and transportation in the United States and in their native countries.

Presentation

1. Have learners turn to page 57. Ask *Who do you see? What do you think they are talking about? What are some good places for families to go on vacation?* List words and comments on the board.
2. Have learners discuss the questions at the bottom of the page.
3. Have learners hypothesize about the Silvas' trip based on what is known about the family members. (Learners can look back at Units 1–4 for information about the Silvas.) *What are their jobs? What activities are they involved in? Where are they from? What do you think the children would enjoy?*
4. On a large sheet of paper, have learners make a list of things that need to be planned for a trip. (destination, form of travel, route, luggage and articles to pack, money needed, length of stay, things to see and do on the trip, etc.) Learners may want to work in small groups or pairs.

1 2 3 4 **5** 6 7 8 9 10 11 12
Travels in America ■ ■ ■ ■ ■ ■ ■

Planning a Trip

What do you think the Silvas are going to do?   Answers will vary.
Have you ever planned a trip? Where did you go?
How did you plan your trip?

Expansion/Extension

See **TRF HANDOUT 5.7,** *You Win a Vacation!*

- On a U.S. map or world map, learners can find and mark different places they have visited. Learners can talk about the places and what they liked or did not like about them.

- Ask learners to write individually about a dream vacation. Learners can use the trip-preparation list to guide their writing. Learners can keep a copy of their writing in their portfolio.

- Learners can visit a local tourist information center. They can pick up tourist guides, fliers, and information packets about the area. Learners may want to plan a field trip or weekend trip to one of the tourist sites.

- Learners can make up conversations based on the picture and role-play them for the group.

Comparing Transportation

Purpose: To give practice in comparing and contrasting; to give practice with descriptive adjectives and with superlatives

Teacher Preparation and Materials

1. Sample train, plane, and bus schedules, fare information, and tickets
2. Copies of TRF Handout 5.4, *Travel Bureau (Expansion/Extension)*
3. Travel sections of local newspapers *(Expansion/Extension)*
4. Local yellow pages *(Expansion/Extension)*

Warm-up

1. Have learners look back at page 57 for the types of transportation that the Silvas are considering. List them on the board.
2. Ask learners about experiences they have had using the different forms of transportation. *Did you ever travel by bus? What was it like? Did you enjoy traveling that way? Why or why not?* Make a list of adjectives to describe transportation. FOR EXAMPLE: *cheap, expensive, fast, slow, comfortable.* Have learners compare two forms of transportation, using comparatives. Have learners compare all the forms of transportation, using superlatives.
3. Bring in tickets, schedules, and fare information for buses, planes, and trains. Elicit/explain types of tickets and fares: *one-way, round-trip, half-price, child's, senior citizen's.*

Presentation

1. Have learners read the story and Adela's notes on page 58. Have learners underline words they do not know. Elicit/explain the meanings of new words: *coach, layover.*
2. Ask literal and inferential questions. FOR EXAMPLE: *What questions do you think Adela asked when she called the bus and train stations? Which form of transportation has more daily departure times? If they take the train, when will they arrive in Atlanta?*

---

58 Comparing Transportation

Roberto and Adela are going to visit relatives in Atlanta. They are taking Eddy and Cruz with them. Marco is going on the trip too. He's excited about seeing his family again. The Silvas want to know the best way to go to Atlanta. Adela called the airport, train and bus stations and made some notes. She wants to share the information with the family.

Plane	Train	Bus
9:00, 11:30 2:45, 5:00, 7:30	Lv. daily @ 11:00	8:00, 10:00, 2:00, 6:00
Nonstop 2 hrs. $238 round-trip kids full fare	Coach $108 one-way $135 round-trip kids 2-15 ½ price Extra $ for sleeping car 14 hrs.	Change in Richmond 2 hr. layover 16 hr. trip Can go through different cities Can interrupt trip anywhere $87 one-way $150 round-trip kids ½ price

Use Adela's notes. Check (✔) the answer.

Which way is . . .

	Plane	Train	Bus
1. the fastest?	✔		
2. the slowest?			✔
3. the most comfortable?		Answers may vary.	
4. the least comfortable?		Answers may vary.	
5. the most expensive?	✔		
6. the cheapest (round trip)?		✔	
7. the most flexible (time)?	✔		
8. the most flexible (route)?			✔

---

3. Ask *How much does it cost for two adults to go one-way by bus to Atlanta? How much does it cost for two children to go round-trip by bus to Atlanta?* Have learners calculate the answers. Then ask learners to use comparatives to summarize the information.
4. Elicit statements using superlatives about Adela's notes. *Which trip would be the cheapest? Which would be the most expensive?* Introduce the word *flexible.* Elicit/explain its meanings when used with transportation. (getting on and off the bus where you want, being able to leave at different times)
5. Have learners complete the exercise and explain their answers with information from the lists on the board and from their own experiences.
6. Ask learners to discuss which form of transportation they think the Silvas should use and to explain why.

Expansion/Extension

See **TRF HANDOUT 5.4,** *Travel Bureau*

More *Expansion/Extension* on page 104

Tips from
Some Friends

Purpose: To give practice with descriptive adjectives, with the past tense, with prepositions of location, and with prepositional phrases; to introduce *while* clauses

Teacher Preparation and Materials

1. Pictures of vacation areas: beach/coast, mountains, forest, lake, city, resort, campground, theme park
2. Auto club brochures and information
3. ▣▣ Audiotape for Level 3
4. Local yellow pages *(Expansion/Extension)*
5. Road atlas or map of the United States *(Expansion/Extension)*

Warm-up

1. Show pictures of vacation areas. On the board, have learners list possible activities for each location and a list of adjectives to describe each area. Be sure to include *swimming, boating, fishing, riding, camping, hiking, beautiful, lovely, awful, interesting, great, expensive,* and *boring.*
2. Learners can choose one of the vacation areas and try to persuade another person to go there, using the lists of activities and descriptive words. Encourage use of expressions of persuasion. FOR EXAMPLE: *I really think you should go here. It's a lovely place. You can . . . and . . . . You'd love it.*
3. Bring in information on auto clubs. Ask learners if they belong to an auto club. Elicit/explain different services commonly offered, such as towing, travel information, and some repairs.

Presentation

1. Have learners turn to page 59 and look at the questions in exercise A. Ask learners to predict what the conversation will be about. Ask *What advice or suggestions do you think Stan and Diep will give Roberto?*
2. ▣▣ Play the first few lines of the audiotape. Stop after Roberto says: "How did

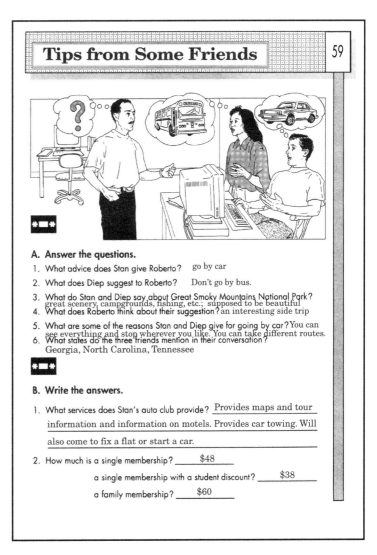

Tips from Some Friends

A. Answer the questions.

1. What advice does Stan give Roberto? go by car
2. What does Diep suggest to Roberto? Don't go by bus.
3. What do Stan and Diep say about Great Smoky Mountains National Park? great scenery, campgrounds, fishing, etc.; supposed to be beautiful
4. What does Roberto think about their suggestion? an interesting side trip
5. What are some of the reasons Stan and Diep give for going by car? You can see everything and stop wherever you like. You can take different routes.
6. What states do the three friends mention in their conversation? Georgia, North Carolina, Tennessee

B. Write the answers.

1. What services does Stan's auto club provide? Provides maps and tour information and information on motels. Provides car towing. Will also come to fix a flat or start a car.

2. How much is a single membership? $48

   a single membership with a student discount? $38

   a family membership? $60

you get to Atlanta, Diep?" Have learners hypothesize how Stan and Diep traveled, who they traveled with, and what the good and bad points of their trips might have been.

3. ▣▣ Play the rest of the conversation. Ask literal and inferential questions. FOR EXAMPLE: *Which form of transportation do Diep and Stan recommend? Are Stan and Diep persuasive? Do you think Roberto likes their ideas? Why do you think so?*

4. Have learners discuss the questions in exercise A. ▣▣ If necessary, replay the conversation.

5. Have learners brainstorm questions that Roberto might ask Stan about car trips.

6. ▣▣ Play the second conversation. Have learners summarize the information that Stan gives about the auto club.

7. Have learners answer the questions in exercise B. Ask learners if they think Roberto should join Stan's auto club.

Expansion/Extension on page 104

Mapping a Route

Purpose: To give practice in interpreting maps; to give practice with prepositions of location

Teacher Preparation and Materials

1. Map of the United States
2. Compass (optional)
3. Copies of TRF Handout 5.2, *Planning a Trip to the American West* (Expansion/Extension)

Warm-up

1. Tape a U.S. map on the wall. Have learners locate states and cities they already know. On the board, make a chart with the headings *Cities* and *States.* List places under the appropriate headings. Have learners write both the full name and two-letter abbreviation of the states. Be sure to include *Washington, D.C.; Atlanta, Georgia (GA); Virginia (VA); Tennessee (TN);* and *North Carolina (NC).*

2. Use the map to elicit/explain directional words: *north, south, east, west.* Point out the directional key on the map or use a compass to help clarify meanings. Refer to the map on the wall and ask questions that use directions and city/state names. Have learners identify the correct state or direction. FOR EXAMPLE: *If I'm in Washington, D.C., and go south, what state do I go through first? If I go from Florida to Georgia, in what direction am I traveling?* Introduce secondary points on the compass: *northeast, northwest, southeast, southwest.* Ask questions involving these words.

Presentation

1. Have learners turn to page 60. Have a volunteer read the title and introductory paragraph. Have learners locate Washington, D.C., and Atlanta, Georgia, on their maps. Ask learners what other place the Silvas want to visit on their trip. Have learners locate it on their maps.

2. Have learners read the directions and find the places mentioned. Then have learners go through the directions again, filling in the blanks. Learners can work in pairs or small groups.

3. After checking their work, have learners find the distance measurements on the map of the United States. Learners can calculate the total distance of the trip.

4. Have learners write directions for another route between Washington, D.C., and Atlanta, based on the map. In pairs, have learners practice giving and following directions. Have one learner give new directions while the partner traces the route on the map. Then have learners switch roles. 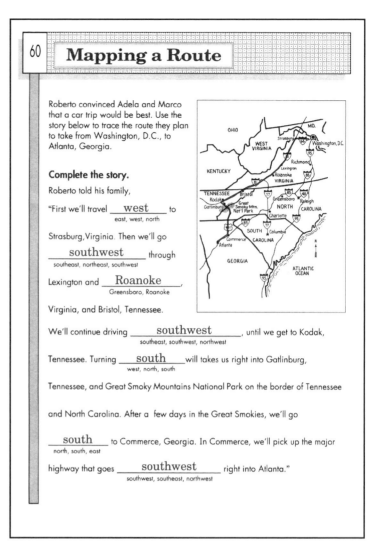 In a one-to-one situation, have the learner give directions for you to follow. Then give directions for the learner to follow.

Expansion/Extension

See TRF HANDOUT 5.2, *Planning a Trip to the American West*

- Learners can reverse the directions on page 60 and tell someone how to get from Atlanta to Great Smoky Mountains National Park and then to Washington, D.C.

More *Expansion/Extension* on page 104

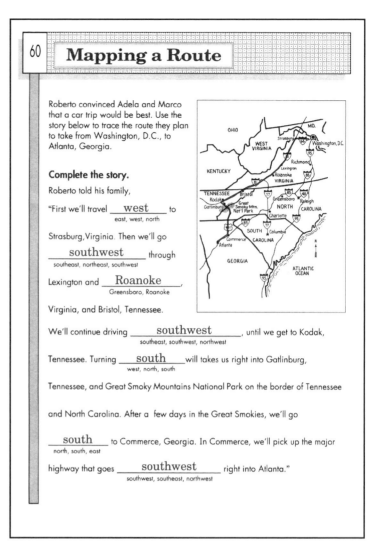

60 **Mapping a Route**

Roberto convinced Adela and Marco that a car trip would be best. Use the story below to trace the route they plan to take from Washington, D.C., to Atlanta, Georgia.

Complete the story.

Roberto told his family,

"First we'll travel ___west___ to
<small>east, west, north</small>

Strasburg, Virginia. Then we'll go

___southwest___ through
<small>southeast, northeast, southwest</small>

Lexington and ___Roanoke___,
<small>Greensboro, Roanoke</small>

Virginia, and Bristol, Tennessee.

We'll continue driving ___southwest___, until we get to Kodak,
<small>southeast, southwest, northwest</small>

Tennessee. Turning ___south___ will takes us right into Gatlinburg,
<small>west, north, south</small>

Tennessee, and Great Smoky Mountains National Park on the border of Tennessee

and North Carolina. After a few days in the Great Smokies, we'll go

___south___ to Commerce, Georgia. In Commerce, we'll pick up the major
<small>north, south, east</small>

highway that goes ___southwest___ right into Atlanta."
<small>southwest, southeast, northwest</small>

Many Miles to Go

Purpose: To introduce reading map keys and distance charts; to give practice with the past tense, with prepositional phrases, and with *How + many/much/far;* to give practice with comparing and contrasting

Teacher Preparation and Materials

1. Road map of the United States with distance chart
2. Calculators (optional)
3. Copies of TRF Handout 5.1, *U.S. Geography (Expansion/Extension)*
4. Road maps or city maps with distance charts *(Expansion/Extension)*

Warm-up

1. Have learners look back at the map on page 60 and calculate (or estimate) distances between different places. Ask *What is the distance between Washington, D.C., and Atlanta, Georgia? Is it easy or difficult to figure it out? Why?*
2. Have learners look at the road map of the United States and find the distance chart. Point out that the distances given are for the most direct route.

Presentation

1. Have learners turn to page 61 and read the title of the page and the chart. Have learners predict what the story is about. Ask *How old is Cruz? What kind of plans do you think she would make?*
2. Have learners read the story and underline words they do not know. Elicit/explain the meanings of new words: *mileage, general idea,* and *science museum.*
3. Ask literal and inferential questions. FOR EXAMPLE: *Where did Cruz want to go? What did Roberto say about her plans? How far is it from Washington, D.C., to Los Angeles? How many days would it take to drive that far? What do the X's mean on the chart?*
4. Have learners complete the exercises. Learners can use calculators if they have them. Have learners prove their answers in exercise C.

Many Miles to Go — Student Page 61

Roberto examined a chart on his map that listed the mileage from one city to another. It gave him a general idea of how many miles his trip would be. Then he showed the chart to Cruz, who began planning their next trip right away. She wanted to visit her cousins in Miami and her aunt and uncle in New York City. After that, she wanted to go to Disneyland, with a side trip to a great science museum in Chicago she'd heard about.

Roberto loved her plans, but he said they would involve too much driving. He showed her just how many miles her trips would take.

Driving Distances for Cruz's Vacation Plans

	Atlanta	Chicago	Los Angeles	Miami	New York City	Wash., D.C.
Atlanta	XXX	583	1,935	610	747	542
Chicago	583	XXX	1,741	1,190	711	594
Los Angeles	1,935	1,741	XXX	2,355	2,446	2,295
Miami	610	1,190	2,355	XXX	1,095	927
New York City	747	711	2,446	1,095	XXX	204
Wash., D.C.	542	594	2,295	927	204	XXX

A. Use the chart to calculate the trips Cruz wants to take.
1. Washington, D.C.–Miami–New York City–Washington, D.C., is 2,226 miles.
2. Washington, D.C.–Los Angeles–Chicago–Washington, D.C., is 4,630 miles.

B. Use the chart to complete the sentences.
1. The cities that are farthest apart are New York City and Los Angeles .
2. The cities that are closest together are New York City and Washington, D.C.

C. Check the answers.
1. Which trip is the shortest distance?
   __ Miami to Atlanta to Los Angeles
   ✔ Washington, D.C., to New York City to Chicago
   __ New York City to Chicago to Washington, D.C.
2. Which trip is the greatest distance?
   __ Atlanta to Washington, D.C., to Los Angeles
   __ Chicago to Miami to New York City
   ✔ Los Angeles to New York City to Atlanta

---

5. Learners can create their own distance-related questions based on the mileage chart.

Expansion/Extension

See TRF HANDOUT 5.1, *U.S. Geography*

- Ask learners to compare the distance listed on the chart for Washington, D.C., to Atlanta with the mileage for the route that the Silvas plan to take through the Great Smoky Mountains. Have learners discuss how much time it will take to travel from Washington, D.C., to Great Smoky Mountains National Park and then to Atlanta. Ask *How many hours will the trip take? How far do you think the Silvas will travel in one day? Do you think it's worth the extra time and mileage?* Ask learners how long it would take to travel by car from one city to another based on the driving distances on the chart on page 61.

More *Expansion/Extension* on page 104

What's the Weather Like?

Purpose: To introduce reading a weather map; to give practice with prepositional phrases

Teacher Preparation and Materials

1. Pictures representing weather conditions: sunny, rainy, stormy, cloudy, snowy
2. Map of the United States
3. Indoor/outdoor thermometer
4. Weather maps from a local newspaper for several days
5. Local newspapers
6. ▇▇▇ Audiotape for Level 3

Warm-up

1. Using the pictures, elicit/introduce weather terms (*sun, rain, clouds, snow, overcast, thunderstorm*) and related adjectives (*sunny, rainy, cloudy, snowy, stormy*). Tape a U.S. map to the wall. Give national weather "broadcasts" and have learners place the correct pictures on the appropriate parts of the map. FOR EXAMPLE: *There's going to be heavy snow in Denver, Colorado, and the surrounding area. Rain is expected for the East Coast from Washington, D.C., up to Boston, Massachusetts.*

2. Show a thermometer. Have learners determine the temperature inside and outside the building. Talk about the usual temperature ranges for your area in different seasons.

3. Show examples of local weather maps. Ask *Have you ever seen or looked at weather maps? Where? What information is given on the map? Why do you think people want weather information?*

Presentation

1. Have learners turn to page 62, read the title, and look at the map. Have learners predict what the listening activity will be about.

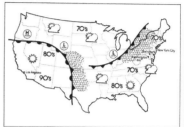

2. On the weather map, have learners find the places that the Silvas plan to visit. Have learners describe the type of weather shown on the map for those areas.

3. Have learners read the story and underline words they do not know. Elicit/explain the meanings of new words.

4. Make a chart with the headings *Washington, Virginia,* and *Tennessee* on the board. ▇▇▇ Play the audiotape. Have learners summarize the weather forecasts for those areas and fill in notes on the chart.

5. Have learners complete exercise A. ▇▇▇ Replay the audiotape for learners to check their answers. Have learners correct false statements.

6. Have learners discuss the questions in exercise B. Bring in a current edition of a local newspaper so learners can check the weather forecast.

Expansion/Extension on page 104

Packing for the Trip

Purpose: To introduce making inquiries; to give practice in stating preferences

Teacher Preparation and Materials

1. Pictures of vacation areas, used for page 59
2. Pictures of lodgings: motel, cabin, hotel, campsite

Warm-up

1. Tape the pictures of vacation areas to the board. Have learners brainstorm types of clothing and equipment you would need for a trip to those places. Have learners classify the items under the headings *Clothing, Toiletries,* and *Other Necessities.*
2. Use pictures to review/introduce types of lodging. Have learners suggest different packing needs for travelers using each of the types of lodging. (FOR EXAMPLE: At a campsite you might need a sleeping bag or blankets, towels, and cooking utensils.)

Presentation

1. Have learners turn to page 63. Have a volunteer read the title and introductory paragraph. Ask what types of things an eight-year-old would want to take on a trip and what they think of her packing style.
2. Have learners complete exercise A and have them explain their responses. Learners can discuss their lists of other items that she should take and can suggest the quantity of each item that she might need.
3. Have learners list in exercise B other items the family might need. Learners can work in pairs or small groups. When checking answers, list the items on the board. Learners can practice making inquiries about specific items. (FOR EXAMPLE: Why should they take a flashlight? Do they really need an umbrella?)

Packing for the Trip

All of the Silvas are busily packing their suitcases for their trip. Even Cruz is trying to pack her own suitcase. She made a list of what she needs to bring with her.

pajamas	underwear
jeans	swimsuit
T-shirts	cookies
red dress	doll
snowsuit	toothpaste
boots	umbrella
mittens	sneakers

A. Help Cruz pack for the trip.   Answers will vary.
1. Underline the things that you think Cruz should take. Put an X through the things that she doesn't need.
2. Make a list of other things that you think Cruz should take.

_____   _____

_____   _____

B. Make a list of other things that the Silvas should take on their trip.

Clothing	Toiletries	Other Necessities
socks	comb	Flashlight
	Answers will vary.	

Expansion/Extension

- Ask learners to make a list of items needed for travel to their native countries. Learners should be prepared to justify the items. Be sure to include different travel documents.
- Play an alphabet chain game about taking a trip to the Smoky Mountains. Say *I'm going on a trip to the Smoky Mountains and I'm going to take an atlas.* Have the next person in the chain repeat your item and add an item that begins with the letter *B.* Continue the chain, adding an item for each letter of the alphabet.
- Ask learners to make a list of suggested items to pack and recommended activities for travelers with small children.

A Night Out

Purpose: To give practice in reading travel brochures, in stating preferences, and in comparing and contrasting; to give practice with *while* clauses and with *would + like*

Teacher Preparation and Materials

1. Brochures or newspaper listings of local tourist attractions
2. Audiotapes of different types of music: bluegrass, country, gospel, pop *(Expansion/Extension)*

Warm-up

1. Bring in brochures or newspaper listings of local attractions and events. Have learners look through them and talk about ones they have been to and ones they would like to see/go to sometime.
2. Write category headings on the board: *Museums, Theaters, Musical Performances, Sports Events, Amusement/Theme Parks, Rodeos.* Elicit/explain the meanings of the words. Have learners name and categorize leisure activities and special events from the brochures and newspaper listings. Encourage learners to add other events and attractions that they know.

Presentation

1. Have learners turn to page 64. Have a volunteer read the title and introductory paragraph. Ask *What did Marco offer to do? Is Gatlinburg a large city? Is it by the coast or in the mountains? What types of attractions and events do you think there will be in and around Gatlinburg?*
2. Have learners read the brochure information and underline words they do not know. Elicit/explain the meanings of new words: *theme park, sing-along, comedy, rodeo, restricted schedule, admission, not recommended for children, bluegrass.*
3. Have learners discuss the questions at the bottom of the page. In large classes, have learners work in small groups, with one learner acting as the recorder and another as the reporter. ■ In a one-to-one situation, discuss the questions together.

---

64 **A Night Out**

The Silvas arrived in Gatlinburg, Tennessee. They checked into a nice motel and decided to stay there a couple of days while they visited Great Smoky Mountains National Park. Marco offered to take care of Cruz and Eddy so that Adela and Roberto could go out alone. They wanted to have a special time together, but they didn't want to spend too much money. They looked through the brochure of activities in the area.

Dixie Gardens. This theme park and craft center provides thrilling rides, live craft demonstrations, picnic facilities, and a petting zoo to ensure fun for all ages. Open daily 9–9, June–Aug. Restricted schedule other seasons.
ADMISSION: adults, $19.75; children 4–11, $14.25
PARKING: $2

Great Smoky Roundup. Nightly performances include music, comedy, and Wild West fun! A sing-along fest is followed by rodeo demonstrations and contests. Regional and country specialities make dinner a treat. Shows begin nightly at 7 p.m. Dinner served continuously from 6 p.m. Open mid-Mar. through Dec.
ADMISSION: adults, $24.50 children 4–11, $15.25

Mountainview Music Theatre. See local and professional talent perform bluegrass, country, gospel, and pop music. Monday through Saturday at 8:15 p.m. from mid-May through October. Matinees Wednesdays and Saturdays at 2:30 p.m.
ADMISSION: adults, $9; adults over 55, $7, children 7–12, $5. (Not recommended for children under 7.)

Think and talk about the questions. Answers will vary.
1. Where do you think Roberto and Adela went while Marco took care of Eddy and Cruz? Why do you think they picked that activity?
2. What attractions would appeal to you? Why?
3. Do you think these activities are worth the money they cost?
4. How can you find out about less expensive activities when you take trips?

---

4. Ask learners to choose an activity from the brochure that they think is interesting. Ask them to write the reasons for their choice. In pairs, have learners try to persuade their partner to go to that activity.
5. Have learners write about Roberto and Adela's night out. Ask *Where did they go? What did they do? What do you think it was like?*

Expansion/Extension

- Introduce idioms for inexpensive travel, such as *traveling on a shoestring.* Ask learners to make a list of inexpensive tourist activities for the local area. Learners can look through newspapers or tourist brochures for ideas.
- Play audiotapes of different types of music, such as bluegrass, country, gospel, and pop. Learners can suggest or do research to find names of musicians and musical groups for the different categories.

More *Expansion/Extension* on page 105

An Introduction to the Great Smokies

Purpose: To give practice in reading travel brochures and scenic route information

Teacher Preparation and Materials

1. Pictures of national parks, such as Great Smoky Mountains National Park, Yellowstone, Yosemite, Zion, Grand Teton
2. Copies of TRF Handout 5.5, *Historical Sites (Expansion/Extension)*
3. Copies of TRF Handout 5.6, *Along the Freedom Trail (Expansion/Extension)*
4. Arrange a field trip to a local park. *(Expansion/Extension)*
5. Arrange a field trip to a science or natural history museum. *(Expansion/Extension)*

Warm-up

1. In the center of the board, write the word *Environment*. Elicit/explain the meaning. Have learners brainstorm components of the environment, such as air, water, land, plants, and animals. Make a semantic web using the words. Expand the web to include specific types of wild animals, trees, bodies of water, and land masses.
2. Have learners talk about animals and plants they have seen. Ask *Which are in your area? Where can you find other animals?*
3. Bring in pictures of national parks. Elicit/ explain what a national park is and why these parks have been created. Elicit outdoor activities associated with the different parks.

Presentation

1. Have learners turn to page 65. Have a volunteer read the title and introductory paragraph. Have learners predict what information might be in the pamphlet.
2. Have learners read the pamphlet information and underline words they do not know. Elicit/explain the meanings of new words: *protect, acres, summits, haze, hemisphere, varied, deciduous, profusion, banned, abundant, wonders, lodging,*

lectures, park rangers, tourist seasons, stables, magnificent, scenic.

3. Ask literal and inferential questions. FOR EXAMPLE: *What are some examples of plant life and wildlife of the Great Smokies? Why do you think hunting was banned? What kind of lectures do you think are given? Do you think this would be an interesting place to visit? Why or why not?*
4. Have learners complete exercise A. Have learners share and explain their answers.
5. Have learners discuss the question in exercise B. Together make a list of ideas. Learners may want to check books or encyclopedias for more information about the purpose of national parks and the rules for using national parks. Learners can write an essay on the topic.

Expansion/Extension

See TRF HANDOUT 5.5, *Historical Sites*
TRF HANDOUT 5.6, *Along the Freedom Trail*

More *Expansion/Extension* on page 105

An Introduction to the Great Smokies | 65

Protecting the environment will be the theme of the coming year at Eddy's school. He wants to learn about the national park so that he can report about his trip when he goes back to school. He has learned a lot from reading a pamphlet called *An Introduction to the Great Smokies*.

WELCOME TO GREAT SMOKY MOUNTAINS NATIONAL PARK

The Great Smoky Mountains National Park covers over a half-million acres in North Carolina and Tennessee. It was named for the blue, smoky haze that almost always covers its peaks. Many summits rise over 6,000 feet and are home to some of the most varied plant life in the hemisphere. There are 180,000 acres of virgin forest, with thousands of evergreen and deciduous trees. Other plant life includes wild rhododendron, myrtle, azalea, dogwood, and wild flowers in profusion.

Hunting was banned in the Great Smokies in 1934. Wildlife is abundant and includes deer, grouse, wild turkey, and bear. Miles of hiking trails and paved roads provide access to the wonders of nature in the park.

The Great Smoky Mountains National Park is open all year, and admission is free. Lodging is available atop Mount LeConte and at many campgrounds in the park. Hikes on many trails and lectures by park rangers are available during the main tourist seasons. Horses can be rented for trail rides at several stables. Mount LeConte offers magnificent views. Newfound Gap Road is a scenic road that crosses the park. Miles of streams provide excellent trout fishing.

A. Write your answer. Answers may vary.
What things would you like to do in the Great Smokies?

_____

_____

_____

_____

B. Discuss the question. Answers may vary.
How can national parks help protect the environment?

Asking for Directions

Purpose: To give practice in making inquiries, in clarifying and verifying, in interpreting a map, and in following directions; to give practice with prepositions of location

Teacher Preparation and Materials

1. Local road map
2. ▄▄▄ Audiotape for Level 3
3. Copies of TRF Handout 5.3, *Signs along the Way (Expansion/Extension)*

Warm-up

1. On the board, have learners brainstorm and list different types of roads. Be sure to include *avenue, road, boulevard, route, interstate,* and *street.* Have learners classify roads. Ask *Which roads are usually in towns and cities? What types of roads are for long-distance traveling?* Have learners look on a map for the names and numbers of interstates and state highways in your local area.
2. Ask learners if they have ever needed to ask for directions. Ask *Have you ever asked for directions? Were you able to follow them? Why do you think you could or couldn't? Did you have a map of the area? Were you in a car or on foot?* Allow learners to share their experiences.

Presentation

1. Have learners turn to page 66 and look at the map. Have learners find different points on the map, such as Interstate 20, Foster Historical Museum, and the X that marks where the Silvas' car is.
2. ▄▄▄ Play the first part of the audiotape. Stop at the point where the woman completes her directions the first time. Ask questions about the exchange and the directions she gives. FOR EXAMPLE: *Do you think you could remember all these directions without the map? What do you think the rest of the conversation will be about?*

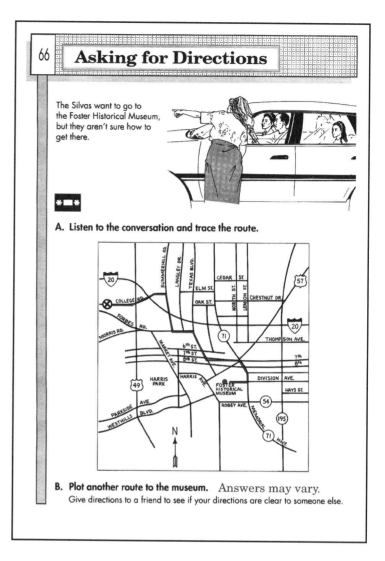

66 **Asking for Directions**

The Silvas want to go to the Foster Historical Museum, but they aren't sure how to get there.

A. Listen to the conversation and trace the route.

B. Plot another route to the museum. Answers may vary.
Give directions to a friend to see if your directions are clear to someone else.

3. ▄▄▄ Play the rest of the audiotape and have learners trace the route on their maps. ▄▄▄ Replay the audiotape if necessary.
4. Have learners discuss questions related to the directions. Ask *Do you think Roberto couldn't find the museum on the map? How do you react when someone asks you for directions? How well marked are tourist sites in your area? Are there signs from major roads to museums, historical sites, and other tourist attractions?*
5. Have learners do exercise B. Learners can add additional phrases and direction words (*north, south, east, west*).

Expansion/Extension

See* TRF HANDOUT 5.3, *Signs along the Way

- Ask learners to plot routes on local road maps and then practice giving their directions for others in the group to follow.

More *Expansion/Extension* on page 105

Practicing Your Skills

Purpose: To give practice in writing letters and postcards and in describing events; to give practice with the past tense, with prepositional phrases, and with descriptive adjectives

Teacher Preparation and Materials

None

Warm-up

1. Have learners look back through the unit and list all the things the Silvas did during their visit to the Great Smoky Mountains National Park area. Ask *What do you think they saw and did? What do you think each person enjoyed the most? Why?*

2. Ask *Have you ever sent a postcard to anyone? If so, to whom? What types of postcards did you send? Why did you send a postcard? Why didn't you send a letter? What types of postcards do you think you could buy at Great Smoky Mountains National Park? Who do you think the Silvas would send a postcard to?*

Presentation

1. Have learners turn to page 67, read the postcard, and underline words they do not know. Elicit/explain the meanings of new words: *spectacular, geography, history, region.*

2. Ask literal and inferential questions about the postcard. FOR EXAMPLE: *Did the Silvas go swimming on their trip? Why do you think Roberto wrote to Stan?*

3. Ask learners to tell about a trip or vacation they have taken. If learners have not traveled, they can talk about a class field trip, a visit to a tourist attraction or event, or a trip they would like to take. Have learners make a list of places and activities for their trips.

4. Have learners write a postcard to a friend or relative about the trip. If necessary,

review addressing mail. Point out that return addresses are not usually put on postcards.

5. Have learners share their cards with the group.

Expansion/Extension

- Ask learners to calculate the approximate cost of the Silvas' trip, using the list of their activities. Learners should also include mileage (gasoline), cost of activities for the family, meals, lodging, souvenirs, postcards, and so on.

- Have learners discuss ways of paying for things while on vacation. Review information about checks, cash, and credit cards. Bring in information on travelers' checks. Ask *What are the advantages and disadvantages of using the different methods of payment on trips?*

Dear Stan,
You were right about Smoky Mts. National Park! We all loved it! We took a trail ride by horseback up Mt. LeConte. The scenery was spectacular! We took several hikes with a park guide who taught us a lot about the geography and history of the region. Eddy was so interested that he started collecting rocks from the region. The weather was good, and we went swimming every day. Cruz is ready to move down here permanently. Hope you're not working too hard!
                    Roberto

Stan Wolanski
42 Baxter Road
Herndon, VA 22070

Write a postcard to a friend or relative.   Answers will vary.
Tell about a trip or vacation that you've taken or that you'd like to take.

More *Expansion/Extension* on page 105

Questions: *How much/many/far?/* Prepositions of Place

Purpose: To give practice with questions using *how* plus *much, many,* or *far* and with prepositions of place

Teacher Preparation and Materials

1. Pictures of vacation areas, used for page 59 *(Warm-up, Expansion/Extension)*

2. Information on fares, used for page 58, or on hotel costs *(Expansion/Extension)*

Warm-up

1. Show learners the pictures of vacation areas. Ask questions with *how many, how much,* and *how far.* FOR EXAMPLE: *How many people are lying on the beach? How many lakes are in this area? How far is it from here to the beach? To the mountains? How much time does it take to get there? How much do you think it costs for a vacation there?*

2. Elicit information about travel that learners have done, in the United States or in their native country. Ask, *How many people went on the trip? How much time did you spend? How many miles did you travel? How far did you go? How many cities did you visit?*

3. Review prepositions of place by eliciting descriptions of the classroom, noting relative positions of people and things. FOR EXAMPLE: *Where is the teacher's desk?* (It's in front of the blackboard.) *Where is Armando?* (He's sitting next to Julia.)

Presentation

1. Have learners turn to page 68. Review the meanings of the question words and the example questions and answers in the chart.

2. Have learners complete the first exercise. Review answers by having one learner ask the question and another give the answer. Discuss any differences in responses.

3. Have learners look at the picture on page 68 and identify the people. Have them complete the second exercise. Review

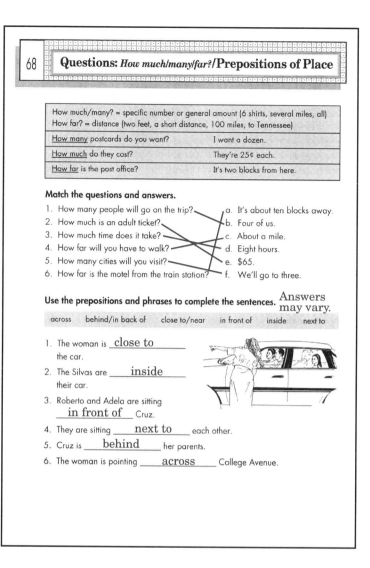

answers by asking *where* questions to elicit the sentences (FOR EXAMPLE: *Where are the Silvas? Where is the woman pointing?*)

Expansion/Extension

- Each learner can plan a trip or a weekend activity. They can use information or brochures about fares and hotel costs if appropriate. Have learners work in pairs to ask and answer questions about their plans, eliciting information about how many people will take part, how much time it will take, how far the people will travel, how much it will cost, and so on.

- Have learners select a picture of a vacation area and write a description of it. Encourage them to use prepositions of place to give details about the relative positions of things in the picture.

- Learners can write descriptions of familiar places, such as a workplace, a spot in their native country, or a room in their home. Have them share their descriptions, in writing or orally, with a partner or small group. The partner or group can ask questions to elicit more details. Learners may wish to draw a picture (or bring in a photograph) of the place being described.

Adjectives: Superlatives

Purpose: To give practice in forming and using superlative adjectives

Teacher Preparation and Materials

1. Sets of three pictures showing comparable people or things (*Warm-up*)

2. Pictures of vacation places, used for page 59 (*Expansion/Extension*)

Warm-up

1. Show learners two pictures from each set of three comparable people or things. Elicit descriptions using comparative forms of adjectives. (FOR EXAMPLE: The man on the left is taller than the man on the right. The red sofa looks more comfortable than the green sofa.)

2. Add the third picture to each set, and elicit descriptions using superlative forms. Prompt with questions, if necessary, to model the appropriate superlative form. (FOR EXAMPLE: *Which sofa do you think is the most comfortable? Which man is the tallest?*)

Presentation

1. Have learners turn to page 69 and look at the chart. Point out the differences in the way comparatives and superlatives are formed or spelled for different types of adjectives.

2. Look at the example in the first exercise, and have learners complete the exercise. Review answers. Have volunteers write the superlative adjectives on the board to check spelling.

3. Go over the example in the second exercise. Make sure learners understand how to use the cues under the write-on lines.

4. Have learners complete the exercise, and review answers.

tall	taller	the tallest
cheerful	more cheerful	the most cheerful
slim	slimmer	slimmest
friendly	friendlier	friendliest

A. Complete the sentences with the superlative form.

Example: The Southwest has _____ the highest _____ (high) temperatures in the country.

1. It also has ____ the driest ____ (dry) weather.
2. The North Central states have ____ the heaviest ____ (heavy) snowfalls.
3. They often have ____ the wettest ____ (wet) springs, too.
4. The South usually has ____ the mildest ____ (mild) winters.
5. But it often has the most humid (humid) summers.
6. The Northwest usually has ____ the rainiest ____ (rainy) weather in the nation.
7. But it also has ____ the greenest ____ (green) summers.

B. Write sentences with superlatives.

Example: ___Adela is the neatest and the slowest packer___ in the family.
Adela/neat/slow/packer

1. __She takes the newest clothes__ _____ when she travels.
She/new/clothes

2. __Cruz is the fastest packer__ _____ in the family.
Cruz/fast/packer

3. __She is the messiest and most careless one__, too.
She/messy/careless/one

4. That's because __she is the most impatient member__ of the family.
she/impatient/member

Expansion/Extension

- Have learners create a description of their class, using comparative and superlative adjectives as much as possible. Encourage exaggeration if desired. (FOR EXAMPLE: Our class has the smartest learners in the whole school. We work harder than any other class.)

- Have learners write about their families, comparing people as much as possible. (FOR EXAMPLE: My brother Jamil is the oldest child in the family. He has the most children. My sister lives farthest away from home now. My brother Khalid is younger than I am, but he is also taller.)

- Learners may wish to compose sentences about the weather in their native countries or in the area where they currently live. They can use the sentences in the first exercise as models. (FOR EXAMPLE: This area is drier and hotter than the rest of the state in summer. Our city gets the most snow in the country.)

- Have learners select two or three pictures of vacation areas and write or talk about them using comparative or superlative forms. Encourage them to compare the areas in terms of weather, things to do, costs, and so on.

UNIT 5: Travels in America
Expansion/Extension

Comparing Transportation
More *Expansion/Extension* for SB page 58

- Learners can role-play calling for information and making travel reservations using the bus, train, and plane schedules.

- Learners can look through local newspapers for ads on plane, train, or bus fares. Elicit/explain restrictions that may apply. (FOR EXAMPLE: Travel must be on Tuesday, Wednesday, or Thursday, and include a Saturday night stay. Special rates are not available on holidays.)

- Ask learners to look in the yellow pages for the names and phone numbers of bus, train, and airline companies. Learners can also look for local stations, airports, and depots. Ask *Why do some companies have 800 numbers for information and reservations?* Learners can call and request time schedules and fare information for different destinations.

- Learners can discuss ticket prices. Ask *Why do children and seniors get discounts? What are the differences in price and accommodations between first class and coach? What are "price wars"? What types of discounted fares are available?* (FOR EXAMPLE: excursion, supersaver) *What are additional costs related to each form of transportation?* (cost of getting to and from the station/airport, cost of meals, cost of parking)

Tips from Some Friends
***Expansion/Extension* for SB page 59**

- Ask learners to look through local auto club brochures and to compare costs and services with the information that Stan talks about.

- Bring in a U.S. map or road atlas. Ask learners to find the states mentioned in the conversations. Learners can look for recreation areas, national and state parks, campgrounds, and other attractions.

- Learners can write or call the National Park Service for information about the Great Smoky Mountains or other national parks. Learners can also contact state tourist offices for information about places of interest.

Mapping a Route
More *Expansion/Extension* for SB page 60

- Ask learners to chart a possible return trip route for the Silvas, going through a city on the Atlantic coast.

- Make a list of major cities and/or state capitals. Ask learners to name the appropriate states. Alternatively, make a list of states and have learners write the state capitals. Ask learners to use a large U.S. map to plot and write directions for a travel route between any two cities. Ask other learners to read and follow the routes on the map.

Many Miles to Go
More *Expansion/Extension* for SB page 61

- Learners can discuss metric measurements. Ask *Why are both miles and kilometers used on some highway signs? What is a kilometer? What is a mile? How do they compare? What countries use metric measurements? Do you think the United States should change to all metric measurements? Why or why not?*

- Ask learners to find distance charts and keys on road maps or city maps. Ask learners to identify types of roads and places of interest, using the keys and charts, and to calculate distances between places. If appropriate, have learners use the street listings and grid marks on the map to locate places.

- Give learners a U.S. road map and a list of cities in various parts of the country. Ask learners to arrange the cities in a logical order for a one-way trip and to calculate the total distance.

- Learners can match tourist attractions with states and/or cities. Some places might be the Grand Canyon, Niagara Falls, Walt Disney World, the Statue of Liberty, Kennedy Space Center, the White House, and the Golden Gate Bridge.

What's the Weather Like?
***Expansion/Extension* for SB page 62**

- Learners can collect weather maps or listen to radio and TV forecasts for a few days and compare the forecasts with the actual weather in the area. Discuss the accuracy of the forecasts. Ask *Why are forecasts sometimes wrong?*

- Ask learners to prepare a weather report for another part of the country based on the weather map information on page 62.
- Ask learners to find newspaper articles on weather. Introduce other weather terms: *tornadoes, hurricanes, blizzards, snow flurries, showers, frost, fog, ice storm, high/low (pressure), cold/warm front, air quality, pollen count, humidity.* Learners can talk about weather conditions that make it dangerous to travel and that cause school closings. Ask *When do schools close due to weather? How do you find out if schools are closed? When do airports close? What conditions are dangerous for air travel?*
- Ask learners about seasons and climates in their native countries. Ask *Are seasons and weather in your native country different from what exists where you live in the United States? What differences are there? How are daily life and lifestyle (work day, clothing, housing, travel, and so on) different because of the climate?*
- Learners can practice changing temperatures from degrees Fahrenheit to degrees Celsius and vice versa. $°F = (°C \times \frac{9}{5}) + 32$ and $°C = (°F - 32) \times \frac{5}{9}$. Ask *Which measurement system is used in your native country?*
- Introduce idioms and expressions about weather. FOR EXAMPLE: *It's raining cats and dogs. The wind nearly blew me off my feet. There will be showers off and on all day.*
- Learners can share folk methods and sayings for predicting weather. FOR EXAMPLE: It's going to be a cold winter because the squirrel's tail is so bushy. "Red sky at night, sailors delight. Red sky at morning, sailors take warning."

A Night Out
More *Expansion/Extension* for SB page 64

- Ask learners if they ever visit local craft shops when they travel. Have them make a list of crafts, such as basketry, quilting, woodcarving, pottery, and weaving. Ask learners to look in the library for information on designs and patterns used in various regions of the United States. Learners can compare regional American patterns and designs to those used in their native cultures.

An Introduction to the Great Smokies
More *Expansion/Extension* for SB page 65

- Learners can take a field trip to a local park to look for and identify trees and animals. Learners may want to borrow some field guides from the library.
- Learners can research the national park system, including President Roosevelt's creation of the first national park, names of different parks, and points of interest.
- Ask learners about parks and protected areas in their native countries. Ask *Who controls these areas? Why are they protected? What is interesting about each of the places?*
- Learners can take a field trip to a local science/natural history exhibit or museum to learn more about the local environment, wildlife, and plant life.
- Elicit/introduce information about endangered species. Ask *What animals are on the endangered list? Why are they endangered? What has caused their decrease in population? What animals used to live in the United States but are now extinct?* Learners can debate the pros and cons of protecting certain types of animals.

Asking for Directions
More *Expansion/Extension* for SB page 66

- Learners can practice giving directions, using time clauses. (FOR EXAMPLE: When you see the sign for the interstate, turn left. Just before you get to the church, you bear right. As soon as you get to Seventh Avenue, go right. You turn right again, just after you reach the bus station. Stay on the road until you get to the museum.)

Practicing Your Skills
More *Expansion/Extension* for SB page 67

- Ask learners to compile a vocabulary list for the unit. Learners can create categories and categorize the new words. Some categories might be Maps and Directions, Weather, Travel Costs, Sights and Entertainment, Lodging/Places to Stay, and Miscellaneous.

Discovering Patterns

Objectives

- To help learners discover grammatical patterns
- To teach and give practice with those patterns
  The structures covered are:
  - the past tense in time clauses
  - *How* questions (*How far? How long? How often?*)
  - separable two-word verbs
  - inseparable two-word verbs
  - dependent clauses (*who, that, which*)

About the Structures

- **Verbs: Past Tense in Time Clauses**

  Adverbial time clauses are connected to the main clauses and cannot stand by themselves. They give information about when things happened. If there is a verb in the past tense (simple past, past continuous) in the time clause, then there needs to be a verb in the past tense in the main clause.

- **Questions: *How far? How long? How often?***

  The question word *how* may be confusing, because it can be used with adjectives (e.g., *old, big, sweet*) as well as adverbs (e.g., *quickly, often*). This unit focuses on the use of *how* in questions of frequency, length of time and distance, and duration of time.

- **Two-Word Verbs: Separable**

  These verbs are made up of a verb and a preposition but they function as a unit. Objects of separable verbs can be placed after the verb-plus-preposition units or, with nouns or noun phrases, in the middle of the units. Two-word verbs are difficult because the choice of prepositions is arbitrary in many cases.

- **Two-Word Verbs: Inseparable**

  These inseparable verbs differ from the separable ones in that objects of the verbs can be placed only after the two-word verbs.

- **Dependent Clauses: *Who, That, Which***

  In these exercises, the dependent clauses (also called relative clauses) modify nouns or pronouns that function as subjects, objects of verbs, and objects of prepositions. Learners may have difficulty in determining the appropriate relative pronouns to use and where the dependent clauses should be placed.

Verbs: Past Tense in Time Clauses

Purpose: To give practice in using the past tense in time clauses

Teacher Preparation and Materials

Pictures of people: talking on the telephone, watching TV, looking out a window, eating dinner, talking to a neighbor, lighting a candle

Warm-up

1. On the board write the sentence *The lights went out last night.* Then make a chart with the headings *Before, When,* and *After* and the pictures of people.

FOR EXAMPLE:

	Before	When	After
Diep	(talking on the phone)	(looking out the window)	(talking to a neighbor)
Marco	(watching TV)	(eating dinner)	(lighting a candle)

Model sentences with time clauses based on the chart. Have learners practice forming sentences.

2. Ask *When* questions about the chart. Have learners respond with complete sentences. FOR EXAMPLE: *When did Diep talk to her neighbor?* (She talked to her neighbor after the lights went out.)

Presentation

1. Have learners turn to page 70 and look at the examples in the box. Learners can identify past tense verbs in the main clauses and time clauses.

2. Ask *Which part of each sentence talks about time? What differences do you see between the first two sentences? When is a comma used? What words usually start time clauses? Is the subject the same in both parts (or clauses) of the sentences?*

3. Have learners complete the exercises. If necessary, ask questions about the To Do list in exercise B to elicit vocabulary needed to complete the sentences.

Verbs: Past Tense in Time Clauses

> While Roberto tried to connect the VCR, Eddy read the manual.
> Eddy read the manual while Roberto tried to connect the VCR.
>
> Before I worked full-time, I had a part-time job.
> I had a part-time job before I worked full-time.
>
> After his boss passed out, Stan drove himself to the hospital.
> Stan drove himself to the hospital after his boss passed out.
>
> When Diep got home, she called her brother.
> Diep called her brother when she got home.

A. Underline the time clause in each sentence.

1. After Diep finished work, she stopped at the bank.
2. She deposited her paycheck after she paid her bills.
3. Before she left, Diep checked the balance of her savings account.
4. When she left, she took a brochure about long-term savings.
5. She read the information while she waited for the bus.

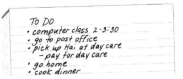

```
TO DO
• computer class 2-3:30
• go to post office
• pick up Hai at day care
   – pay for day care
• go home
• cook dinner
```

B. Read Diep's TO DO list from last Friday.
Complete the sentences. Use time clauses in the past tense.

1. Diep went to the post office after _____she finished class_____.
2. Before _she picked up her son_, she got stamps and mailed some letters.
3. She gave a check to the day-care worker when _she picked up her son_.
4. After _____she picked up her son at day care_____, she went home.
5. Her son watched TV while _____Diep cooked_____.

Expansion/Extension

- Ask learners to rewrite the sentences in the exercises, changing the order of the main and time clauses.

- Learners can write a *Wh-* question for each of the sentences. (FOR EXAMPLE: What did Diep do after she finished work? When did Diep read the information on long-term savings?)

- Ask *When* questions about story lines from Units 1–5. Have learners look through their books and give answers using time clauses. FOR EXAMPLE: *When did the Silvas visit Great Smoky Mountains National Park?* (They visited the park before they went to Atlanta.)

- Ask learners to complete sentences about interesting things that have happened to them. FOR EXAMPLE: *When I . . . , I saw . . . . Before I arrived in the United States, ...*

Questions: *How far?* *How long? How often?*

Purpose: To give practice with question formation and with question words for distance, duration, and frequency

Teacher Preparation and Materials

1. Blank index cards *(Expansion/Extension)*
2. Map of the United States *(Expansion/Extension)*

Warm-up

1. On the board write question words as column headings: *How Far? How Long? How Often?* Ask questions about the Silvas' trip from Unit 5. Have learners answer the questions. Learners can look through Unit 5 for specific information.
2. Ask questions about learners' trips to the United States or another trip they may have taken.

Presentation

1. Have learners turn to page 71 and look at the *How* questions in the box.
2. Ask questions using *How* to elicit appropriate responses. FOR EXAMPLE: *How often do we have class? How long have you been in the United States?*
3. Give statements and have learners respond with appropriate *How* questions. FOR EXAMPLE: *I studied last night.* (How long did you study?)
4. Point out the two possible meanings for *How long?* (measurement and length of time)
5. Have learners complete the exercises.

Expansion/Extension

- Learners can brainstorm and list other examples of answers to the *How* questions in the box.
- Learners can write the questions and answers on sets of index cards and then play a game of Concentration.

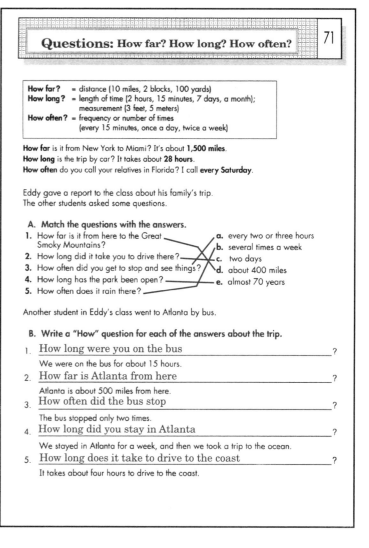

- Ask learners to measure distances and time related to the classroom. FOR EXAMPLE: *How far is it from your desk to the door? How long is the class in seconds? How many pages are in Unit 6 of your book?* If learners are interested, ask them to research other measurements, such as the distance to the moon, the time needed to travel to (name of a place, city, or country) by car, and the number of people living in a specific state or city.
- Introduce other adjectives/adverbs used in *How* questions: *tall, much, many, old, quickly, fast, big,* and so on. Model questions about the class setting. FOR EXAMPLE: *How many people are in the class? How tall is the bookcase in the corner? How much time do we have left in class?* Have learners practice asking and answering questions using these words.
- On index cards write answers to questions about the Silvas' trip or about a class field trip. As a group, play a game like Jeopardy. Have learners choose an answer card and then say an appropriate question.

Two-Word Verbs: Separable

Purpose: To give practice in using separable two-word verbs

Teacher Preparation and Materials

1. Large sheet of paper, marker
2. Key and key ring

Warm-up

1. On the board write several sets of instructions. Have learners compare the meanings. FOR EXAMPLE: *Turn the knob. Turn off the machine. Pick a class. Pick up a book.*

2. Have learners think of other verbs whose meanings change when a preposition is added. Make a list of those two-word verbs on a large sheet of paper. Tell learners that they will be using and adding more verbs to this list later. (**Note:** Learners may suggest some two-word verbs that are inseparable. These can be included on the list, but they will be discussed in the next lesson.)

Presentation

1. Have learners turn to page 72 and look at the expressions in the box. Ask questions about meanings. FOR EXAMPLE: *Find the two-word verb that means "to complete."*

2. Have learners compare the sentences under the box. Point out that object pronouns, such as *it* and *them,* are placed between the verb and preposition. (**Note:** Long object noun phrases are usually placed after the two-word verbs. Short object noun phrases can be placed between or after the two-word verbs.)

3. Introduce the term *separable.* Demonstrate the meaning with a key and a key ring. Show that the key can be used both when it is attached to the ring and when it is taken off the ring. Point out that the two-word verbs studied on this page are also separable. They can be connected as a unit or disconnected without changing the meaning.

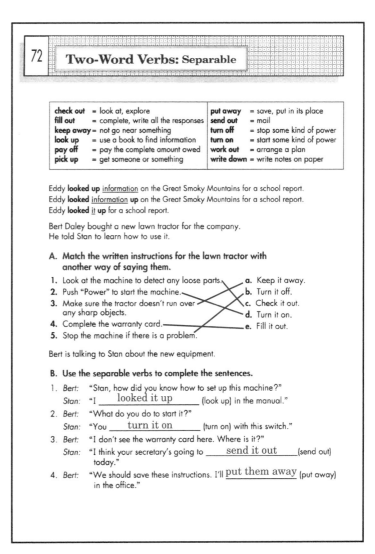

4. Have learners complete the exercises. Have learners say their responses aloud to see if the sentences sound correct.

Expansion/Extension

- Ask learners to rewrite the answers in exercise A, using nouns instead of pronouns.

- Learners can rewrite both sets of the sentences in exercise A to make the object nouns or noun phrases plural.

- Ask learners to look through Units 1–5 for examples of other separable two-word verbs. They can also make a list of pronouns (such as *it, them, those, these, this, that*) used to replace object nouns or noun phrases.

- Learners can use some of the separable two-word verbs in the box to write a description of how to do something, such as budgeting, operating a machine or tool, paying bills, and registering for classes. Alternatively, learners can make up instructions for an imaginary activity or machine.

Two-Word Verbs: Inseparable

Purpose: To give practice in using inseparable two-word verbs

Teacher Preparation and Materials

Large sheet of paper with two-word verbs, used for page 72

Warm-up

1. Write on the board *separable* and *inseparable*. Review the meaning of *separable* and elicit/introduce the meaning of *inseparable*. Explain that some two-word verbs are separable and some are inseparable. On the board write sentences with separable and inseparable verbs. FOR EXAMPLE:

Separable	Inseparable
Turn off the light./ Turn the light off.	Go over the next lesson.

Ask learners what they think the difference is between the two categories. Have learners try to say the sentence with the inseparable verb as if the verb were separable. (Go the next lesson over.)

2. Ask learners to look at the list of two-word verbs used for page 72 and to mark the two-word verbs that are inseparable. To check the work, ask learners to use the two-word verbs in sentences as if the verbs were separable and identify those that can't be separated.

Presentation

1. Have learners turn to page 73 and look at the expressions in the box. Ask questions about the inseparable two-word verbs. *Which verb means "to be careful"? If you "go over" your homework, what does that mean?*

2. Have learners look at the examples. Elicit/explain that these verbs cannot be separated by objects or object pronouns.

3. Ask learners to complete the exercises. Have learners say their responses aloud to see if the sentences sound correct. Have learners create other sentences using the two-word inseparable verbs.

---

break down	= stop operating, stop working	**go over**	= study or review
cut back	= reduce or lower (the amount)	**keep on**	= continue
eat out	= buy meals at a restaurant	**move in**	= begin living in a place
get along	= manage, meet one's needs	**run into**	= meet by chance
get off	= leave (the bus or train)	**run out of**	= use up the supply
get up	= rise from bed	**watch out**	= be careful

Examples: Diep gets up at about 5:00 in the morning.
Will Stan keep on working for Bert?
I have to get off the bus at Center Street.

Yolette and Al talked about ways to reduce their expenses.

A. Rewrite the sentences, using inseparable verbs.

1. Tomorrow morning we'll rise from bed early and start making a plan.
   Tomorrow morning we'll get up early and start making a plan

2. We need to lower the number of long-distance phone calls.
   We need to cut back (on) the number of long-distance phone calls.

3. We need to stop eating at restaurants so much.
   We need to stop eating out so much.

4. We need to continue saving money.
   We need to keep on saving money.

5. We need to review our budget from time to time.
   We need to go over our budget from time to time.

6. Let's hope the car doesn't stop working. That would ruin our budget.
   Let's hope the car doesn't break down. That would ruin our budget.

B. Complete the sentences, using inseparable verbs.

1. Yolette and Al know they have to ____cut back____ on their spending.
2. They'll ____watch out____ for unnecessary expenses.
3. They don't want to ____run out of____ money.
4. They'll just have to ____get along____ on a tight budget.

Expansion/Extension

- Learners can write questions for the sentences in exercise A. The questions can ask for more specific budget information. (FOR EXAMPLE: How often should Al and Yolette go over their budget? What can they do if the car breaks down?) In pairs, learners can exchange questions and write answers for their partners' questions.

- Ask learners to look through Units 1–5 for examples of other inseparable two-word verbs and add them to the list on the paper.

- Learners can write their own lists of money-saving suggestions, using separable and inseparable two-word verbs.

- Introduce/explain that some of the two-word verbs have double meanings. FOR EXAMPLE: *break down* means "stop working" or "divide something into smaller parts" (break down the expenses); *cut back* means "to reduce, lower" or "to trim" (cut the bushes back about six inches). Ask learners to use these two-word verbs in sentences to illustrate both meanings.

Dependent Clauses: *Who, That, Which*

Purpose: To give practice in using dependent clauses with *who*, *that*, and *which*

Teacher Preparation and Materials
Three books of different sizes or colors

Warm-up
Place three books on a table or desk. Say to a volunteer *Please give me a book*. The volunteer should ask for clarification as to which book you want. (Which book?) Rephrase the request, using a dependent clause. FOR EXAMPLE: *Please give me the book that has a green cover*. Practice with other books and objects in the room. *Please put the book on a chair*. (Which chair?) *Please put it on the chair that is next to the door*. Write the rephrased requests on the board.

Presentation
1. Have learners turn to page 74 and look at the examples in the box. Ask questions to help point out patterns. FOR EXAMPLE: *Which men did Bert pay? Which book is it?*

2. Have learners compare the sentences with dependent clauses to the two explanatory sentences. Ask *What word refers to "the men"? What word refers to "the book"?* Summarize by showing learners that *who* refers to people, *which* refers to things, and *that* refers to people or things.

3. Have learners complete the exercises. Learners can act out the conversations in the exercises and/or add more lines to the conversations.

Expansion/Extension
- Ask learners to look through Units 1–5 for other examples of dependent/relative clauses.
- Play a game of "Who/What Is It?" Have a volunteer think of a person or thing in the room. Other learners can ask *Yes/No* questions with dependent clauses to try to identify the person or thing. (FOR EXAMPLE: Is it the man who is from Kiev? Is it the red book that is under the bag?)

- Introduce and have learners practice using the relative pronoun *whom*. (FOR EXAMPLE: That's the worker whom I was talking about.) Point out that in informal speech, *whom* is often replaced by *who*. Depending on the learners' skills, show examples of sentences where the relative pronouns are omitted. (**Note:** Relative pronouns can sometimes be left out in some types of restrictive clauses.)

- Learners can write a *Which* question for each sentence in the exercises. (FOR EXAMPLE: Which people are on the list? Yolette, which names do you want? Which customers should be included on the list?)

---

74 — Dependent Clauses: *Who, That, Which*

Bert paid the money to the men **who (that)** did the work. =
Bert paid the money to the men. The men did the work.

Here is a book **which (that)** describes the Great Smoky Mountains. =
Here is a book. The book describes the Great Smoky Mountains.

Yolette and her boss Lou are talking about the new customer database.

A. Fill in the first word of each dependent clause: who, that, or which.

1. *Yolette:* "Lou, are there any other names <u>that/which</u> should be added to the mailing list?"

2. *Lou:* "The customers <u>who/that</u> came in yesterday should probably be included."

3. *Lou:* "I left the information <u>that/which</u> you need next to the computer."
   Yolette: "Thanks. I want to finish the list this morning."

4. *Lou:* "Do you think we can try to get the addresses of customers <u>who/that</u> buy children's shoes?"

5. *Yolette:* "Sure. I'll do it right after I input the names <u>that/which</u> you just gave me."

B. Combine the two sentences, using dependent clauses.

> **Example:** *Yolette:* "The salesman was very nice. He gave me directions."
> *Yolette:* "<u>The salesman who gave me directions was very nice.</u>"

1. *Yolette:* "Here's the list of people. The people buy children's shoes."
   Yolette: "<u>Here's the list of people who buy children's shoes.</u>"

2. *Lou:* "The list looks good. You made the list."
   Lou: "<u>The list that you made looks good.</u>"

3. *Lou:* "OK, here are the fliers. They need to be sent out."
   Lou: "<u>OK, here are the fliers that need to be sent out.</u>"

4. *Yolette:* "I know the man. He designed and printed the fliers."
   Yolette: "<u>I know the man who designed and printed the fliers.</u>"

5. *Yolette:* "Mr. Jones is a friend. You can trust him."
   Yolette: "<u>Mr. Jones is a friend who you can trust.</u>"

Problems on the Job

Objectives

Functions
- Giving and accepting apologies
- Expressing emotions
- Expressing uncertainty and confusion
- Expressing embarrassment
- Reporting and describing
- Predicting

Life Tasks
- Reading job evaluations
- Explaining company policies and rules
- Reading magazine advice articles
- Preparing for a meeting with a work supervisor
- Reading advice columns
- Writing an advice letter

Structures
- *If/then* statements (*If* + past tense + modal)
- *What* + *if*
- *Should have* + past participle

Culture
- Responses and reactions to embarrassing situations
- Apologies
- Polite language

Vocabulary

Key words:

accuracy	knowledge
apologize	performance
apology	evaluation
approved	problem solving
authorized	promotion
company policy	raise
confidential	recommendation
criteria	rejected
evaluation	required
interview	satisfactory
habit	termination
judgment	unsatisfactory

Related words:

accurately	efficient
ambitious	embarrassed
annoyed	expectation
apologetic	frustrated
appropriately	furious
ashamed	outraged
bragging	overall
conflict	permitted
confused	perplexed
consistently	provoke
contact	relationship
cooperative	satisfied
cover up	shocked
deserve	temper
discriminated	under pressure
dishonest	

Making Mistakes

Purpose: To introduce dealing with embarrassment, apologizing, and talking about mistakes

Teacher Preparation and Materials
Large sheet of paper, markers

Warm-up
1. At the top of a large sheet of paper, write *How do you feel when . . . .* Make two columns under the title and label them *you make a mistake?* and *someone makes a mistake that affects or bothers you?* Have learners suggest feelings for the two situations. Write learners' suggestions on the paper. Some feelings might be *embarrassed, surprised, worried, annoyed, frustrated, furious, ashamed,* and *apologetic.* (**Note:** This chart will be used again for pages 76 and 84.)
2. Ask learners if they have had any embarrassing experiences or if they have experienced any of the feelings listed on the chart. Allow learners to talk about what happened, what they said or did, and what other people said or did.

Presentation
1. Have learners turn to page 75. Ask questions about the picture. FOR EXAMPLE: *How would you describe this restaurant? Who are the people at the table? What do you think Roberto was carrying on the tray?* List words and comments on the board.
2. Have learners discuss the questions at the bottom of the page.
3. Ask learners to guess how the customer feels. Have learners suggest reasons why the accident happened and predict how Roberto and the customer will react to the accident.
4. On the board, write *If I were Roberto, I'd . . . . If I were the customer, I'd . . . .* Have learners use words from the chart to describe the possible feelings and actions of Roberto and the customer.

1 2 3 4 5 6 7 8 9 10 11 12
Problems on the Job ■ ■ ■ ■ ■ ■ ■

Making Mistakes
What's happening here?
How do you think Roberto feels?
What should he do?

Answers may vary.

Expansion/Extension
- Ask learners to role-play the restaurant scene. Learners can refer to the sentence completions on the board for ideas.
- Learners can discuss other situations in which it would be appropriate to say, "I'm sorry." Some settings to consider are in a supermarket, at school, at work, and at home.
- Learners can describe and write about an embarrassing situation that they have had. They can keep a copy of their writing in their portfolio.
- Ask learners to complete conditional sentences using the words from the semantic web. (FOR EXAMPLE: *I'd be shocked if . . . . I'd be furious if . . . .*)
- Learners can compare different cultural behaviors that may surprise, embarrass, or bother people. (FOR EXAMPLE: *I'm shocked when Americans . . . . Americans seem shocked when I . . . .*) Learners can discuss the cultural differences and ways to handle or avoid possible misunderstandings.

Roberto's Apology

Purpose: To give practice in giving and accepting apologies

Teacher Preparation and Materials

1. Chart of feelings, used for page 75
2. ▓▓▓ Audiotape for Level 3
3. Copies of TRF Handout 7.1, *Conversation Bytes (Expansion/Extension)*

Warm-up

1. Have learners look again at the picture on page 65 and the chart of feelings created for that page. Ask them to suggest how Roberto and the customer probably feel and how they will react. On the board, list things Roberto could do to apologize and then list possible reactions/responses from the customer.

2. Ask learners about experiences they have had apologizing to someone or having someone apologize to them. Add other appropriate actions or expressions to the lists on the board.

Presentation

1. Have learners turn to page 76 and read the questions in part A to focus their listening. Have learners predict answers.

2. ▓▓▓ Play the audiotape. Ask literal and inferential questions about Roberto. FOR EXAMPLE: *What do you think made Roberto slip? What did he get for Mr. Jansen?*

3. Ask questions about Mr. Jansen. FOR EXAMPLE: *How did Mr. Jansen react? Why wasn't Mr. Jansen angry? Why didn't Roberto apologize again after cleaning up the spilled soup? Do you think Roberto apologized too much or too little?*

4. Have learners answer the questions in exercise A. ▓▓▓ Learners can listen again to the conversation to check their responses.

5. Ask *Why did Roberto offer to have the restaurant pay for the dry cleaning? Why did he offer the people at Mr. Jansen's table free desserts? How do you think Roberto's boss will react?*

76 **Roberto's Apology**

▓▓▓ **A. Write the answers.**

1. Why did Roberto apologize to the customer? <u>because he spilled soup on his suit</u>
2. How did the customer respond? <u>politely</u>
3. What did Roberto tell the customer to do? <u>have his suit drycleaned and send the bill to the restaurant</u>
4. What did Roberto offer the customer? <u>a free dessert for everyone in the party</u>

B. Answer the questions.

1. How do people apologize? What do they say? How do people accept apologies? **Answers may vary.**

Write different ways to . . .

apologize	accept an apology

2. What happens when people don't want to accept an apology? What kinds of things can they say or do? **Answers may vary.**

C. Complete the sentence. **Answers will vary.**
How do you feel when something goes wrong?
Complete the sentence below. You can give more than one answer.

When something goes wrong, I feel _____

6. Have learners complete the chart in exercise B. ▓▓▓ Learners can listen again to the conversation and write expressions that were used. Learners can ask friends or neighbors for other appropriate expressions. Together compile a list of expressions for apologizing and accepting an apology. Discuss reasons why a person might not accept an apology and how to handle such situations.

7. Have learners discuss the question in exercise C. In large classes, have learners work in small groups, with one learner acting as the recorder and another as the reporter. Have the groups share their responses. ▓▓ In a one-to-one situation, discuss the question together and have the learner complete the sentence in several different ways. Have learners expand on their answers by talking about situations when things go wrong. (FOR EXAMPLE: When something goes wrong at work, I feel worried because I might get fired. When something goes wrong with the car, I feel angry because I can't fix it myself.)

Expansion/Extension **on page 126**

Talking to the Boss

Purpose: To give practice in reporting and describing an error and a solution

Teacher Preparation and Materials

1.  Audiotape for Level 3
2. Copies of TRF Handout 7.2, *Corporate Culture (Expansion/Extension)*
3. Copies of TRF Handout 7.3, *More Conversation Bytes (Expansion/Extension)*

Warm-up

1. Have learners look back at their answers to exercise C on page 76. Ask learners about experiences they have had with mistakes on the job (or if learners do not work, with problems or misunderstandings with day-care providers, social service workers, bank workers, store clerks, and so on). *Who do you talk to when something goes wrong? Does anyone come to ask if they can help? Do people get angry if you make a mistake? Who gets angry? Why do you think they get angry?*

2. Ask learners about Roberto's mistake. Ask *How do you think Roberto's boss will react?* Review answers to this question from discussion of page 76.

Presentation

1. Have learners turn to page 77 and look at the picture. Ask learners to predict what the manager will say to Roberto. Then have learners read the questions in exercise A.

2. Play conversation #1 on the audio-tape. Ask questions to help learners describe the tones and attitudes of Roberto and Marcel. FOR EXAMPLE: *What kind of person does Roberto sound like in this version of the conversation? Is he effective in dealing with the situation? Why or why not?*

3. Play conversation #2 and again ask questions to help learners describe the tones and attitudes of the speakers. FOR EXAMPLE: *What kind of person does Roberto sound like here? What is different about Marcel's reaction? Why?*

Talking to the Boss 77

Marcel Dulac manages the restaurant. Marcel is worried that Mr. Jansen won't eat there again because of what Roberto did.

A. Listen to two versions of the conversation between Marcel and Roberto. Think and talk about the questions. Answers may vary.
1. What did Roberto say that was different in the second conversation?
2. How did Marcel treat Roberto in each conversation?
3. How do you know which conversation was more successful?

B. Describe Roberto in . . . Answers may vary.

	conversation 1	conversation 2
1.		
2.		
3.		

---

4. Have learners discuss the questions in exercise A. Play the conversations again if necessary.

5. Have learners complete the chart in exercise B. Learners can work individually or in pairs. Have learners use information from the conversations to explain their responses.

Expansion/Extension

See TRF HANDOUT 7.2, *Corporate Culture*
TRF HANDOUT 7.3, *More Conversation Bytes*

• Learners can write different versions of reports that Marcel might make about the incident based on information in the two conversations.

• Ask learners how else Roberto could have handled the conversation with Marcel. Learners can role-play variations of the conversations.

More *Expansion/Extension* on page 126

No Promotion for Diep

Purpose: To give practice in expressing feelings, uncertainty, and confusion; to introduce *what + if* and *If/then*

Teacher Preparation and Materials

1. Large sheet of paper, marker
2. Equal Employment Opportunity notice (*Expansion/Extension*)
3. Local phone book (*Expansion/Extension*)
4. Complaint or grievance form from a workplace or labor union (*Expansion/Extension*)

Warm-up

1. On the large sheet of paper, write the words *raise* and *promotion*. Elicit/explain the meanings of the words. Then ask *Do all jobs give raises? When do workers get raises? How do supervisors decide who gets a raise? What are some reasons why people might want a promotion? How do supervisors decide who gets a promotion? What are some reasons why people might not get a promotion? What types of workers get raises and promotions?* List learners' ideas on the paper for requirements for getting raises and promotions.

2. On the board, write:

   If I work hard, then maybe I will get a raise. But I didn't get a raise. If I got more training, then maybe I would get a raise.

   Have learners compare the sentences and then practice creating their own conditional sentences about job promotions and raises, using the requirements listed on the paper.

Presentation

1. Have learners turn to page 78. Have a volunteer read the title. Ask *What do you know about Diep? How do you think she will react to not getting a promotion?*

2. Have learners read the passage. Have learners underline words they do not know. Elicit/explain the meanings of new words: *enrolled, efficient, discriminated, satisfied, deserve.*

| 78 | No Promotion for Diep |

Diep has worked at City Hospital for two years. She has worked hard at her job and has always tried to improve her skills. She enrolled in computer classes so that she would be even more efficient at work. Diep hoped that she would receive a promotion, or at least a raise, and she was very upset when she didn't get either one. She tried to understand why.

When Diep talked to her brother Quang about it, he got angry. He said she was being discriminated against. He thought she was passed over because she was a woman. But Diep said that her supervisor was also a woman. Quang got angrier. He said she didn't get the raise because she was Vietnamese. Diep said other Vietnamese workers got promotions and raises, so that couldn't be the reason either.

"Ms. Morris is just not satisfied with my work," Diep said sadly. "If I spoke English better, she'd give me a promotion. If I understood directions better, I'd do things faster. If I worked more hours, she'd take me more seriously."

Quang said, "You always work hard. You never miss work. You're never late or rude. You have to tell your supervisor that you deserve a promotion and that you need that raise."

Diep thought Quang was right, but she didn't think she could tell her supervisor. She thought she would have to look for another job.

A. Answer the question. Answers will vary.

What would you do if you didn't get a raise or promotion that you thought you deserved?

_____

_____

B. Interview.

Talk to a friend or someone in your family. Ask him or her to complete these sentences. Answers will vary.

1. If I were late for work, _____.
2. If I disliked my boss, _____.
3. If _____, I'd quit my job.
4. I'd look for another job if _____.

---

3. Ask literal and inferential questions, such as *Why does Diep want the promotion? What reasons does Quang give for her not getting it? Why does Diep think she wasn't discriminated against, either sexually or racially? Do you agree with her or disagree? Do you think Quang's suggestion is a good or bad one? Why? What do you think about Diep's solution?*

4. Have learners discuss options that people have if they do not get a raise or promotion. Have learners write an answer to the question in exercise A and explain their response.

5. Ask learners to interview friends or family members and to complete exercise B. Have learners share responses that they think are unusual or interesting.

Expansion/Extension

- Discuss discrimination on the job. Elicit/explain different bases of discrimination: race, age, sex, ethnic group/national origin, religion, handicap/disability.

More *Expansion/Extension* on page 126

Following Company Policy

Purpose: To give practice in reporting and describing and in expressing feelings

Teacher Preparation and Materials

1. ▨▨▨ Audiotape for Level 3
2. Copies of TRF Handout 7.5, *Coping with an Unfriendly Person (Expansion/Extension)*
3. Employee policy manual or list of job responsibilities *(Expansion/Extension)*

Warm-up

1. Ask *What did Roberto offer Mr. Jansen along with the apology? Did Roberto need to check with his boss if this was OK, or was Roberto authorized to do it himself?* On the board write the word *authorized.* Ask *Why did Roberto offer these things to Mr. Jansen? Was it Roberto's own idea, or was it the company policy?* Write on the board *company policy.* Ask *Did Roberto tell his boss how much money Mr. Jansen gave as a tip, or is the amount confidential?* Write on the board *confidential.*

2. Ask learners why employees should know company policies and why all employees are not authorized to perform the same tasks. Ask what types of information may be considered confidential. Learners can give examples from their own work situation or from experiences in dealing with workers in stores, post offices, banks, and schools.

Presentation

1. Have learners turn to page 79, read the title, and look at the picture. Ask questions to help learners predict what the conversation will be about. FOR EXAMPLE: *What do you think Diep is carrying? Why does she have it? Why do you think the patient is excited?*

2. ▨▨▨ Play the first few lines of part A of the audiotape. Stop after the patient says: "You must have read it! What did it say?" Ask learners what the problem is and what they think Diep will do.

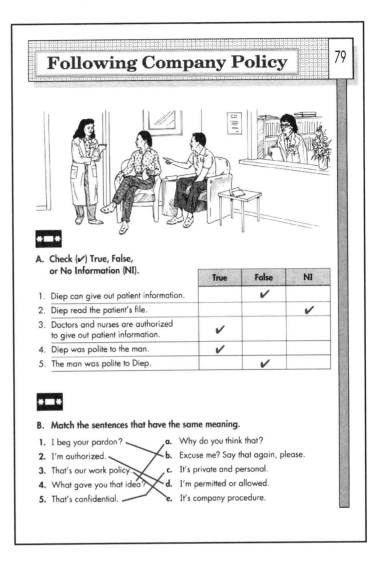

3. ▨▨▨ Listen to the rest of part A of the conversation. Ask *What did the man want from Diep? Why didn't she want to give him his file? Why did Ms. Morris interrupt? What did she do? How do you think Ms. Morris feels about Diep's handling of the situation? How do you think Diep feels about the incident?*

4. Have learners complete exercise A. ▨▨▨ Learners can listen again to the conversation to verify answers.

5. ▨▨▨ Play part B of the conversation. Ask *How do you think Diep felt about Ms. Morris helping her? Why did Diep apply for a different job in the hospital? Do you think Ms. Morris is satisfied with Diep's work? Why or why not?*

6. Have learners read the expressions in the first column of exercise B. ▨▨▨ Play the two conversations again and have learners listen for the expressions and key words. Then have learners match the phrases.

Expansion/Extension

See TRF HANDOUT 7.5, *Coping with an Unfriendly Person*

More *Expansion/Extension* on page 126

Performance Evaluation

Purpose: To introduce reading job evaluations

Teacher Preparation and Materials

1. Large sheet of paper, marker
2. Samples of different job evaluation forms
3. Copies of TRF Handout 7.6, *Filling Out an Employee Evaluation Form (Expansion/Extension)*

Warm-up

1. Have learners brainstorm qualities, behavior, and attitudes that are characteristic of a good worker. List ideas on a large sheet of paper. Be sure to include *knowledge, problem solving, quantity, accuracy, judgment,* and *output.* Label the list *Criteria.* Have learners suggest ways to rate a worker's performance. (Yes/No, 1–5, A–F, narrative, and so on)

2. Bring in samples of different job evaluation forms. Have learners compare what is rated and the rating systems. Ask learners if they have ever been evaluated, either on the job or in school. Allow learners to share experiences they have had with evaluations.

Presentation

1. Have learners turn to page 80 and read the title and introduction. Ask learners to predict if Diep's evaluation will be generally good or poor. Have learners explain the reasons for their predictions.

2. Have learners read the evaluation form and underline words they do not know. Elicit/explain the meanings of new words: *adheres, contact, accurately, efficiently, overall, consistently, exceeds, recommendation, termination, approved, rejected.*

3. Ask *What are Diep's strong points? What are her weak points? Which criteria need to be rated for promotions? Did Ms. Morris recommend Diep for a promotion? Was Ms. Morris's recommendation approved or rejected? Why do you think it was rejected?*

Performance Evaluation — page 80

Here is Diep's job evaluation. What kind of worker is she?

CITY HOSPITAL

Employee's Name *Diep Tran* Current Position *Lab Ass't.*
Dept. *Laboratory* Supervisor *Joan Morris*

Please rate all criteria 1–5 (lowest to highest) or **N/A** in each category. For promotions, required criteria marked (**R**) cannot be rated **N/A**.

Criteria	1	2	3	4	5	N/A
• knowledge of work (R)	1	2	3	4	⑤	N/A
• quantity of work (R)	1	2	3	④	5	N/A
• accuracy of output (R)	1	2	3	4	⑤	N/A
• 15 hours of computer training (R)	1	2	3	4	5	Ⓝ/Ⓐ
• good patient contact	1	2	③	4	5	N/A
• problem solving	1	2	3	④	5	N/A
• adheres to hospital policies (R)	1	2	3	4	⑤	N/A
• uses independent judgment	1	2	③	4	5	N/A
• completes paperwork accurately and in a timely fashion	1	2	3	4	⑤	N/A
• plans own work efficiently	1	2	3	④	5	N/A

Overall evaluation (check one)
___ Consistently exceeds expectations
✓ Fully meets expectations
___ Meets some expectations
___ Does not meet expectations

Supervisor recommends (check one)
✓ Step promotion to *2/0* job category
___ Continue in present job category
___ Additional supervision/training
___ Termination

Recommendation: ☐ approved ☒ rejected

A. Write the answers.
1. Why didn't Diep get the promotion? *because the evaluation didn't have the computer training listed*
2. What should she have told Ms. Morris? *that she was taking a computer course*

B. Think and talk about the question. Answers may vary.
What would you do about a problem like this?

4. Have learners write their answers to exercise A and discuss the question in exercise B. In large classes, have learners work in small groups, with one learner acting as the recorder and another learner as the reporter. Have the groups share their responses. ▪ In a one-to-one situation, discuss the questions together.

Expansion/Extension

See TRF HANDOUT 7.6, *Filling Out an Employee Evaluation Form*

• Ask learners to rewrite Diep's evaluation in a narrative form. Learners can use the information on the form on page 70 and other information that they have learned about Diep.

• Learners can choose a job and make a list of criteria that could be considered in evaluating a worker's performance. Ask learners to explain why each item might be important for that particular job.

More Expansion/Extension on page 127

Preparing for a Job Review

Purpose: To give practice in reading magazine advice articles and in preparing for a job review meeting

Teacher Preparation and Materials
None

Warm-up

1. On the board, write two column headings: *Things I Do Really Well* and *Things I Would Like to Do Better*. Have learners list their skills and abilities for each category. Have learners identify skills and abilities that relate to their present job or to a job they might like to have. Ask questions to elicit/explain that friends, co-workers, and supervisors do not always know about your strengths and goals. FOR EXAMPLE: *What can you do well? Does your boss know about that? Why or why not? Do your friends know that you can . . . ?* Learners can share their lists with others in the group and explain why they listed certain skills and abilities.

2. Ask learners to look back at Diep's evaluation form on page 80. Have learners suggest things that Diep does well and things that she might like to do better. Elicit/explain that a supervisor might discuss these things in a job review after an evaluation form has been completed. Have learners suggest other questions or information that might be discussed.

Presentation

1. Have learners turn to page 81. Have a volunteer read the title of the page, the title of the article, and the introductory paragraph. Ask if anyone has had a meeting with a supervisor. If so, ask what happened and what types of questions the supervisor asked.

2. Have learners read the article and underline words they do not know.

Preparing for a Job Review 81

Timely Tips for Meeting with Your Supervisor

Is it time for your annual job review? Whether you're a counter clerk or a crew chief, there are standard questions that you can expect every time. Here's what to expect and how to make the most of your time with your supervisor.

- **What do you already know how to do well?**

  This is your opportunity to shine! Point out what you do well, what you enjoy doing, what you've trained others to do, and so on. If you don't feel comfortable bragging, think about *what you'd like to hear* someone say about your work and tell *that* to your supervisor.

- **What would you like to do better in this job?**

  Admit that there's always room for improvement. Show that you're aware of your (minor) weaknesses and let your supervisor know how you've already started to work on them. Don't be ashamed of mistakes or problems. Just show that you're

aware of them and are doing something about them.

- **What new tasks would you like to do or to learn next?**

  You need to figure out your *own* goals to answer this one. Are you happy where you are, doing what you're doing? Do you want a change, new challenges, or a promotion? These questions should be answered in your mind *before* the performance review. This is a chance for you to remind your supervisor of what you've already accomplished and stress that you want to advance. If possible, show how your goals will benefit the company (or better yet, the supervisor).

  It also helps to have some questions for the supervisor. Ask how you can improve your performance and what your chances are for getting new responsibilities. Finally, be sure to thank your supervisor at the end of the interview. You always want to end a meeting on a positive note.

A. Think and talk about the questions. Answers will vary.

1. Do you agree with the advice in this article?
2. Think about your job or one that you've had. How would you answer the questions if you had a job review?

B. Choose one of the questions from the article. Write an answer that you'd give to your supervisor.

Answers will vary.

Elicit/explain the meanings of new words: *annual, standard, opportunity, bragging, admit, aware of, tasks, challenges, accomplished, benefit, positive note.*

3. Ask *What is the purpose of this article? Does the article sound formal or informal? Do you think you need to tell your boss what you do well or should your boss know that already? Do you feel comfortable talking about things that you cannot do well? Would this advice be appropriate in your native country? Why or why not?*

4. Have learners discuss the questions in exercise A. In large classes, have learners work in small groups. Have the groups share their responses. ◼ In a one-to-one situation, discuss the questions together.

5. Have learners complete exercise B individually. Volunteers can share their answers with the group. Have others in the group comment on the answers, make suggestions for improvement, or ask for further explanation or clarification.

Expansion/Extension **on page 127**

Hot under the Collar

Purpose: To give practice in expressing feelings

Teacher Preparation and Materials

1. ▪▪▪ Audiotape for Level 3
2. Copies of TRF Handout 7.7, *Discussing Problems at Work (Expansion/Extension)*

Warm-up

1. On the board, write *At work, it really makes me angry when . . . .* Have learners work in pairs or small groups listing things that make them angry at work. If learners do not have jobs, have them write things that bother or anger them at home, in school, or in their daily life. Learners can share their lists and tell interesting stories related to the lists.
2. Have learners think of synonyms for *angry*. List words and phrases on the board. Be sure to include *hot under the collar*.

Presentation

1. Have learners turn to page 82, look at the picture, and make hypotheses about the situation. *Who is Stan arguing with? Who else is with them? What do you think is the problem? Whose fault do you think it is? What do you think could be done about the problem?*
2. ▪▪▪ Play the audiotape. Ask *Who's hot under the collar? Why do the other workers want Stan to do more work? What do you think it means to cover for another person? Do you think Stan should help his co-workers or leave the mistake as it is? Why? Do the workers respect Stan's honesty? Why do you think they don't like Stan?*
3. ▪▪▪ Have learners complete exercise A and then listen again to the conversation to verify responses.
4. Ask learners to discuss the questions in exercise B. In large classes, have learners work in small groups, with one learner acting as the recorder and another as the reporter. Have the groups share their

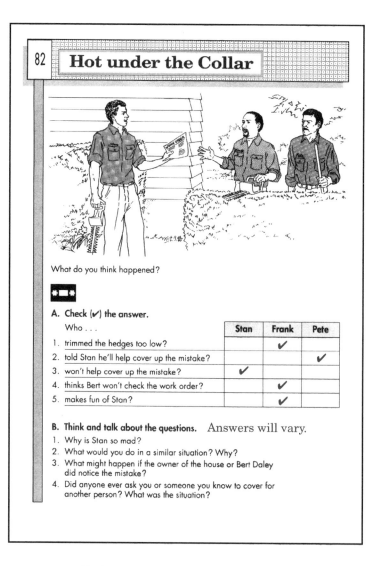

82 **Hot under the Collar**

What do you think happened?

▪▪▪

A. Check (✔) the answer.

Who . . .	Stan	Frank	Pete
1. trimmed the hedges too low?		✔	
2. told Stan he'll help cover up the mistake?			✔
3. won't help cover up the mistake?	✔		
4. thinks Bert won't check the work order?		✔	
5. makes fun of Stan?		✔	

B. Think and talk about the questions. Answers will vary.
1. Why is Stan so mad?
2. What would you do in a similar situation? Why?
3. What might happen if the owner of the house or Bert Daley did notice the mistake?
4. Did anyone ever ask you or someone you know to cover for another person? What was the situation?

answers. ▪▪ In a one-to-one situation, discuss the questions together.
5. Ask learners to list the good and bad aspects of Stan's reaction. Ask *What does it say about him? What does it tell you about Stan's loyalty to his co-workers? What does it tell you about Stan's pride in his work?*

Expansion/Extension

See **TRF HANDOUT 7.7,** *Discussing Problems at Work*

- Have learners role-play the conversation. Learners can make a list of other possible reactions for Stan and discuss the pros and cons of the different choices. Have learners role-play variations of the conversation, based on the list of reactions.
- Ask learners to role-play a conversation between the workers and Bert. *What will the workers tell Bert about the hedges? Will Stan point out the error? How do you think Bert will react to the mistake? Will he tell the customer? Will he have the workers retrim the hedges?*

More *Expansion/Extension* on page 127

A Recommendation for Stan

Purpose: To give practice in reading job evaluations

Teacher Preparation and Materials

Sample employee manuals or personnel policies *(Expansion/Extension)*

Warm-up

1. Have learners list on the board what they know about Stan's work performance.
2. Ask learners to imagine that they are Stan's supervisor and that they need to evaluate Stan's work. This can be done as a whole group or in small groups or pairs. Learners can use Diep's evaluation form on page 80 or your class evaluation form to guide the activity. Have learners explain their evaluations of Stan.

Presentation

1. Have learners turn to page 83. Have a volunteer read the title and introductory paragraph. Have learners predict if Stan's evaluation will be positive or negative and explain why.
2. Have learners read Stan's job evaluation and underline words they do not know. Elicit/explain the meanings of new words: *complaining, temper, provoke, cooperative, conflicts, satisfactory, unsatisfactory, habits, maintains, appropriately, unavailable, relationships.*
3. Ask literal and inferential questions, such as *What does Stan do well? poorly? Why do you think Bert rated him only S/U for "uses good judgment"? Do you think Stan would agree or disagree with his job evaluation? What might he say to Bert about the evaluation?*
4. Have learners discuss attributes that make a good worker and a good supervisor. List learners' ideas on the board. Have learners comment on similarities and differences between the lists.

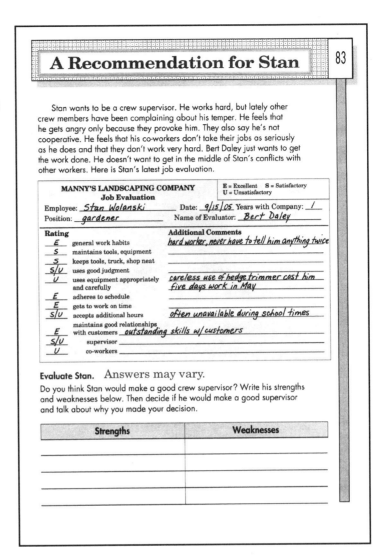

5. Have learners complete the exercise at the bottom of the page. Ask learners to evaluate Stan as a potential supervisor. Learners should explain their opinions.

Expansion/Extension

- Learners can rewrite Stan's evaluation in narrative form.
- Learners can role-play a review meeting between Stan and Bert. Learners can prepare answers for Stan to use, based on the tips on page 81.
- Ask learners to discuss Stan's options if he does not agree with his supervisor's remarks. Learners can look through employee manuals for policies and procedures for grievances. Ask learners to find out what happens with job evaluations. *Where are they kept? Are they confidential? Who has access to them? Why does the company need to keep them?*

How Do You Act under Pressure?

Purpose: To give practice in expressing feelings and in self-evaluation

Teacher Preparation and Materials

1. Chart of feelings, used for pages 75 and 76
2. Copies of TRF Handout 7.4, *Personal Priorities at Work (Expansion/Extension)*
3. Employee manuals or personnel policies *(Expansion/Extension)*
4. Invite a personnel manager to speak to the class. *(Expansion/Extension)*

Warm-up

1. Use the stories of Roberto, Diep, and Stan in this unit to elicit/explain the meaning of *pressure situation*. Have learners brainstorm and list other pressure situations that can occur at work. If learners do not work, encourage them to think of pressure situations in their daily lives or in the lives of family members and friends.
2. Ask learners how they would feel if they were in each of the situations listed. Learners may want to look back at the chart of feelings for vocabulary. Add other vocabulary to the chart.

Presentation

1. Have learners turn to page 84. Have a volunteer read the title and introductory paragraph.
2. Ask learners to read through the phrases listed in exercise A and underline new words. Elicit/explain the meanings of new words: *argues, solutions, defends, calm.* Have learners suggest other ways people may respond to difficult or pressure situations. Learners can add these responses to the list in exercise A.
3. Have learners complete the column for Roberto individually or in pairs. If necessary, ask learners to look back at pages 75–77 and to recall how Roberto acted when he spilled the soup. Then have

---

84 How Do You Act under Pressure?

Roberto, Diep, and Stan all act differently during difficult situations. The list below gives some of the words that describe how people act when they are under pressure or embarrassed.

A. Write the words that you think describe each character. Then write the words that describe the way you act.

Add some words of your own. Answers may vary.

becomes shy	gets angry	is thoughtful	gets embarrassed
avoids situations	argues back	defends self	apologizes
accepts apologies	thinks out solutions	stays calm	gets confused
annoys others	makes situation worse	improves situation	

Roberto	Diep	Stan	Me

B. Interview some friends or members of your family. Write their answers. Answers will vary.

Name	What would you do if a co-worker asked you to do something dishonest?
1.	
2.	
3.	
4.	

---

learners complete the rest of the exercise. Have learners share and explain their answers.

4. Ask learners to think of questionable or dishonest things that a co-worker or client might ask them to do. (FOR EXAMPLE: Stan was asked to trim the hedges lower than they were supposed to be. Diep was asked to give out confidential information.) Ask learners how they would respond if asked to do something dishonest or contrary to company policy. List reactions on the board and have learners evaluate the pros and cons of the reactions. Have learners discuss if there is ever a good reason for not following company policies.
5. Have learners interview others to find more ways of responding to the same problem. Have learners share their findings with the group and discuss which responses might be effective. Learners can role-play situations based on their interview answers.

Expansion/Extension

See TRF HANDOUT 7.4, *Personal Priorities at Work*

More *Expansion/Extension* on page 127

Practicing Your Skills

Purpose: To give practice in problem solving and in reading and responding to advice columns

Teacher Preparation and Materials
No Smoking sign

Warm-up

1. Place the No Smoking sign at the front of the class. Ask learners to name buildings or rooms where they have seen the sign. Ask if there are other places where they think the sign should be posted. Ask if there are places where the sign should not be posted. Have learners explain their answers.

2. Ask learners what their reaction would be to someone who is smoking in a nonsmoking area. For example: *Would you ask the person not to smoke? Would you point out the sign to the smoker? Would you ignore the situation?* As a group, make a list of expressions for confronting the smoker. Then, have learners role-play confronting a person who is smoking in a nonsmoking area, using the list of expressions.

Presentation

1. Have learners turn to page 85, read the letter, and underline words they do not know. Elicit/explain the meanings of new words: *elegant, insist, nonsmoking customers.*

2. Ask literal and inferential questions about the letter. *What is the problem? What is your opinion of people who sit in a nonsmoking area and insist on smoking? What do you think of people who drop ashes on plates? Is "the customer always right"? Would you feel differently if this happened in a more informal restaurant?*

3. Have learners brainstorm and list possible solutions to the manager's problem. Then have learners individually write a response. Ask volunteers to share

---

A. Read this letter in the advice column "Dear Gabby."

> Dear Gabby,
> I am the manager of a very elegant restaurant. I only allow smoking in the smallest, least pleasant area of the restaurant. When customers who smoke come in and are seated there, they usually complain and want to sit in the nonsmoking area. Or when the smoking area is full, they don't want to wait and insist on sitting in the nonsmoking area. These customers often demand ashtrays or drop ashes on their plates. Then my nonsmoking customers complain that they can't breathe. I believe that "the customer is always right." My problem is, which customer? How can I handle my customers and keep them all happy?
> ***Confused Manager***
> Des Moines, IA

B. What would you do?
Answer the letter to "Dear Gabby." Use the questions to help write your letter.

- What could the manager do when someone wants to smoke in a nonsmoking area?
- Would you allow ashtrays in nonsmoking areas?
- Which customers do you agree with?
- Would you change the areas of the restaurant so smokers would feel more comfortable?
- Explain any ideas you have for solving this problem.

Answers may vary.

> Dear Manager,
> _____
> _____
> _____
> _____
> _____
> _____
> Sincerely,
> _____
> (your name)

---

their responses aloud. Have others in the group evaluate the potential effectiveness of the different solutions.

Expansion/Extension

- Ask learners to write letters to an advice column about a problem they have faced on the job or about a problem that one of the characters had in this unit. Learners can exchange letters and then write responses to the letters. Volunteers can share the different problems and possible solutions.

- Learners can role-play a restaurant scene with the manager who wrote the letter, talking to various vocal customers who are not pleased with their seats or with the smoking/nonsmoking policy.

- Ask learners to compile a vocabulary list for the unit. Learners can create categories and categorize the new words. Some categories might be Feelings, Work Rules, Job Evaluation Terms, and Miscellaneous.

Verbs: "Unreal" Conditional

Purpose: To give practice with *if/then* sentences expressing unreal conditions

Teacher Preparation and Materials
None

Warm-up

1. Use contrasts to review *if/then* sentences that express unreal conditions. Present learners with several true statements about yourself, their class or program, or the area in which you live. FOR EXAMPLE: *This program offers classes in the evenings, during the day, and on weekends. This area gets a lot of snow every winter.* Contrast these with unreal conditionals. FOR EXAMPLE: *If I couldn't teach ESL, I would be very disappointed. If the program offered classes only during the day, a lot of learners wouldn't be able to study. More people would come here to live if we didn't get so much snow.* Put examples on the board, and focus attention on the verb forms in each clause.

2. Elicit from learners true sentences and contrasting unreal conditionals about themselves, their work, their families, and so on. Ask questions if necessary to elicit and model the sentences. Put examples on the board, and focus attention on the verb forms in each clause.

Presentation

1. Have learners turn to page 86 and review the example sentences in the box. Focus attention on the verb forms in each clause.

2. Tell learners they are going to read more about Diep and the outcome of her performance evaluation. Review pages 78 and 80 if necessary. Tell learners that Mr. Myers, mentioned in the exercise, is director of the lab in which Diep works.

3. Review the example in the first exercise, and have learners complete the sentences. Review answers.

4. Ask learners to give Diep advice, based on information in the exercise. (FOR EXAMPLE:

---

86 **Verbs: "Unreal" Conditional**

I**'d feel** happy **if** I **had** a good job.
(would feel)

If Marco **had** a good job, he**'d feel** happy.
(would feel)

I **wouldn't be** happy **if** I **lost** my job.
(would not be)

If he **lost** his job, he **wouldn't be** happy.
(would not be)

A. Complete the sentences with a verb from the box.

not be	explain	✔get	look	tell	take

Example: Diep would feel better if she _____**got**_____ a promotion.

1. She **'d look**_____ for another job if she felt unappreciated.
2. If Diep asked, Mr. Myers **would explain**_____ his recommendation.
3. If Mr. Myers explained the evaluation, Diep _____**wouldn't be**_____ so upset.
4. If Diep _____**told**_____ Mr. Myers about the computer course, she'd receive a promotion.
5. Mr. Myers wouldn't be happy if Diep _____**took**_____ another job.

B. Imagine you work in a restaurant. Answer the questions. Use an unreal conditional. Answers will vary.

What would you do . . .

1. if a customer complained about your service?

   _____

2. if a customer said you'd brought the wrong sandwich?

   _____

3. if a customer asked for extra salad?

   _____

4. if a customer didn't leave a tip?

   _____

Diep, ask Mr. Myers to explain the evaluation. Tell him about the computer course. Tell him you are going to look for another job if you don't receive a promotion.)

5. Have learners work in pairs or small groups to complete the second exercise. Review responses as a class. Write or have learners write their suggestions on the board. Then discuss and evaluate them as a class.

Expansion/Extension

- Have learners discuss or write what they would do if they won the lottery.

- Have learners complete the sentence "If I were mayor, I would . . ." or "If I were president, I would. . . ." Have them give reasons for the actions they would take.

- Ask learners to identify problems in other work settings, similar to the restaurant in the second exercise. Have them imagine that they work in those other settings and tell what they would do if the problems arose. You may want to have each learner identify problems typical of his or her own job and then exchange papers with a partner in a different job.

Verbs: *Should have* + Past Participle/ Polite Forms

Purpose: To give practice in using *should have* + past participle and in distinguishing polite language

Teacher Preparation and Materials

▪▪▪ Audiotape for Level 3

Warm-up

1. Tell learners about a morning on which a lot of things went wrong. Tell what the person in the story should have done but didn't and what the consequences were. FOR EXAMPLE: *I should have set my alarm last night, but I didn't, so I overslept. I should have gotten up at six o'clock. Instead, I got up at seven-thirty. I didn't have time for breakfast, but I should have eaten something, because now I'm very hungry. I shouldn't have rushed out of the house. I forgot papers I needed for a meeting at work.*

2. Put examples of sentences with *should/ shouldn't have* + past participle on the board. Discuss what they mean, and focus learners' attention on the form of the verbs.

Presentation

1. Have learners turn to page 87 and read the example sentences. Draw attention to the forms of the past participle in each one.

2. Review the story on page 82 of Stan and his co-workers. ▪▪▪ Play the audiotape. Ask questions to remind learners of what happened. Ask if they think the men should have behaved differently

3. Explain that learners are going to write about what the men should or should not have done. Read the example in the first exercise. Ask, *Did Pete ask Stan to cover for Frank's mistake?* (Yes.) Discuss why Pete shouldn't have done this.

4. Have learners complete the exercise. Review answers. Discuss why the men should or should not have done each one,

and if not, what they should have done instead.

5. Ask learners if they have ever met someone, at work or in the community, who was rude to them. Ask what those people said or did that was rude.

6. Look at the example in the second exercise. Discuss why answer *b* is more polite than *a*.

7. Have learners complete the exercise. Review answers. Discuss any differences in responses, and discuss why learners feel the chosen answer is more polite than the other choice.

Expansion/Extension

- Have learners work in pairs or small groups to create conversations between a customer and a store clerk, waiter, or telephone operator; between neighbors; or between a parent and a child. Learners should create two versions of their conversation. In the first, one or both parties can speak rudely, while in the second both parties should speak politely.

- Have learners role-play their conversations. Help them use appropriate intonation to reinforce the rudeness or politeness in the conversation.

Verbs: *Should have* + *Past Participle*/Polite Forms — 87

He **should have been** careful with the saw.
They **should have talked** to their supervisor.
You **shouldn't have left** early yesterday.

Think about the story on page 82. Listen to the tape again if necessary. Complete the following sentences.

Example: Pete ___shouldn't have asked___ (not ask) Stan to cover for Frank's mistake.

1. Frank ___should have read___ (read) the work order.
2. He ___should have done___ (do) the work more carefully.
3. He and Pete ___shouldn't have trimmed___ (not trim) the hedges so low.
4. Stan ___shouldn't have yelled___ (not yell) at them.
5. He ___shouldn't have made___ (not make) Frank angry.
6. The three co-workers ___should have found___ (find) a better solution.

Check the polite form.

Example: _____ a. Excuse me, but it's your fault.
　　　　　✔ b. Perhaps we can find a solution together.

1. ✔ a. Pardon me. Please let me help with that.
　 _____ b. Here! Give it to me!
2. ✔ a. That's very kind of you.
　 _____ b. Yeah, thanks.
3. _____ a. I want you to help me now.
　 ✔ b. Excuse me, may I ask you a question?
4. _____ a. You can't have that! That's none of your business.
　 ✔ b. I'm not authorized to give out that information.
5. ✔ a. I appreciate your position, but I really need to see those forms.
　 _____ b. They're mine, and I demand that you give them to me right now.

UNIT 7: Problems on the Job
Expansion/Extension

Roberto's Apology
Expansion/Extension for SB page 76

See TRF HANDOUT 7.1, Conversation Bytes

- Learners can discuss Roberto's handling of the situation. Ask *How well do you think Roberto handled the apology? Did he seem sincere? In this type of situation, how important do you think it is that he remained calm? How long do you think Roberto has been working in a restaurant? Why?*

- Ask learners to categorize by formality the expressions from exercise B that are used to apologize and to accept apologies. FOR EXAMPLE:

	INFORMAL EXPRESSIONS	FORMAL EXPRESSIONS
Apologies	Oh, dear./Oh, no! I feel terrible. Uh oh. I didn't mean it/ to do it.	Excuse me. Please forgive me. I beg your pardon. I'm so/very/ terribly sorry. Pardon me.
Responses/ Acceptances	That's OK/all right. Don't worry about it. No problem. Forget about it. It happens all the time/to everybody.	You're forgiven. I accept your apology. I understand. You're excused.

- Learners can discuss how to tell if someone is being sincere or sarcastic. Elicit/explain meanings of the two terms. Say the different expressions from the chart, changing the tone and register. Have learners decide if you are being sincere or sarcastic.

Talking to the Boss
More *Expansion/Extension* for SB page 77

- Learners can discuss Marcel's handling of the situation. Ask *Do you think he overreacted to the situation in version 1? in version 2? Do you think he was right to wait until the restaurant was closed to approach Roberto about the incident? Do you think Marcel is a supportive or unsupportive manager? Why?*

No Promotion for Diep
More *Expansion/Extension* for SB page 78

- Bring in an Equal Employment Opportunity notice. Ask learners to find names of laws and agencies that protect workers from discriminatory practices. Learners can look through a local phone book for federal and state agencies that deal with job discrimination.

- Bring in copies of a workplace or labor union complaint form. Learners can discuss procedures for filing complaints and the types of information needed to file complaints or grievances with personnel offices or labor unions.

- Ask learners about promotions and raises. *Did you ever get a promotion or raise? How do different companies determine who receives promotions and raises and when to give them? Who can you ask for information about promotions and raises at your workplace? Do you think you deserve a promotion or raise?*

- Learners can write and/or role-play two conversations between Diep and her supervisor. FOR EXAMPLE: In one conversation, learners can have Diep question why she did not receive a promotion. In the other, learners can have Diep tell her supervisor that she is going to look for another job.

Following Company Policy
More *Expansion/Extension* for SB page 79

- Ask learners to role-play the two conversations using the expressions in exercise B.

- Prepare an oral True/False/No Information quiz. Learners can listen to the conversations again. Dictate statements and have learners mark their answers on a sheet of paper. FOR EXAMPLE: *Diep was annoyed that Ms. Morris interrupted the man. Ms. Morris can give out confidential information. Only doctors or nurses can give out test result information. Ms. Morris doesn't like Diep's work. Diep applied for a transfer. Ms. Morris knows why Diep didn't get the promotion. Diep leaves work at 4:00.*

- Ask learners to discuss Diep's and their own personal experiences in dealing with hostile customers, clients, bosses, or co-workers. *Why do you think the patient acted the way he did toward Diep? Have you ever had to work with someone who was hostile? How did you handle the situation? Do you think you handled the situation effectively? What are things you might have done differently? How did you feel after the confrontation?*

- Learners can brainstorm and list examples of assertive behavior. They can discuss how Diep might have handled the situation better by being more assertive and then rewrite the ending to the first conversation, making Diep more assertive.
- Bring in a sample employee manual or list of responsibilities for a particular job. Elicit/ explain why some workplaces have such material and what information is included.

Performance Evaluation
More *Expansion/Extension* for SB page 80

- Ask learners to make a performance evaluation form for their class. Learners can decide on criteria for evaluating class work and a rating system. Individually, learners can use the form to rate their own performance. If desired, learners can review their self-evaluation with you.
- List the following verbs on the board: *recommend, evaluate, terminate, promote, expect.* Say the verbs and have learners mark the accent or stress for each of the words. Ask learners to scan the evaluation form for nouns formed from the verbs. Write the nouns next to the appropriate verbs. Say the nouns and have learners mark the accent or stress. Ask learners to compare spellings and stress in the words. Learners can practice using the different forms in sentences about work or class evaluations.

Preparing for a Job Review
Expansion/Extension for SB page 81

- Learners can role-play a job review, with one learner asking questions and another learner answering from personal work or class experience.
- Learners can make a list of their own tips for talking with supervisors. Learners can write an advice article based on the list.
- Ask learners to prepare answers to the questions in the article for Diep to use for her meeting with Ms. Morris. Learners can role-play Diep talking

with Ms. Morris. Learners can also prepare answers for Roberto to use with his supervisor.

- Learners can talk or write about experiences they have had with job review meetings. Ask *Were the questions from this article used? What other questions were asked? Who did most of the talking? How did you feel after the review? Why? How might you have handled it differently?*

Hot under the Collar
More *Expansion/Extension* for SB page 82

- Learners can discuss loyalty in the workplace. Ask *Which is more important: honesty or loyalty? If you had to choose, do you think it is more important to get along with co-workers or to perform your work accurately? Why?*

How Do You Act under Pressure?
More *Expansion/Extension* for SB page 84

- Learners can look through employee manuals or personnel policies for information on consequences of dishonesty.
- Arrange for a supervisor or personnel manager to talk to the group about company policies and related personnel issues. Questions for discussion might include *Should you report a co-worker who is not following rules? Who can you talk to about problems with co-workers? about problems with supervisors?*
- Ask learners to discuss alternative actions by the characters in dealing with their workplace problems. *What would have happened if Roberto had gotten angry at Marcel? What would have happened if Diep had gotten angry? What if Stan had been thoughtful or stayed calm?*

Saving the Environment

Objectives

Functions
- Describing
- Giving directions
- Persuading
- Expressing agreement and disagreement
- Stating a position
- Expressing opinions

Life Tasks
- Reading and following recycling instructions/information
- Classifying recyclable materials
- Making charts
- Preparing a report
- Reading newspaper editorials
- Considering the impact of industrial development
- Disposing of hazardous waste

Structures
- Present perfect tense
- Reported speech with *that*
- *Wh-* questions: *why*
- *Should* vs. *must/have to*
- Dependent clauses

Culture
- Individual rights vs. the common good
- Making of local laws

Vocabulary

Key words:

chemical
city council
clean-up project
conservation
contamination
dispose
dump
energy
environment
environmentally sound

hazardous waste
persuade
pollution
recycle
recycling bins
recycling center
recycling symbol
toxic waste
trash

Key abbreviation:

EPA–Environmental Protection Agency

Related words:

acid rain
biotech industry
carpool
commuting
cut down
energy-efficient
EPA-registered
incineration
landfill disposal
nonpolluting
nontoxic
ozone layer

permit
proposed
research and development branch
secondary packaging
shrink-wrap
site
smokestack
substance
talk-show host
tax base

At the Recycling Center

Purpose: To introduce recycling vocabulary

Teacher Preparation and Materials

1. Large sheet of paper, marker
2. Local newspapers, scrapbook
   (Expansion/Extension)

Warm-up

1. In the center of the large sheet of paper write *Garbage*. Have learners suggest and list on the board items that are considered garbage. Elicit/introduce categories of garbage, such as Paper, Metal, Plastic, Glass, Chemical, Cloth, and Food. Create a semantic web, using the categories and names of garbage items.

2. Have learners comment on amounts and types of garbage. Ask *How often is trash/ garbage picked up in your area? Which category from the web makes up most of your garbage? How do you get rid of your garbage? Where does it go? Is everything really garbage or can some things be used again?* Write on the board *Recycle*. Elicit/ explain the meaning. Have learners check items on the semantic web that can be recycled and explain possible uses for the items. (**Note:** The semantic web will be used again for pages 89, 90, 96, and 98.)

Presentation

1. Have learners turn to page 88. Ask questions about the picture. *What do you see? What types of items are recycled here? How much work is it for people to recycle? Should people have to wait in line to get rid of their garbage? Why do you think these people want to recycle their garbage?* List words and comments on the board.

2. Ask learners to discuss the questions at the bottom of the page.

3. Have learners discuss how the title of the page relates to the unit title. If necessary, elicit/explain the meaning of *environment*. Learners can look back at page 65 for components of the environment. Ask *What is the environment? What makes up our*

At the Recycling Center

What are Cruz and Eddy doing?　　Answers will vary.
What is Adela doing?
Does your town recycle?
What can you recycle? What can't you recycle?

environment? What do you think is wrong with it? What are we "saving" it from? How serious do you think the problem is? How does recycling affect the environment? Do you think it makes a big difference?

Expansion/Extension

- Ask learners to research products that are made from recycled materials. Ask *What is done with the glass and bottles? What are newspapers used for? What can recycled plastic be used for? Are there recycling factories in your area? What types of materials do they use and what do they make?*

- Ask learners to write about their experiences or opinions about recycling. To help them prepare for writing, ask *Do you recycle any materials? Are materials recycled in your native country? What materials are recycled and how are they recycled? Do you think it is a good idea to recycle? Why or why not? How does it help the environment?* Learners can keep a copy of their writing in their portfolio.

More *Expansion/Extension* on page 142

Why Do We Sort Trash?

Purpose: To introduce expressing agreement and disagreement, reported speech with *that,* and *should* vs. *must/have to;* to give practice in describing and in giving directions; to give practice with dependent clauses and with *Wh-* questions with *why*

Teacher Preparation and Materials

1. Samples or pictures of recyclable products, nonrecyclable products, and products with the recycling symbol
2. Semantic web, used for page 88
3. ▄▄▄ Audiotape for Level 3
4. Large sheet of paper, marker

Warm-up

1. Bring in samples or pictures of products that have recycling symbols, other recyclable products, and some products that cannot be recycled. Have learners look at the semantic web to categorize the items by the materials they are made of. Ask learners to decide which products they think would be easier to recycle and to explain why.
2. Have learners look at products, such as plastic detergent containers, soda bottles, and plastic bags, for the recycling symbol. Ask *Why do you think the symbol uses arrows?*

Presentation

1. Have learners turn to page 89. Ask *What are they doing? What do you think they are talking about?* If learners have been to a recycling center, ask about what they saw and did there. Ask how and what things are recycled in your area.
2. ▄▄▄ Have learners listen to the audiotape. Ask literal and inferential questions, such as *What rules did they talk about? What reasons do they give for the rules? Do you think Adela is convinced that the rules are necessary?* ▄▄▄ Have learners listen again to the conversation. Make two columns on a large sheet of paper and list rules and

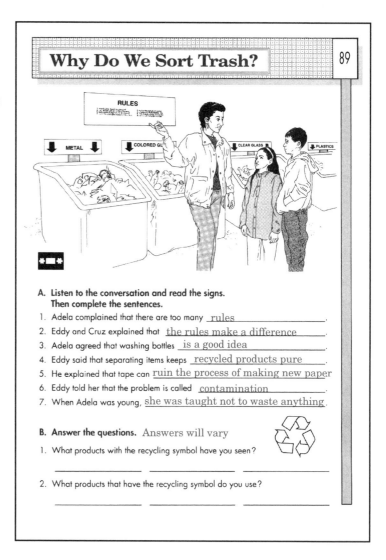

reasons. (**Note:** This list will be used again for page 90.) Elicit/explain the meaning of new words: *rinsing, makes sense, pure, contamination.*

3. Ask learners to complete exercise A. ▄▄▄ They can listen again to the conversation to verify answers.
4. Have learners discuss recycling. Ask *How much work is it to recycle? Should recycling be optional or mandatory?*
5. Ask learners to complete exercise B. This can be a homework assignment. Have learners share their findings.

Expansion/Extension

- Learners can go to a store and look for other products with the recycling symbol. Many plastic containers have a number inside the symbol. Learners can find out what the numbers signify and how they relate to recycling policies.

A Guide to Recycling

Purpose: To introduce reading and following recycling instructions/information; to give practice in classifying recyclable materials; to give practice with dependent clauses

Teacher Preparation and Materials

1. Brochures on recycling
2. List of recycling rules, used for page 89
3. Semantic web, used for pages 88 and 89
4. Copies of TRF Handout 8.1, *Reuse, Recycle, or Reject (Expansion/Extension)*

Warm-up

1. Bring in brochures on local recycling rules. Have learners scan the brochures for graphics and symbols. Elicit/explain the meanings of the symbols. Have learners look for recycling rules similar to the ones on the list they wrote for page 89.
2. If there is recycling in your area, review how it operates. Ask *Is there a recycling or drop-off center in this area? Do people put recyclable materials out with their trash in separate containers? How did you learn about the recycling policies?* Have learners suggest reasons why a particular method of collection is used in your area.

Presentation

1. Have learners turn to page 90. Have a volunteer read the title and the introduction. Have learners compare using recycling bins with going to a recycling center. Ask *Which do you think is easier for residents to use: recycling bins or recycling centers? Why? Which is more work for the recycling company? Which method would people be more likely to use if they had a choice?*
2. Ask learners to read the brochure. If necessary, have learners look at the semantic web used for pages 88 and 89. Have learners decide which products on the web could be recycled, according to the chart on page 90.
3. Have learners work in pairs or small groups to complete the exercise. Learners

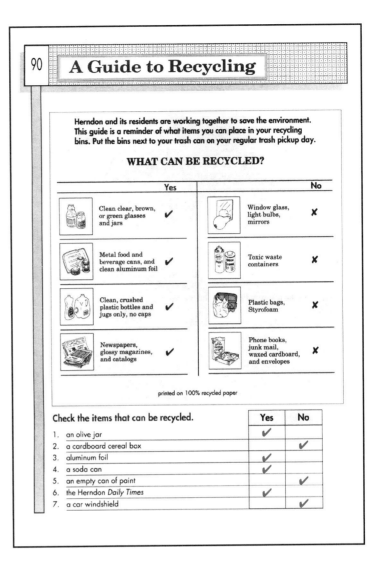

can suggest other items and decide if they are recyclable or not.

4. Ask learners to explain their answers by finding the category description in the brochure for each item.
5. Have learners underline new vocabulary words. Elicit/explain the meaning of new words: *beverage, crushed, glossy, aluminum foil, toxic waste, Styrofoam, waxed cardboard, recycled paper.* Use samples or pictures of products from page 89 to clarify meaning.
6. Ask learners to guess why certain products are not recyclable. (FOR EXAMPLE: Toxic waste containers may have some toxic waste inside that cannot be completely removed. Mirrors may have metal components and it would be difficult to separate the metal from the glass.)

Expansion/Extension

See TRF HANDOUT 8.1, *Reuse, Recycle, or Reject*

More *Expansion/Extension* on page 142

Too Much Packaging

Purpose: To give practice in describing; to introduce stating a position; to give practice with reported speech with *that*

Teacher Preparation and Materials

1. Samples of packaging materials: boxes, clear plastic wrap, shrink-wrap, aluminum foil, Styrofoam trays
2. ▄▄▄ Audiotape for Level 3
3. Copies of TRF Handout 8.3, *Cost, Convenience, or the Environment? (Expansion/Extension)*

Warm-up

Bring in samples of packaging materials. Elicit/introduce the names of the materials. Have learners name different products that are packaged with the materials.

Presentation

1. Have learners turn to page 91, read the title, and look at the picture. Ask *What do you think Adela and Roberto are talking about? What might have "too much packaging"?*
2. ▄▄▄ Play the audiotape. Ask literal and inferential questions about the conversation, such as *How much packaging is on the meat? What reasons does Adela give for using all the wrapping? What reasons does Roberto give for not using them? Why might people be worried about too much packaging? Why do you think Eddy and Cruz talked to their parents about environmental issues?*
3. Have learners read the questions in exercise A. Elicit/explain the meaning of *environmentally sound.*
4. ▄▄▄ Replay the audiotape. Ask learners to complete exercise A and to share their answers. Discuss various unnecessary packaging used in everyday life, such as giftwrapping and extra plastic bags for deli items. Ask *Which wrappings do you think people should give up? What types of wrapping are used in your native country?*

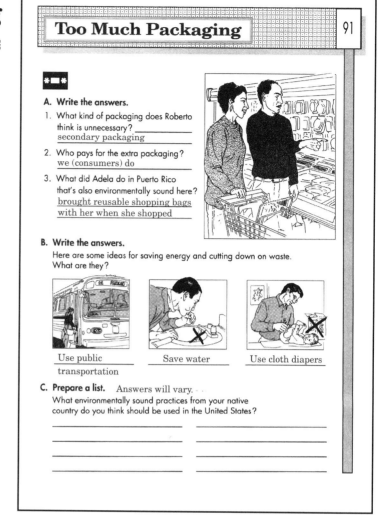

5. Have learners look at the pictures in exercise B and discuss how each idea saves energy or protects the environment. Ask learners to write the answers.
6. Ask learners to complete exercise C individually or in small groups. Bring learners together to share their lists. Compile a class list of environmentally sound practices.

Expansion/Extension

***See* TRF HANDOUT 8.3,** *Cost, Convenience, or the Environment?*

- Learners can find out about natural resource problems in the United States. Ask *What are some natural resource problems in the United States? What are some of the causes of the problems? Should natural resources be protected even if people will lose their jobs?*

A Field Trip

Purpose: To give practice in classifying recyclable materials and in making charts; to give practice with dependent clauses

Teacher Preparation and Materials

Picture of a polluted beach or riverfront (from a newspaper, magazine, or library book)

Warm-up

Have learners look at a picture of a polluted beach or riverfront. Ask *Why is there so much garbage in the picture? How do you think it got there? What dangers or problems are caused by the garbage? Who do you think should clean it up?*

Presentation

1. Have learners turn to page 92, look at the picture, and read the title of the page. Ask *What kind of a field trip do you think this is? What will the children learn from this field trip? Why do you think they are wearing work gloves? What do you think they will find to put in the garbage bags?*

2. Have learners read the story, including the list of items collected, and underline words they do not know. Elicit/explain the meanings of new words: *participate, Clean-up Project, reduce, pollution, deposit.*

3. Ask literal and inferential questions, such as *Why do you think the children are working with the Clean-up Project? What are the goals of the project? What are the bags for? Which bag do you think will have the most items? Why?*

4. Have learners look at the chart. Ask volunteers to name an item from the list for each of the categories on the chart. Have learners complete the exercise individually or in pairs. Bring learners together and have them explain their answers.

5. Have learners think of additional items that might be found near or in a river. Ask learners to sort them by the categories on the chart.

---

92 **A Field Trip**

Each child in Cruz Silva's class had to do a project about helping the environment. Cruz and several of her classmates decided to form a team and participate in Herndon's Annual Riverbank Clean-up Project.

The Clean-up Project had three purposes: to pick up trash on the riverbank, to reduce pollution in the river, and to recycle as much of the trash as possible. Cruz and her friends each used a large bag to pick up various items on the riverbank. They had separate bags for glass; for plastic; for items that can be reused or returned, such as deposit bottles and cans or usable sports equipment; and for items that cannot be recycled or reused.

Here's some of what they found. Put each item in the right bag.

1 shoe	a bicycle tire	a shoelace
a pickle jar	18 deposit cans	2 tennis balls
a juice bottle	a torn sweatshirt	a plastic football
5 gum wrappers	11 deposit bottles	an empty detergent bottle
2 plastic milk bottles	a broken fishing pole	an empty jug of windshield cleaner

Glass That Can Be Recycled	Plastic That Can Be Recycled	Items That Can Be Reused or Returned	Items That Cannot Be Recycled or Returned
juice bottle	jug of windshield cleaner	11 deposit bottles	5 gum wrappers
pickle jar	detergent bottle	bicycle tire	1 shoe
	2 plastic milk bottles	18 deposit cans	a torn sweatshirt
		2 tennis balls	a shoelace
		plastic football	broken fishing pole

Expansion/Extension

- Have learners list ways to prevent the accumulation of litter and trash in public areas. They can call or write to local or national environmental groups for information and ideas. Learners can check with the appropriate local agency on how to request additional trash receptacles and what the consequences and fines are for littering and illegal dumping.

- Learners can identify a local site that needs to be cleaned up and write a letter to the editor of the local paper about it. Ask learners to include suggestions for how the clean-up could be done, who could participate, when it could be done, and so on.

- Ask learners to arrange their own class clean-up project. They can select a place, such as a school yard or local park and collect trash. They can compile a list of items collected and arrange for the return, recycling, or disposal of the items. Check with local government to see if permission is needed and if supplies (garbage bags, bins, etc.) might be available.

More *Expansion/Extension* on page 142

Conservation Reports

Purpose: To give practice in stating a position, in describing, in problem solving, and in preparing a report

Teacher Preparation and Materials

1. Large sheet of paper, marker
2. Information on water filters (*Expansion/Extension*)
3. Copies of TRF Handout 8.2, *Energy Quiz* (*Expansion/Extension*)
4. Copies of TRF Handout 8.4, *Your Electrical Appliances and Your Electric Bill (Expansion/Extension)*
5. Magazines with pictures of conservation methods, scissors, tape, posterboard, and glue for all (*Expansion/Extension*)

Warm-up

On the board write the word *conservation*. Elicit/explain the meaning or have learners look it up in a dictionary. Write a simple definition after the word, such as *protection from loss, waste,* or *harm*. Have learners brainstorm things in the environment that need to be protected. Make a list of ideas on the board. Have learners explain why each needs to be protected and what some conservation solutions might be.

Presentation

1. Have learners turn to page 93. Have a volunteer read the title and introductory paragraph. Ask *Who decided the topics for the reports? Where are the students going to get information for their reports? Who are they going to interview for the reports? What do you think the students will do with the information?*
2. Have learners read the three topic headings. Ask volunteers to restate the problems in their own words. Have learners suggest reasons for the problems.
3. Have learners think of another solution for each of the problems and record it.

Conservation Reports

93

Cruz and her classmates had to write a report about helping the environment. The teacher gave them several environmental problems. She asked the students to interview their family and friends to help find some solutions to the problems.

Interview. Then complete the class reports. Answers will vary.
Each problem is followed by one solution. Interview some friends or family members and record their solutions.

Water Conservation: How to Use Less and Keep It Pure

Name	Solution
Roberto	*Motor oil and paint can poison the drinking water, so don't pour them down the drain.*

Air Pollution: How Can We Make the Air Better to Breathe?

Name	Solution
Adela	*Organize a car pool or use public transportation instead of driving alone.*

Energy Conservation: The Less We Use, the More We Save

Name	Solution
Eddy	*Replace regular bulbs with energy-efficient bulbs. They cost more to buy, but they last longer and save money on your energy bills.*

Then ask learners to interview others in the class and record their solutions on the report form. ■ In a one-to-one situation, have the learner interview friends or co-workers.

4. Have learners share the interview responses. Record solutions on a large chart for the entire class. Depending on learners' skills and interests, ask them to write a paragraph on each of the problems and to suggest appropriate solutions.
5. Have learners choose the problem they think is the most important. Ask learners to explain their choices. (FOR EXAMPLE: I think energy conservation is the most important problem here. Oil and gas supplies are limited. We need new sources for energy.)

Expansion/Extension

See TRF HANDOUT 8.2, *Energy Quiz*
TRF HANDOUT 8.4, *Your Electrical Appliances and Your Electric Bill*

More *Expansion/Extension* on page 142

MediKit Deserves to Build

Purpose: To give practice in reading newspaper editorials, in stating a position, in persuading, and in evaluating point of view; to introduce present perfect tense; to give practice with reported speech with *that*

Teacher Preparation and Materials

1. Picture of a factory with smokestacks and lots of cars and trucks in the parking lot
2. Large sheet of paper, marker

Warm-up

1. Bring in a picture of a large factory. Have learners imagine that this factory is being built next to their apartment building or house. Have learners brainstorm the pros and cons of living next to a factory. List learners' ideas on a large sheet of paper. (**Note:** This list will be used again for page 95.)
2. Ask if some types of factories would be more acceptable than others. Elicit/ introduce names of different industries. Be sure to include *biotech* and *chemical*.

Presentation

1. Have learners turn to page 94. Have a volunteer read the title and first paragraph. Ask *Do you think town and city councils should give permits to everyone who wants to construct a building? What are some reasons why they would grant a permit to a business? What types of questions do you think the Herndon Town Council has about MediKit?*
2. Have learners read the editorial and underline new words. Elicit/explain the meanings of new words: *facility, biotech, beneficial, sterile, site, tax base, economic stability, potential, components, acres, sensitivity, contribute, densely populated, effect, profound, pumped into, ignore, commence, specifies, multiple.*
3. Ask literal and inferential questions, such as *How long has MediKit been in*

business? *Do you think MediKit has problems with its other facilities? What does MediKit say it will bring to Herndon? Is this editorial for or against the new business? Which argument do you think is the most convincing for the company? Why? What is the difference between an editorial and a news article?*

4. Discuss the questions at the bottom of the page. In larger classes, have learners work in small groups. Have learners explain their responses. ▪ In a one-to-one situation, have the learner answer the questions and then discuss his or her responses.
5. Have learners brainstorm a list of questions that the town council might want MediKit to answer.

Expansion/Extension

- Learners can write a letter to the editor of the local paper in Herndon, urging the town council to ask MediKit some questions (prepared in *Presentation* #5) about the proposed biotech facility.

---

94 | MediKit Deserves to Build

MediKit Deserves to Build

There has been a lot of discussion about the pros and cons of allowing MediKit Technical International to build a new facility in Herndon. MediKit is pressing the Herndon Town Council to grant the permits it needs to begin building. Meanwhile, the town council is currently considering whether or not to grant MediKit the permits.

The development of a new biotech industry in Herndon is wholly beneficial to our community. MediKit produces a valuable medical product: sterile blood-test kits for medical laboratories in the mid-Atlantic states. MediKit's choice of Herndon as the site for expanding production can only offer our community more jobs, a wider tax base, and greater economic stability.

Some in the community fear that a company which uses chemicals in a manufacturing process is a potential air or water polluter. They don't know MediKit. MediKit's president, Alfred Gomez, assures us that almost 50 years in the business has given the company the opportunity to learn how to reuse or recycle all possible components of its chemical products.

MediKit has chosen three undeveloped acres in southeast Herndon as its new site. This is another example of the corporation's sensitivity to the community. MediKit has assured the town council that it will not contribute to the traffic problems in our densely populated town.

A spokesperson for MediKit estimates that the company will provide up to 500 direct jobs for local citizens and almost as many indirect jobs to support those employees, in such fields as food service, construction, personal service, and education. The effect on the economy will be profound. MediKit estimates that between one and two million dollars a year will be pumped into the local economy. These are numbers that we should not ignore. We urge the town council to grant the necessary permit for our new neighbor to commence operations speedily.

Opponents of this permit are sensible people. Once MediKit specifies how it recycles and disposes of its waste and people understand the multiple benefits of a new, local company, we believe these reasonable people will surely change their minds.

Think and talk about the questions. Answers may vary.

1. How does this editorial try to persuade the Herndon Town Council to grant the permit for MediKit?
2. Where did most of the facts from this editorial come from?
3. How does the editorial deal with its opponents?
4. Can you think of any reasons to disagree with the editorial?

Different Viewpoints

Purpose: To give practice in stating a position, in expressing agreement and disagreement, and in evaluating point of view; to introduce considering the impact of industrial development

Teacher Preparation and Materials

1. List used for page 94
2. 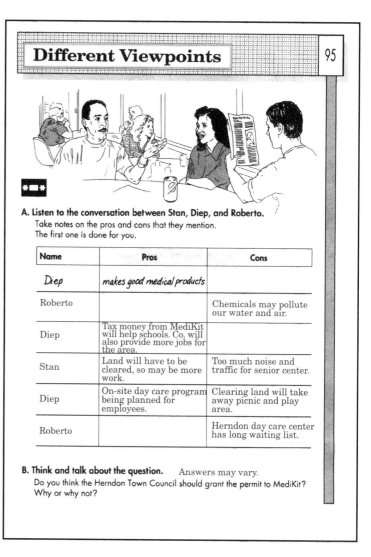 Audiotape for Level 3
3. Copies of TRF Handout 8.5, *What's Important to You? (Expansion/Extension)*

Warm-up

Have learners look at the list used for page 94. For each of the pros and cons listed, have learners name who or what in the vicinity of the factory might be affected. (FOR EXAMPLE: More trucks on the roads might be dangerous to children playing nearby and might make more noise for everyone. More jobs might be helpful for unemployed people.)

Presentation

1. Have learners turn to page 95. Ask learners to read the title and to look at the picture. Have learners predict possible viewpoints of each of the characters based on their jobs and other known information.

2. Ask learners to read the instructions for exercise A and to look at the chart. Play the audiotape and have learners take notes on another sheet of paper.

3. Ask learners to use their notes to summarize the information that they heard. Have learners copy their notes into the student book. If necessary, have learners listen to the audiotape again to fill in any missing information.

4. Ask literal and inferential questions about the conversation, such as *Who is in favor of MediKit and why? Who disapproves? Name some of the things that the characters are concerned about. Which of their concerns do you think are the most important? Why? Why are the issues so complicated?*

A. Listen to the conversation between Stan, Diep, and Roberto.
Take notes on the pros and cons that they mention.
The first one is done for you.

Name	Pros	Cons
Diep	makes good medical products	
Roberto		Chemicals may pollute our water and air.
Diep	Tax money from MediKit will help schools. Co. will also provide more jobs for the area.	
Stan	Land will have to be cleared, so may be more work.	Too much noise and traffic for senior center.
Diep	On-site day care program being planned for employees.	Clearing land will take away picnic and play area.
Roberto		Herndon day care center has long waiting list.

B. Think and talk about the question. Answers may vary.
Do you think the Herndon Town Council should grant the permit to MediKit? Why or why not?

5. Have learners discuss the question at the bottom of the page. Learners should be prepared to defend their positions.

6. Learners can brainstorm and make a list of additional information that the Herndon Town Council should request from MediKit to make a more informed decision on the permit. Point out to learners that in this stage of business planning, everything is negotiable. The town council and MediKit can make a compromise, MediKit may decide on another location, and so on.

Expansion/Extension

See TRF HANDOUT 8.5, *What's Important to You?*

- Learners can work in small groups to rank the pros and cons on page 95 in the order of importance. Bring the groups together and have learners present and explain their rankings. As a class, come to an agreement on the rankings.

More *Expansion/Extension* on page 142

Hazardous Waste: Handle with Rubber Gloves

Purpose: To introduce disposing of hazardous waste; to give practice in describing, in persuading, in stating a position, and in evaluating points of view; to give practice with reported speech with *that*

Teacher Preparation and Materials

1. Semantic web, used for pages 88, 89, and 90
2. Samples or pictures of containers for toxic or hazardous materials, such as insecticides, antifreeze, disinfectants, bleach, and turpentine
3. [cassette] Audiotape for Level 3
4. Information on lead poisoning *(Expansion/Extension)*

Warm-up

1. Have learners refer to the semantic web. Ask learners which items are poisonous or could be dangerous. Elicit/introduce new vocabulary: *hazardous waste, toxic, nontoxic.*
2. Ask learners how to find out if a product is hazardous or not. Have learners look on containers for household cleaning products, gardening products, or automotive products for warnings and cautions.

Presentation

1. Have learners turn to page 96, read the title, and look at the pictures. Ask *Who is Stan calling? What do you think they will talk about? Have you ever heard a radio call-in program? Do you think they give useful information?* Point out that radio shows often bring in experts with opposing viewpoints.
2. [cassette] Play part A of the audiotape. Have learners summarize the conversation. Then have learners do exercise A. [cassette] Learners can listen again to the conversation to verify responses.
3. Have learners discuss the questions in exercise B. Learners can refer to the

---

96 Hazardous Waste: Handle with Rubber Gloves

A. Answer the questions.

1. What hazardous substances does Stan want to dispose of? paint brushes, paint thinner, floor cleaners, weed killer
2. What steps should Stan take when he's disposing of hazardous household substances? Tighten caps and lids; pack items upright in a box; don't mix chemicals and hazardous waste products; never smoke.

B. Think and talk about the questions. Answers will vary.

1. What hazardous household substances do you have at home?
2. How do you dispose of them?
3. Can you think of any ways to reuse or recycle them?

C. Complete the story.

Richard Rivera works for MediKit. He said that the __amount__ of chemicals
                                                      1
his company uses has __declined__ 85 percent since 1949. Most of the
                          2
__chemicals__ that MediKit now uses are nontoxic and nonpolluting. The
      3
__toxic__ chemicals that MediKit does use are __disposed__ of by high
    4   5
temperature incineration. Talk-show host Ron Fisher asked if incineration
__affects__ the ozone layer or causes acid __rain__. Rivera said that
    6   7
there were __problems__ with incineration but it was better than __landfill__
                8   9
disposal. He also mentioned the motto __Reduce__, Reuse, and Recycle.
                                          10

---

semantic web for names of substances and look on containers for information on proper disposal.

4. [cassette] Play part B of the audiotape. Ask literal and inferential questions, such as *What company does Richard Rivera work for? Are all the chemicals that MediKit uses toxic? Where do the toxic chemicals go? Do you think the talk-show host is for or against MediKit? Why?*
5. [cassette] Replay the conversation. Have learners complete exercise C. Point out that there is more than one correct way to complete some of the sentences.
6. Have learners underline new words in the story. Elicit/explain the meanings of new words: *declined, nonpolluting, incineration, ozone layer, acid rain, motto.*
7. Ask learners to identify the differences between the two guest speakers on the talk show. Ask *Which guest gave more precise information and was more objective? Which guest was trying to persuade people? Do you trust the information that each of the guests gave? Why or why not?*

Expansion/Extension on page 142

Problems and Solutions

Purpose: To give practice in problem solving; to give practice with *should* vs. *must/have to*

Teacher Preparation and Materials

1. Copies of TRF Handout 8.6, *Town Proposal (Expansion/Extension)*
2. Copies of TRF Handout 8.7, *It's Your Vote! (Expansion/Extension)*

Warm-up

Have learners look back at the editorial on page 94 and the list of pros and cons on page 95. Have learners summarize the major problems of the proposed MediKit factory. Ask learners if they think the problems can be solved and, if so, how.

Presentation

1. Have learners turn to page 97. Have a volunteer read the title and introductory paragraph. Ask *Why doesn't the town council give MediKit the permit and let MediKit solve the problems after the completion of the building? What do you think will happen if the council doesn't like MediKit's proposed solutions?*

2. Have learners read the first problem and underline new words. Elicit/explain the meanings of *proposed site* and *commuting*. Have learners restate the problem in their own words. Then have them identify the people, places, or things involved in the problem and how they might be changed to solve the problem. (FOR EXAMPLE: narrow streets—make streets wider; two-way streets—make streets one-way; employees commuting—provide alternative transportation)

3. Repeat the procedure for the other two problems and exercise B.

4. Have learners discuss their proposed solutions for the problems. In large classes, have learners work in small groups, with one learner acting as the recorder and another as the reporter. Encourage learners to come up with as

many different solutions as possible. Have the groups share their answers and explain why they think the proposed solutions will work. Have others ask for clarification and/or raise objections. Compile a list of suggested solutions and have learners vote on which one they think is the most effective and practical. ■ In a one-to-one situation, have the learner think of several solutions for each problem, then choose one and present or write a report on it.

Expansion/Extension

See TRF HANDOUT 8.6, *Town Proposal*
TRF HANDOUT 8.7, *It's Your Vote!*

- Learners can role-play a meeting between representatives for the MediKit company and the Herndon Town Council. The MediKit representatives can offer their proposed solutions to the problems and try to persuade the council members to accept them. The council members should question how each proposal would address all the issues involved.

There are some problems that must be solved before the Herndon Town Council will permit MediKit to build its new plant.

A. Read each problem and think about possible solutions. Then write your ideas for each one. Answers will vary.

1. The narrow, two-way streets around MediKit's proposed site cannot handle the increased traffic of employees commuting to work and trucks carrying materials in and out of the factory.

   Possible solution(s): _____

2. Daytime truck noise and factory noise will interfere with activities in the senior center across from the new site.

   Possible solution(s): _____

3. MediKit would have to cut down an extra acre of trees in order to build the planned on-site day-care center for employees' children.

   Possible solution(s): _____

B. What else can MediKit do to help the community? Write your idea. Answers will vary.
Explain what it will require and how it will benefit the town and/or the company.

_____

Practicing Your Skills

Purpose: To give practice in describing an idea and in reading company announcements

Teacher Preparation and Materials

Semantic web used for pages 88, 89, 90, and 96

Warm-up

1. Have learners look at the semantic web. Then have learners review types of materials that can be recycled.

2. Ask *Are there any places in town that have signs about recycling or have containers for recycling?* If necessary, provide some examples, such as the supermarket that asks customers to bring in plastic shopping bags for recycling and automotive stores that accept used car oil. Have learners suggest other places that might encourage the recycling of different products or materials.

Presentation

1. Have learners turn to page 98 and read the hospital announcement and Diep's winning application. Have learners underline words they do not know. Elicit/explain the meanings of new words: *implemented, promotes, letterhead, computerizes, discards, supplement*.

2. Ask literal and inferential questions, such as *Why do you think the hospital had the contest? Will this idea cost the hospital any money?* (pay for workers to store, load, and transport the paper; mileage and fuel costs to transport the paper; and so on) *Will the hospital save any money with this idea?*

3. Have learners brainstorm ideas for starting a class/school/learning center recycling plan for improving a local recycling project. Make a list of the ideas on the board. Have learners individually write a draft of their idea or one of the ideas listed on the board. In pairs, have learners exchange drafts. Learners should read, ask questions about, and review the

| 98 | **Practicing Your Skills** |

Dear Hospital Employees:
City Hospital announces a $100 reward to Diep Tran for her winning idea for reducing waste in our hospital. Congratulations, Ms. Tran!

Here is Ms. Tran's winning application. Her idea will be implemented immediately.

Name: Diep Tran
Employee #: 021323

Idea for Conservation:

Every month, some department changes a form, promotes someone and prints new letterhead, or computerizes information and discards stacks of file cards. I suggest we donate the old forms, letterhead, and file cards to local public schools. They can use old forms to practice math problems, use the backs of letterhead to photocopy messages home to parents, and use file cards to make flash cards. Not only do we reduce paper and help supplement school budgets, but every time the paper is reused, someone is reminded that City Hospital cares about our schools and environment.

Imagine that your town offers a prize for the best way to start or improve recycling in your area.

Write your idea here. Answers will vary.
Here are some questions that will help.

- What's the idea?
- What aspect of the environment does it help? (saving energy or other resources, reducing pollution, reducing trash)
- How would it work?
- Who would be involved?
- How much would it save (or cost)?
- Are there any other benefits from this idea?

_____
_____
_____
_____

drafts for clarity, grammar, spelling, and punctuation. Then have learners rewrite the idea in their books.

Expansion/Extension

- Learners can rewrite their ideas as an editorial or letter to the editor of a local newspaper.

- Set up a school or class contest similar to the hospital contest. Learners can prepare an announcement for the contest and set up a place/box for collecting entries. Arrange for an impartial person or panel of people to read and judge the entries. If possible, have a prize for the best entry.

- Ask learners to compile a vocabulary list for the unit. Learners can create categories and categorize the new words. Some categories might be Environmental Problems/Solutions, Garbage Disposal, Agencies/Businesses, and Miscellaneous.

Verbs: Present Perfect Tense

Purpose: To give practice in forming and using the present perfect tense

Teacher Preparation and Materials

1. Brochures on recycling, used for page 90
2. A report or history of local recycling efforts, if available *(Warm-up)*
3. Addresses of politicians at the local, state, and federal levels *(Expansion/Extension)*

Warm-up

1. Review use of the present perfect tense with a simple time line. Show learners when you moved to your current city or town; then use the time line to demonstrate how long you have lived there. Similarly, show on the time line when you started teaching in your current position and how long you have taught there. Write sentences about this information on the board, contrasting the past and present perfect tenses and focusing attention on verb forms.

2. Use a report or history of local recycling efforts to create a time line showing when recycling of various products began in your area, how long it has been going on, and how much has been recycled in that period. Write sentences relating this information, contrasting the tenses and focusing attention on present perfect forms.

Presentation

1. Have learners turn to page 99 and read example sentences from the chart.

2. Review or explain new vocabulary from the exercise, such as *electricity usage, usage savings, lower-watt bulbs,* and *reminders.*

3. Read the first sentence of the exercise to explain the topic of the paragraph and to make sure learners understand how to use the prompts under the write-on lines.

4. Have learners complete the exercise. Review answers, then ask questions to check comprehension. Ask learners if they think the projects are useful, and if so, why.

| I
You
We
They | **have** | **recycled** | newspapers every week. |
| He
She
It | **has** | **done** | it for many years. |

Complete the paragraph with verbs in the present perfect. Then write about yourself.

Cruz and Eddy's school ___**has held**___ an Environment Day program
                              hold

for several years. The school **has encouraged** all students to participate.
                                  encourage

The students ___**have asked**___ their parents to help, too. Each grade
                    ask

___**has chosen**___ one issue. Eddy's grade ___**has worked**___ on
   choose   *work*

reducing electricity usage in their school and homes.

Eddy ___**has made**___ a usage-savings chart with three friends.
           make

They ___**have written**___ directions for their chart. Each student
            write

___**has taken**___ a chart home. All the groups **have developed**
   take   *develop*

good ideas. One group ___**has replaced**___ the lights with lower-watt bulbs.
                            replace

Another ___**has drawn**___ reminders to shut off lights in empty rooms.
              draw

How have you helped the environment?
Answers will vary.
_____

5. Have learners discuss and then write personal answers to the question *How have you helped the environment?*

6. As learners share their answers, compile responses on a chart identifying the ways in which the class as a whole has helped the environment. Learners can discuss if they have benefited personally from their efforts, and if they have learned new ideas that they can apply at home, at work, or in their community.

Expansion/Extension

• If learners began a class clean-up project from *Expansion/Extension* for page 92, they may be ready to report on what they have accomplished so far.

• Learners may wish to learn what local, state, or federal politicians representing their area have done to help the environment. Learners can research positions and voting records by contacting the politicians' offices (by phone or mail), checking government web sites, or contacting environmental organizations.

• Learners could compose a letter to politicians expressing their own positions on environmental issues and asking *How have you helped the environment?*

Modals: *Should, Must/Have to/* Reported Speech

Purpose: To give practice in using *should* vs. *must* or *have to* and in using reported speech

Teacher Preparation and Materials

1. Flyers, memos, or brochures listing local ordinances (such as parking regulations) or school rules (such as dress codes or attendance policies) *(Warm-up)*
2. ▣▣▣ Audiotape for Level 3
3. Brochure or flyer listing local recycling and hazardous waste policies (This information may also be in a local phone book.) *(Expansion/Extension)*

Warm-up

1. Have learners read one or more lists of ordinances or school rules. Mention examples from the lists, and ask, *Is this something I am required to do, or is it something that's just a good idea?* Leash laws or parking regulations are examples of requirements. Locking a bicycle or holding a handrail when using a school staircase is a good idea but not required.
2. As learners respond, rephrase the item using *should* or *must / have to.* FOR EXAMPLE: *Lock your bike when you leave it in the bike rack.* (Good idea.) *Yes, you should lock your bike in the bike rack. Walk your dog on a leash.* (Required.) *Yes, you must have a leash on your dog.*
3. In some cases, rules will already be expressed with *should* or *must / have to.* Have learners skim the lists, circling rules expressed with *should* and putting a star next to ones that use *must* or *have to.*

Presentation

1. Have learners turn to page 100 and review the examples in the charts. Discuss why reusing paper bags is only a suggestion or good idea, while recycling newspapers is a requirement (in most parts of the country).

---

100 | **Modals:** *Should, Must/Have to/* **Reported Speech**

I You He She It We They	**should**	reuse paper bags.

I You We They	**have to/must**	recycle newspapers.
He She It	**has to/must**	

Rules for Herndon's Trash and Recycling Station

▶ Herndon residency required for Trash and Recycling permits.
▶ Brush and tree stumps can be no longer than 4'.
▶ Please rinse all bottles, cans, and plastics before recycling.
▶ Dispose of lightbulbs and ceramics with trash. Do not recycle.
▶ Please put deposit bottles and cans in specially marked bins.
▶ Tie or bag magazines and newspapers before recycling.
▶ Disposal of hazardous waste or batteries is prohibited at this Station.

Complete the sentences. Use *should* or *must/have to, has to.*

1. Al and Yolette ____must____ live in Herndon to use this Station.
2. Al ____has to____ cut up a 6' branch before he throws it away.
3. He ____should____ keep deposit bottles separate from other glass.
4. Yolette ____should____ wash out her cans before recycling them.
5. Al ____must____ put a broken mixing bowl in his trash.

What did Cruz tell her mother? Use reported speech. Answers will vary.

Example: recycling rules
____Cruz told her mother that recycling rules are important.____

1. dirty bottles or cans

_____

2. leaving caps on bottles

_____

---

2. Read the rules for Herndon's trash and recycling station. Elicit/explain new or difficult vocabulary *(residency, permits, stumps, specially marked bins, to bag, hazardous waste).*
3. Read item 1 in the first exercise. Have learners identify the rule that determines the answer to this item ("Herndon residency required").
4. Have learners complete the exercise. Review answers, and ask learners to identify the rule that determines the answer in each case.
5. ▣▣▣ Play the audiotape for page 89. Have learners listen to the conversation, then complete the second exercise by using reported speech to write what Cruz told her mother about recycling. ▣▣▣ If necessary, replay the tape so learners can check what Cruz said.

Expansion/Extension

- Have learners read recycling regulations for the area in which they live. Elicit examples of what they must or should do with their trash to follow local regulations.

UNIT 8: Saving the Environment
Expansion/Extension

At the Recycling Center
More *Expansion/Extension* for SB page 88

- Learners can look through local newspapers for articles on environmental issues. Learners can collect articles in a scrapbook or on a bulletin board. Throughout the unit, learners can add articles and categorize them by the types of environmental problems. (recycling and trash, air pollution, water pollution, energy conservation, etc.)

A Guide to Recycling
More *Expansion/Extension* for SB page 90

- Learners can set up a class or group recycling project. They can decide what items to collect for recycling, where to store items, and how to get items picked up or to the recycling center. Learners can prepare a chart describing items to be collected and a list of recycling rules. After the project, they can write a report about their recycling efforts for a local newspaper or school newsletter.

A Field Trip
More *Expansion/Extension* for SB page 92

- Ask learners to write a report about their local clean-up project, describing why it was held and what effect it has had/will have on the environment and community.

Conservation Reports
More *Expansion/Extension* for SB page 93

- Learners can find out where their water comes from. Ask *Is there a water reservoir in your area? How is the area protected? How is the water made clean?* Learners may want to contact local or state agencies, such as natural resource agencies, environmental conservation departments, or water resource authorities.

- Ask learners to contact local natural gas and electric companies for conservation ideas. Have learners gather information that is sent out periodically with bills.
- Ask learners to make posters or ads to promote conservation. Posters can be displayed in the classroom or on bulletin boards in the school.

Different Viewpoints
More *Expansion/Extension* for SB page 95

- ▨ Learners can listen again to the audiotape and make a list of phrases used to express and ask for opinions. (FOR EXAMPLE: I think it's great! I'm not so sure that I want the company there. I just don't want . . . .) Then ask learners to practice using the expressions to give their opinions or to ask others about their opinions on Medikit or a similar issue. Learners can brainstorm and list additional phrases. (FOR EXAMPLE: What about the fact that . . . ? How do you know . . . ? I heard that . . . . That's one thing I'm not too happy about.)
- Learners can prepare a debate on a conservation versus development issue that is relevant to the local area. Learners can choose sides and prepare their arguments and counterarguments.
- Ask learners to write a letter to the editor of the local paper or a local official to present their point of view on the issue that was debated in the previous activity.

Hazardous Waste:
Handle with Rubber Gloves
Expansion/Extension for SB page 96

- Ask learners to list suggestions for storing hazardous substances at home. (FOR EXAMPLE: Don't leave containers open. Keep containers out of reach of children. Keep containers locked up.)
- Bring in information on lead poisoning. Discuss or have learners find out what causes lead poisoning, why it is dangerous, how people can be tested for lead poisoning, how people can find out if lead paint was used in their homes, and what community services/agencies are concerned with lead poisoning.
- Learners can check on local guidelines and procedures for disposal of hazardous substances, from both households and companies.

Real Costs of a Car

Objectives

Functions
- Explaining and describing (problems, events)
- Dealing with numbers

Life Tasks
- Questioning a repair bill
- Checking a procedure in a maintenance manual
- Reading an insurance policy
- Using consumer reports to get information on new cars
- Reading classified ads
- Comparing bank loan information
- Asking for an estimate
- Figuring costs
- Understanding abbreviations

Structures
- *Should*
- Dependent clauses of reason
- Dependent clauses of time
- *Wh-* questions
- Past continuous tense

Culture
- Reasons for buying insurance
- Consumer protection

Vocabulary

Key words:

bodily injury liability	labor
body work	list price
brakes	matching down payment
claim	property damage liability
collision	
comprehensive	quarterly payment
coverage	rate
deductible	rebate
discount	registration fees
down payment	responsibility
fender	routine maintenance
finance	surcharge
garage	tow truck
guaranteed	trade
insurance company	uninsured motorist

Related words:

4-speed	make
air bag	manual
air conditioning	maximum
AM/FM stereo	model
antilock	mpg (miles per gallon)
automatic	
cargo area	odometer
dented	oil
dipstick	oil change
drain pan	oil filter
drain plug	registration number
flexible	shop around
impersonal	transmission
incentive	transmission fluid
intersection	wrench
jack	year

Checking Out a Car

Purpose: To give practice in explaining and describing problems; to introduce car repair and car maintenance vocabulary

Teacher Preparation and Materials

1. Large sheet of paper, marker
2. Pictures of different types of cars
3. Copies of TRF Handout 9.1, *Parts of a Car (Expansion/Extension)*
4. Local yellow pages *(Expansion/Extension)*

Warm-up

1. In the center of the large sheet of paper write *Car*. Have learners suggest car-related vocabulary. List it on the board. Elicit/introduce categories, such as Car Parts, Types of Cars, and Car Problems. Create a semantic web, using the categories and car vocabulary. (**Note:** The web can be used throughout the unit to record new vocabulary in appropriate categories.)
2. Show learners pictures of different types of cars. Ask them to tell which cars they like and to explain why. Ask *Which cars do you think are good? Which are best for families? Which type of car do you think is the most dependable? Why?*

Presentation

1. Have learners turn to page 101, read the title, and look at the picture. Ask questions, such as *What do you see? Whose car do you think it is? What do you think they are talking about? Why do Adela and Marco look upset?* List words and comments on the board.
2. Have learners discuss the questions at the bottom of the page. Ask them to explain their answers.
3. Learners can brainstorm and make a list of questions that Adela and Marco may want to ask the mechanic about the car. Ask learners to role-play a conversation among the three characters.

1 2 3 4 5 6 7 8 **9** 10 11 12

Real Costs of a Car ■ ■ ■ ■ ■ ■ ■ ■

Checking Out a Car

Where are Adela and Marco?
What do you think happened to the car?
How do you think they feel?

Answers may vary.

Expansion/Extension

See TRF HANDOUT 9.1, *Parts of a Car*

- Learners can write in their writing journals about experiences they have had with auto repair shops.
- Learners can share ideas and advice on how to find a reliable mechanic or repair shop. Ask *How do you choose a repair shop for your car?* (or *How would you choose a repair shop if you owned a car?*)
- Learners can look in local yellow pages for advertisements and names of auto repair shops. Learners can look for shops that specialize in particular car makes or specific car problems.
- Learners can talk about experiences with owning a car. Ask *Do you or does someone you know have a car? What kind is it? Where did you/he/she get it? Do most people in this area have their own cars? Why/why not? Did you have a car in your native country?*

On the Way to Work

Purpose: To give practice in describing events; to give practice with dependent clauses; to introduce the past continuous tense

Teacher Preparation and Materials

1. Picture of a car accident
2. Sets of eight strips of paper with one line of the story on page 102 written on each strip (one set for each group of 3–5 learners)
3. Copies of TRF Handout 9.5, *Car Accident (Expansion/Extension)*
4. Copies of accident report forms *(Expansion/Extension)*
5. Driver's manuals, insurance cards, auto club brochures *(Expansion/Extension)*

Warm-up

Mime different actions associated with driving a car. Have learners describe the actions. Make a list of the verbs on the board or add them to the semantic web started for page 101. Elicit/introduce appropriate words, such as *turning, braking/ stopping, driving/steering, swerving, signaling,* and *passing.*

Presentation

1. Have learners turn to page 102 and look at the picture. Have learners describe what they think might have happened to cause the accident. Learners can use the list of verbs on the board as reference.
2. Have a volunteer read the introductory paragraph and directions. Have learners scan the sentences and underline words they do not know. Elicit/explain the meanings of new words: *destinations, swerved, avoid, smashed, meanwhile, unaware, tow truck, intersection, statements, slammed on the brakes, cut in front of.*
3. Arrange learners in small groups. Give each group a set of strips of paper with one line of the story written on each strip. Ask the groups to arrange the strips in sequence. Have learners compare stories.
   ■ In a one-to-one situation, have the

102 **On the Way to Work**

Marco was driving to work. He was going to drop his aunt, Adela, off at her friend's house, but they didn't get to their destinations.

Why didn't Marco and Adela get to their destinations?

To find out what happened, put the story in order.

- _3_ Next he swerved right to avoid hitting the other car and smashed into a tree instead.
- _5_ Meanwhile, the other driver drove off when the light changed, unaware that he had caused an accident.
- _8_ Before the police officer finished talking to Marco and Adela, the tow truck arrived.
- _1_ As Marco was driving to work, a driver cut in front of him at an intersection.
- _7_ While one officer called for a tow truck, the other one recorded Marco's and Adela's statements about the accident.
- _2_ Then Marco slammed on the brakes, but they didn't hold.
- _6_ A police car arrived a few minutes after the other car left.
- _4_ Slowly they got out of the car. Although the car was damaged, they were unhurt.

learner arrange the strips in sequence and read the story aloud to check the order. Then have learners number the sentences in the student book in the correct order.

4. Ask literal and inferential questions, such as *What caused the accident? What else could Marco have done when the brakes didn't work? Do you think Marco should have swerved to avoid the other car? Why did the police come? What questions do you think the police asked?*
5. Have learners consider alternatives that Marco could have taken. Ask *What would have happened if Marco had hit the other car instead of the tree? What else would have been different in the story?*
6. Learners can work individually or in pairs, writing an alternative story. Have learners share their stories with the class.

Expansion/Extension

See TRF HANDOUT 9.5, *Car Accident*

More *Expansion/Extension* on page 157

Bad News about Repairs

Purpose: To introduce asking for an estimate

Teacher Preparation and Materials

1. Picture of a car (mounted on a large sheet of paper), marker
2. 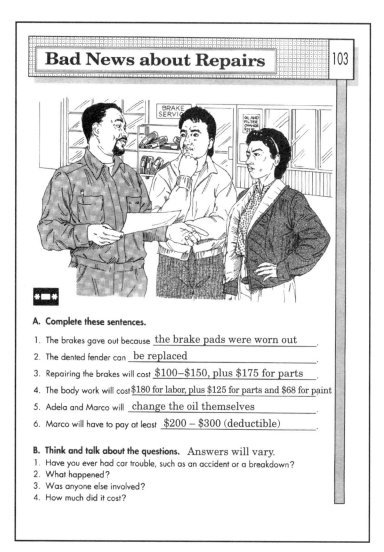 Audiotape for Level 3
3. Car manual or car repair book *(Expansion/Extension)*
4. Picture of car dashboard *(Expansion/Extension)*
5. Invite a mechanic or someone familiar with car repair to speak to the class about car maintenance. *(Expansion/Extension)*

Warm-up

Have learners identify and label a picture of a car. Learners can refer to the semantic web used for page 101 for names of parts. Be sure to include *fender*.

Presentation

1. Have learners turn to page 103, read the title, and look at the picture. Ask *What do you think they are going to talk about? What do you think the bad news is?*

2. Have learners read the sentences in exercise A to focus their listening. Play the audiotape. Ask literal and inferential questions, such as *What needs to be fixed? Why did Marco's brakes squeal? What body work has to be done on the car? Do you think Marco knows a lot about cars? Why or why not? What types of things should drivers know about cars?* Encourage learners to guess the meanings of new words from the context: *body work, dented, squealing.*

3. Have learners complete exercise A. Have learners listen again to the conversation to verify their responses.

4. Have learners discuss the questions in exercise B. Learners can brainstorm and write a list of suggestions for handling car troubles.

Bad News about Repairs 103

A. Complete these sentences.

1. The brakes gave out because ___the brake pads were worn out___.
2. The dented fender can ___be replaced___.
3. Repairing the brakes will cost ___$100–$150, plus $175 for parts___.
4. The body work will cost ___$180 for labor, plus $125 for parts and $68 for paint___
5. Adela and Marco will ___change the oil themselves___.
6. Marco will have to pay at least ___$200 – $300 (deductible)___.

B. Think and talk about the questions. Answers will vary.
1. Have you ever had car trouble, such as an accident or a breakdown?
2. What happened?
3. Was anyone else involved?
4. How much did it cost?

Expansion/Extension

- Learners can make a list of common car troubles and approximate costs for repairs. If learners do not own or are not interested in cars, have them choose an appliance, machine, or housing feature and make up a list of appropriate problems and repair costs.

- Ask learners to role-play the conversation among the three characters using the information in exercise A.

- Learners can look at a picture of a car dashboard and identify the symbols and gauges. Ask *What do the gauges measure? What does it mean if a symbol lights up? Which symbols are warnings?*

- If possible, invite a mechanic or someone familiar with car repair to speak to the group about the basics of car maintenance. Learners can prepare questions beforehand.

- Ask why some people might get a second estimate or opinion about car repairs before authorizing the work. Ask learners when it might be suitable or wise to get a second estimate or opinion about repairs.

The Bill

Purpose: To introduce reading a car repair bill and analyzing costs; to give practice in asking for clarification and in reporting errors on bills

Teacher Preparation and Materials

1. Samples of car registrations
2. Samples of car repair bills
3. 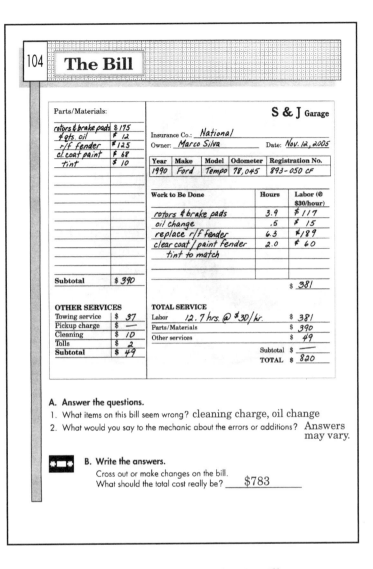 Audiotape for Level 3

Warm-up

1. Have learners look back on page 103 for repairs to be done on Marco's car. On the board list car parts that are needed and work that needs to be done. *(parts: brake pads, fender, paint; work: replace fender, change brake pads, paint fender)*

2. Learners can look at the sample car registrations (or their own) to find the year, make, model, and registration number. If possible, have learners look at and copy the number of miles recorded on a car odometer.

3. Bring in samples of car repair bills. Have learners look for sections that list car parts, work done, and car registration information.

Presentation

1. Have learners turn to page 104 and look at the bill. Ask learners about information on the bill. *What work was done? How much did the towing cost? Which car part was the most expensive?*

2. Ask learners if there are any differences between the estimated work written on the board and the work listed on the bill. Have learners suggest reasons why there might be differences between the two versions. (FOR EXAMPLE: Estimates are not the actual cost.)

3. Have learners answer the questions in exercise A. Learners can brainstorm and write expressions on the board that can be used to point out errors to the mechanic.

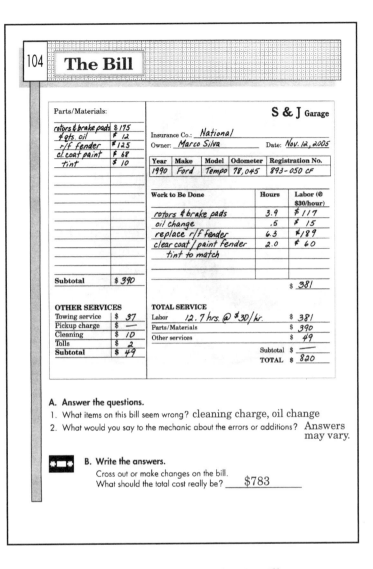

4. Have learners guess how the mechanic will react to questions about the bill. 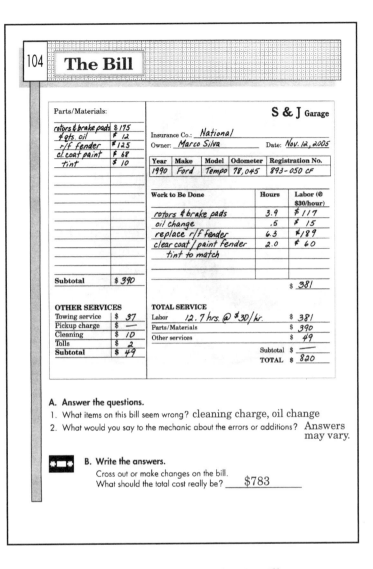 Then play the audiotape. Ask learners to cross out the errors on the bill and to recalculate it.

5. Have learners role-play the conversation between the mechanic and Marco and Adela.

Expansion/Extension

- Learners can discuss additional questions about the conversation and car insurance procedures. Explain that some insurance companies require an estimated bill before they agree to cover a claim. Ask *Why do you think an insurance company would want to know approximately how much the repairs will cost before they are actually done?*

Maintaining a Car:
Forms A and B

Purpose: To give practice with *Wh-* questions and with *should*

Teacher Preparation and Materials

1. Pictures of tools and equipment for car maintenance, such as a wrench, pliers, jack, drain pan, rags
2. Copies of TRF Handout 9.7, *Operating the Self-Serve Gasoline Pump (Expansion/Extension)*
3. Car manual or repair book with diagrams of engine and information on car maintenance *(Expansion/Extension)*
4. Arrange for learners to look at a car engine. *(Expansion/Extension)*

Warm-up

1. Have learners brainstorm and list on the board tasks that need to be done periodically on a car. Elicit/introduce tasks, such as *put gasoline in, check battery, check/ put in oil, wash car, check/rotate tires,* and *check transmission.* Have learners think of types of tools and equipment that would be needed to complete the tasks, such as a wrench, pliers, rag, jack, and empty drain pan. Use pictures to clarify meanings.
2. Ask if learners have performed any of the tasks or watched someone else doing them. Allow learners to share their experiences with car maintenance.

Presentation

1. Divide learners into two groups. Have one group look at page 105 (Form A) and the other group look at page 106 (Form B). Have learners read the titles of their pages and look at the pictures. Ask a volunteer to read the introductory paragraphs. Ask *What's Marco looking at? What do you think he is trying to do? What is Adela doing? Do you think there is a problem?* Elicit/explain the meaning of *maintaining*.

Maintaining a Car: Form A   105

Work with a partner.
One person uses Form A.
The other uses Form B.

Marco and Adela are working on Marco's car. They need to change the oil and the transmission fluid.

You are Marco.
Your partner is Adela.

Adela is helping Marco change the oil. Marco has some questions.

A. Ask your partner for instructions.
1. Ask how often you should change the oil.
2. Ask what tools you need to do the job.
3. Ask when the best time is to drain the oil.
4. Ask how you loosen the drain plug.
5. Ask what you use the wrench for.

Now Adela is changing the transmission fluid. She isn't sure how to do it and has some questions. She asks Marco to find the information in the automobile repair manual.

B. Find the information for your partner in the steps below.
(Note: The steps are not in the correct order.)   Answers: e, d, a, f, b
a. Shift the car to neutral or park and put on the parking brake.
b. Do not overfill the transmission fluid. Overfilling causes severe problems.
c. Check that the transmission fluid is red.
d. The car should be parked with the engine on.
e. Check the fluid when the transmission is hot.
f. The fluid level should be between the second and third notches.

---

2. Have learners look over the information and instructions in exercise A for their role in the information gap exercise. Learners with Form A should try to guess the meanings of new words from the context before checking in a dictionary or manual. Some new words might be *transmission fluid, oil,* and *drain plug.* Have learners prepare questions to use in the role play. Be sure that learners with Form B understand the vocabulary. Some new words might be *normal operating temperature, oil filter, wrench, drain pan, jack,* and *hoist.* ◼ In a one-to-one situation, have the learner look over Form A. Explain new vocabulary as necessary and have the learner prepare questions for exercise A.
3. Have learners work in pairs: one learner uses Form A while the other uses Form B. Learners with Form A should ask questions and record the answers for exercise A. Learners with Form B should choose the appropriate answers for the questions. ◼ In a one-to-one situation, have the learner use Form A and you use Form B.

4. Check the work together by asking questions about changing oil in a car. Learners with Form A should respond with the information they obtained in the pair work. Learners with Form B can verify the responses.

5. Have learners complete exercise B, following the same procedure, but switching roles. People who asked questions should now give instructions, and vice versa. Some new vocabulary might be *shift, neutral, parking brake, overfill, transmission, notches, gear,* and *dipstick.*

6. Have learners discuss what was easy or difficult about the activity. Ask *Was it easier to ask questions or answer the questions? Was it difficult to understand the maintenance procedures? Why or why not? Do you think you would be able to perform these maintenance tasks on a car? Why or why not? Can you think of ways that would make it easier to learn about car maintenance procedures?*

Expansion/Extension

See **TRF HANDOUT 9.7,** *Operating the Self-Serve Gasoline Pump*

- Learners can look in a car manual or repair book for diagrams and/or additional instructions on the care and maintenance of cars.

- If learners are interested, they can look at a car or diagram of a car and find the parts that are mentioned in the information gap activity. Learners may need to check an engine diagram to help identify the various parts. Learners can identify other parts of the car or engine and discuss how they function.

- Ask learners to explain orally or in writing how to perform a routine maintenance or emergency task, such as checking tire pressure, replacing windshield wipers, changing a tire, changing headlight bulbs, and jump-starting an engine. If learners do not own or are not interested in cars, have them choose an appliance or other household maintenance task to describe. Some procedures might be defrosting a freezer, checking and replacing a battery in a smoke detector, changing a washer on a leaky faucet, or replacing glass in a window.

| 106 | **Maintaining a Car: Form B** |

Work with a partner.
One person uses Form A.
The other uses Form B.

Marco and Adela are working on Marco's car. They need to change the oil and the transmission fluid.

You are Adela.
Your partner is Marco.

Adela is helping Marco change the oil. Marco has some questions.

Answers: b, e, a, f, c.

A. Find the information for your partner in the steps below.

(Note: The steps are not in the correct order.)

a. Change the oil only when the engine is at the normal operating temperature.

b. Change the oil every 4,000 miles or every six months.

c. Remove the oil filter with the wrench and empty the oil into the drain pan.

d. Use the jack to hoist up the car.

e. You need a wrench, a drain pan for used oil, and a jack.

f. Turn the drain plug to the left by hand.

Now Adela is changing the transmission fluid. She isn't sure how to do it and has some questions. She asks Marco to find the information in the automobile repair manual.

B. Ask your partner for instructions.

1. Ask when to check the fluid.
2. Ask whether the car should be turned on or off.
3. Ask what gear the car should be in.
4. Ask what notch the fluid level should be on the dipstick.
5. Ask if it's OK to overfill the transmission fluid.

- Learners can discuss car inspection procedures. Ask *Why do cars have to be inspected regularly? How often are cars inspected? What parts are checked? How much does it cost? Where can cars be inspected? What happens if the car doesn't pass inspection?*

- Ask learners to compare the prices of gasoline, motor oil, tires, antifreeze, and other common car expenses. Learners can check prices at service stations, automotive supply stores, department stores, and so on. Ask *What do the different grades of gas mean? How do you know what type of tires or oil to use in a particular car?*

- Learners can ask about rates for tune-ups at local car repair shops or look through car maintenance books for information about doing their own tune-ups. Learners can make a list of what can be done to make a car last longer and perform better.

What the Accident Cost

Purpose: To introduce reading an insurance policy

Teacher Preparation and Materials

1. Sample of a car insurance policy
2. Copies of TRF Handout 9.6, *The Real Costs of a Car (Expansion/Extension)*

Warm-up

1. Bring in a sample of a car insurance policy. Elicit/explain information about insurance. Ask *What is insurance? Why do you need insurance for cars? How does it protect people?*
2. On the board make a chart with four headings: *Injuries or Damage, Property Damage, Bodily Injury, Collision.* Ask *Who can be hurt in accidents? What can be damaged in accidents?* In the first column, list people and things that may be hurt or damaged. (FOR EXAMPLE: passengers in your car, people in other cars, pedestrians, your car, another person's car, buildings) Elicit/explain the meanings of the other column headings. Go through the list of injuries and damage and have learners check on the chart which insurance coverage applies for each of the situations. (FOR EXAMPLE: passengers hurt in your car—*Bodily Injury;* another person's car—*Property Damage*)

Presentation

1. Have learners turn to page 107. Have a volunteer read the title and introductory statement. Ask *Why do you think Marco is reading his insurance policy now? What was damaged in the accident? What type of coverage is Marco checking on?*
2. Have learners look at the policy and find the components and coverage limits. Elicit/explain the meanings of new words: *discounts, surcharge, uninsured, liability, claim, comprehensive, vandalism.*
3. Ask *How much is his annual insurance premium? What is the largest amount that*

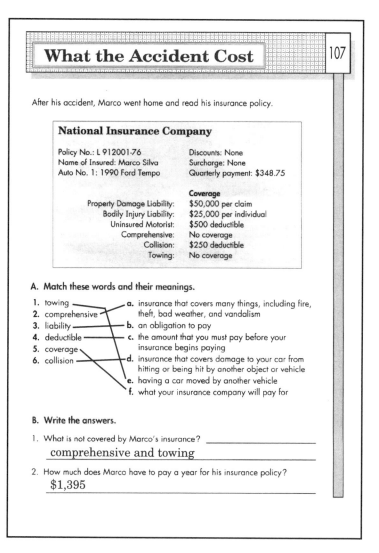

the company will pay? What isn't covered by this policy? Why do you think that the deductible is so high?
4. Have learners complete exercise A. Ask if Marco's insurance company would cover certain situations and, if so, how much coverage would be given. FOR EXAMPLE: *Someone broke a window in Marco's car to steal his radio. Would the insurance company cover the repairs and replacement? Marco hit the car instead of the tree. The other car was damaged and the driver broke his arm. Would Marco's insurance company cover the costs?*
5. Have learners complete exercise B. Learners can look back at the bill on page 104 and calculate the approximate amount that the insurance company will pay and the amount that Marco will have to pay. Ask learners to explain their answers using information from the insurance policy.

Expansion/Extension

See **TRF HANDOUT 9.6,** *The Real Costs of a Car*

More *Expansion/Extension* on page 157

150 • UNIT 9

Buying a Van

Purpose: To introduce reading consumer reports on new cars

Teacher Preparation and Materials

1. Pictures of two new vans (similar in size and style but made by different companies)
2. Copies of TRF Handout 9.2, *Find the Differences (Expansion/Extension)*
3. *Consumer Reports* or newspaper sections with reviews of new cars *(Expansion/Extension)*

Warm-up

1. Show pictures of two different vans. Ask learners to compare the vans. *What features are similar? What are the differences between the two vans?* Ask learners which van they think is better and if they have enough information about the vehicles to decide which is better.
2. Learners can brainstorm and list on the board additional information they would like to know about the vans. Be sure to include *safety features, mileage, handling, brakes,* and so on.

Presentation

1. Have learners turn to page 108. Have a volunteer read the title and introductory paragraph. Ask *What type of information can Stan find in the library about vans? What section of the library would he look in? Why doesn't he just go to some car dealers and ask for information?*
2. Have learners work in two groups, one group reading about the AstroChief and the other group reading about the TurboMaster. Ask learners to scan the text and to circle parts of the description they consider to be pros and underline parts they consider to be cons. Specific vocabulary will be studied later in the lesson. Have each group complete their half of the chart in exercise A.
3. Have each group prepare a salesperson's talk or advertisement about their van, using the pros listed on their charts. Have volunteers from one group try to persuade the other group to buy their van and vice versa. As a class, discuss which group was more persuasive and why.
4. Have each group talk about the cons of their vans. Ask *Do you think a car dealer would tell a buyer about these things? Why or why not? Do you think it's important for people to know about the weak points? How can people find out about good and bad points of cars they want to buy?*
5. Have each group read the description of the van that they did not read before. Have learners point out any additional pros or cons that were not mentioned before. Elicit/explain the meaning of new vocabulary, such as *mpg, automatic, manual, decent, routine, standard, modest, set you back, handling,* and *recommended.*
6. Have learners discuss the questions in exercise B. Have learners explain their answers.

Expansion/Extension

See **TRF HANDOUT 9.2,** *Find the Differences*

More *Expansion/Extension* **on page 157**

---

108 Buying a Van

Stan wants to trade in his sports car for a van. Although he loves his car, he thinks a van would be more practical. He did some research at the library to find out more about vans.

The AstroChief
(list price: $21,550) starts and runs well, but it only gets 17 mpg—low even for a van. A five-speed manual transmission is standard. Its four-speed automatic transmission ($750) shifted smoothly when test-driven. **Brakes** continue to be decent, although stopping distances are still a bit long. **Routine handling** is clumsier than in earlier models, and this AstroChief is slow to respond in emergencies. There's no improvement in the ride of the new model. It remains hard and noisy. **Air bags** have been standard since the 2002 model. **Air conditioning** is a modest $420. **The cargo area** is enlarged, but it takes two people to remove the back bench (89 lbs).

The TurboMaster
(list price: $22,357) starts easily and runs well. An overall 20 mpg is a great improvement over last year's model. A three-speed automatic transmission is standard. Manual transmission is no longer available. **Routine handling** is satisfactory, but emergency handling is still clumsy on hard turns. **A new package** ($1,250) will include antilock brakes and air bags (both highly recommended) and air conditioning. If purchased separately, these three items would set you back $2,228. **Brakes** are firm and quick. Even without a full load, the ride is comfortable. **Cargo area** is excellent, but removing the 100-pound rear seat is a tough job.

A. Evaluate the vans. Answers may vary.
List the pros and cons for each van.

	AstroChief	TurboMaster
Pros		
Cons		

B. Think and talk about the questions. Answers may vary.
1. Which van would you choose?
2. Which features would make you choose one van over the other?

Reading the Ads

Purpose: To give practice in using abbreviations; to give practice with *Wh-* questions

Teacher Preparation and Materials

1. New and used car advertisements from a local newspaper
2. Copies of TRF Handout 9.3, *Autos for Sale (Expansion/Extension)*
3. Copies of TRF Handout 9.4, *I'm Calling about the Car for Sale (Expansion/Extension)*

Warm-up

1. Have learners look back at page 108 for the prices of the vans. Ask *Do you think Stan can afford to buy one of these on his part-time salary? What other options does he have? Where else can he look for cars that are more reasonably priced?*
2. Bring in the auto ads section of a local newspaper. Have learners look for car dealer ads and ads from individuals selling cars. Ask *What differences do you see between these two types of ads? What extras can dealers offer?* Elicit/introduce the meanings of new words: *factory rebate, dealer rebate, trade-in.*

Presentation

1. Have learners turn to page 109. Have a volunteer read the title and introductory paragraph. Ask *What kinds of questions would you ask about a new car? What kinds of questions would you ask about a used car?* Learners can brainstorm possible questions. List them on the board. Questions might include age of car, number of owners, and mileage.
2. Have learners look at the ads. Point out that some ads may have misleading information or abbreviations and terms that are confusing. Ask learners to scan the ads and circle any unfamiliar vocabulary or questionable information. Have learners think of questions they could ask, using the circled words and questionable information from the ads.

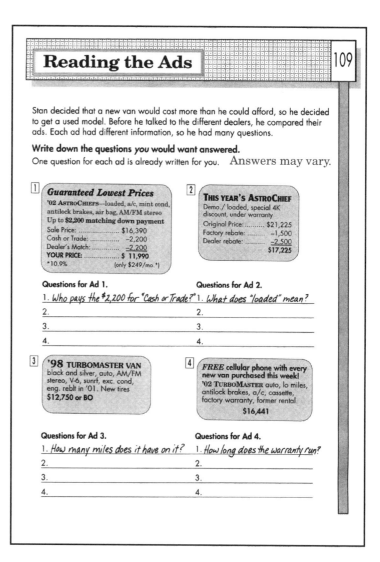

3. Have learners write questions that they would like answered about each of the advertised vans.
4. List learners' questions for each ad on the board. Elicit/explain the meaning of new words and abbreviations, such as *mint cond, down payment, demo, 4K, sunrf,* and *former rental.*
5. Ask *Which vans sound like good deals? Why? Which vans have more attractive features? Do you think these prices are final or can prices be negotiated? How might you negotiate a lower price?*
6. Have learners role-play a potential customer talking to a dealer about one of the advertised vans.

Expansion/Extension

See TRF HANDOUT 9.3, *Autos for Sale*
TRF HANDOUT 9.4, *I'm Calling about the Car for Sale*

• Ask learners to write a mock ad for their own car or for a car they want to buy.

More *Expansion/Extension* on page 157

Getting a Car Loan

Purpose: To introduce asking for bank loan information; to give practice in taking notes

Teacher Preparation and Materials

1. Bank loan fliers, local newspaper ads for banks
2. ▆▆▆ Audiotape for Level 3
3. Bank loan applications *(Expansion/Extension)*

Warm-up

1. Show learners copies of bank fliers or newspaper advertisements about loans. Elicit/review the meanings of words, such as *rates, down payment, monthly payments, loan, credit union, terms, interest,* and *balance.* Have learners consider why banks offer different terms and why interest rates change. Introduce the meaning of *incentive.* Ask learners why banks may offer incentives.

Presentation

1. Have learners turn to page 110 and look at the picture. Have a volunteer read the introductory paragraph. Ask *Why is Stan calling several places? What questions do you think Stan will ask? What information will he need to give the banks?*
2. Have learners look at the chart to focus their listening. ▆▆▆ Then play the audiotape and have learners fill in the loan information for the three banks. Stop after each conversation and ask literal and inferential questions.
3. Have learners underline the incentives that are offered by the banks. ▆▆▆ If necessary, replay the audiotape. Ask learners to explain how each incentive might benefit a loan customer.
4. Have learners complete exercise B. They should be prepared to explain their choices with information from the charts or the conversations. (**Cultural note:** Many car dealers offer "deals" on car loans, but the deals may not always be the best. Banks set their own rates and loan standards, and it often pays to shop around. Also, it

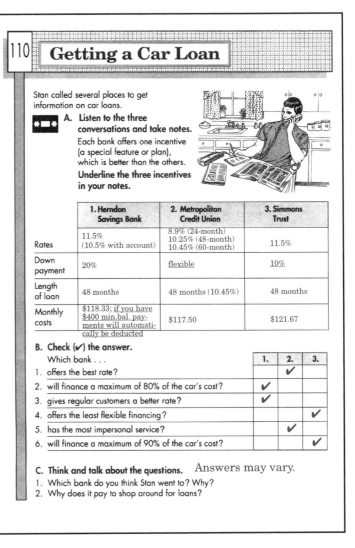

is sometimes necessary to have an account in a particular bank to get a car loan from that bank.)

5. Have learners discuss the questions in exercise C. Learners can write a story about Stan's experiences in looking for and choosing a bank for his car loan.

Expansion/Extension

- Have learners work in pairs to role-play Stan calling each of the banks, requesting loan information, and getting information from a bank employee.
- Learners can call local banks or credit unions and ask about current rates for car loans. As a group, make a chart to compare and contrast rates and other loan information.
- Have learners look at sample bank loan applications and identify the type of information that is requested. (personal, employment, financial, credit history, and so on) Ask learners why banks need this information before approving a loan.

Practicing Your Skills

Purpose: To give practice in figuring costs

Teacher Preparation and Materials
None

Warm-up
Have learners look through the unit for the costs involved with owning a car. Make a list of expenses on the board and their approximate costs.

Presentation
1. Have learners turn to page 111. Have a volunteer read the introductory paragraph.
2. Have learners read the list of costs and compare it with the one on the board. Have learners decide which costs are one-time expenses and which are recurring expenses. If learners are not interested in cars, they can choose another topic and make an appropriate list of costs. Some topics might be Going to School, Raising Children, or Owning a House.
3. Have learners write a story about financial responsibilities based on their own experiences or on Marco's experiences in the unit. Learners can explain the importance of the different costs and the consequences of neglecting responsibilities.
4. Have learners share their stories with the class.

Expansion/Extension
- Learners can compare the costs of driving and owning a car in the United States with the costs in their native countries. Ask *Are cars more expensive in this country than in your native country? What types of registration and insurance are required in your native country?*

Practicing Your Skills

111

Marco has been taking evening classes. His English class was given a writing assignment. The topic is "Having a . . . Is a Big Financial Responsibility." Marco chose to write about the thing that has been most on his mind lately. His essay, "Having a Car Is a Big Financial Responsibility," got an A–.

Write a story about the expenses and responsibilities of owning a car. The following list of possible costs should help.

purchase price	maintenance
interest on loan	repairs
registration fees	garage rental
taxes	gasoline
insurance	parking fees

Answers will vary.

- Learners can discuss and/or write about ways to make driving and owning a car safer and more economical. Learners can suggest ideas to complete the following sentences:
  Cars would be safer if . . .
  People would be better drivers if . . .
  Roads and highways would be better if . . .
  Costs for repairing cars would be lower if . . .
  Car insurance costs would be lower if . . .

  If learners are not interested in cars, have them choose another topic and make up appropriate sentence completions about safety considerations and economizing.

- Ask learners to compile a vocabulary list for the unit. Learners can create categories and categorize the new words. Some categories might be Car Parts/Features, Car Insurance, Repair/Maintenance, Buying or Financing, and Miscellaneous.

Verb: Past Continuous Tense/Dependent Clauses of Reason

Purpose: To give practice with the past continuous tense and contrast it with simple past tense; to give practice recognizing reason clauses

Teacher Preparation and Materials
None

Warm-up

1. Give examples to show the contrast between simple past and past continuous tenses. FOR EXAMPLE: *When I got to class today, Mary was sitting next to Jules. They were both talking to Stefan. Marissa was erasing the blackboard when I got here.*

2. Elicit similar sentences from learners. Ask, *When you got to school today, what was happening in the parking lot? In the hallway? In the classroom?* Put selected responses on the board, and focus on verb forms.

Presentation

1. Have learners turn to page 112 and read the examples in the box at the top of the page.

2. Review the story of Marco's accident on page 102. Have learners retell the story in their own words. Encourage use of simple past and past continuous where appropriate.

3. Read item 1 in the first exercise, and elicit the answer. Explain that Adela is telling the story of the accident to her friend Keiko.

4. Have learners complete the exercise. Review answers by having one or more pairs of learners role-play the conversation.

5. Ask *why* questions about the story of the accident. FOR EXAMPLE: *Why did Marco slam on his brakes? Why did the other driver leave the scene? Why did a police officer talk to Marco and Adela?* Put answers on the board, using conjunctions that signal reason *(because, so, so that).*

6. Have learners read the example sentences in the box in the middle of the page, and point out the use of *because* clauses to give the reason for the event in the main clause.

7. Have learners complete the second exercise, and review answers.

Expansion/Extension

- Have learners tell or write a story about an accident or other notable event they experienced.

- Using the conversation between Adela and Keiko, have learners create a role play in which Keiko retells the story of the accident to someone else (another friend, for example). Encourage learners to use reported speech.

- Have learners use the sentences in the second exercise as a model for a similar discussion of how they care for a car, a household appliance, or a machine at work. Have them include clauses giving reasons for their actions.

---

112 | **Verbs:** Past Continuous Tense/Dependent Clauses of Reason

Marco **was going** to school.
Adela **wasn't driving** this morning.
They **were talking** about the weather.
They **weren't watching** for other drivers.

Complete this conversation between Adela and her friend Keiko.

1. Keiko: What happened? When I called this morning, you ___were leaving___ (leave) the house.

2. Adela: While Marco ___was driving___ (drive), another car cut him off.

3. He slammed on the brakes, but they ___weren't holding___ (not hold).

4. Next thing we knew, we ___were heading___ (head) for a tree!
   Keiko: How awful! What happened to the other driver?

5. Adela: Nothing! While we ___were sitting___ (sit) there, stunned, he drove off without a scratch!

6. Keiko: Did he know that he ___was leaving___ (leave) the scene of an accident?

7. Adela: I don't think so. He ___wasn't paying___ (not pay) attention.

Marco's car hit a tree **because the brakes weren't holding.**
Because the brakes weren't holding, Marco's car hit a tree.

Underline the reason clause in each sentence.

1. It's important to change a car's oil regularly so that the engine stays clean.
2. Marco tries to change his oil every 3,000 miles because his car is old.
3. Because he wants to save money, he usually changes the oil himself.
4. He always checks his equipment so he can do the oil change safely.
5. His car runs well because he takes good care of it.
6. Because he can't afford a new car, he wants his old car to last.

Wh- Questions: Past Tense

Purpose: To give practice with forming and using *wh-* questions in the past tense

Teacher Preparation and Materials

1. Auto insurance policy, including an explanation of how premiums are calculated and any special programs that offer reductions (such as the "Safe Driver Plan" mentioned on page 113) *(Warm-up)*
2. Learners' stories written for *Expansion/Extension* from page 112 *(Expansion/Extension)*

Warm-up

1. Review *wh-* questions in the past tense by asking questions about Marco's accident. Use information from pages 102 and 112. FOR EXAMPLE: *When did the accident happen? Who caused the accident? Why did Marco hit a tree? What happened to Adela?*
2. Ask learners if anyone in their family has a car, and if so, what kind of car insurance they have. Discuss factors that influence premiums. If information is available, have learners review how premiums are calculated for a specific policy and any special programs that can lower premiums.
3. Ask learners what, in their opinion, makes a driver safe. List their criteria on the board. Compare their criteria to those listed in a specific insurance policy. Discuss any differences.

Presentation

1. Have learners turn to page 113 and review the sample questions in the chart. Focus on word order and verb forms.
2. Look at the chart that explains the Wolanskis' "Safe Driver Plan" on their auto insurance. Explain/elicit the meaning of *deductions* and *credits* in this plan. Review each driver's record. Discuss why Ana lost credits for a speeding ticket. Discuss why a speeding ticket results in a smaller deduction than a major accident. Predict the effect of the deductions on insurance costs for Ana and Stan.

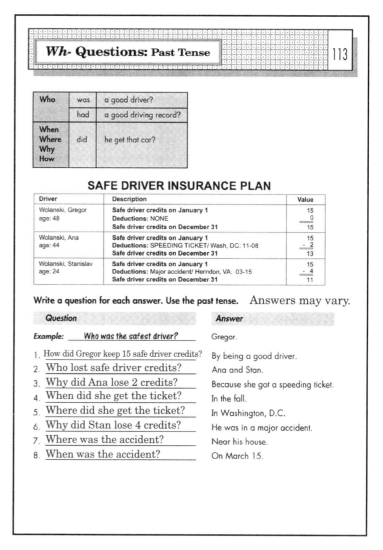

3. Review the example in the exercise, and make sure learners understand how to form questions based on the answers given.
4. Have learners complete the exercise. Review answers by having one learner ask the question and another give the answer. Discuss any differences in learners' responses.

Expansion/Extension

- Have learners work in pairs to create questions about the stories they wrote for *Expansion/Extension* from page 112, then exchange questions and stories with another pair. After reading the new stories, learners can answer the questions orally or in writing.
- Discuss other types of insurance that learners have or might need (homeowners', flood, health, dental, and so on). Elicit learners' ideas on reasons why each type is or is not important and the factors that influence premiums.

UNIT 9: Real Costs of a Car
Expansion/Extension

On the Way to Work
More *Expansion/Extension* for SB page 102

- Bring in copies of accident report forms. Have learners use the information from Marco and Adela's story to fill in the form. Learners can make up additional information about the story and use it to complete the form. (FOR EXAMPLE: Marco was driving 30 mph. The accident happened at 9:50 a.m. The road was dry. There were two cars coming from the opposite direction.)
- Ask learners to make a list of procedures for reporting accidents. Learners can look in driver's manuals, on insurance cards, and in auto club brochures for ideas.
- Learners can role-play Adela and Marco reporting the accident to the police officer.

What the Accident Cost
More *Expansion/Extension* for SB page 107

- If learners have cars, ask about their insurance. Learners can bring in copies of their policies and compare costs and coverage. Ask learners how they chose their insurance company.
- Learners can check on insurance in their state. Ask *What types of coverage are required or mandatory? What coverage is optional? Does this state have no-fault insurance? What is no-fault insurance and what does it cover? Does this state give safe driver points? Do traffic violations affect insurance costs? How long do they stay on your record? What are the* consequences of driving under the influence of alcohol and how does it affect car insurance? What other factors are taken into consideration in determining insurance costs? (age of driver, location, value of car, number of miles driven per year, personal or commercial use, etc.) (**Note:** Some states offer defensive driving courses. Drivers that complete the courses are entitled to lower car insurance rates.)

Buying a Van
More *Expansion/Extension* for SB page 108

- Bring in magazines, such as *Consumer Reports,* or special newspaper sections with reviews of new cars. Ask learners to look for information about particular types of cars. Ask *What types of features are discussed? Which features do you think are the most important?*
- Ask learners to write a "consumer report" for a car (or an appliance) that they know about or own. Ask *What features does it have? How well does it work? What are some of the weak points? What's your overall evaluation of the item?*
- Learners can discuss *mpg.* Ask *What does* mpg *mean? How do you calculate miles per gallon? Why is it usually different for city driving and highway driving?*

Reading the Ads
More *Expansion/Extension* for SB page 109

- Learners can brainstorm other important questions to ask when buying a car, house, or other expensive item. (FOR EXAMPLE: Why are you selling it? How long have you had it? Is there anything wrong with it? What repairs/improvements have you made on it? Can I see your repair or utility bills?)

Under the Law

Objectives

Functions
- Reporting events
- Expressing surprise
- Expressing emotions
- Giving advice

Life Tasks
- Reporting a crime
- Reading a newspaper article
- Filing a complaint
- Reading and understanding legal rights
- Recognizing deceptive advertising
- Writing an article for a newsletter

Structures
- *Wh-* questions
- Prepositions of time and place
- Intensifiers
- *When* clauses
- Present perfect tense
- Passive voice
- *Yes/no* questions

Culture
- Changing sex roles
- Legal aid/legal services
- Cross-cultural views of discipline

Vocabulary

Key words:

800 number	mugging
arrest	precaution
arrest warrant	press charges
assault and battery	prevention
	rights
beating up	robbery
burglary	search warrant
crime	sexual harassment
criminal	vandalism
guilty	victim
harassed	weapon
Miranda rights	

Key abbreviation:

EEOC–Equal Employment Opportunity Commission

Related words:

accuse	physical contact
attorney	pressure
calm	resist
cooperate	robber
deceptive advertising	scream
	shelter for battered women
easy target	
file a complaint	subordinate
forced confession	Supreme Court
hitchhiker	suspect (n.)
interrogate	threaten
panic	violent

Questioned by the Police

Purpose: To introduce law enforcement vocabulary; to give practice in expressing feelings, in answering questions, and in reporting events

Teacher Preparation and Materials

1. Large sheet of paper, marker
2. Local phone book *(Expansion/Extension)*

Warm-up

(**Note:** Crime and related issues may be frightening. In this unit learners consider preventive and cautionary actions for protecting themselves and their families. Learners practice handling and responding to specific types of incidents and threats. Activities introduce agencies and offices that offer help to crime victims. The goals of the unit are to empower learners to handle situations and to join with neighbors and co-workers to create a safer community.)

In the center of a large sheet of paper, write *Crime*. Elicit/explain the meaning. Have learners suggest and list on the board types of crimes, people involved, punishments, and so on. Be sure to include *robbery, mugging, burglary, beating, criminal, victim,* and *police*. Create a semantic web on the sheet of paper, using the categories and crime-related vocabulary. (**Note:** This semantic web will be used again for pages 115, 117, and 123.)

Presentation

1. Have learners turn to page 114. Ask questions about the picture, such as *What's the matter with Quang? How do you think he got hurt? Why is the police officer at Diep's apartment? What do you think they are talking about?* List words and comments on the board.
2. Ask learners to discuss the questions at the bottom of the page.
3. Have learners predict what might have happened to Quang and who might have been involved.

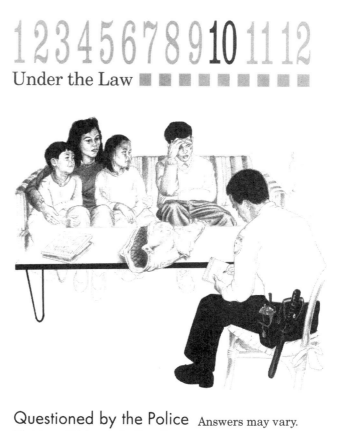

123456789 **10** 1112

Under the Law ■ ■ ■ ■ ■ ■ ■ ■ ■ ■

Questioned by the Police   Answers may vary.

What do you think happened to Quang?

What is the police officer doing?

Do you think the police officer will be able to help Quang? Why or why not?

4. Have learners role-play a conversation between the police officer and Quang. Suggest ways to begin the role play, such as *I'm Officer Hunt. Can you tell me what happened to you tonight?*

Expansion/Extension

- Ask learners to check the local phone book for numbers of police or other community services related to crimes listed on the semantic web. Learners can role-play calling for assistance or reporting incidents.
- Learners can discuss what would be different in the picture if Quang were in trouble or being arrested. Ask questions to begin the discussion. FOR EXAMPLE: *Do you think Quang is in trouble with the police? Would the police officer be talking to Quang in Diep's apartment if Quang were in trouble? Where would they be?*

A Mugging

Purpose: To give practice in reporting events and in giving advice; to give practice with adverbs of description, with *When* clauses, with the passive voice, and with the present perfect tense

Teacher Preparation and Materials

Semantic web used for page 114, marker

Warm-up

1. Have learners review the vocabulary on the semantic web. Have learners suggest and list on the board names of places where crimes occur and verbs/actions related to crimes. Add branches to the web, using the new words listed on the board.

2. Have learners turn to page 114 and review their predictions about what happened to Quang.

Presentation

1. Have learners turn to page 115, read the title, and look at the picture. Ask *Would you want to get off a bus in this neighborhood? Why or why not? Why might this be a dangerous place?*

2. Have learners read the first two paragraphs. Ask *Do you think the man really has a gun? What would you do if you were Quang?* Make a list of possible reactions on the board.

3. Ask learners to finish reading the story and to underline new words. Elicit/explain the meanings of new words: *raspy, shove, resisting, took off.*

4. Ask literal and inferential questions, such as *What did Quang do? Do you think his reactions were sensible? What might you have done differently? Do you think the mugger was nervous or calm? Why? What things did Quang notice about the mugger?*

5. Have learners answer the questions at the bottom of the page.

6. Ask learners to suggest ways that the neighbor might have helped Quang. Ask *What do you think the neighbor said or did? What do you think Quang told the neighbor?* Learners can role-play the situation.

A Mugging

Quang Tran came home late from work. When he got off the bus, he was thinking about his dinner. Suddenly a man jumped out and poked something hard in Quang's back.

The man spoke in a deep, raspy voice: "Don't make a sound. I have a gun. Give me your wallet and your jewelry. Quick."

Quang stayed calm. He knew that resisting was foolish. "OK. I'm not going to try anything. My wallet is in my back pocket. I'm reaching in to get it. Here it . . ." The man interrupted, "Shut up and move fast. Give me your watch and your rings." As the man spoke, Quang smelled cigarette smoke.

Quang slipped the watch off his wrist and passed it backward. Then he held up his hands so the mugger could see he wasn't wearing a ring. "I don't have any rings."

"Bah! Shut up! Don't turn around!" The mugger gave Quang a powerful shove. Quang lost his balance, fell, and banged his head on the pavement. The mugger took off. Quang could hear the man running down the street because his shoes made so much noise.

Quang started shouting, "Help! I've been mugged!" A neighbor came to his aid.

Write the answers.

1. Why didn't Quang notice the mugger? _____
   because he was thinking about his dinner

2. What did the mugger want from Quang? his wallet and jewelry

3. How did the mugger try to scare Quang? _____
   He said he had a gun.

4. How did Quang hit his head? The mugger shoved him. He lost his balance and fell.

5. What did Quang notice about the mugger? He smelled cigarette smoke. The mugger's shoes made a lot of noise.

Expansion/Extension

- Ask learners about Quang's reactions and feelings throughout the incident and what their own reactions might be in a similar situation. Ask *How do you think Quang was able to stay calm during the mugging? How do you think he felt? How would you feel in a similar situation? How do you think you would behave?* Learners can make a list of advice for mugging victims.

- Ask learners to identify dangerous or potentially dangerous places in their area. Ask *Why are these places dangerous? What can you do to protect yourself if you have to go there?* Learners can suggest how to make these places safer.

- Learners can discuss the pros and cons of getting involved with or helping crime victims. Ask *Would you help one of your neighbors if he or she were being robbed? When would you offer help? How would you help in different types of situations? Do you think your neighbors would help you in similar situations? Why or why not? How are these situations handled in your native country?*

What Did You See?

Purpose: To give practice with *Wh-* questions, with adverbs of description, and with intensifiers; to give practice in answering questions

Teacher Preparation and Materials

1. Magazines with pictures of people (different ages, coloring, clothing, and physical features)
2. 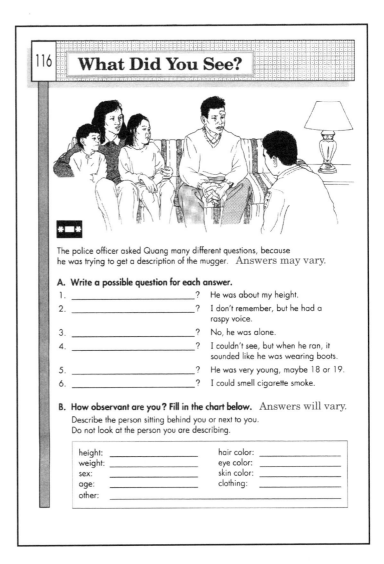 Audiotape for Level 3
3. Copies of TRF Handout 10.1, *Mug Shots (Expansion/Extension)*

Warm-up

1. Elicit/introduce vocabulary to describe physical features and clothing, including hair, eye, and skin colors, and other identifying features. List words and phrases on the board. Describe a person in the room and have learners guess which person fits the description. ◼ In a one-to-one situation, have the learner look through magazines for pictures of people with different features and clothing. Describe a person in one of the pictures and have the learner guess which person fits the description.

2. Ask *What other information can be used to help identify a person?* Elicit/introduce *voice* (accent, tone, words and phrases used), *physical disabilities,* and so on. Add these to the list on the board.

3. Have learners skim the story on page 115 for descriptive words and phrases about Quang's attacker. Check items on the board that fit the attacker's description. Add other characteristics of the mugger from the story to the list on the board.

Presentation

1. Have learners turn to page 116, read the title, and discuss what might have made it difficult for Quang to see very much.

2. ▦ Play the audiotape. Have learners summarize the conversation.

3. Ask literal and inferential questions, such as *What did Quang remember about the*

116 **What Did You See?**

The police officer asked Quang many different questions, because he was trying to get a description of the mugger. Answers may vary.

A. Write a possible question for each answer.

1. _____? He was about my height.
2. _____? I don't remember, but he had a raspy voice.
3. _____? No, he was alone.
4. _____? I couldn't see, but when he ran, it sounded like he was wearing boots.
5. _____? He was very young, maybe 18 or 19.
6. _____? I could smell cigarette smoke.

B. How observant are you? Fill in the chart below. Answers will vary.
Describe the person sitting behind you or next to you.
Do not look at the person you are describing.

height: _____	hair color: _____
weight: _____	eye color: _____
sex: _____	skin color: _____
age: _____	clothing: _____
other: _____	

mugger? How did he know the mugger was strong? What does the police officer think about muggers?

4. ▦ Replay the audiotape and have learners listen for the types of questions asked. Have learners complete exercise A.

5. Have learners role-play the police officer asking Quang questions. Suggest ways to begin the role play, such as *Quang, do you remember anything about the mugger?*

6. Arrange learners in pairs, making sure learners cannot see their partners. Have them fill in the chart in exercise B with information about their partners. Have pairs compare charts and check which characteristics were correct. ◼ In a one-to-one situation, have the learner fill in the chart about a friend or a family member.

7. Discuss the descriptions. Ask *Which characteristics were easy to guess? Which were difficult? Were you able to remember many specific details? How easy would it be to describe a stranger that you met or observed in a dark place?*

***Expansion/Extension* on page 172**

Preventing Street Crime

Purpose: To provide practice in giving advice; to provide practice with prepositions of place

Teacher Preparation and Materials

1. Samples of "Police Blotter" columns (found in local or small-town newspapers)
2. Semantic web used for page 115
3. Large sheet of paper, marker
4. Posterboard, markers *(Expansion/Extension)*
5. Invite a local police officer to speak to the class about ways to protect themselves and their homes. *(Expansion/Extension)*

Warm-up

Give learners samples of local "Police Blotter" columns. Have learners skim the columns for types of crimes reported. Add any new crime vocabulary to the semantic web for the unit. Ask *Why do you think the newspaper lists the different crimes in the area?*

Presentation

1. Have learners turn to page 117 and read the titles of the page and newspaper article. Ask *What do you think this newspaper article will be about? What does "Mugger Hits Herndon" mean? What do you think are some ways to avoid muggings and other street crimes?*
2. Have learners read the article and underline new words. Elicit/explain the meanings of new words: *logged calls, crime prevention, asserted, precautions, criminal, easy target, common sense, victim, surroundings, shadows, notify.*
3. Ask literal and inferential questions about the article, such as *Do you think the police were able to arrest all the criminals involved in the incidents? What are some things that make a person an easy target of street crime? Can you think of any other advice that isn't in the article?*

POLICE BEAT: Mugger Hits Herndon

During the week of December 2, the Herndon Police Department received reports of 12 muggings, out of a total of 44 logged calls. Police also listed a purse snatching, made 15 arrests, responded to 13 accidents, and answered 3 calls of vandalism.

Herndon Police Chief Edward Dowd suggests that all citizens of Herndon follow some simple guidelines to avoid being mugged on the street. "Every citizen has a role to play in crime prevention," he asserted. "There are sensible precautions that everyone can take to be safer on the street."

Street robberies are a quick way for a criminal to make money. Muggers are always looking for an easy target. Common sense can help you avoid being the next victim.

- Be aware of your surroundings and stay in well-lighted areas at night. Muggers always prefer shadows.
- Stay with a crowd. There's safety in numbers.
- Hold your bag or purse close to your body to make it hard to snatch. Keep your wallet in a pocket, not in your bag or purse.
- Don't carry large sums of cash.
- Notify the police of strangers who are hanging around your home or apartment for no apparent reason, especially at night.
- Lock your car doors when driving your vehicle and whenever you leave it, no matter for how short a time.

Think and talk about the questions. Answers will vary.

1. Have you or someone you know been a victim of a street crime? What happened?
2. Do you think the ideas for avoiding muggings are sensible ones?
3. What other precautions do you use to protect yourself?
4. What precautions do you take to avoid burglaries at your home?
5. Why do you have to take special precautions when you go on vacation?
6. What else can be done to prevent street crime?

4. Have learners discuss the questions at the bottom of the page in small groups. ⬛ In a one-to-one situation, the learner can answer the questions individually and then discuss his or her responses with you.
5. As a group, have learners share their responses. Compile a class list of precautions on a large sheet of paper. (**Note:** This list will be used again for page 123.)

Expansion/Extension

- Learners can make a list of safety precautions for children. (FOR EXAMPLE: Never get in a car with strangers. Don't accept gifts or candy from strangers.) Learners can discuss at what age children can be left at home alone or can be responsible for taking care of younger children.
- Ask learners to make and illustrate posters to display the safety precautions.
- Invite a local police officer to speak to the class about ways to protect themselves and their homes.

Harassed by the Boss

Purpose: To give practice in expressing feelings; to give practice with the present perfect tense

Teacher Preparation and Materials

1. Information or brochures on the Equal Employment Opportunity Commission
2. Local phone book (*Expansion/Extension*)

Warm-up

1. On the board write *harass*. Elicit/explain the meaning or have learners look it up in a dictionary. Write a simple definition after the word, such as *to disturb or bother someone continually*. Have learners brainstorm things that people do to harass others. Make a list of ideas on the board. Have learners explain which types of harassment they think are illegal and which types are not serious.

2. Bring in information or brochures on the Equal Employment Opportunity Commission (EEOC). Elicit/explain how and why the commission protects workers. Have learners look through the information and brochures for the types of harassment and discrimination that the commission handles. Ask *Why are these problems found in workplaces? Why can't workers protect themselves?*

Presentation

1. Have learners turn to page 118, read the title, and look at the picture. Ask *Who do you see?* (Learners can look back at Unit 7 for the name of Diep's supervisor.) *Why do you think Joan (Ms. Morris) looks miserable? What do you think the doctor is saying? Do you think this is a form of harassment? Why or why not? What do you think Joan should do?*

2. Have learners read the story and underline words they do not know. Elicit/explain the meanings of new words: *grateful, compliment, file a complaint, ignore.*

3. Ask literal and inferential questions, such as *Has Joan told Dr. Landers how she*

---

118 **Harassed by the Boss**

Diep's supervisor, Joan Morris, works for Dr. Landers. Dr. Landers has been bothering Joan for a long time. She's told him many times that she doesn't like being touched or cornered. She doesn't like him to tell her she's beautiful and smells nice. He just laughs and says she should be grateful for the compliment. She gets upset and angry, but she's been afraid to do anything because she needs her job. She's been afraid she'll get a bad evaluation from him if she complains to the hospital. Joan is also afraid that everyone at work thinks she doesn't mind or that she encourages his attention. She's worried that people won't believe that she's being harassed.

Lately Joan has noticed that Dr. Landers has been harassing female student nurses, too. Joan can't ignore Dr. Landers any longer. She's going to file a complaint with the Equal Employment Opportunity Commission (EEOC).

A. Write your answers.

1. Why did Joan Morris wait so long to file a complaint about Dr. Landers?

   <u>She was afraid she'd get a bad evaluation or lose her job.</u>

2. What finally made her decide to file the complaint?

   <u>She has seen Dr. Landers harassing female student</u>
   nurses.

B. Think and talk about the questions. Answers will vary.

1. Why do you think Dr. Landers keeps bothering Joan Morris even though she's asked him to stop?
2. How do you think she feels?
3. Why is it so hard for Joan to make him stop?
4. Have you ever had a problem with someone giving you attention you didn't want? Who was involved? What did you do?

---

feels? Why do you think he doesn't take her seriously? What is Joan afraid of? What has made her change her mind about reporting the harassment? What do you think the hospital's policy is on this type of harassment? Do you think there are other people Joan could contact or report this situation to?

4. Have learners answer the questions in exercise A.

5. Ask learners to discuss the questions at the bottom of the page in small groups. Bring the groups together and have them share their ideas with the class. ◼ In a one-to-one situation, the learner can answer the questions individually and then discuss his or her responses.

Expansion/Extension

- Learners can look in the local phone book for the number of the EEOC or the appropriate state agency that deals with job discrimination and sexual harassment. If possible, have learners call for information and procedures for filing complaints.

More *Expansion/Extension* on page 172

How Can I Be Sure?

Purpose: To give practice in expressing feelings, in reporting events, and in giving advice

Teacher Preparation and Materials

1. 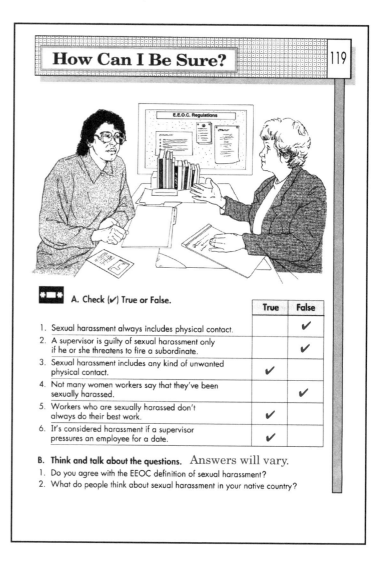 Audiotape for Level 3
2. EEOC complaint form
   (Expansion/Extension)
3. Sample company policies and information or brochures about sexual harassment
   (Expansion/Extension)
4. Invite a guest speaker, such as a lawyer or EEOC representative, to speak to the class about sexual harassment.
   (Expansion/Extension)

Warm-up

Have learners summarize Joan's problem from the story on page 118. Have learners guess how Joan is feeling about herself and the situation. Ask learners why they think Joan hesitated before reporting the situation, what Joan thinks the EEOC can do, and what fears Joan may still have about the situation.

Presentation

1. Have learners turn to page 119, read the title, and look at the picture. Ask *Why is Joan in the EEOC office? What do you think they are talking about? What do you think Joan wants to be sure about? Do you think it is easy for Joan to file a complaint against her supervisor? Why or why not?*
2. Play the audiotape. Have learners summarize the conversation.
3. Ask learners to read the sentences in exercise A and underline new vocabulary. Elicit/explain the meanings of new words: *guilty, subordinate, unwanted, pressures.* Replay the audiotape. Have learners complete the exercise.
4. Have volunteers share and explain their answers. Learners can listen to the audiotape again to verify responses. Ask learners to rewrite or orally rephrase the false sentences to make them true.

5. Have learners restate the meaning of *sexual harassment* and write a definition on the board. Ask learners to discuss the questions in exercise B in small groups. Bring groups together and have them share their ideas with the class. In a one-to-one situation, have the learner answer the questions individually and then discuss his or her responses. Discuss any disagreements or reservations that learners may have with the EEOC definition.

Expansion/Extension

- Bring in a copy of an EEOC complaint form. Learners can find out what information is needed to file. Elicit/explain the types of documentation that are helpful to have when filing a sexual harassment complaint or any type of legal complaint. Documentation should include date(s) of harassment, place(s), description of what was said or done, and the names of any witnesses.

More *Expansion/Extension* on page 172

A Family Fight

Purpose: To give practice in reporting events; to give practice with the present perfect tense

Teacher Preparation and Materials

1. Copies of TRF Handout 10.4, *Difficult Situations (Expansion/Extension)*
2. Copies of TRF Handout 10.5, *The Rights of Children (Expansion/Extension)*
3. Copies of Amendment IV of the U.S. Constitution *(Expansion/Extension)*

Warm-up

On the board write the word *Family*. Have learners suggest words to describe feelings about the family group or individual family members. List learners' ideas on the board. Identify the feelings as positive or negative. Ask *What makes people feel good about their families? What makes people feel stressed or upset with their families? Should other people try to help families that may be having problems? What types of problems should they help with?*

Presentation

1. Have learners turn to page 120, read the title, and look at the picture. Ask *Who are the members of each character's family? Do you think these families ever have fights? Why might some family members fight?*
2. Have learners look at the thought bubble next to Yolette. Ask *Who do you think these women are? What is Yolette talking about? Why is the police officer talking to the other woman? What do you think has happened to her?*
3. Have learners read the story and underline words they do not know. Elicit/explain the meanings of new words: *warrant, beating up, cooperate.*
4. Ask literal and inferential questions, such as *Why did Al call the police? Was Marty legally right in his response to the police? Do you think it was easy for Sara to talk to the police? What do you think Sara told the police? How do you think Sara feels*

120

A Family Fight

Three friends have been comparing stories about their week. Diep talked about Quang's mugging and her supervisor's problem at work.

Roberto talked about his son, Eddy, who thought he had won a free trip to Florida.

Yolette told her friends about a sad event that happened to her neighbor. Last night Al called the police because their neighbor, Marty Evans, was beating up his wife, Sara.

"We heard terrible noises and yelling. When the police got there, Marty didn't want to let them in. He said they couldn't enter his apartment without his permission or without a warrant. Marty wouldn't cooperate with the police. Finally Sara managed to step out in the hall to talk with the police. She was crying because Marty had broken her arm. The police took her to the hospital. I hope she's going to be all right," Yolette said.

Diep, Roberto, and Yolette discussed what happens in their native countries when husbands beat wives or parents beat children. They agreed that some ideas and laws in this country are different from those in other countries.

Think and talk about the questions.   Answers will vary.

1. Did Al and Yolette do the right thing?
2. What else could they have done?
3. How do you think Sara feels? How do you think Marty feels?
4. What would you have done if you were Al or Yolette?
5. Do you think it is all right for men to beat women?
6. Do you think it is all right for parents to beat children?

about Marty? How do you think Marty feels about Sara? When do you think family problems become the concern of the police?

5. Have learners discuss the questions at the bottom of the page in small groups. ◼ In a one-to-one situation, have the learner answer the questions individually and then discuss his or her responses.
6. Ask learners about the possible outcomes of the situation. Ask *What might happen if Sara goes home? Where could Sara go if she doesn't go home? What could happen to Marty? If there are children in the family, what might happen to them?*

Expansion/Extension

See TRF HANDOUT 10.4, *Difficult Situations*
TRF HANDOUT 10.5, *The Rights of Children*

- Learners can role-play situations from the story. (FOR EXAMPLE: Marty answering the door and talking to the police; Sara talking to the police after entering the hall; Al calling the police to report the alleged beating)

More *Expansion/Extension* on page 172

Know Your Rights

Purpose: To give practice in expressing surprise and in giving advice

Teacher Preparation and Materials

1. ▣▣▣ Audiotape for Level 3
2. Copies of TRF Handout 10.3, *Speeding Ticket (Expansion/Extension)*
3. Copies of TRF Handout 10.6, *A Day in Court (Expansion/Extension)*
4. Copies of Amendment IV of the U.S. Constitution *(Expansion/Extension)*
5. Copies of local/state laws regarding spouse and child abuse *(Expansion/Extension)*
6. Local phone book *(Expansion/Extension)*

Warm-up

Have learners summarize the story from page 120. Ask learners to make predictions about what will happen. List learners' ideas on the board.

Presentation

1. Have learners turn to page 121. Have a volunteer read the title and introductory paragraph. Elicit/explain the meanings of new words: *shelter, battered, violent, press charges, arrest warrant.*
2. Ask *Were our predictions (on the board) right? What do you think about Sara's decision? What other options does she have? Do you think this is the first time Marty has beaten her? Why do you think the volunteer says that it is hard for violent people to stop? When a woman presses charges against her husband, what effects might that have on the family?*
3. Have learners look at the picture. Ask *What is happening? What do you think the police officer is saying to the person? Why?*
4. ▣▣▣ Play the first part of the audiotape. Stop after the police officer says: "Sara Evans is charging you with assault and battery." Have learners guess what Marty's reaction will be. Ask *Will Marty get angry? Do you think Marty will deny*

hitting Sara? Should Marty say anything? What does the police officer have to say when someone is arrested?

5. ▣▣▣ Play the rest of the conversation. Ask *What did the police officer read to Marty? What do you think it means? What did the police officer tell Marty before reading the Miranda rights?*
6. Have learners look at the explanation of the Miranda rights. Ask volunteers to read each sentence and restate the information in simpler terms.
7. Ask learners to complete the vocabulary exercise at the bottom of the page.
8. Have learners discuss issues related to the Miranda rights. Ask *How can a lawyer help during police interrogations? What could happen if the police do not read someone his or her rights? Why does the Supreme Court protect the rights of people who are accused of committing a crime?*

After Sara Evans was released from the hospital, the police took her to a shelter for battered women. A volunteer worker told Sara that it was against the law for Marty to beat her. The volunteer also said that it's very hard for violent husbands to stop. Sara knew the woman was right and decided to press charges. The police went to Sara's apartment with an arrest warrant for Marty.

▣▣▣

MIRANDA RIGHTS

In 1966, the Supreme Court of the United States decided that police officers had to follow certain procedures when interrogating someone accused of a crime. Miranda rights protect people against forced confessions. According to the Miranda decision, criminal suspects must be told the following:

1. they do not *have* to answer a police officer's questions until their attorney is present;
2. they have the right to hire an attorney to defend them; and
3. if they can't afford to pay, the court will assign an attorney to defend them for free.

Find the word or phrase that means the same as . . .

1. lawyer: attorney
2. asking questions: interrogating
3. blamed: accused
4. protect or help: defend
5. steps or actions: procedures
6. be able to pay for: afford
7. employ: hire

Expansion/Extension on page 172

Watch Out: Deceptive Advertising

Purpose: To give practice in expressing surprise and in reporting events; to give practice with the present perfect tense

Teacher Preparation and Materials

1. Direct mail advertisements (if possible, both legitimate and deceptive/illegitimate offers)
2. Copies of TRF Handout 10.7, *An Offer You Can Refuse (Expansion/Extension)*

Warm-up

Bring in advertisements or offers received in the mail. Have learners look through them and comment on which ones they think are effective and which appear to be misleading or too good to be true. Ask *Have you ever received this type of mail? Do you think all of the offers are true? Do you ever buy things because of advertisements? Do you think advertisers can say things that are not true about their products or services? Would you want to see something before buying it, or would you order something over the phone or by mail without seeing it? Why or why not?*

Presentation

1. Have learners turn to page 122, read the title, and look at the picture. Elicit/explain the meaning of *deceptive.* Ask *Who do you think Eddy is calling? What do you think he is asking about? Do you think his parents know what he is doing?*
2. Have learners read the story and underline any new words. Elicit/explain the meaning of new words: *processed, 800 number, service fee.*
3. Ask literal and inferential questions, such as *Why didn't Eddy receive information from the company after he sent the $20? What lesson did Eddy learn? Do you think the company tricked other people the same way as Eddy?*
4. Have learners reread the story to find things that are suspicious. (Eddy wins a free vacation from a company he never

heard of. A money order is used. Eddy was asked to send money to a company with no written guarantee for anything in return.)
5. Have learners complete exercise A. Then have learners work individually or in small groups to discuss the questions at the bottom of the page.

Expansion/Extension

See TRF HANDOUT 10.7, *An Offer You Can Refuse*

- Ask learners to role-play Eddy telling Roberto about the situation.
- Learners can discuss what Roberto and Eddy could do to prevent this from happening to other people. (FOR EXAMPLE: give a talk at school, write a letter to the editor of a local paper)

---

122 · Watch Out: Deceptive Advertising

Roberto told his friends at school about an incident that happened to his son, Eddy. Eddy received a postcard in the mail that said that he and his family had won a free trip to Florida. The postcard was from a company called Vacation Trips, Inc.

Eddy was very excited. He knew that his family would be so pleased that he had won this fabulous vacation. The card instructed Eddy to call a special 800 number in order to claim his prize. He called the number and spoke to a woman who asked him to send a $20 money order made out to Vacation Trips, Inc. She explained that the money was a service fee and that Eddy would be receiving more information about the trip once the fee was processed.

Eddy took $20 from his savings, purchased the money order, and mailed it. Weeks went by and Eddy didn't hear anything more about the free vacation. Finally he told his father what had happened. Roberto realized that Eddy had been tricked.

Eddy was disappointed and angry that he hadn't really won a Florida vacation. But he learned a lesson from the experience.

A. What happened? List each thing Eddy did in the story.
1. *Eddy received a postcard that said he and his family had won a free trip to Florida.*
2. He called an 800 number to claim his prize.
3. He took $20 from his savings.
4. He purchased a money order for $20 and mailed it.
5. Finally, after weeks of hearing nothing, he told his father.

B. Think and talk about the questions. Answers will vary.
1. Why do you think Eddy responded to the postcard in this way?
2. Could Roberto have done anything to help his son?
3. Have you ever been told that you had won a big prize? If so, did you believe it?
4. How can you avoid problems like this?

Expansion/Extension on page 172

What's Your Safety IQ?

Purpose: To give practice in giving advice

Teacher Preparation and Materials

1. Semantic web and list of precautions, used for page 117
2. Samples of magazine or newspaper self-quizzes
3. Copies of TRF Handout 10.2, *Neighborhood Crime Watch (Expansion/Extension)*

Warm-up

1. Have learners review the crime vocabulary from the semantic web and the list of safety precautions. Have learners suggest additional crime situations and precautions from the unit and add these to the semantic web and list.
2. Show samples of self-quizzes from magazines or newspapers. Ask learners if they have ever taken any quizzes like the samples and, if so, what the quizzes were about. Elicit/explain that the purpose of these types of quizzes is to give information or test knowledge in an informal and self-assessing format. Have learners look over the quizzes to see the types of questions (true/false, multiple choice, matching, and so on) and the rating systems that are used.

Presentation

1. Have learners turn to page 123. Have a volunteer read the title and introductory paragraph. Elicit/explain the meaning of *IQ*.
2. Ask learners to skim the quiz and underline words they do not know. Elicit/explain the meanings of new words: *weapon, panic, hitchhikers, search warrant*.
3. Have learners work individually or in pairs to complete the quiz.
4. Point out the answers to the quiz at the bottom of the page. Ask learners to check their own answers and give reasons for their responses.

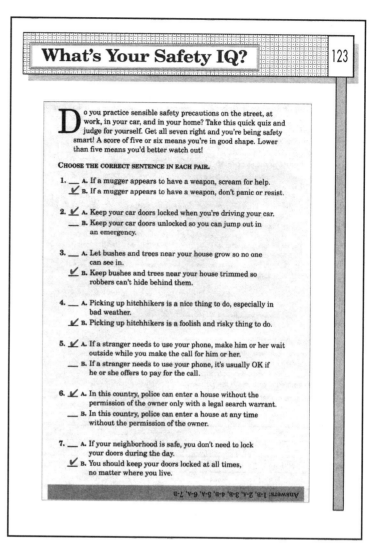

5. Ask *Why do you think that newspapers and magazines have quizzes like this? Which would you be more likely to look at and read: a list of do's and don'ts or a short quiz?*
6. Have learners prepare their own safety quizzes and then exchange them with others in the class.

Expansion/Extension

See TRF HANDOUT 10.2, *Neighborhood Crime Watch*

- Learners can role-play the situations described in items #5 and #6 of the quiz. Learners can practice expressions for refusing, such as *I'm sorry, but . . . . I'd really like to help you out, but . . . . No! I cannot let you do that.*
- Ask learners how they decide whether or not to help someone and when it might not be wise. Learners can also discuss how to choose a person to ask for help if they ever need assistance. Ask learners to compare how people help others and what caution is needed in the United States and in their native countries.

Practicing Your Skills

Purpose: To give practice in reporting events and in giving advice; to give practice with the present perfect tense

Teacher Preparation and Materials
None

Warm-up
Ask learners to look at the picture on page 115 and to suggest things that might improve the safety of the bus stop. Ask about local areas that have high crime rates and what improvements could be made. List learners' ideas on the board.

Presentation
1. Have learners turn to page 124. Have a volunteer read the introductory paragraph. Ask *Why did Diep write the letter? Do you think the hospital workers would be concerned about a mugging near the hospital? Do you think the letter will stop crime near the hospital, or will the letter make people more cautious?*

2. Have learners read the letter and underline words they do not know. Elicit/explain the meanings of new words: *disturbing, fortunately, bruises, extension.*

3. Ask literal and inferential questions about the letter, such as *What is the first paragraph about? What does Diep suggest in the second paragraph? Do you think a committee will be formed?*

4. Learners can brainstorm and add to the list on the board workplace or neighborhood conditions that are dangerous but not crime-related. Ask learners to explain why these conditions are dangerous and what might be done to solve the problems. Add learners' ideas for solutions to the list on the board.

5. Ask learners to pick from the list a problem that is important to them. Have learners individually write a draft of an article or letter to fellow learners or co-workers explaining their ideas for improving the condition or situation.

---

124 **Practicing Your Skills**

After Quang was mugged, Diep became very concerned about her safety and the safety of her family and friends. She didn't want others to be victims of a crime like Quang had been. Diep decided to tell her brother's story in the hospital newsletter.

> **An Open Letter to My City Hospital Co-Workers:**
>
> Some of you may have heard that my brother, Quang Tran, was mugged last week on Highland Street, right near the hospital. The street was dark and no one was around, so it was the perfect spot for a crime. Fortunately, Quang only received minor cuts and bruises, but the mugger took his wallet and watch.
>
> This experience has been very disturbing for our entire family. I think that it's about time that we voiced our opinions about the lack of safety in this neighborhood. We need more lights on the streets, and we also need more police officers in the area.
>
> Anyone interested in forming a committee to help make our streets safer, please call me at extension 2471.
>
> Sincerely,
> Diep Tran

Write a short article for a newsletter. Answers will vary.
Possible subjects include:
• safety or unsanitary conditions in your neighborhood, school, or workplace
• building or street maintenance
• communication with the police

Be sure to mention why you are interested in the subject. If you write about a current problem, try to convince others to help you correct the situation.

_____

_____

_____

_____

_____

_____

---

6. In pairs, have learners exchange drafts. Learners should read, ask questions about, and comment on the drafts in terms of clarity. Then have learners rewrite their own ideas in their books or on separate sheets of paper. Learners can keep a copy of their writing in their portfolio.

Expansion/Extension
• Learners can rewrite their ideas as a letter to an appropriate local government agency or elected official. Learners can find the addresses and mail the letters.

• Learners can find out about the types of Neighborhood Watch programs in their city or town.

• Ask learners to compile a vocabulary list for the unit. Learners can create categories and categorize the new words. Some categories might be Crimes, People and Places, Descriptive Words, Court and Legal Terms, and Miscellaneous.

Verbs: Present Perfect Tense – Questions/ Passive Voice

Purpose: To give practice with *yes/no* questions and answers in the present perfect tense and with forming and using the passive voice

Teacher Preparation and Materials

Newspaper stories about muggings or other crimes *(Expansion/Extension)*

Warm-up

1. Review the present perfect tense. Ask questions about learners' experiences in their community. Use key time phrases, such as *ever, yet,* or *before today,* to elicit answers in the present perfect. Contrast these with questions that elicit answers in the simple past. FOR EXAMPLE: *Have you ever been to City Hall? Why did you go there? Have you ever used public transportation? How many times have you ridden city buses?*

2. Tell a story about a crime in your neighborhood. Use active voice, but refer to vague or unidentified persons who committed the crime. FOR EXAMPLE: *Someone robbed my neighbor last month. The robber broke a window in the back of the house. He took some jewelry, a CD player, and most of my neighbor's CDs. The robber didn't take the TV, probably because it is very big, but he smashed the TV screen. The police recovered some of the jewelry, but they didn't catch the robber.* Write the story on the board. Then, to review use of the passive voice, retell the story focusing on what happened, rather than on what the robber did. FOR EXAMPLE: *My neighbor was robbed last month. A window in the back of the house was broken. Some jewelry, a CD player, and most of my neighbor's CDs were taken.* Point out to learners that the passive is often used to focus on what happened rather than on who did something.

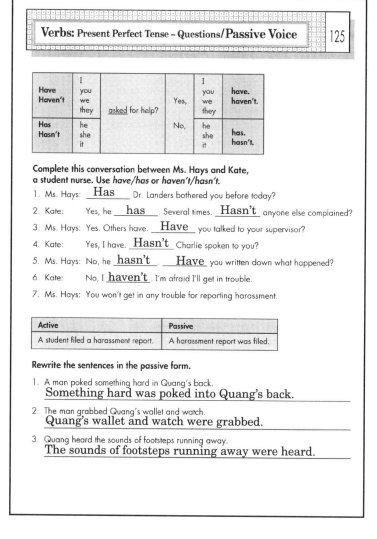

Presentation

1. Have learners turn to page 125 and review question and answer forms in the chart.

2. You may wish to have learners review the story on page 118 of Joan Morris's experience with sexual harassment. Explain that the first exercise refers to another case of harassment at the hospital.

3. With learners, complete item 1 as an example. Then have learners complete the exercise.

4. Review answers by having pairs of learners role-play the conversation between Ms. Hays and Kate.

5. Review the sample active and passive sentences in the second chart. Then have learners complete the second exercise. Review answers by having learners, in round-robin format, use passive voice to tell what happened to Quang.

Expansion/Extension

- Learners may want to rewrite Quang's story from page 115 in the style of a police report, referring to "the victim" and "the suspect" and using passive voice frequently.

Wh- Questions: Past Tense/Prepositions of Time and Place

Purpose: To give practice with *wh-* questions in the past tense and with prepositions of time and place

Teacher Preparation and Materials

List of safety precautions developed for *Expansion/Extension* on page 117 (Expansion/Extension)

Warm-up

1. Use Quang's story on page 115 to review *wh-* questions in the past tense. Put *wh-* words on the board: *who, what, when, where, why,* and *how.* Have learners reread Quang's story and, if they wish, prepare *wh-* questions about the events. Point to one of the *wh-* words at random and call a learner's name. The learner must give a correctly formed question with that word, and, if the question is grammatically correct, can call on another learner to answer it. Point to another *wh-* word. The learner who answered must give another question with the new word and can call on a third learner to answer. The activity should move briskly to provide quick review of the question forms.

2. Review the article on street crime on page 117. Have learners circle prepositions of time and place as they read. Elicit and list prepositional phrases. The article has examples of phrases with *during, at, close to, in, on,* and *with.* Add examples of phrases with *before* and *after* to complete the set of prepositions used in the Student Book exercise. Clarify meanings if necessary.

Presentation

1. Have learners turn to page 126 and review the questions in the charts. Focus on word order and verb forms.

2. Have learners reread Eddy's story on page 122. Look at the first item in the first exercise on page 126 and write a question. Then have learners work individually or in pairs to complete the exercise.

---

126 | **Wh- Questions:** Past Tense / Prepositions of Time and Place

Who	filed	a report?	What / When / Where / Why	was/were	filed? / it/they filed?	How / What	did	it get filed? / it say?

Read the story on page 122. Then write questions for these answers. Answers may vary.

Question	Answer
Who received a postcard?	Eddy did.
What did he think?	He thought he'd won a vacation.
Where was the vacation?	In Florida.
Who did he speak to?	A woman at Vacation Trips, Inc.
When did he tell his father?	Weeks after he sent the money order.
Why was he disappointed and angry?	Because he really didn't win a prize.
How did Vacation Trips, Inc. make money?	By cheating people.
What did he learn?	To be very careful about "free offers."

Prepositions of Time	Prepositions of Place
Yolette had questions before class.	She sat close to the door.
She raised her hand during class.	She was in the front row.
Her question was answered after the demonstration.	She sat with some friends.

Complete each sentence with an appropriate preposition.

1. Light the hallway **during** the night.
2. Stay **in** well-lighted places.
3. Walk **with** other people whenever possible.
4. Keep your purse or bag **close to** your side.
5. Don't let strangers enter an empty hallway **after** you.
6. Check the backseat of your car **before** getting in.

---

3. Review the exercise by having one learner read a question and another give the answer. There may be more than one way to form a question for a given answer. Have learners discuss and evaluate variations in the questions they create.

4. Have learners read the example sentences in the prepositions chart. Then have them complete the exercise and review answers.

Expansion/Extension

- Have learners create and role-play a conversation between Eddy and a friend. Eddy tells his friend about his experience with the deceptive advertising, and his friend asks questions to get additional details.

- Have learners review the list of safety precautions they developed for page 117 and add to that list any further ideas based on the safety quiz on page 123 and the second exercise on this page. If they have not yet done so, encourage them to think about safety in different places around town (parking garages, shopping malls, and so on) and at all times of day and night.

UNIT 10: Under the Law
Expansion/Extension

What Did You See?
Expansion/Extension for SB page 116

See TRF HANDOUT 10.1, *Mug Shots*

- Learners can brainstorm and list other characteristics and features to use to describe people. (FOR EXAMPLE: face/skin—rash, mustache, beard, scar, tattoo; voice—lisp, accent, stutter) Learners can include other clues used by police investigators to help identify people, such as fingerprints, hair, semen, skin, or blood type.

- Ask learners what constitutes a race-related crime. Ask *Do you think the mugger attacked Quang because of his race? Why or why not? What are some characteristics of racially motivated crimes? What are racial epithets? Is there a police unit in your area that deals with race-related crimes?*

Harassed by the Boss
More *Expansion/Extension* for SB page 118

- Learners can suggest ways that Joan Morris could confront Dr. Landers about the harassment and then role-play the confrontation. Learners playing Joan should explain to Dr. Landers what behavior is offensive, how she feels about it, and what she wants changed. Learners should have Joan be firm in talking to her harasser: "If you don't . . . , I will . . . ."

How Can I Be Sure?
More *Expansion/Extension* for SB page 119

- Learners can look at company policies, brochures, or other information about sexual harassment. Ask learners what other action Joan might take.

- Invite a lawyer or EEOC representative to speak to the class about sexual harassment.

A Family Fight
More *Expansion/Extension* for SB page 120

- Ask learners to read Amendment IV of the U.S. Constitution. Ask learners to restate the amendment in their own words.

- Learners can discuss discipline for children. Ask *How and why are children disciplined in your native country? What types of discipline are used in the United States? If you have children in school, do you think the teachers discipline the children appropriately? Why or why not?*

- Ask learners to suggest reasons why Marty became violent. Ask *What types of problems and stresses can cause people to become violent? What can people do to prevent themselves from becoming violent? What can family or friends do to help potentially violent people deal with situations and control their behavior?*

Know Your Rights
Expansion/Extension for SB page 121

See TRF HANDOUT 10.3, *Speeding Ticket*
    TRF HANDOUT 10.6, *A Day in Court*

- Ask learners why the police did not arrest Marty when Al reported the problem. Learners can refer to Amendment IV of the U.S. Constitution.

- Bring in copies of local or state laws regarding spouse and child abuse. Ask learners to compare Marty's and Sara's situation with local laws. Ask *What are the rights of the victims? the accused? What can/can't the police do?*

- Ask learners to look in the community services pages of the local phone book to find names and numbers of agencies or shelters that deal with domestic violence and related issues. Learners can discuss why the addresses for the shelters are not listed.

Watch Out:
Deceptive Advertising
More *Expansion/Extension* for SB page 122

- Learners can brainstorm and list situations or offers that may be suspicious or fraudulent. Some examples might be chain letters, money pyramids, credit card scams, "miracle" medicines, and so on. Learners can suggest and role-play ways to handle the different situations.

Can I Buy a House?

Objectives

Functions
- Comparing and contrasting
- Computing costs
- Expressing preferences
- Hypothesizing
- Giving and getting advice

Life Tasks
- Reading real estate listings
- Using mortgage rates to calculate mortgage costs
- Reading house inspection reports
- Calculating home improvement costs
- Reading housing grant information and using eligibility scales
- Evaluating advice column information
- Interpreting newspaper apartment ads

Structures
- Comparative adjectives
- *Ask* + infinitive
- Descriptive adjectives
- *What about . . . ?* questions
- *What if . . . ?* questions

Culture
- Owning property in the United States
- Housing grants
- Remodeling and improving housing
- Living arrangements with roommates in the United States

Vocabulary

Key words:

assessment	own/owner
condition	principal and
exterior	interest
housing grant	qualify
improvement	real estate agent
inspector	real estate listing
interest rate	remodeling
lease	rent/renter
long-term	roommate
investment value	security deposit
lot size	subsidy
major investment	unit measure
mortgage	

Related words:

amenity	pension
approval	pressure-treated
asking price	wood
asphalt shingle	property
attic	ranch
boiler	residential
deck	spacious
dividend	starter home
downspout	storm window
expectation	suburb
furnished	terrace
gutter	unfinished
habit	unfurnished
inclination	vacant
instinct	veteran
insulate	vinyl siding
living	walk-in closet
arrangement	wall-to-wall
negotiable	carpeting

For Sale

Purpose: To introduce housing and real estate vocabulary

Teacher Preparation and Materials

1. Pictures of different types of houses, apartment buildings, and residential areas
2. Large sheet of paper, markers
3. Copies of TRF Handout 11.2, *My New Home (Expansion/Extension)*
4. Real estate fliers and/or newspaper real estate sections *(Expansion/Extension)*

Warm-up

1. Show pictures of different types of houses, apartment buildings, and residential areas. Ask learners to brainstorm and to list on the board types of housing. Be sure to include *apartment, ranch house*, and kinds of housing that are common in the area.
2. Have learners discuss different rooms, fixtures, and appliances. Ask *What rooms do you have in your house/apartment? What appliances and fixtures were in your home before you moved in? What types of appliances did you bring with you? What housing features are most important to you?*

Presentation

1. Have learners open their books to page 127. Ask questions about the picture. *Who are Al and Yolette talking to? Why do you think they are standing in front of this house? How would you describe this house? How much do you think it would cost? What do you think Al is thinking about? What questions would you have about this house?*
2. Have learners discuss the questions at the bottom of the page.
3. Learners can brainstorm and list on a large sheet of paper things that Al and Yolette should consider before buying a house, such as location, commuting distance, services, condition, size,

1 2 3 4 5 6 7 8 9 10 **11** 12

Can I Buy a House? ■ ■ ■ ■ ■ ■ ■ ■

For Sale   Answers may vary.
What are Al and Yolette doing?
What are they talking about?

and price. (**Note:** This list will be used again in the *Expansion/Extension* for page 136.)

4. Have learners role-play Al and Yolette talking to the real estate agent about their list of housing considerations. (**Note:** If learners are not familiar with real estate agents, you may want to play that role and ask appropriate questions.)

Expansion/Extension

See TRF HANDOUT 11.2, *My New Home*

- Learners can write a description of a house that they believe Al and Yolette might be interested in. They can take into consideration what they already know about the Jamisons and can speculate on their future plans.
- Ask learners to look through real estate fliers and/or newspaper real estate sections for pictures of the different styles of houses that are listed on the board.

Which Is Better for You?

Purpose: To give practice in expressing preferences, in comparing and contrasting, and in giving and getting advice

Teacher Preparation and Materials

None

Warm-up

1. Ask learners if they rent or own their homes and what their reasons are for renting or owning. On the board make a chart of reasons why people rent and reasons why people own their homes.

2. Have learners turn to page 127. Ask them to guess why Al and Yolette are thinking about buying a home.

Presentation

1. Have learners turn to page 128. Have learners read the page title and the article title. Ask *What do you think this article is going to tell you? What do you think the biggest difference is between buying and renting a place?*

2. Have learners read the introductory paragraph. Ask *What are the biggest expenses for homeowners? Do people who rent have to pay for these? What are the biggest expenses for renters?*

3. Have learners read the chart and underline words they do not know. Elicit/explain the meanings of new words: *deductions, deduct, federal tax, long-term investment value, limited responsibility, approval, at your own discretion.*

4. Have learners scan the chart to determine who has the advantage for each of the categories. Ask *Who has better tax advantages: the renter or owner?* and so on.

5. Learners can brainstorm and list additional topics or subtopics to compare, such as building expansion, remodeling, property taxes, insurance costs, income from renting/leasing property, legal responsibilities, and insurance responsibilities. Have learners work in small

groups to discuss the questions at the bottom of the page. Bring groups together and compile a class list of additional advantages and disadvantages. ▪ In a one-to-one situation, have the learner answer the questions and then discuss his or her responses.

6. Have learners write their answer to question #3 as an entry in their writing journal. If learners do not plan to buy, have them write about their reasons for the decision.

Expansion/Extension

- Learners can brainstorm and list different tasks related to home maintenance, emergency problems, and improvements. (FOR EXAMPLE: maintenance—removing garbage, replacing light bulbs, mowing the lawn, fixing leaky faucets; improvements—additional electrical outlets, landscaping) If learners rent, ask which tasks are the responsibility of the owner or building manager and which are the responsibility of the renter.

---

128 Which is Better for You?

TO BUY OR TO RENT?
That Is the Question.

Many people thinking about the purchase of a house wonder whether it's better to rent or to buy. Down payments, mortgage and interest costs, regular maintenance, and unexpected expenses sometimes scare off potential home owners. According to Marsha Decter, president of Decter Real Estate in Herndon, "Buying a home is the major investment of most people's lives. Traditionally, it's the American dream." But is it right for everyone? And what are the benefits of renting? Let's look at some of the facts:

	RENTER	OWNER
TAX ADVANTAGES	You have no deductions or very limited state deductions.	You can deduct all mortgage interest on your federal tax return.
LONG-TERM INVESTMENT VALUE	You have no investment value.	Your investment value is usually very good.
MAINTENANCE RESPONSIBILITY	You are usually not responsible at all or have very limited responsibility.	You are fully responsible for all maintenance.
EMERGENCY PROBLEMS	You usually have very limited responsibility when problems occur.	You are fully responsible for all problems.
IMPROVEMENTS	You need your landlord's approval. You may have to pay or share cost. Improvements remain with property.	You make improvements at your own discretion. You pay full cost. Improvements may add value to your investment.

Think and talk about the questions. Answers will vary.

1. What are some other advantages of renting and owning? What are some other disadvantages?
2. In your native country, did you own or rent your home?
3. If you rent, do you plan to buy a home someday? If so, what kind of home would you like?

Talking to a Real Estate Agent

Purpose: To give practice in asking for information and in expressing preferences; to give practice with descriptive adjectives, with *prefer* with object, and with *What about . . . ?* questions

Teacher Preparation and Materials
1. Large sheet of paper, marker
2. Sample of a real estate information sheet
3. ▰▰▰ Audiotape for Level 3
4. Copies of TRF Handout 11.1, *Location, Location, and Location (Expansion/Extension)*
5. Copies of TRF Handout 11.3, *Real Estate Listing (Expansion/Extension)*

Warm-up
1. Have learners look at the picture on page 127. Review/introduce information about a real estate agent's job and reasons why a person buying a house might or might not want to work with an agent.
2. Learners can brainstorm and list on a large sheet of paper questions that real estate agents should be able to answer about homes or buildings they are trying to sell. (FOR EXAMPLE: What is the size of the property? What type of fuel is used for heat? How many rooms are there?) For learners who are not interested in buying, point out that many of the questions are also applicable for renters. (**Note:** This list will be used again in the *Expansion/Extension* for page 136.)
3. Bring in a sample of a real estate information sheet. Ask why it might be useful to both real estate agents and potential buyers/renters.

Presentation
1. Have learners turn to page 129. Have a volunteer read the title and introductory paragraph. Ask *Why do you think Al and Yolette went to several different real estate agents? How do you think they chose agents to talk to? What characteristics do you think helped them choose one agent to*

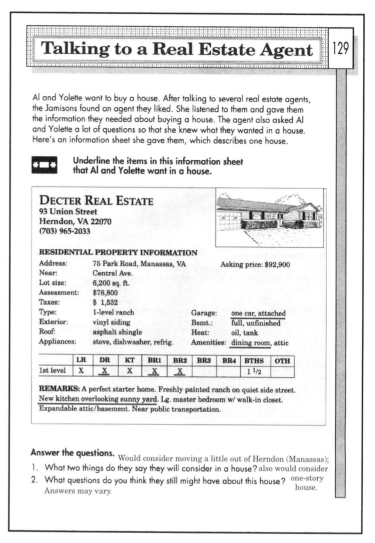

Talking to a Real Estate Agent 129

Al and Yolette want to buy a house. After talking to several real estate agents, the Jamisons found an agent they liked. She listened to them and gave them the information they needed about buying a house. The agent also asked Al and Yolette a lot of questions so that she knew what they wanted in a house. Here's an information sheet she gave them, which describes one house.

▰▰▰ Underline the items in this information sheet that Al and Yolette want in a house.

DECTER REAL ESTATE
93 Union Street
Herndon, VA 22070
(703) 965-2033

RESIDENTIAL PROPERTY INFORMATION

Address:	75 Park Road, Manassas, VA		Asking price: $92,900
Near:	Central Ave.		
Lot size:	6,200 sq. ft.		
Assessment:	$78,800		
Taxes:	$ 1,532		
Type:	1-level ranch	Garage:	one car, attached
Exterior:	vinyl siding	Bsmt.:	full, unfinished
Roof:	asphalt shingle	Heat:	oil, tank
Appliances:	stove, dishwasher, refrig.	Amenities:	dining room, attic

	LR	DR	KT	BR1	BR2	BR3	BR4	BTHS	OTH
1st level	X	X	X	X	X			1 1/2	

REMARKS: A perfect starter home. Freshly painted ranch on quiet side street. New kitchen overlooking sunny yard. Lg. master bedroom w/ walk-in closet. Expandable attic/basement. Near public transportation.

Answer the questions.
1. What two things do they say they will consider in a house? Would consider moving a little out of Herndon (Manassas); also would consider one-story house.
2. What questions do you think they still might have about this house? Answers may vary.

work with? How else can you get information on an agent?

2. Learners can brainstorm and add to the list questions that the real estate agent will ask the Jamisons and questions that the Jamisons may ask the agent.
3. ▰▰▰ Play the audiotape. Ask learners to check off the questions on the list that were asked and to add questions from the conversation. Have learners describe the type of house the Jamisons are looking for.
4. Have learners look at the information sheet in the book. Ask literal and inferential questions about the sheet. Elicit/explain the meanings of new words: *residential, lot size, assessment, asking price, exterior, vinyl siding, asphalt shingle, amenities, starter home, expandable.*
5. ▰▰▰ Replay the audiotape and have learners listen for the Jamisons' preferences. Have learners answer the questions at the bottom of the page.

Expansion/Extension on page 187

Can We Get a Mortgage?

Purpose: To introduce computing costs; to give practice in comparing and contrasting, in asking for information, and in problem solving

Teacher Preparation and Materials

1. Copies of TRF Handout 11.7, *Paying the Loan (Expansion/Extension)*
2. Bank loan/mortgage information *(Expansion/Extension)*
3. Samples of bank or other mortgage applications *(Expansion/Extension)*

Warm-up

1. Have learners look at page 110 for information to consider when shopping for a loan. Write on the board *mortgage*. Elicit/explain the meaning. Ask learners what differences there might be between a car loan and a mortgage. *What amounts of money might people borrow to buy a car? to buy a house? How much of a down payment might there be? How long would it take to pay back the loan/mortgage?*

2. Have learners look at the worksheet on page 32, which shows the Jamisons' monthly expenses, and find how much of their take-home income is spent on rent. Ask learners how much they think the Jamisons could afford to pay each month for a mortgage.

Presentation

1. Have learners turn to page 130. Have a volunteer read the title and introductory paragraph. Ask *How much was the down payment that they made? Why do you think banks want customers to make a down payment? Why do you think there are different interest rates listed?*

2. Have learners look at the first chart. Ask *How much income is needed to borrow $100,000 at 9%? $50,000 at 10%? $75,000 at 8%?* Elicit/demonstrate how to estimate approximate amounts, using the chart information. FOR EXAMPLE: *How much*

---

130 **Can We Get a Mortgage?**

Al and Yolette are buying a house for $86,500. They made a 7.5% down payment and applied for an $80,000 mortgage. Their combined annual income before taxes and deductions is $34,865. A chart from the bank showed them that they easily qualify for an $80,000 mortgage at the current rate of 9%.

Income Needed to Qualify for a Mortgage

Loan Amount	$50,000	$75,000	$100,000
Interest Rate	**Income Needed***		
8%	$15,724	$23,568	$31,447
9%	$17,242	$25,863	$34,484
10%	$18,085	$28,208	$37,611

*30-year loans; monthly payments (principal and interest) cannot exceed 28% of gross income.
Source: National Association of Realtors

A. Answer the questions. $100,000
1. What is the largest mortgage amount that Al and Yolette can borrow at 9%?
2. Why do you think banks and mortgage companies assume that people spend 28% of their income on mortgage payments? Answers may vary.

Another chart showed Al and Yolette what their monthly payments will be.

Mortgage Payment Table at Various Interest Rates

	8%	9%	10%
Amount Borrowed	**Monthly Payments* (principal + interest)**		
$ 40,000	$294	$322	$351
$ 60,000	$440	$483	$527
$ 80,000	$587	$644	$702
$100,000	$734	$805	$878

* rounded off to nearest whole dollar Source: Federal Trade Commission

B. Answer the questions.
1. How much would monthly payments be on a $60,000 mortgage at 8%? 9%? 10%? $440, $483, $527
2. How would you figure monthly payments for a $90,000 mortgage at 9%?
$724.50 (Find the difference between $805 and $644 = $161.00. Divide by 2 = $80.50. Add that sum to $644 = $724.50.)

---

income is needed to borrow $60,000 at 10%? (Divide $18,000 [income—rounded off—needed for $50,000 at 10%] by $50,000, then multiply by $60,000. Estimated income needed is $21,600.) Have learners estimate income needed for other mortgage amounts at various interest rates.

3. Have learners work individually or in small groups to answer the questions in exercise A.

4. Have learners look at the second chart. Ask questions about the chart. *How much is the monthly payment for a $40,000 mortgage at 10%? What do you think the monthly payment would be for a $70,000 mortgage at 8%?* Elicit/explain the meaning of *principal + interest*.

5. Have learners work individually or in groups to answer the questions in exercise B. Ask *Why do you think a chart like this is useful?*

Expansion/Extension

See TRF HANDOUT 11.7, *Paying the Loan*

More *Expansion/Extension* on page 187

What Will It Cost?

Purpose: To give practice in computing costs

Teacher Preparation and Materials

1. Measuring tape or yardstick
2. Hardware store fliers
3. Pictures of parts of a house: gutters, downspouts, storm windows, insulation, deck, boiler
4. Copies of TRF Handout 11.5, *Home Improvement Tips (Expansion/Extension)*
5. Copies of TRF Handout 11.6, *Do It Yourself (Expansion/Extension)*

Warm-up

1. Have learners use a measuring tape or yardstick to find the length and width of the floor of the room, the top of a desk, or other places/things in the room. Introduce the word *unit* and make a list on the board of unit measurements: *inch, foot, yard*. Elicit/explain how to calculate the perimeter ([length + width] x 2) and area (length x width). Introduce and list on the board square unit measurements (used for measuring area): *square inch, square foot, square yard*.
2. Have learners look through hardware store fliers for materials and items needed to build or repair different parts of a house. (FOR EXAMPLE: roofs—asphalt or wood shingles, metal sheeting, tar) Have learners find materials that are sold by units of length and by square units.

Presentation

1. Have learners turn to page 131. Have a volunteer read the title and introductory paragraph. Elicit/explain the meaning of *inspector*. Explain that buyers have a house inspected to find out what repairs may be needed and what the costs will be before they decide if they want to purchase the house or not.
2. Learners can brainstorm and list on the board things that an inspector might look for or notice during an inspection.

What Will It Cost? 131

Al and Yolette had an inspector look at the house they planned to buy. They wanted to know if the house had any major problems and, if so, how much the repairs would cost. They also wanted to find out what some remodeling projects would cost. The inspector gave Al and Yolette this chart. They studied the information and decided to purchase the house.

Inspection Report
Property: 75 Park Road, Manassas, VA

Item	Condition/ Comments	Unit of Measure	Average Cost/unit
Replace roof with asphalt shingles	within 5 yrs.	sq. ft.	$ 1.50
Install new gutters and downspouts	1 yr.	foot	$ 1.75
Install new boiler	satisfactory	each	$ 3,150.00
Run electric line for dryer/range	satisfactory	each	$ 225.00
Install new storm windows	now	each	$ 115.00
Insulate attic	now	sq. ft.	$ .90
Remodel kitchen	optional	each	$ 10,500.00
Remodel bath	optional	each	$ 6,250.00
Add full bath	optional	each	$ 7,000.00

A. Answer the questions.

1. What things do Al and Yolette have to do to put the house in good condition? __install new storm windows; insulate attic__

2. What things could they do if they wanted to improve the value of the house? __Answers may vary.__

B. Calculate the cost.

Al and Yolette decided to make the following improvements in their new home. Calculate the average cost of each and then the total cost.

1. insulation in attic floor, 18' x 30' $ __486.00__
2. 12 storm windows $ __1,380.00__
3. new gutters and downspouts in rear of house, 30' $ __52.50__
4. Total $ __1,918.50__

---

3. Have learners read the chart and underline words they do not know. Elicit/explain the meanings of new words: *gutters, downspouts, boiler, storm windows, optional, insulate, run a line, condition*. If possible, use pictures to illustrate the meanings of the words.
4. Ask literal and inferential questions, such as *Which items listed on the board did the inspector comment on? Why do you think the inspector didn't comment on the other items? Do you think this house is in good or poor condition? Why? Which improvements do you think are the most important? How much would it cost to replace 100 square feet of the roof? to replace 300 square feet of the roof?*
5. Have learners complete the exercises and then explain their answers.
6. Have learners decide which improvements they would make if they were buying the house and explain when and why they would make them. Ask learners to calculate the costs of their recommended improvements.

Expansion/Extension on page 187

Thinking about a Move

Purpose: To give practice in expressing preferences, and in giving and getting advice; to give practice with descriptive adjectives

Teacher Preparation and Materials
■■■ Audiotape for Level 3

Warm-up
1. Have learners talk about experiences they have had with moving. Ask *How long have you lived in your present home? How often have you moved? What were some reasons why you/your family moved? Do you think you will move again? Why or why not?*
2. Discuss the differences between moving within a country and moving from one country to another. Have learners describe the issues involved in each type of move. Ask *What did you take with you when you moved to the United States? If you have moved since then, what did you take with you?*

Presentation
1. Have learners turn to page 132, read the title, and look at the picture. Ask *Who do you think might be considering a move? Why might he or she want to move? What types of living arrangements might each of the families be interested in?* (Learners may want to look back at page 6 for information on the characters.)
2. ■■■ Play the audiotape. Have learners summarize the conversation. Ask questions as necessary. *Who is moving? Who has been looking for an apartment? Why hasn't Stan found any places yet? Why would Diep like to move? Why hasn't she been looking for a place? What does Roberto suggest to Diep? What does Roberto suggest to Stan?*
3. Have learners read the sentences in exercise A. ■■■ Replay the audiotape and have learners complete the exercise. ■■■ Learners can listen to the audiotape again to verify responses. Have learners

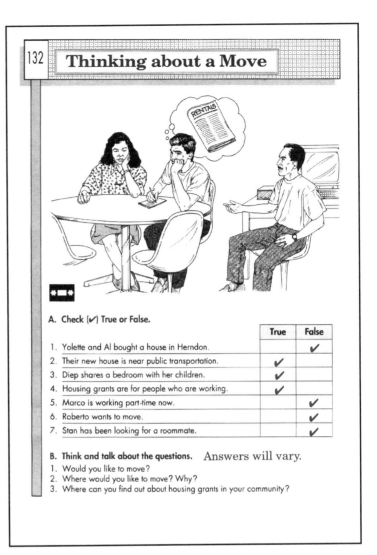

change the false sentences orally or in writing to make them true.
4. Have learners work in small groups to discuss the questions in exercise B. ■ In a one-to-one situation, have the learner answer the questions and then discuss his or her responses.

Expansion/Extension
- Learners can discuss or write about a place they would like to move to. Ask *What would your dream house or apartment be like? Where would it be?*
- Learners can discuss and compare the cultural acceptability of roommates. Ask *Is it customary for people to live with roommates in your native country? Why or why not? Do unmarried family members live with their parents or with other people? At what age do unmarried family members move out? Is it more acceptable for men or women to have roommates? Is it acceptable to have roommates of the opposite sex?*

Housing Grants Program

Purpose: To give practice in asking for information and in problem solving; to give practice with *What if . . . ?* questions

Teacher Preparation and Materials

1. Local phone book *(Expansion/Extension)*
2. Information (including eligibility requirements) on housing grants and subsidies *(Expansion/Extension)*

Warm-up

1. On the board write *grant*. Elicit/explain the meaning. Ask learners what they think a housing grant is. Ask *Who do you think would qualify for a housing grant? Who do you think gives housing grants? Why are housing grants given?*

2. Have learners look back at page 23 for the eligibility scale for legal services. Ask *What information was used to determine eligibility for free legal services? Do you think the same information would be used to help determine eligibility for housing grants? What other information might be needed to determine housing grant eligibility?*

3. Learners can brainstorm and list sources of income that should be considered to determine eligibility. Elicit/introduce *salary/job income, unemployment compensation, worker's compensation, welfare, Social Security, dividends, veterans' benefits, pension, interest, self-employment income, student grants, gifts.*

Presentation

1. Have learners turn to page 133 and skim the flier. Ask *What questions does this flier answer? What does the chart show?*

2. Have learners read the flier and underline words they do not know. Elicit/explain the meanings of new words: *subsidies, county residents, gross income, minimum, maximum.*

3. Ask literal and inferential questions, such as *Can single people with children apply?*

Can single people without children apply? Do you have to be over 55 years old to be eligible? What's the income limit for a family of six? Who is this program supposed to help? Why might people need this program?

4. Have learners work individually or in small groups to complete the exercise. Ask learners to explain their answers.

5. Depending on learners' skills, have them use the information they already know about Diep to decide if she would be eligible for assistance or not. Have learners explain their answers. Learners can also calculate how much of a grant she might receive.

Expansion/Extension

• Ask learners to look in local phone books for names and numbers of the government offices or departments that give housing grants. (These often can be found in the community services guide.)

More *Expansion/Extension* on page 187

Choose a Roommate with Care

Purpose: To provide practice in giving and getting advice, expressing preferences, and describing personal characteristics

Teacher Preparation and Materials

Newspaper classifieds with ads for roommates *(Expansion/Extension)*

Warm-up

Have learners talk about their living arrangements. Ask *Do you live alone or with other people? What do you like best/least about your living arrangement? What are the advantages/disadvantages of living with other people? Do you think it is easier to live with your family and relatives or with friends? Why?* Elicit/explain the meaning of *roommate.*

Presentation

1. Have learners turn to page 134, read the title, and write on the board a list of ideas on how to choose a roommate. Ask *What type of person would make a good roommate? What characteristics would he or she have?*

2. Have learners scan the article for main ideas. Ask *Why are more people living with roommates rather than living alone? What does this article suggest that people consider when choosing a roommate?*

3. Have learners read the article and underline words they do not know. Elicit/explain the meaning of new words: *college dormitories, polled, census, nonromantic attachments, matching services, screeners, habits, inclinations, instincts, references, commitment, trial period.*

4. Ask literal and inferential questions, such as *In 1990 what percentage of adults lived with roommates? Was this more or less than in 1970? What are some ways that people find roommates? Which ways do*

---

134 Choose a Roommate with Care

LIVING WITH A ROOMMATE

Once upon a time, roommates were people you lived with in college dormitories. Nowadays, living with a roommate is a growing trend for many young (and not-so-young) adults. Almost 5% of adults polled during the 1990 census reported living with roommates (nonromantic attachments), up from a little over 3.5% 10 years earlier and almost triple 1970's figures of about 1.5%. A major reason for this increase in roommate situations is economic: Rents, utility costs, and food prices have far outpaced the rise in individual income, so people are learning to share their living space along with their expenses.

A growing number of people are relying on bulletin boards or roommate-matching services to find roommates. When you don't know the potential roommate well or at all, you need to be very choosy. Here are some useful recommendations from professional roommate screeners.

- Be honest about your expectations and needs. Ask about the other person's habits: late hours; sharing food, clothes or belongings; how to deal with overnight guests; dishwashing and bathroom-cleaning inclinations.
- Trust your instincts. If something tells you it won't work out, it probably won't.
- Check references of the other person (especially any previous living arrangement).
- Ask to see the lease so that you know the full amount of the rent.
- A written agreement with a trial period of two to six months will give both sides a chance to get to know each other before deciding on a longer commitment. Get the agreement in writing to protect yourself legally.

Write the answers.   Answers will vary.

1. Why were more people living with roommates in 1990 than 20 years earlier?

2. What kind of person would you pick if you were going to share your home?

3. What questions would you ask that person?

4. What would be the hardest thing for you about sharing your home?

---

you think would be best? Why? Why is a temporary written agreement useful?

5. Ask learners to answer the questions and to share their responses. As a group, compile a list of questions to ask prospective roommates.

6. Have learners role-play a meeting or interview between prospective roommates. Have learners discuss the role play. Ask *What types of questions are easy to ask? Which questions do you think tell the most about a person?*

Expansion/Extension

- Learners can brainstorm and make a list of issues to consider in a written agreement between roommates. (FOR EXAMPLE: length of time of the agreement, amounts to be paid jointly, amounts to be paid separately, behavioral expectations, purchases to be made jointly) Learners can write sample agreements based on the list.

More *Expansion/Extension* on page 187

Can We Get Along?

Purpose: To give practice in expressing preferences and in asking for information; to give practice with *What if . . . ?* questions, with *What about . . . ?* questions, with comparative adjectives, and with questions with *do/does*

Teacher Preparation and Materials

Index card for each learner (each card has a different set of characteristics for the learner to role-play and a statement about the characteristics desired in a potential roommate) *(Expansion/Extension)*

Warm-up

Have learners look at the roommate screeners' recommendations on page 134. Have learners review questions that potential roommates might ask each other to determine compatibility.

Presentation

1. Have learners turn to page 135. Have a volunteer read the title and introductory paragraph. Ask *What types of questions do you think they will ask? What do you know about these two? Would you guess that they are compatible? Why or why not?*

2. Have learners read the answers. Ask *What are the topics that Marco and Stan asked each other about?*

3. Have learners individually write questions for each of the answers. As a group, review questions that learners wrote. Discuss how learners determined suitable questions.

4. Learners can brainstorm and list other possible questions on a separate sheet. Then have learners role-play the situation.

Expansion/Extension

- Elicit/introduce phrases and expressions that could be used to express reactions to a potential roommate. Learners can practice the phrases and expressions in role-plays about roommate decisions. (FOR EXAMPLE: I'm sure/certain/positive that we would get along fine. I definitely think it will work. There's no question in my mind. I'm not so sure this would work. I don't know yet. I don't think this would be a good idea right now. I doubt this would work out. I'm a little worried/concerned/anxious/nervous about . . . . Maybe we'd better think about it. I'd prefer someone more . . . . I'd rather . . . .)

- Elicit/introduce idioms and other vocabulary that might come up in interviewing potential roommates. (FOR EXAMPLE: night person, morning person, neat, messy, loner, social butterfly, outgoing, conservative, liberal, happy-go-lucky, frugal, materialistic) Learners can role-play interviewing potential roommates. Give each learner an index card with several characteristics about the person they are role-playing and a statement about the characteristics desired in a potential roommate. (FOR EXAMPLE: You are a night person, happy-go-lucky, and outgoing. You want to find a roommate who has similar characteristics.) Ask learners to interview others in the class to find suitable matches for the people they are role-playing.

Stan and Marco are talking about rooming together. They want to make sure they can get along, so they're asking each other lots of questions. Their answers are written below. Complete the missing questions.   Answers may vary.

1. Stan: "Why _do you want to move_____?"
   Marco: "I need a quieter place to live. I love Eddy and Cruz, but they sure can make noise."

2. Stan: "How much _____?"
   Marco: "I can afford between $300 and $350 for my share."

3. Stan: "What if _____?"
   Marco: "My aunt and uncle will give me a short-term loan."

4. Stan: "Where _____?"
   Marco: "I'd prefer to stay in Herndon, but I'm willing to look at other towns too."

5. Marco: "What do _____?"
   Stan: "Most nights I'll be working or studying, but I'll still be able to play basketball on Tuesdays. And of course, I like to see my friends on weekends."

6. Marco: "Do you _____?"
   Stan: "No, I prefer to get up early and go for a run."

7. Marco: "Do you _____?"
   Stan: "Not much. Just spaghetti and meatballs, bacon and eggs, you know. I guess we'll have to learn. Or eat out a lot."

8. Marco: "Now, where _____?"
   Stan: "Well, let's take a look at the newspaper and see what apartments are available!"

Finding a Place

Purpose: To give practice in comparing and contrasting, and in expressing preferences; to give practice with abbreviations and with *What if . . . ?* questions

Teacher Preparation and Materials

1. Local housing rental ads
2. 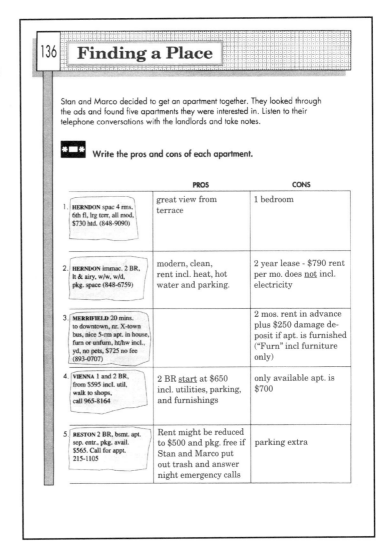 Audiotape for Level 3
3. Copies of TRF Handout 11.4, *Nice View, Quiet Neighbors (Expansion/Extension)*
4. Lists of housing considerations and questions, used for pages 127 and 129 *(Expansion/Extension)*

Warm-up

1. Ask learners to brainstorm what they would want in an apartment. List their ideas on the board. For appropriate words on the list, elicit/introduce abbreviations that are commonly used in ads. (FOR EXAMPLE: two bedrooms = 2 BR; heat included = ht. incl.)
2. Bring in local housing rental ads. Ask *Have you ever looked at newspaper ads for apartments or other types of housing? What types of information do you think should be included in ads? Can you tell a lot about an apartment or house from an ad? How can you find out more about an advertised place?*

Presentation

1. Have learners turn to page 136. Have a volunteer read the title and introductory paragraph. Ask *What types of things are important when considering an apartment? What information should Stan and Marco try to get?* Add any new ideas to the list on the board.
2. Have learners look at the ads. Ask *Do all the ads include the rent? Do you think the ads tell you everything you need to know to make a decision? Why?/Why not? What else do you need or want to know?*
3. On the board write the words *crosstown, parking, heated, wall-to-wall carpeting,*

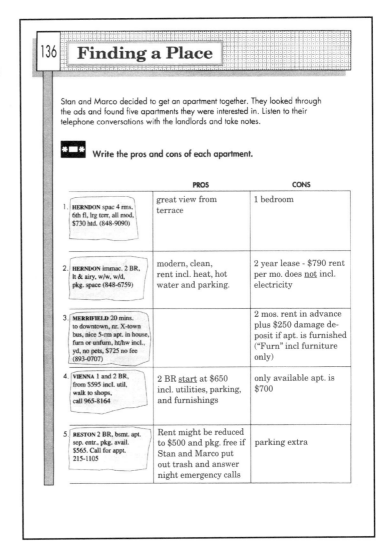

136 Finding a Place

Stan and Marco decided to get an apartment together. They looked through the ads and found five apartments they were interested in. Listen to their telephone conversations with the landlords and take notes.

Write the pros and cons of each apartment.

	PROS	CONS
1. **HERNDON** spac 4 rms, 6th fl, lrg terr, all mod, $730 htd. (848-9090)	great view from terrace	1 bedroom
2. **HERNDON** immac. 2 BR, lt & airy, w/w, w/d, pkg. space (848-6759)	modern, clean, rent incl. heat, hot water and parking.	2 year lease - $790 rent per mo. does <u>not</u> incl. electricity
3. **MERRIFIELD** 20 mins. to downtown, nr. X-town bus, nice 5-rm apt. in house, furn or unfurn, ht/hw incl., yd, no pets, $725 no fee (893-0707)		2 mos. rent in advance plus $250 damage deposit if apt. is furnished ("Furn" incl furniture only)
4. **VIENNA** 1 and 2 BR, from $595 incl. util, walk to shops, call 965-8164	2 BR <u>start</u> at $650 incl. utilities, parking, and furnishings	only available apt. is $700
5. **RESTON** 2 BR, bsmt. apt. sep. entr., pkg. avail. $565. Call for appt. 215-1105	Rent might be reduced to $500 and pkg. free if Stan and Marco put out trash and answer night emergency calls	parking extra

utilities included, appointment, heat and hot water included, immaculate, rooms, floor, large, modern, bedroom, light, washer and dryer, near, furnished, unfurnished, yard, basement, separate entrance, and *available.* Ask learners to look through the ads for the appropriate abbreviations and to write the abbreviations next to the words. Elicit/explain the meanings of new words: *crosstown, wall-to-wall carpeting, immaculate.*

4. 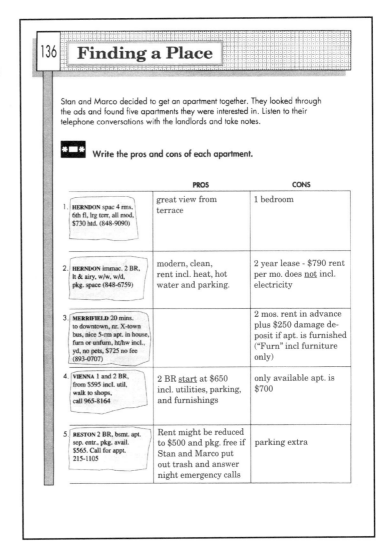 Have learners listen to the first conversation. Ask *Does the landlord add any new information that is not found in the ad? Does this apartment sound appropriate for Stan and Marco? Why or why not?*
5. 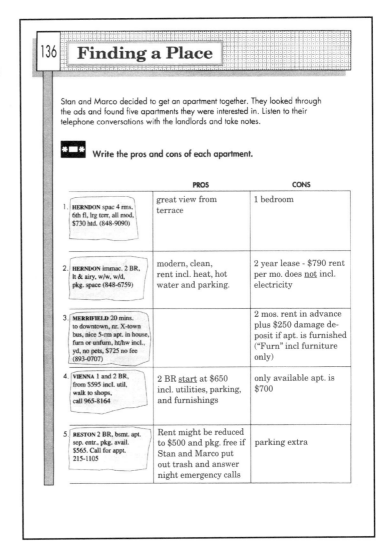 Repeat step #4 for the other conversations.
6. 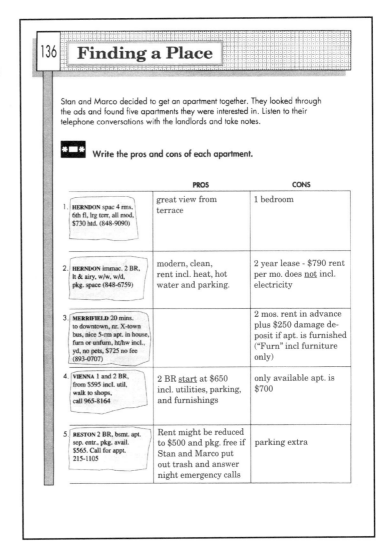 Have learners listen again to the conversations and take notes on the pros and cons of each apartment. Learners can add their own ideas about the apartments.
7. Ask learners to rank the apartments from best to worst individually. As a group, compare rankings to see how many came to the same conclusions.

Expansion/Extension **on page 187**

Practicing Your Skills

Purpose: To give practice in comparing and contrasting; to give practice with descriptive adjectives

Teacher Preparation and Materials

Pictures of houses, used for page 127 and, if possible, pictures of housing in different parts of the world

Warm-up

Show learners pictures of different types of housing in the United States and in different parts of the world. Ask learners about the houses. Ask *How are different houses suited to different climates? lifestyles? local resources? Would the type of houses in your native country be appropriate in the United States? Why or why not? Would the type of houses used in the United States be appropriate in your native country? Why or why not?*

Presentation

1. Have learners turn to page 137 and look at the pictures. Ask learners if there are pictures of the types of housing that they had in their native country and types that they now have in the United States.

2. Ask learners to describe the types of housing that they are familiar with, including features, materials that are used, and locations.

3. Have learners read the instructions and list of questions. Ask learners to brainstorm additional questions for comparing homes. List these on the board.

4. Have learners individually write a comparison of their past and present homes. They can use the list of ideas on the board or the questions in the book as prompts.

5. Have pairs of learners exchange drafts. Learners should read, ask questions about, and comment on the drafts in terms of clarity and detail. Then have learners rewrite their own drafts in their books or on separate sheets of paper. Learners can keep a copy of their writing in their portfolios.

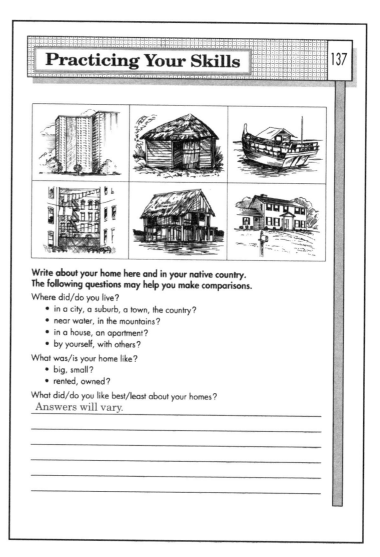

Practicing Your Skills 137

Write about your home here and in your native country. The following questions may help you make comparisons.

Where did/do you live?
- in a city, a suburb, a town, the country?
- near water, in the mountains?
- in a house, an apartment?
- by yourself, with others?

What was/is your home like?
- big, small?
- rented, owned?

What did/do you like best/least about your homes?

Answers will vary.

Expansion/Extension

- Ask learners about costs (property taxes, mortgage fees) involved in purchasing a house in the United States and in their native countries. Learners can write a comparative essay about these and/or add them to their writing for page 137.

- Learners can compare regulations related to property ownership in the United States and in their native countries. Ask *What rights do the town or city have regarding people's property? Can the town/state/federal government ever take your land? Under what circumstances is this possible?*

- Ask learners to compile a vocabulary list for the unit. Learners can create categories and categorize the new words. Some categories might be Home Improvement, Mortgage Information, Buying or Renting, and Miscellaneous.

Descriptive Adjectives/ Questions: *What... about?/What... if?*

Purpose: To give practice in using descriptive adjectives and in forming questions with *what... about* and *what... if*

Teacher Preparation and Materials

Pictures of houses used for page 127, and pictures of rooms, furnished and unfurnished (*Expansion/Extension*)

Warm-up

1. Present a very basic description of the classroom, including only a catalog of the space and the objects in it, with no adjectives. This can be presented to learners orally sentence by sentence, or written on the board or on a handout. Use this description to elicit descriptive adjectives. Have learners insert adjectives in the sentences where appropriate. If this is done orally or on the board, learners can discuss which adjectives to use and why.

2. Model formation and use of questions with *what... about* and *what... if* by telling learners about a plan for a vacation trip or a weekend activity. FOR EXAMPLE: *I was planning to take a short trip this weekend to the mountains. I packed my camping gear in the car, and then I started to have second thoughts. "What if it rains this weekend?" I asked myself. "What will I do if the campground is flooded or my tent leaks? And what about wild animals? What would I do if I met a bear in the woods?"* The story can be extended with additional examples. In the end, learners can vote on whether you should go on the camping trip or not.

Presentation

1. Have learners turn to page 138 and read the examples in the box at the top of the page.

2. Learners can work individually, in pairs, or in small groups to complete the exercise and identify the descriptive adjectives.

---

138 — Descriptive Adjectives/Questions: *What... about?/What... if?*

The <u>new</u> house is in Herndon. The rooms are <u>spacious</u>. All the windows have <u>insulated</u> glass. <u>Friendly</u> neighbors welcomed them.

Read this description of the Jamisons' new house. Underline the descriptive adjectives. On separate paper, write about your home. Use descriptive adjectives.

The house is on a <u>single</u> floor. You enter through a <u>narrow</u> hallway. On the right is an <u>airy</u> living room. It has a <u>picture</u> window that looks out on an <u>attractive</u> garden. On the left is a <u>formal</u> dining room. It has a <u>corner</u> cabinet for dishes. Behind the dining room is a <u>sunny</u> kitchen. There is a broom closet with a <u>deep</u> shelf. The stairs to the <u>finished</u> basement are in the kitchen, too. There are three bedrooms on the other side of the house. The <u>master</u> bedroom has <u>generous</u> closets, but needs a coat of <u>fresh</u> paint. The other bedrooms have <u>worn</u> wallpaper and <u>modest</u> closets.

<u>What</u> did the banker say <u>about</u> our mortgage? <u>What about</u> our mortgage?	The banker said that it has been approved.
<u>What</u> can we do <u>if</u> we don't get this house? <u>What if</u> we don't get this house?	She said that the approval can be transferred to another house.

Complete the conversation with *What... about* or *What... if*.

1. Stan: <u>What</u> did the landlord say <u>about</u> the apartment?

   Marco: He said that it's available. But it's expensive.

2. Stan: <u>What if</u> we took an apartment on a lower floor?

   Marco: He said that 12A is the only one available on Green Street.

3. Stan: <u>What about</u> trading the parking space for lower rent?

   Marco: I think that he'd consider that idea.

---

3. Ask questions to check comprehension and review responses. FOR EXAMPLE: *How many floors does the house have? What kind of hallway is there? Is the living room dark? Where can you put dishes? How many bedrooms are there?*

4. Have learners write descriptions of their own homes, using the paragraph as a model. Volunteers can read their descriptions to the class.

5. Have learners read the questions and answers in the chart at the bottom of the page. Then have them complete the second exercise. Review answers by having pairs of learners role-play the questions and answers between Stan and Marco.

Expansion/Extension

- Learners can choose a picture of a house or a room that appeals to them and write a detailed description of it. To follow up, post the pictures on the board or wall. Then have volunteers read their descriptions and have other learners guess which picture is being described.

Adjectives: Comparatives

Purpose: To give practice in forming and using comparative adjectives

Teacher Preparation and Materials

1. Sets of pictures with two versions of household objects, furniture, or appliances (including any appropriate sets of pictures used for page 69) *(Warm-up)*

2. Store ads for household objects, furniture, or appliances *(Expansion/Extension)*

3. Yard or garage sale notices from newspapers or flyers *(Expansion/Extension)*

Warm-up

Show pictures of two versions of household objects, furniture, or appliances. Elicit comparisons. (FOR EXAMPLE: This coffee maker is bigger than that one. The red sofa looks more comfortable than the green one.) Ask questions if necessary to prompt descriptions and comparisons. Focus on forms of comparative adjectives.

Presentation

1. Have learners turn to page 139 and review the chart of adjectives and comparative forms. Point out the spelling changes in adjectives ending in *-y* and review irregular forms *(bad / worse, good / better)*. If additional practice is needed, elicit comparisons of people and objects in the classroom.

2. Read the ads that Stan and Marco are considering. Make sure learners understand any abbreviations. Focus on the items available, the condition of each, and the prices. On the board, create a chart with two columns, headed *Herndon* and *Reston*. List the items available at both places down the left side. Elicit the condition and price of each item, and note the information in the appropriate columns.

3. Review the example in exercise A. Then have learners complete the exercise, using the ads and the information in the chart. Review answers.

4. Have learners use the information in the ads and the chart to complete the sentences in exercise B. Discuss learners' choices and reasons. To follow up, ask learners where they would buy pots, pans, and utensils, and why.

Expansion/Extension

- Have learners look at store ads for household items. Have them compare advertised items (FOR EXAMPLE: This washing machine is roomier than that one, but that one is cheaper.) and decide which item or store they would prefer and why.

- Have learners look at ads for local yard, garage, or moving sales. In pairs or small groups, they can compare selection, condition of items, and prices, particularly if comparable items are available at two or more sales. Have learners decide which sale they would go to and give reasons.

- Have learners discuss the pros and cons of shopping at yard, garage, or moving sales. They can create a set of guidelines for effective shopping at these sales, including possible pitfalls and suggestions for getting a good deal.

Adjectives: Comparatives 139

Regular		Irregular	
Adjective	*Comparative*	*Adjective*	*Comparative*
small	smaller	roomy	roomier (than)
comfortable	more comfortable (than)	bad	worse

Stan and Marco need things for their new kitchen. Here are two ads they can check out.

YARD SALE IN HERNDON
Clean refrigerator: $100. small appliances/ good condition: $10: hairdryer, blender, automatic coffee maker + box of pots, pans & utensils, all fair condition: $35 for whole box.
GARAGE SALE

RESTON—MOVING SALE
Kitchen gear: sm. appliances: good to excel. condition: $15 each; self-cleaning stove: $75. Deluxe side-by-side refrig. still under warranty ($800 new) asking $350, freezer needs defrosting. Assorted pots/pans/ flatware/dishes $50.

A. Complete the sentences with comparative forms.

Example: The sale in Reston is _____closer than_____ (close) the one in Herndon.

1. The items are __more expensive__ (expensive).
2. But they seem to be in __better__ (good) condition.
3. The refrigerator in Reston seems to be __fancier__ (fancy), too.
4. But the one in Herndon is a lot __cheaper__ (cheap).
5. It seems to be __cleaner__ (clean), too.
6. They decide to check out the __more convenient__ (convenient) sale first.

B. Look at the ads. Then complete the sentences. Answers will vary.

I'd buy the coffee pot from _____ because _____

I'd buy the refrigerator from _____ because _____

UNIT 11: Can I Buy a House?
Expansion/Extension

Talking to a Real Estate Agent
Expansion/Extension for SB page 129

See TRF HANDOUT 11.1, *Location, Location, and Location*
TRF HANDOUT 11.3, *Real Estate Listing*

- Learners can role-play Al and Yolette asking the real estate agent about the house described on the information sheet. The real estate agent should try to persuade Al and Yolette to consider this house despite their preferences. Ask learners if they think the Jamisons will want to see the house or not.

Can We Get a Mortgage?
More *Expansion/Extension* for SB page 130

- Learners can look at bank loan information for other types of loans and terms available. Ask *What is the difference between adjustable and fixed rates? What lengths of time are commonly offered for mortgages? What differences would there be in the total amount of interest paid to the bank?*
- Learners can look at samples of mortgage applications and find out the types of information required. Discuss the relevance of this information.

What Will It Cost?
Expansion/Extension for SB page 131

See TRF HANDOUT 11.5, *Home Improvement Tips*
TRF HANDOUT 11.6, *Do It Yourself*

- Learners can look through hardware store fliers for the costs of materials for the remodeling and improvement ideas listed on page 131. Point out that the Jamisons can save money by buying the materials and doing some of the work themselves. Ask *Which improvements do you think Al and Yolette could do themselves? How much time would it take for these jobs? Is the money saved worth the time, work, and mess? Why or why not?*

Housing Grants Program
More *Expansion/Extension* for SB page 133

- Learners can look through information on local housing grants and subsidies to find out the qualifications for assistance and how to apply.
- Ask learners to look at local program eligibility scales and requirements and to determine if the families described on page 133 would qualify for assistance. Learners should explain their answers. Learners can role-play conversations between a housing grant worker and an applicant, using the descriptions of families on page 133.

Choose a Roommate with Care
More *Expansion/Extension* for SB page 134

- Ask learners to look on bulletin boards and in newspaper classifieds for ads about roommate situations. Discuss the pros and cons of finding a roommate through bulletin boards, personal ads, signs, and referrals from friends or relatives.

Finding a Place
Expansion/Extension for SB page 136

See TRF HANDOUT 11.4, *Nice View, Quiet Neighbors*

- Ask learners about other ways to find housing, such as bulletin boards, word of mouth, and housing agencies. Learners can share experiences they have had using the various methods.
- Learners can look at the lists used for pages 127 and 129 of things to consider before buying a house and questions to ask about a house. Ask learners to compare those lists with the list prepared for page 136 of what to look for in a rental apartment.
- ▣▣ Ask learners to listen again to the conversations and discuss the responses of the landlords. Ask *Did the landlords seem eager/cautious/apprehensive about renting to Stan and Marco? What are legitimate reasons for not renting to a particular person? What reasons would be discriminatory? What can you do if a real estate agent seems to be steering you away from housing in certain areas?* Learners can check with the local housing authority on illegal rental methods and what to do if they feel they have been discriminated against.

1 2 3 4 5 6 7 8 9 10 11 12 Summary

Discovering Patterns

Objectives

- To help learners discover grammatical patterns
- To teach and give practice with those patterns
  The structures covered are:
  - past and present participles of verbs
  - the present perfect tense
  - the passive voice
  - the present perfect continuous tense
  - the "unreal" conditional

About the Structures

• Verbs: Past and Present Participles

In this unit, learners begin categorizing regular and irregular verbs and comparing their past and present participles. Learners may have difficulty applying spelling rules and remembering irregular verb forms.

• Verbs: Present Perfect Tense

This tense, frequently used in conversation, is used to talk about activities or situations that began at an unspecified past time. When this tense is used with *since* or *for,* it is used to talk about an activity that began in the past, continues in the present, and will probably go on in the future. In this unit, the meanings of the past tense and the present perfect tense are compared, but learners are not expected to master the distinction yet.

• Verbs: Passive Voice

The passive voice is used to stress an action. Passive voice sentences start with the receiver or object of the action, not the doer of the action. They always include a form of the verb *be* and a past participle. Only verbs that can take a direct or indirect object can be used in the passive voice. Learners often make errors related to the use and form of the past participle.

• Verbs: Present Perfect Continuous Tense

The present perfect continuous tense expresses or implies duration of an action that is in progress. It is similar in meaning to the present perfect, but the present perfect denotes repeated actions in the past and suggests probable continuation of the action without referring to duration. Learners have difficulty understanding the difference in meaning between the two tenses, since they are often used interchangeably, and with some verbs, like *live* and *work,* they are essentially interchangeable.

• Verbs: "Unreal" Conditional

This structure consists of two clauses: an *if* clause that expresses something that is hypothetical and a main clause that proposes a possible outcome. The past tense is used in the *if* clause. The main clause contains *would* and a base form of a verb. Learners may have difficulty remembering to use *were* for all subjects when the verb *be* is in the *if* clause. In colloquial English, *was* is often used.

Verbs: Past and Present Participles

Purpose: To give practice in recognizing and in forming past and present participles

Teacher Preparation and Materials

Large sheet of paper, marker

Warm-up

Ask questions about different characters in the Student Book or about learners in the group. Have learners answer with complete sentences using appropriate verb forms. On the board list the main verbs and their forms as they are used in the answers. FOR EXAMPLE: *What family moved to Manassas?* (move, moved) *Are Stan and Marco planning to move soon?* (plan, planning) *Do you recycle bottles?* (recycle) *What types of materials are Cruz and Eddy recycling on page 88?* (recycle, recycling) *Have you ever recycled papers?* (recycle, recycled) *Where did Diep and her family go on vacation?* (go, went)

Presentation

1. Have learners open their books to page 140 and look at the chart. Elicit/explain that English verbs have four main forms: the present tense, the past tense, the present participle, and the past participle. Ask learners to identify the forms that were written on the board in the *Warm-up.*

2. Ask questions to elicit verb form endings, spelling changes, and irregular verb patterns. FOR EXAMPLE: *What ending is used to form the past participle for regular verbs? Which irregular verbs have different forms for the past tense and past participle?*

3. On the board write the verbs *speak, write,* and *think.* Ask learners to look at page 114 and to use the verbs to talk about the picture. If necessary, use questions to elicit different verb tenses. FOR EXAMPLE: *Who was Quang speaking to? Why did Quang speak with the police officer? What did the police officer write? What did Quang think the mugger looked like?* Make a chart on the board similar to the

one on page 140 and write the different forms of these three verbs on the chart.

4. Repeat the procedure with other sets of verbs and pictures in the book. FOR EXAMPLE: *move, wait, plan* (page 127), *sit, do, start* (page 75). Alternatively, have learners build a story using the verbs and write the verb forms on the board. If necessary, use questions to elicit different verb forms.

5. Have learners individually complete the verb list in their books. On a large sheet of paper, compile a class verb list based on learners' charts.

Expansion/Extension

- Ask learners to write a description of one of the pictures used in the *Presentation.* Learners can identify different verb forms used. If past and present participles are used, ask learners to determine which (auxiliary) verbs precede the different participles. (**Note:** Past participles follow *have, has,* or *had;* present participles follow *be, am, is, are, was, were,* or *been.*)

123456789101112
Discovering Patterns

Verbs: Past and Present Participles

Verbs: Past and Present Participles

	Present Tense	Past Tense	Past Participle	Present Participle
Regular	turn	turned	turned	turning
	arrive	arrived	arrived	arriving
	stop	stopped	stopped	stopping
	study	studied	studied	studying
Irregular	be	was/were	been	being
	go	went	gone	going
	have	had	had	having
	find	found	found	finding
	take	took	taken	taking
	give	gave	given	giving

Complete the verb list.

	Present Tense	Past Tense	Past Participle	Present Participle
Regular	1. use	used	used	using
	2. clean	cleaned	cleaned	cleaning
	3. start	started	started	starting
	4. plan	planned	planned	planning
	5.	} Answers will vary.		
	6.			
	7.			
Irregular	1. see	saw	seen	seeing
	2. think	thought	thought	thinking
	3. speak	spoke	spoken	speaking
	4. come	came	come	coming
	5. write	wrote	written	writing
	6. get	got	got(ten)	getting
	7. know	knew	known	knowing
	8. do	did	done	doing
	9. make	made	made	making
	10.			
	11.			
	12.	} Answers will vary.		
	13.			
	14.			

Verbs: Present Perfect Tense

Purpose: To give practice in using the present perfect tense

Teacher Preparation and Materials
Large sheet of paper, marker

Warm-up
1. Make a time line on a large sheet of paper. FOR EXAMPLE: Say *I came to the United States in 1987*. On the time line, mark 1987 with an X and write *came to the U.S.* Then say *I lived in Chicago from 1987 to 1990*. On the time line, mark the span of years and write *lived in Chicago*. Say *In 1990 I moved to Texas. I have lived here (in Texas) since 1990*. On the time line, mark 1990 with an X and write *moved to Texas*. Then draw an arrow from 1990 to the present year and write *have lived in* (name of town/city).
2. Have learners make their own time lines with similar information and explain the time lines to the group, using the past tense and present perfect tense.

Presentation
1. Have learners turn to page 141 and look at the examples in the box.
2. Ask questions about the patterns, such as *Which tense has one word? Which tense has two words? What is the first part of a verb in the present perfect? What verb form is the second part of the present perfect tense?* (Learners can refer back to page 140.) *What time expressions are used with the past tense? with the present perfect tense?*
3. Elicit/explain that when an exact time is stated (such as *last week, yesterday, in 1990*), the past tense is used. When the exact time is not given, the present perfect tense is usually used. (**Note:** The prepositions *for* and *since* can be used with both the present perfect and past tenses, depending on whether or not the

action is completed. FOR EXAMPLE: *I lived in New York for three years and then I moved to Chicago. I've lived here in Chicago for two years.*)
4. Learners can brainstorm and list on the board other sentences in the past and present perfect tenses. If appropriate, learners can chart them on a time line.
5. Have learners complete the exercises. Ask learners to act out the conversations in the exercises.

Expansion/Extension
- Ask learners to make lists of time words associated with the two tenses. (FOR EXAMPLE: past tense—*ago, in, last, this morning, year;* present perfect tense—*so far, until now, up to the present, all his life, just, already, yet*)
- Learners can ask each other questions about activities in the past. They should respond using the appropriate tense: present perfect or past. FOR EXAMPLE: *Did you write your report?* (No, I haven't written it yet./Yes, I wrote it last night.)

Verbs: Present Perfect Tense |141|

Past	Present Perfect
I **worked** there from 1995 to 2000.	I've **worked** here since 1995.
Al **went** to New York in March.	Al **has gone** to New York for a few days.
They **saw** the movie last week.	They **have seen** the movie three times.
We **had** a meeting last month.	We **haven't had** another meeting yet.
I **used** a computer in my last job.	**Have** you ever **used** a computer?

A. Stan is talking to Quang about moving. Underline the present perfect sentences.

1. *Stan:* "Marco and I have finally found an apartment that we both like."
2. *Quang:* "That's great. Have you signed the lease yet?"
3. *Stan:* "Yes. We met with the landlord yesterday."
4. *Quang:* "Are you going to move into the apartment soon?"
5. *Stan:* "In two weeks. I've waited a long time to get a place of my own."
6. *Quang:* "Have you started to pack yet?"
7. *Stan:* "Not really, but I've already gotten some boxes."
8. *Quang:* "Were you planning to rent a van or truck for the move?"
9. *Stan:* "No. We both have cars, so we're using them. We might have to take several trips, but that's not a big problem."

B. Joan Morris and Diep Tran are going over Diep's evaluation. Complete the sentences, using the present perfect.

1. *Diep:* "Good afternoon. I ___have come___ (come) to talk about my evaluation."
2. *Joan:* "Yes. Have a seat please. I ___have got___ (get) your evaluation back from the personnel office, so let's go over it together. Here's a copy for you."
3. *Diep:* "Thank you. I ___have___ n't ___seen___ (see) it yet."
4. *Joan:* "It shows that you ___have been___ (be) a dependable member of our team."
5. *Diep:* "I think that I ___have learned___ (learn) a lot in the past year."
6. *Joan:* "___Have___ you ___thought___ (think) about taking any business courses?"
7. *Diep:* "I ___have___ just ___completed___ (complete) a computer course at the Community College. It's not mentioned on the form."
8. *Joan:* "Probably the personnel office ___has___ n't ___received___ (receive) that information yet. Did you tell them about it?"
9. *Diep:* "No, I ___have___ n't ___spoken___ (speak) to them yet."

Verbs: Passive Voice

Purpose: To give practice in using the passive voice with the present, past, present perfect, and future tenses

Teacher Preparation and Materials
Newspapers *(Expansion/Extension)*

Warm-up

1. Have learners turn to page 88 and tell you about the recycled materials. If necessary, use questions to elicit sentences in the passive voice. FOR EXAMPLE: *What is done to the papers? Where are the papers piled? What are the papers tied with? What are the bottles used for?* List learners' responses on the board.

2. Repeat the procedure with page 101 and have learners tell you about the repairs that were done to Marco's car.

Presentation

1. Have learners turn to page 142 and look at the examples in the box. Have learners identify the forms of the verbs used in each of the sentences. Point out that the passive voice has a form of the verb *be* and the past participle of the action verb.

2. Ask learners to compare the active and passive sentences in the chart. Ask *What differences do you see between the two sentences? Do you know who did each of the activities in the active voice? Do you know who did the activities in the passive voice? Do you think the sentences mean the same thing?*

3. Have learners look at the sentences on the board. Ask *Is it important to know who sorted all the bottles or who tied all the papers?* Point out that in the passive voice, the action is more important than who did the action. You might also want to show learners how the doer of the action can be added to the passive sentence. (FOR EXAMPLE: *The paper is reused by the company.*)

4. Have learners complete the exercises.

---

142 | **Verbs: Passive Voice**

Tense	Active	Passive
Present	The company **reuses** the paper.	The paper **is reused**.
	The teacher **assigns** the children to teams.	The children **are assigned** to teams.
Past	Someone **stole** our car.	Our car **was stolen**.
	Some thieves **took** our TV and VCR.	The TV and VCR **were taken**.
Present perfect	The landlord **has fixed** the sink.	The sink **has been fixed**.
Future	Someone **will repair** the roof.	The roof **will be repaired**.
	I am **going to clean** the bottles.	The bottles **are going to be cleaned**.

The Silvas bought a house. There was a lot of work to do.

A. Underline the passive sentences.

1. The furniture was moved to the new house last weekend.
2. The kitchen appliances were hooked up on Saturday.
3. The kitchen hasn't been remodeled yet.
4. The seller added a new bathroom two years ago.
5. The gutters on the roof were replaced.
6. The Silvas repainted the bedrooms.

B. Help Adela complete a form for the realty company. Use the passive voice.

DECTER REAL ESTATE
We are taking a survey of our clients. Please tell us what was done to your house before you moved in and what will be done in the next two years.

Done
1. The bedrooms ___were painted___. (paint)
2. The attic ___has been insulated___. (insulate)
3. The living room carpet ___was cleaned___. (clean)
4. The grass ___was cut___. (cut)
5. New storm windows ___have been installed___. (install)

To Be Done
1. A family room ___will be added___. (add)
2. Old wallpaper ___will be removed___. (remove)
3. A deck ___will be built___. (build)
4. The kitchen cabinets ___will be refinished___. (refinish)
5. The refrigerator ___will be replaced___. (replace)

Expansion/Extension

- Learners can rewrite active voice sentences in the exercises to be in the passive voice and passive voice sentences to be in the active voice.

- Ask learners to write questions in the passive voice for the remodeling projects listed on the real estate form. (FOR EXAMPLE: When were the bedrooms repainted? What color were the bedrooms repainted?)

- Learners can make their own list of things done and to be done relating to household projects, recycling chores, holiday preparations, school/class projects, work, etc.

- Ask learners to look at newspaper articles and readings in the student book for examples of the use of the active and passive voice. Ask about stylistic differences. *Which voice is better for telling about exciting and interesting events? Which voice is usually used for more formal readings and information?*

Verbs: Present Perfect Continuous Tense

Purpose: To give practice in using the present perfect continuous tense

Teacher Preparation and Materials
None

Warm-up
1. Elicit sentences in the past and present perfect tenses, using verbs such as *study, talk, plan, come,* and *try.* Write some of the sentences on the board.
2. On the board write *Marco has tried to call many times. Marco has been trying to call all evening.* Have learners compare the two sentences. Ask *Is there a difference in meaning between the two sentences? Which sentence suggests an action that extends over a period of time?*
3. Ask learners to look on the board at the sentences they provided. Ask *Which ones suggest an action that extends over a period of time?*

Presentation
1. Have learners turn to page 143 and look at the examples in the box. Ask questions about the sentences. *What form of* have *is used? What form of the verb* be *is used?* (Learners can refer to the chart on page 140.) *What verb form is the last part?*
2. Point out that the present perfect continuous tense is not usually used with adverbs of frequency like *usually, just, already, never, finally,* and *always.*
3. Have learners complete the exercises. Learners can act out the conversations in the exercises and/or add more lines to the conversations.

Verbs: Present Perfect Continuous Tense | 143

> Eddy and Cruz **have been studying** about the environment at school.
> They **haven't been working** on the some research projects.
> The class **has been cleaning** up part of the river.
> How long **has** the town council **been considering** the new proposal?
> Why **has** MediKit **been looking** at Herndon as the site for its new factory?

Al is talking to the mechanic about his car.

A. Underline the sentences in the present perfect continuous tense.
1. *Mechanic:* "So what's wrong with your car?"
2. *Al:* "I've been noticing a strange clicking noise in the engine."
3. *Mechanic:* "How long have you been hearing this noise?"
4. *Al:* "It just started a couple of days ago. But I've also been having trouble starting the car."
5. *Mechanic:* "That could just be the battery. We'll check it out. Have any of the lights been blinking on the dashboard?"
6. *Al:* "No, that hasn't been a problem. But the car has been stalling a lot even after the motor has been running for a while."

B. Complete the sentences. Use the present perfect continuous tense.
1. *Mechanic:* "I have been working (work) on this car since 2:00. I think we got rid of the clicking sound. We put in a new belt."
   Al: "Is the motor still stalling when you start it?"
2. *Mechanic:* "No. It has been running (run) fine all afternoon—no stalling, no problem starting it."
   Al: "That's great."
3. *Mechanic:* " Have you been using (use) the car for long trips or just around town?"
   Al: "Both. We took a trip to Atlanta a few months ago."
4. *Mechanic:* "What kind of gas have you been (put) in your car?"
   Al: "I usually use premium." putting
5. *Mechanic:* "It looks like you have been taking (take) good care of the car."
   Al: "I have been teaching (teach) my nephew Marco the basics, so he has been helping (help) me with the maintenance."

Expansion/Extension
- Learners can look through Units 1–5 for examples of the present perfect continuous tense.
- Ask learners to use the present perfect continuous tense to write about things they have been doing to learn English, to get a job, to get a new apartment, or other activities.
- Learners can imagine that Stan is writing to a friend about looking for an apartment and roommate or buying a used van. Learners can use the present perfect continuous tense to describe what he has been doing.

Verbs: "Unreal" Conditional

Purpose: To give practice in using "unreal" conditionals

Teacher Preparation and Materials

Three books of different sizes or colors

Warm-up

1. On the board write the *If* clauses of future conditional statements. (FOR EXAMPLE: If I stay home tomorrow, ... If Stan and Marco become roommates, ...) Have learners suggest possible completions to the sentences. Have learners identify the verb tenses used in the *If* and main clauses.

2. On the board write some *If* clauses for "unreal" conditional sentences. (FOR EXAMPLE: If Stan owned a van, ... If we had a test right now, ...) Have learners suggest main clauses to complete the sentences. Have learners identify the verb tenses used in the *If* and main clauses.

Presentation

1. Have learners turn to page 144 and look at the examples in the box. Ask *Did Marco lose his job? Do you have a vacation now?* Have learners suggest other completions for the *if* clauses in the box.

2. Ask questions about the verbs in the clauses. *Which verb tense is used in the If clause? What word/verb/modal is used in the other clause?*

3. Point out that *were* is used for all subjects in "unreal" conditional clauses. (FOR EXAMPLE: If I/he/you/we/they were rich, ...)

4. Ask learners to individually complete the exercises. As a group, compile the answers for exercises B and C. Learners can vote on which answers they think are the best.

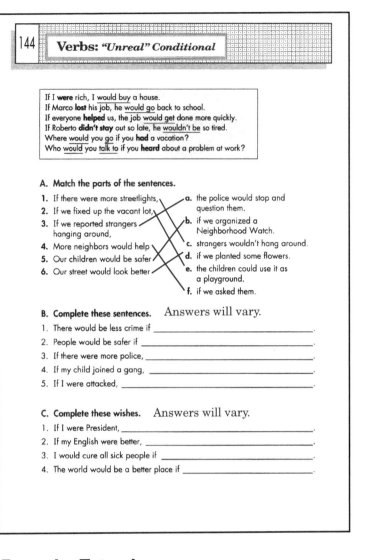

Expansion/Extension

- Learners can create their own *What would you do if . . .* questions. (FOR EXAMPLE: What would you do if you met the president? What would you do if you found $1,000?) Learners can ask their questions of others in the group, record responses, and report their findings to the group.

- Ask learners to choose a situation or problem discussed in one of the units. Learners can use "unreal" conditional sentences to give advice about the situation or problem. (FOR EXAMPLE: If I thought my boss was harassing me, I would . . . . If I needed to buy a car, I'd look in the newspaper for ads.)

- Learners can rewrite the sentences in exercise A in the negative. (FOR EXAMPLE: If there weren't any streetlights, strangers would hang around all the time. If we didn't fix up the vacant lot, the children wouldn't have a suitable playground.)

Verbs: Present Perfect Tense – Regular and Irregular Verbs

Purpose: To give practice in forming and using the present perfect tense with regular and irregular verbs

Teacher Preparation and Materials

Time lines created for page 141 (*Warm-up*)

Warm-up

1. Review use of the present perfect tense. Model with your time line created for page 141. Remind learners how long you have lived in your current city. Then expand the time line to reflect other experiences and recent changes in your life. FOR EXAMPLE: *I moved into a new house two years ago. I have lived there for two years. I plan to visit Mexico this summer, so I started studying Spanish a few months ago. I have studied Spanish for three months now.*

2. Have learners review their personal time lines from page 141. Guide them in expanding the information to reflect recent changes or accomplishments in their lives or the lives of family members. Elicit statements contrasting past tense and present perfect. Encourage learners to tell what they have done and what they haven't yet done. (FOR EXAMPLE: My youngest child recently started kindergarten. She has been in school for a month. I want to get a better job. I have prepared a new resume, and I have applied for several jobs, but I haven't gotten one yet.)

Presentation

1. Have learners turn to page 145. Review the verb forms in the chart.

2. Have learners list some of Stan's goals that were discussed in preceding units. (FOR EXAMPLE: He said he wanted to take business courses and eventually have his own landscaping business. He wanted to do better in his current job. And he wanted to move into an apartment with a friend.)

3. Read the example sentence together. Then

have learners complete the exercise individually or with a partner. Review answers.

4. Have learners discuss and then write about a goal they have accomplished and one they have not yet accomplished. They can refer to their time lines for ideas or write about different accomplishments. Or learners may prefer to write about steps that they have or have not completed towards a long-term goal.

Expansion/Extension

• Learners can use statements of their accomplishments as the basis for a resume. Provide examples of resumes, or have learners find their own examples in resources from the public library, a career counseling agency (preferably one that provides free resources), or job-search web sites.

• Learners who plan to find jobs (or better jobs) can create and role-play interviews with career counselors or potential employers. If possible, invite colleagues to participate as interviewers, rather than other learners, to lend greater authenticity to the role plays.

I You We They	have haven't	had	all the prerequisites.
He She It	has hasn't	finished	

Complete the sentences. Then write a sentence about a goal you have accomplished and one you haven't.

Example: Stan ___has accomplished___ (accomplish) some of his goals.

1. He ___has taken___ (take) two computer courses and ___has gotten___ (get) good grades.
2. He ___has carried___ (carry) a full academic load so far.
3. But he ___hasn't begun___ (not begin) the business sequence yet.
4. He and Marco ___have found___ (find) a nice apartment.
5. They ___have made___ (make) a lot of improvements in it, too.
6. Stan ___has learned___ (learn) new "people" skills this year.
7. So far he and Marco ___have not had___ (not have) any serious arguments.
8. He ___has changed___ (change) his attitude at work, too.
9. His boss thinks he ___has become___ (become) a better worker.

I have ___Answers will vary.___

I haven't ___

Modals: *Should, Can, Must*

Purpose: To give practice in using modals *should, can,* and *must*

Teacher Preparation and Materials

1. Troubleshooting guides for computers, household appliances, or workplace machines; equipment manuals used for pages 49 and 50 *(Expansion/Extension)*

2. Troubleshooting guides created by learners for *Expansion/Extension* on page 50 *(Expansion/Extension)*

Warm-up

Review meaning and use of modals *should, can,* and *must*. To elicit use of these modals, discuss how to run and take care of classroom equipment, including tape or CD players, overhead projectors, electric or manual staplers, computers, TVs and VCRs, even lighting fixtures. Ask learners, *To get this equipment started, what must I do? What should I do if there is a problem? Can I fix it myself? If not, what should I do?* Many learners will know at least how to get the equipment started. Be sure to include questions and discussion of all the pieces used with the equipment (FOR EXAMPLE: You must use headphones to listen to tapes on this portable tape player.)

Presentation

1. Have learners turn to page 146. Read the VCR troubleshooting guide together, and make sure all vocabulary is understood.

2. Do item 1 in the exercise as an example. Have learners identify which point in the guide provides the answer.

3. Have learners work individually or in pairs to complete the exercise. Encourage learners to note which point in the guide gives the answer for each item.

4. Review answers, and discuss reasons for the answers.

---

146 | **Modals:** *Should, Can, Must*

TROUBLESHOOTING

Model JNF-1221 VCR

PROBLEM	POSSIBLE SOLUTION
VCR won't turn on.	1. Check the AC cord and outlet. 2. If the LOCK light is on, press and hold the DISPLAY button for 10 seconds until the LOCK light is off. 3. For further assistance, see Chapter 1, "Your New VCR."
VCR controls don't work.	1. To work safely, turn off the VCR before continuing. 2. Unplug the power cord for at least 2 minutes. Then plug the power cord back in and turn on the VCR. 3. If controls still don't work, see Chapter 1, "Your New VCR."
VCR does not record TV programs.	1. Check the VCR tuning. 2. If the input selection on the VCR reads "L," you must switch it to TUNER by pressing the INPUT button. 3. For additional information, see Chapter 2, "VCR Operations."

Complete the sentences with *can/can't, should/shouldn't,* or *must/mustn't.*

1. If your VCR won't turn on, you __should__ check the AC cord and outlet first.
2. The VCR __can't__ be turned on if the LOCK light is on.
3. The DISPLAY button __must__ be pressed down for at least 10 seconds.
4. If the VCR still won't turn on, you __should__ read Chapter 1 for more help.
5. You __should__ leave the VCR off when you are checking the controls.
6. You __should__ unplug the power cord for two minutes if the controls don't work.
7. Your VCR __can't__ be set to "L" if you want to record programs.
8. To record programs, you __must__ have the input selection on TUNER.
9. To switch to TUNER, you __must__ press the INPUT button.
10. If you need more help, you __should__ refer to the chapter indicated.

Expansion/Extension

- Have learners look at troubleshooting guides for computers, household appliances, or workplace machines. Have them restate information from the guides in standard sentences using *can/can't, should/shouldn't,* and *must/mustn't.*

- If learners have had problems with a machine, have them describe the problems and check the manual for possible remedies, which they can explain in standard sentences.

- Have learners create their own simplified guide to using and repairing an appliance or workplace machine with which they are familiar.

- If learners created troubleshooting charts for *Expansion/Extension* on page 50, use those charts for information gap activities. Copy them, blocking out selected parts. Have learners ask and answer questions about problems with the machines or appliances: what they can check, what they should adjust, and what they must change or repair.

Wh- Questions: Past Tense

Purpose: To give practice with and review *wh-* questions

Teacher Preparation and Materials
Automobile or other insurance policies *(Expansion/Extension)*

Warm-up

1. Review *wh-* questions. Model use of questions with *who, when, where, why, what,* and *how much* by asking learners about their homes, families, schooling, or similar topics. FOR EXAMPLE: *Where do you live? How much does it cost you to study in this program? What school do your children attend? When did you start studying here? Who are your neighbors? Why did you come to this city / town?*

2. Have learners turn to page 129 and review the description of the house for sale. Have learners work in pairs to ask each other questions about the house, using as many *wh-* words as possible. (FOR EXAMPLE: Who is selling the house? Where is it located? How much are the taxes? How much is the assessment? What street is it near?)

Presentation

1. Have learners turn to page 147 and review the questions in the chart. Focus on word order and verb forms.

2. Read the portion of the auto insurance policy shown. Review insurance terminology *(effective, limits, deductible, premium, compulsory, optional, collision, comprehensive)*. Ask questions to check comprehension. FOR EXAMPLE: *What agency insures the Wolanskis? What is the premium for collision insurance? What is the deductible? If one of the drivers is in an accident and injures another person, does that driver have to pay anything? How much money will the insurance company pay for each injured person?*

3. Review the example in the exercise. Point out to learners that there is more than one possible question for most of these answers.

4. Have learners complete the exercise. Review responses by having one learner ask a question and another give the answer. Discuss variations in questions, and decide if all are equally appropriate.

Expansion/Extension

- Learners can look at examples of auto or other insurance policies. Elicit information about features of the policies, including limits, deductibles, and premiums. Have learners compare similar types of policies (such as all the auto policies) and evaluate which seems to provide the best coverage at the lowest premiums.

- Have learners create and role-play a conversation between a customer and an insurance agent discussing one of the policies or comparing two or more policies. The customer should have a lot of questions that the agent must answer.

Who	was/were	insured?
When Where Why	was were	it effective? they covered?
How much		the premium/s?
How much What	did	it cost?

Policy for: Wolanski, Gregor; Wolanski, Ana; Wolanski, Stanislav
Effective: January 1, 2004 to December 31, 2004
Agent: Savemore Insurance Agency, Reston, VA

	Limits	Deductible (Amount you pay)	Premium (Costs)
Compulsory insurance			
Injury to others	$20,000 per person $40,000 per accident	None	$ 238.
Personal injury	$8,000 per person	None	$75.
Optional insurance			
Collision	Actual cash value	$500.	$536.
Comprehensive	Actual cash value	$500.	$102.

Write questions for the answers about the insurance policy.   Answers may vary.

Questions	Answer
Example: What insurance is compulsory?	Injury to others and personal injury.
1. Who is the policy for?	The Wolanski family.
2. When does the policy end?	It ends on the last day of the year.
3. Why is the collision premium so high?	Because collision costs are so high.
4. Where is the insurance agency?	In Reston, Virginia.
5. What does "optional insurance" mean?	It isn't required by law.
6. What is the personal injury limit?	The personal injury limit is $8,000 per person.

Conditional Sentences: *If/Then* Clauses

Purpose: To give practice with *if/then* clauses in conditional sentences

Teacher Preparation and Materials

Information on school lunch programs in local schools, including eligibility requirements and application forms *(Expansion/ Extension)*

Warm-up

1. Review *if/then* clauses. Have learners turn to page 133 and review the eligibility guidelines for the Housing Grants Program. Use *if/then* clauses to ask questions about eligibility. FOR EXAMPLE: *If there are five people in your household and the household income is $28,000, are you then eligible for a housing grant?* (Yes.) *If you are 60 years old, can you apply for a housing grant?* (Yes, if you meet the income eligibility limit.) *If you are working and your children are over 20 years old, are you eligible?* (No.)

2. Have learners use *if/then* clauses to make statements, based on the information in the chart, about who is eligible and what their maximum grant could be. Have volunteers put their sentences on the board. After others check these examples for accuracy, focus on clause structure and verb forms and tenses in the two clauses.

Presentation

1. Have learners turn to page 148 and review the *if/then* sentences in the cause-and-effect chart. Point out that eligibility for free school lunches is based on income limits, like eligibility for housing grants.

2. Review the portion of the application presented in the Student Book. Review key vocabulary *(exceed, monthly income limit)*. Ask questions to check comprehension. FOR EXAMPLE: *Which children can be eligible for a free school lunch?* (Children from elementary through high school) *If there are two people in your household, what is the maximum monthly income you can have*

and still be eligible? ($1,735) If there are eight people in your household, what is the maximum monthly income for eligibility? ($4,419)

3. Have learners work individually or in pairs to complete the exercise. Review answers.

Expansion/Extension

• Have learners create additional *if/then* sentences describing people who may or may not be eligible for free lunches. If appropriate, they can describe their own households and decide if they would be eligible for this program.

• Bring in samples of similar application information and forms for programs in schools in your community, particularly in schools learners' children attend. Review the eligibility limits, and compare then to the ones in the book. Learners can create *if/then* sentences about various families and households. They can decide if those families or households would be eligible for any of the local programs.

---

148 Conditional Sentences: *If/Then* Clauses

Cause		Effect
If Diep makes less than the limit,	then her children	are/will be eligible for free lunches. can get free school lunches. will get free school lunches.
If you make more than the limit,	then your child	isn't/won't be eligible for free lunches. can't get free school lunches. won't get free school lunches.

Application for Free School Lunches
You can apply for free school lunches for students in elementary through high school. Your monthly income level must not exceed these limits.

Number in home	Monthly income limit	Number in home	Monthly income limit
2	$1735	5	$3076
3	2182	6	3523
4	2629	For each add'l family member add $448.	

Complete the *if/then* sentences.

Example: If a single parent has two sons and makes $1,500 a month, _____
   then the boys are eligible for free school lunches.

1. If a couple with four children have a yearly income of $18,000, _then the_ children are eligible for free school lunches.

2. If a family with six children makes $5,000 a month, _then the children_ aren't eligible for free school lunches

3. If a grandmother raising her granddaughter has an income of $10,000, _____ then the girl is eligible for free school lunches.

4. If _Answers will vary._ then all three elementary school girls will be able to get free school lunches.

5. If _Answers will vary._ then my twins won't be eligible for free school lunches.

Tapescripts

UNIT 1
Continuing Education

page 8   What Classes Should I Take?

Narrator: Listen to the conversation between Ron Briggs and Stan.

Ron: How can I help you today, Stan?

Stan: Well, I need some help deciding which classes I should take if I want to own my own business someday.

Ron: OK. What classes have you already taken?

Stan: I'm taking Introduction to Computers and Beginning Word Processing this term.

Ron: Good. And have you taken any math classes?

Stan: Uh, no. Math was not my best subject in high school.

Ron: That's OK. But you *will* have to take Basic Math. It's a prerequisite for all other business courses . . .

Stan: Excuse me, can you explain that?

Ron: Sure. Basic Math is a prerequisite, a required course that you must take before you register for any other business class.

Stan: I see. OK, so I'll take Basic Math. And do I have to take any writing classes?

Ron: You don't have to but you should. We have a great business-writing class. It helps people with all kinds of business letters. Everyone likes the class. It's good to take it with Advanced Word Processing.

Stan: Let's see. Basic Math and Business Writing, plus Advanced Word Processing. Do you think I can take three classes if I'm working part-time, too?

Ron: I don't know. It depends on how much time and energy you have for studying and how many hours you work. Let's look at the course schedule to see if you can do it.

page 10   Getting Help from a Friend
Part A.

Narrator: Listen to the conversation between Diep and Yolette.

Diep: The break is almost over. We'd better get back to class.

Yolette: Have you noticed that Ms. Arno tends to keep our class late all the time?

Diep: I know. She enjoys talking about computers so much that once she gets started, she loses track of the time. Then she makes all of us late for other activities.

Yolette: I really have to watch the time because if she keeps us more than five minutes late, I miss my bus. And if I miss my bus, I'm late for work.

Diep: I know what you mean. Sometimes she makes me late picking up my son at day care. If I pick him up 15 minutes late, I get charged extra.

Yolette: It's hard trying to juggle so many schedules—school, work . . . and you have day care, too.

Diep: You said it! Ms. Arno is a great teacher, but she just doesn't realize that we have lives outside the computer lab.

Yolette: I know what you mean. But it's so hard to just get up and leave when she's still talking.

Part B.

Narrator: Listen to the conversation between Diep and Yolette.

Diep: Next term I'll only be able to take one course. I hear tuition's going up, so I can only afford one course.

Yolette: Have you checked with the financial aid office?

Diep: What's that?

Yolette: It's the office that helps students who are having a hard time paying for school. You should go and find out if you qualify for any aid. They have scholarships that pay for tuition, and of course there are loans that you can pay back later.

Diep:	Have you ever gone to the financial aid office?
Yolette:	Oh, yes. Before I worked full-time, I had a work-study grant. I worked part-time in the school library to help pay for my tuition. And Diep, did you know there's a day care center downstairs?
Diep:	What?
Yolette:	Yes. I don't know if there are any openings, but you should check. It's free for students.
Diep:	That would be great. I'm going to check it out right now. See you later.
Yolette:	Bye.

page 12 **Understanding Computers**

Narrator:	Listen to Ms. Arno, the computer instructor.
Ms. Arno:	First, I'm going to explain about the similarities and differences between hard disks and diskettes. Their most important function is that they both store information, or data. Hard disks are contained within a sealed unit and are housed *inside* your computer. Hard disks are *internal;* they're in your computer and remain in the computer whether the machine is on or off. Diskettes are external; they must be inserted into and ejected from a slot in the computer. They have a rigid case, but you might hear people call them "floppy disks." That's because the disk inside is bendable. You add and delete information in the same way with both hard disks and diskettes. You also have to take care of them in similar ways. Don't let them get dirty, don't let them get too hot or too cold, and don't let them come in contact with magnets. A major difference between the two is their capacity—the amount of information each can hold. Hard disks can hold thousands of times as much information as a diskette. Also, you can get your information much faster from a hard disk than from a diskette. A big advantage of diskettes, however, is that they are portable. You can carry them from computer to computer, and you can easily send information through the mail on diskettes.

page 14 **Using a Computer**

Narrator:	Listen to the conversation between Yolette and Lou.
Yolette:	What's the matter, Lou? You look . . .
Lou:	Look at all these returned fliers! It took hours to address them and we wasted all this money on postage! And now all these customers still don't know about our big sale. Look, there are even duplicate wrong addresses!
Yolette:	You know, we use the company computer for keeping inventory. Why don't we add another database so that . . .
Lou:	Add a database? What does that mean?
Yolette:	Let me finish. We can make a database of the customer mailing list. The list can contain customer names, addresses, kinds of purchases, maybe age, and . . .
Lou:	How would it work?
Yolette:	Hmmm. Let me see . . . Say you're planning a special sale of Speedette shoes. If you figure all the major fields ahead of time—name, address, brand of shoes, sex, age—you can find only those customers who buy Speedette shoes, and send them the mailing. If we target specific customers, we avoid sending ads and fliers to people who aren't interested in Speedettes. That saves money and . . .
Lou:	But won't it take a lot of time to record all those customers?
Yolette:	It will take some time, but only once, not every time we want to send something out. We can print out labels, too, and save the time we spent addressing all of these by hand.
Lou:	Hmmm . . . Not a bad idea. When can you get started?

UNIT 2
What the
Community Offers

page 20 **At the Public Library**

Narrator: Listen to the conversation between Roberto, Stan, and Marco.

Roberto: Hi, Stan. Sorry we're a little late. How are you?

Stan: Pretty good. How are you doing, Roberto?

Roberto: I'm tired. . . . Too much to do. You know how it is.

Stan: I know what you mean.

Roberto: Oh, Stan, this is my nephew, Marco. He's my brother's oldest son.

Stan: Glad to meet you, Marco.

Roberto: Marco just moved here from Atlanta. He's got a job at Hanover Electronics. Marco, this is Stan, a friend of mine at the computer center.

Marco: Nice to meet you, too, Stan.

Stan: I hope you like it here.

Marco: Oh, I do!

Roberto: Hey, Stan. You play a lot of sports, don't you?

Stan: Yeah.

Roberto: Would you mind taking Marco to the recreation center with you some night? He likes sports, too, and I'd like him to see the center.

Stan: Sure. How about going this Friday?

Marco: Great. I'm always ready for sports.

Stan: Me too. But I have to study sometime.

Roberto: Let's get started then. I'm not sure where the books about computers are.

Stan: Excuse me, where can we find information about computers?

Reference
Librarian: Back here in the magazine section there are lots of computer magazines. Or, if you're looking for materials to check out, you can find lots of computer books in the stacks on the second floor.

page 22 **Getting Help**

Narrator: Listen to the conversation between Diep and the telephone operator at the legal services office.

Operator: Good afternoon. Legal Services.

Diep: Good afternoon. My name is Diep Tran. I have a problem with my rent.

Operator: OK, Ms. . . . uh . . .

Diep: Diep Tran. *T* as in *toy, R* as in *robin, A* as in *apple,* and *N* as in *nut.*

Operator: Yes, Ms. Tran. How can I help you?

Diep: I just received a letter from the apartment manager. She says that I haven't paid my rent for two months. But I did. I sent money orders on August 1 and September 1.

Operator: OK. Do you have your receipts?

Diep: That's the problem. I don't have them!

Operator: OK, Ms. Tran. I think we can help. Are you working?

Diep: I only work part-time at the hospital. I don't have enough money to pay a lawyer.

Operator: That's OK. Let's see if we can schedule an appointment for you to come in. Can you come in next Wednesday?

Diep: The letter says I have to pay within five days. Can't I get an appointment today?

Operator: Oh, not today, but tomorrow at 9:30 is open. First I'll need to verify your income, so please bring your last two pay stubs.

Diep: Excuse me, my last what?

Operator: Pay stubs. The receipts attached to your paychecks that show your pay, taxes, and deductions. Bring the last two receipts you have.

Diep: OK. I'll bring them tomorrow at 9:30. Thank you so much for your help.

Operator: OK. We'll see you tomorrow. Bye now.

Diep: Good-bye.

page 27   **Recorded Messages**

Narrator: Listen to the prerecorded message for the public library.

Voice: Thanks for calling the Library Information Line. Our hours are 9 a.m. to 9 p.m., Monday through Friday, and 12 noon to 5 p.m. on Saturdays and Sundays. We hope you will join us for the following special events: On Mondays and Tuesdays from 11 a.m. to 12 noon, there is storytelling in the Children's Room. This Saturday at 9:30 a.m., the whole family can enjoy videos on animals of the rain forest. On Wednesday, March 8, at 4 p.m., we'll sponsor a special lecture on choosing a college. Our guest speaker will talk about local colleges and how to apply for financial aid. High school teens, mark your calendars now! We look forward to seeing you at the library. Stay on the line if you want to hear this message again.

◆◆◆◆

Narrator: Listen to the prerecorded message at the Job Assistance Network.

Voice: You have reached the Job Assistance Network. We're sorry we can't answer your call right now. Our office hours are Monday through Friday, 9 a.m. to 5 p.m. The Job Assistance Network currently has three job-training programs. The first training program is in office skills, where you can learn data entry and basic accounting. Our second training program teaches printing skills, focusing on photocopier operation and maintenance, desktop publishing, and offset printing. The third training program is in computer skills. Our current class is for computer technicians only. For additional information about classes, schedules, and fees, please call during our office hours, Monday through Friday, 9 a.m. to 5 p.m. If you have a touch-tone phone, you can press 1 now for information in Spanish. Press 2 for information in French. Press 3 for information in Russian. Press 4 for information in Japanese. And press 5 for information in Vietnamese.

UNIT 3
Making Ends Meet

page 32   **Monthly Expenses**

Narrator: Listen to the conversation between Al and Yolette.

Al: Yolette, we have to do something about these bills. Every month we owe more. We never catch up. I'm really worried.

Yolette: I know, Al. Let's figure our expenses and try to work out a budget.

Al: That's a good idea. I'll go through the bills and you write down what we owe. First, our rent is $712.

Yolette: Rent: $712. What about the electric bill?

Al: We're on a budget payment of $60 every month with the electric company.

Yolette: What's the phone bill this month?

Al: It's $72.23.

Yolette: Well, at least that's not as bad as last month!

Al: Yeah, but we've got to start cutting back on our long-distance calls.

Yolette: Yeah. It'll be tough, but we have to do better. What about the heating bill?

Al: This month we owe $79.84.

Yolette: Let's round that off to $80. We should look into the budget plan for that, also, so that our bills are more regular.

Al: OK, I'll call tomorrow. Now, the car loan is $56 a month. And we pay $36 a month on our life insurance. Now let's look at our credit cards. Ouch! Look at this. We owe $1,492.95 on our County Bank Credit Card.

Yolette: What?

Al: Well, we charged a lot on vacation, including the tickets and the motel.

Yolette: You're right. What's the minimum payment due?

Al: The minimum payment is $45. Here's another bill. We owe Barron's Discount $125!

Yolette: I *had* to buy some new things for the trip! And here's Miller Department Store. We're charged to the limit there: $400. Good grief!

Al: What's the minimum payment due on . . .

page 39   **A Mistake on the Phone Bill**
Conversation 1.

Narrator: Listen to the first conversation between Al and the operator.

Operator: MATC Long-Distance Service.

Al: This is Albert Jamison. You made a mistake on my phone bill! I didn't call Brooklyn last month. I shouldn't have to pay for calls I didn't make! I wasn't even home then! I was on vacation.

Operator: Excuse me, Mr. Jamison. Can I have your area code and phone number so that I can look up your account? I'm sure we can take care of this matter for you.

Al: Oh, OK. My number is (703) 893-4741.

Operator: Ah, yes, Mr. Jamison. I have your account on the screen. What seems to be the problem?

Al: I don't know anyone in Brooklyn. I rarely call New York at all. My wife sometimes calls her sister in the Bronx. But never Brooklyn.

Operator: Excuse me. What date are you referring to?

Al: The 19th. That call you've got there on March 19.

Operator: I see there's also a call on that day charged to your calling card from South Island, Florida.

Al: There, I told you so! We weren't even home then. My wife and I were in Florida. See? So, how can you charge us for a call from our home when we were in Florida?

Operator: Was someone at your house while you were away?

Al: Are you kidding?

Operator: Let me check that number. It belongs to an L. Ragan.

Al: L. Ragan? I never heard of any Ragans. I'm telling you. You made a mistake!

Operator: All right then. I'll credit your account.

Conversation 2.

Narrator: Listen to the second conversation between Al and the operator.

Operator: MATC Long-Distance Service.

Al: This is Albert Jamison. My phone number is (703) 893-4741. There seems to be an error on my phone bill.

Operator: Did you say your number is (703) 893-4741?

Al: That's correct.

Operator: Ah, yes. Mr. Jamison. I have your account on the screen. What seems to be the problem?

Al: There's a phone call on my account to Brooklyn, New York, on March 19 for $5.73. I'm sure that it's a mistake.

Operator: You're talking about the call to (718) 879-1440?

Al: That's right. My wife and I were in Florida at that time. In fact, we made a calling-card call one hour earlier from South Island, Florida.

Operator: Was someone at your house while you were away?

Al: Absolutely not.

Operator: Let me check that number. It belongs to an L. Ragan.

Al: L. Ragan? No, I don't know any Ragans. We didn't make that call.

Operator: All right then. Sorry for the inconvenience. I'll credit your account.

UNIT 4
Living with Machines

page 45   **Trouble with Machines**

Narrator: Listen to the conversation between Roberto, Yolette, and another student.

Roberto: This machine is out of orange juice, and it won't give me my money back!

Yolette: Call the service company. There's the phone number.

Student: No, kick it again! See, I told you a kick would work!

Roberto: Oh, no! It only gave me back 15 cents! I really want a juice, but I guess I'll have to do without one today. I'll call the service company and see if I can get my money back.

Yolette: Boy, we're not having much luck with machines today. I couldn't get the printer to print out any of my work in class today. It kept jamming—over and over again. I wanted to scream! Machines—can't live with them, can't live without them.

Roberto: Tell me about it. Did I tell you about trying to hook up my new VCR? It was really difficult. . . .

page 47 Watching and Recording

Narrator: Listen to the conversation between Eddy and Roberto.

Roberto: OK, Eddy. Read what the instructions say.

Eddy: First turn on the VCR. Then insert a new tape into the loading slot.

Roberto: First the VCR goes on. Then load a new tape.

Eddy: The VCR must be set at channel 3 at all times.

Roberto: Set the VCR to channel 3.

Eddy: Next you must turn on the cable.

Roberto: Next turn on the cable.

Eddy: Finally turn on the TV.

Roberto: Turn on the TV. OK, now what channel is the movie on?

Eddy: Thirty-six.

Roberto: Set TV to channel 36. OK. If we want to watch the basketball game at the same time, we must have to do something else. Do the instructions say anything about that, Eddy?

Eddy: Yeah, Dad. It says you can watch another station while the VCR's recording, by turning the TV's input dial to B.

Roberto: Turn input to B.

Eddy: Now change the cable box to the channel you want to watch. For the basketball game, it'll be channel 2.

Roberto: Hey, that's great Eddy. It sure helps to have two people on this job.

page 53 An Accident Report

Narrator: Listen to Stan's description of the accident and then Bert's description.

Stan: I started trimming some thick hedges. I told Bert that they should be thinned by hand. He said hand-thinning would take too much time and that I should use the electric hedge trimmer. Soon the hedge trimmer got caught in some thick branches. Luckily, I turned it off before I started to untangle it, but the blade was so sharp I sliced my arm.

When I showed the cut to Bert, he almost passed out. I had to drive myself to the hospital. It took 10 stitches to sew up the cut, and they gave me a tetanus shot, too. Boy, did it hurt! The doctor said the cut wasn't deep but that I shouldn't work until the stitches come out next Monday.

Bert: Stan showed me the hedges he wanted to thin by hand. My mistake was that I thought he was more skilled than he really is. It was stupid to try to grab the blade. No wonder he got cut. Luckily, we always train our workers to turn off machines before they touch them. He could have really hurt himself. Anyway, I couldn't drive him to the hospital because I was responsible for the whole crew, not just for Stan. If his cut isn't deep, there's no reason he needs to take so much time off.

UNIT 5
Travels in America

**page 59 Tips from Some Friends
Part A.**

Narrator: Listen to the conversation between Stan, Roberto, and Diep.

Stan: Do you have any vacation plans yet, Roberto?

Roberto: Yes, Stan. We're going to Georgia to visit my brother's family.

Stan: I've been to Georgia. I went across the country last summer. It was great. I loved it!

Diep: I've been to Atlanta. The city is beautiful, but I hated getting there.

Roberto: We've been trying to decide how to get down there. Plane fare is so expensive, and the train and the bus aren't cheap, either. How did you get to Atlanta, Diep?

Diep: By bus. The scenery was lovely, but the ride was so long and hot that the children got bored and restless. We had to wait three hours in a bus terminal in North Carolina, too. It was awful.

Roberto: How did *you* travel, Stan?

Stan:	I went by car. It's the only way to go. You see everything and you can stop and stay wherever you like. Hey! You'll be going through Tennessee, won't you?
Roberto:	Well, if we drive, I guess we could.
Stan:	You *must* go to Great Smoky Mountains National Park.
Roberto:	What's there?
Stan:	Beautiful scenery, great campgrounds, horseback riding, fishing, swimming, boating, everything! It was the best part of my trip. I stayed for a week.
Diep:	I've heard about the Smokies. They're supposed to be beautiful.
Roberto:	Hmmm. It sounds like an interesting side trip.
Diep:	And if you drive, you can come home by a different route. You could even go to the coast and go swimming in the Atlantic. It's a longer ride, but it might be fun.
Roberto:	Adela and the kids would love that! That's it. I've made up my mind. We'll go by car.

Part B.

Narrator:	Listen to the conversation between Roberto and Stan.
Roberto:	When you went cross-country, Stan, didn't you mind all that driving?
Stan:	Oh, no. I went with two friends, and we shared the driving.
Roberto:	Didn't you worry about whether your car would break down?
Stan:	Not really. You might want to look into an auto club if you're serious about driving.
Roberto:	What does an auto club do?
Stan:	Lots of things. I told them where I wanted to go, and they gave me all these maps and tour information. And when my car broke down next to a cornfield in Kansas, they towed it to a gas station, and I got it fixed there. The auto club also helped me find a motel room while I waited for my car to be fixed.
Roberto:	Hmmm. How much does it cost to join?
Stan:	A single membership is $48 a year, but it's only $38 with a student discount.

Roberto:	I wonder how much a family membership costs?
Stan:	Oh, it's about $60. It covers all the drivers in a family. But it's really worth it.
Roberto:	Do you really think so?
Stan:	Oh, yeah. They'll come any time your car doesn't start, or you have a flat, or you need to be towed. My old second-hand heap sees a lot of the auto club.
Roberto:	Hmmm. My car is pretty old, too. I think I'll give them a call.

page 62   **What's the Weather Like?**

Narrator:	Listen to the weather report.
Reporter:	Good evening, Washington. Here's the weather report for Wednesday, June 10. The high today in Washington was 77° and in Baltimore, 79°. A low front is bringing clouds to the greater Washington area. There's a chance of showers around sunrise tomorrow, but the skies should be clear by noon, and it will be sunny and mild right through the weekend. Virginia is also somewhat cloudy and overcast. Temperatures got as high as 80° in Roanoke today, but it's going to be quite a bit cooler tomorrow. It looks like it's going to rain for most of the day tomorrow, but expect the sun to break through late in the afternoon. Friday will be beautiful, with highs around 83°. Meanwhile, Tennessee is experiencing a much cooler summer than usual this year. Temperatures are in the low- to mid-70s. Humidity is low and the air quality is excellent.

page 66   **Asking for Directions**

Narrator:	Listen to the conversation between Roberto and a woman.
Roberto:	Excuse me. Could you tell me how to get to Division Avenue?
Woman:	Hmmm. Division Avenue? Are you going to the Historical Museum?
Roberto:	That's right. I seem to be a little lost. Do you know how I can get there?
Woman:	Hmmm . . . Let me think about the easiest way to get you there from here. OK. I know. You're on College Road. Go to the end of this street and

take a right onto Summerhill Road. At the end of Summerhill, go left until you get to Texas Boulevard. Take a right on Texas to Seventh Street, where you'll turn left again. Seventh goes into Route 71 heading south. Go right on Division, and you can't miss the museum.

Roberto: Whew! Let's see. Right at the end of this street onto Summerhill.

Woman: That's right. You'll go under the Interstate, so you'll know you're heading in the right direction.

Roberto: At the end of Summerhill, go left, and then right onto Texas Boulevard. Then what?

Woman: Stay on Texas Boulevard to Seventh Street. It's a one-way street, so you'll have to turn left.

Roberto: Then Seventh runs into Route 71.

Woman: 71 *South.*

Roberto: From 71 South, take a right on Division, and we'll see the museum from there.

Woman: You've got it. Good luck!

Roberto: Thanks so much for your help.

UNIT 7
Problems on the Job

page 76 Roberto's Apology

Narrator: Listen to the conversation between Roberto and Mr. Jansen, the customer.

Roberto: Excuse me. I'm terribly sorry, Mr. Jansen. I must have slipped on something on the floor.

Mr. Jansen: Oh, that's all right. It could happen to anyone.

Roberto: Let me get you some napkins. I'll be right back with some soda water to see if we can remove the stain.

Mr. Jansen: Thanks.

Roberto: Well, sir, that looks a little better. Now, please have your suit dry-cleaned and bring us the bill. We'll take care of it.

Mr. Jansen: I will, thanks.

Roberto: And tonight everyone in your party can have a free dessert with their meal.

Mr. Jansen: That's very nice of you.

page 77 Talking to the Boss
Conversation 1.

Narrator: Listen to the conversation between Roberto and Marcel, the manager.

Marcel: Roberto! What happened? The Jansens are regular customers! What was the disturbance about?

Roberto: The floor was slippery. Someone must have spilled something and didn't clean it up. I was lucky I didn't break my neck.

Marcel: Just tell me what happened, Roberto!

Roberto: I spilled a little bit of soup in Mr. Jansen's lap. He didn't mind. He said he was sure the cleaners could get out the stain.

Marcel: Oh, no! What did you do?

Roberto: Oh, I got some napkins and tried to wipe up a bit of the mess.

Marcel: You didn't even apologize? What did he say?

Roberto: He just told me not to worry about it.

Marcel: Did you offer to pay his dry-cleaning bill?

Roberto: Oh, I *think* so. But it's not important.

Marcel: It sure is! That's house policy. Did you at least offer him free dessert or something?

Roberto: Yeah, but I didn't push it.

Marcel: I can't believe what I'm hearing!

Conversation 2.

Narrator: Listen to the conversation between Marcel and Roberto.

Marcel: Roberto! What happened? The Jansens are regular customers! What was that disturbance about?

Roberto: It wasn't a disturbance, Marcel. I slipped on something and spilled some soup in his lap.

Marcel: Oh, no! What did you do?

Roberto: I immediately got clean napkins and wiped up what I could. Then I got some soda water to clean up the stain.

Marcel:	That's all? Have you forgotten the restaurant's policy? Did you lose your memory along with your balance?
Roberto:	No, Marcel. I did not forget the policy. I told him we would pay the cleaning bill and offered the whole table dessert on the house.
Marcel:	And?
Roberto:	Mr. Jansen was very nice about it. He accepted my apology and the dessert offer. He said he'll send us the cleaning bill. Everyone had caramel cream for dessert. And they left me a tip anyway.
Marcel:	Hmmm. You're a good worker, Roberto, but next time, wear rubber-soled shoes.

page 79 **Following Company Policy**
Part A.

Narrator:	Listen to the conversation between Diep, a patient, and Diep's supervisor, Joan Morris.
Patient:	Hey, Miss. That's my file. What are the results of my tests?
Diep:	I beg your pardon, sir? I don't know what you mean.
Patient:	Of course you do! You brought in my file. You must have read it. What did it say?
Diep:	I'm very sorry sir, but I'm not authorized to give out that information. Your doctor or nurse will explain everything.
Patient:	I don't want to wait. Give me the file, and I'll read it myself.
Diep:	I'm afraid I can't do that. I'm very sorry. Please wait for the doctor . . .
Patient:	It's my file. Give it to me now!
Joan:	What's going on here, Diep?
Diep:	Oh, Ms. Morris. Please tell this man I can't give him his file!
Joan:	Of course you can't give out files to patients. I'll give that file to the doctor, and she'll tell this man everything he needs to know. Sir, you'll get the information directly from your doctor.

Part B.

Narrator:	Listen to the conversation between Diep and Ms. Morris.
Diep:	Oh, thank you for helping me, Ms. Morris. The man was so angry when I wouldn't tell him about his tests or give him the file.
Joan:	No problem, Diep. You did the right thing. Hospital policy says only authorized personnel can give out confidential information, and test results are definitely confidential. Even *I'm* not allowed to talk to patients about test results.
Diep:	I appreciate your help.
Joan:	By the way, Diep. I heard a rumor that you've applied for a job in another part of the hospital. I'll be sad to see you go.
Diep:	Uh . . . Yes, Ms. Morris. I thought you weren't satisfied with my work.
Joan:	Whatever gave you that idea?
Diep:	Well, I didn't get the promotion I thought I deserved. I've been meaning to ask you about that.
Joan:	OK, Diep. Why don't you come to my office today before you leave? We'll go over your evaluation and get to the bottom of this.
Diep:	Oh, thank you, Ms. Morris. I'll be there at 4:00.

page 82 **Hot under the Collar**

Narrator:	Listen to the conversation between Pete, Stan, and Frank.
Pete:	It's no big deal, Stan. We all make mistakes sometimes. It's not like we're stealing anything.
Stan:	How could you ask me to do such a thing, Pete? Frank didn't read the work order. Now he wants me to cut my side to match his mistake.
Frank:	All I'm asking is for you to trim the hedges lower. No one will even notice the mistake. I covered for you when you stupidly sliced your arm.
Stan:	What do you mean "covered for me"? You saw the accident. It wasn't my fault!
Pete:	Now he didn't mean that, Stan. We workers have to stick together. All you have to do is trim your side, and no one will notice. We'll help you. It won't take any time at all.
Frank:	You owe me one, Stan. The owner won't notice, and Bert Daley certainly won't check the work order.

Stan: Absolutely not! How can you ask me to lie? You made the mistake. You've got to tell Bert.

Frank: You creep! You're so ambitious, you can't see straight. Mr. Perfect Stan. You never make a mistake, do you? Well, just wait. You may need help one day, and we'll all remember this.

UNIT 8
Saving the Environment

page 89 **Why Do We Sort Trash?**

Narrator: Listen to the conversation between Adela, Cruz, and Eddy.

Adela: My goodness, there are so many rules for recycling.

Cruz: What do you mean, Mom?

Adela: Wash this, separate that, remove the other thing. Do all those rules really make a difference?

Cruz: They sure do, Mom.

Eddy: She's right, Mom. We should separate our trash and remove bottle caps to save time and work for the recycling center.

Adela: I suppose so. Of course, rinsing out bottles and jars is a good idea. That rule makes sense, but other things don't seem to make a difference.

Eddy: We should follow the other rules, too. Separating items keeps recycled products pure.

Adela: Excuse me?

Eddy: We learned that sticky things like tape or envelope glue can ruin the process of making new paper or cardboard. It's called contamination.

Adela: Well, we should reuse as much as we can. When I was your age, I was taught not to waste anything. I guess recycling is another form of saving.

page 91 **Too Much Packaging**

Narrator: Listen to the conversation between Roberto and Adela.

Roberto: Boy, look at that package. Twelve ounces of salami wrapped in plastic, then cardboard, then shrink-wrap! The package probably weighs more than the salami.

Adela: But, Roberto, it keeps the food cleaner, and the meat stays fresher longer.

Roberto: Adela, the meat would stay clean and fresh with a simple plastic wrap. All the secondary packaging is extra.

Adela: Secondary packaging? Oh, you mean the shrink-wrap around the cardboard box around the plastic? But how else would you know what brand you were buying?

Roberto: I wish they would use just one piece of wrap with a label. You know, almost half of the paper and cardboard we have to dispose of comes from packaging. It fills up all the dumps and makes more garbage, *and* we end up paying for the extra wrappings.

Adela: I suppose you mean it's added into the price we pay?

Roberto: Uh-huh.

Adela: Since when did you become an expert on product packaging?

Roberto: Well, I've learned a lot from Eddy and Cruz. It's their school theme this year. They gave me these reusable cloth shopping bags to bring instead of using paper or plastic ones.

Adela: You know, we always brought our own bags when we went shopping in Puerto Rico.

Roberto: Yeah, we were ahead of our time back then. Now we're finally catching up to ourselves.

page 95 **Different Viewpoints**

Narrator: Listen to the conversation between Stan, Diep, and Roberto.

Stan: Did you hear about the new company that wants to open here in Herndon?

Diep: MediKit? Oh, yes. I think it's great! They make good products. We use them at the hospital.

Roberto: I'm not so sure I want a drug company manufacturing anything here in Herndon.

Diep: What are you talking about, Roberto? They're not making illegal drugs. They're a good company.

Roberto:	They use chemicals in those kits, and chemicals pollute. How do we know they're not going to dump their waste into the river? Or burn it out of smokestacks into the air?
Stan:	Gee, I never thought of that. Won't that be controlled?
Roberto:	Maybe, maybe not. I just don't want to take the chance for myself or my kids.
Diep:	I have kids, too. I sure don't want their air or water to be polluted, but I think the schools will be better with the additional money MediKit will pay in taxes. And my brother, Quang, will probably be able to get a good job with them, too.
Stan:	What about the fact that they'll be clearing land? I bet my boss will try to get a contract out of that. That could mean more work for me, too.
Diep:	Actually, that's one thing I'm not too happy about. They say they're clearing undeveloped land. But a lot of kids play in the woods there. It's my favorite picnic area, too.
Stan:	That's true. My neighbors are pretty upset, too. They go to a senior center right across the way from the new site. They're afraid the noise will be awful and the traffic on the surrounding streets will be dangerous.
Diep:	I also heard that they're planning an on-site day care program for the children of their employees.
Roberto:	On-site day care? What about other people who need day care? Herndon's day care center has a long waiting list.

page 96 **Hazardous Waste:**
Handle with Rubber Gloves
Part A.

Narrator:	Listen to the conversation between the talk-show host Ron Fisher, his guest Sheryl, and Stan Wolanski.
Host:	Good afternoon. This is Ron Fisher with "Talk of the Town," WRVA, Herndon. Today's call-in topic is "Hazardous Waste in Herndon: Handle It with Rubber Gloves." Our first guest is Dr. Sheryl Hammet, State Manager of Hazardous Waste Collection. Good afternoon, Sheryl.
Sheryl:	Hello, Ron.

Host:	Sheryl will be answering questions about how you can dispose of hazardous household waste. Our first caller is Stan. Go ahead, Stan.
Stan:	Hello, Ron. I just got a notice about a hazardous-waste collection day for households next month. I have a lot of hazardous materials from around the house and garden that I'd like to bring in.
Sheryl:	What sort of things?
Stan:	Oh, stuff like old brushes, paint thinner, floor cleaners, weed killer. I'm concerned about driving them over there, though. How can I get them to the collection site safely?
Sheryl:	That's a good question, Stan. Before you put hazardous waste products in a car, you should tighten caps and lids. You should pack the items upright in sturdy boxes. Pad the boxes with paper. Never mix chemicals or hazardous waste products, and you should never smoke while handling hazardous waste.
Stan:	Thanks.

Part B.

Narrator:	Listen to the conversation between Ron Fisher, Yolette, and Richard Rivera.
Host:	Good afternoon. I'm Ron Fisher, back with today's call-in show on "Hazardous Waste in Herndon: Handle It with Rubber Gloves." My next guest is Richard Rivera, Director of Chemical Controls with MediKit Technical International. Richard will answer specific questions about how MediKit will dispose of *its* hazardous waste if it gets permission to build its new plant. Yolette is on the line.
Yolette:	Thank you, Ron. I'm interested in finding out more about what MediKit plans to do with the hazardous chemicals left over from the production of sterile blood-test kits.
Richard:	Thanks for giving me the opportunity to tell people about their new neighbor, Yolette. Since MediKit started producing sterile kits in 1949, we've been able to reduce the amount of toxic chemicals we use by 85 percent. That

means most of the chemicals we use are nontoxic and nonpolluting to start with.

Yolette: I'm glad to hear that. What about the 15 percent that *is* toxic?

Richard: Of that 15 percent, we are able to reuse or recycle more than half. That last bit, about 5 percent of all MediKit's chemicals, is taken to an EPA-registered incineration system in the Far West where high-temperature incineration is permitted.

Yolette: So you're saying that *no* toxic chemicals will be disposed of locally?

Richard: I feel confident in assuring you that no chemicals, toxic or not, will be dumped into local rivers or emitted into the air. Don't forget, *we'll* be living here, too.

Host: But Richard, doesn't high-temperature incineration affect the ozone layer? And doesn't incineration, even far away, create pollution and acid rain?

Richard: We understand that our disposal is not perfect, but our studies have shown that high-temperature inciner-ation is *less* likely to pollute the envi-ronment than landfill disposal. We try to live by the motto "Reduce, Reuse, and Recycle" when it comes to our use of chemicals. And each year, our research and development branch is finding new ways to reduce the use of toxic chemicals.

Host: We have another caller on the line. Thank you for . . .

UNIT 9
Real Costs of a Car

page 103 Bad News about Repairs

Narrator: Listen to the conversation between Marco, Adela, and the car mechanic.

Mechanic: Well, you see, it's this way. You have major brake problems. Your rotors are gone because the front disc brake pads on both sides are worn out. You should have heard squealing from time to time.

Marco: I guess I did, but each time, the squealing stopped, so I thought everything was OK.

Mechanic: Nope. You should have checked it out. That's why the brakes gave out on you. Luckily, the body damage isn't so bad. Only one fender's involved, and we can replace it easily. Matching the paint won't be hard, either.

Marco: How much is all this going to cost?

Mechanic: You're looking at something like $100, maybe $150, for the brakes. Parts will be another $175, maybe more. Body work will be about $180 for labor, plus another $125 for parts, and painting it should run another $68.

Adela: Hmmm. Is there anything else wrong with the car?

Mechanic: Well, you should get an oil change.

Adela: We can do that ourselves.

Marco: Do you think so?

Adela: Sure we can. But as for all the rest of the work . . . Will your insurance cover the repairs?

Marco: I don't know. I think I have to pay the deductible first, $200 or $300 or so.

page 104 The Bill

Narrator: Listen to the conversation between Marco, Adela, and the car mechanic.

Marco: Aunt Adela, I think there are some mistakes on this bill.

Adela: Hmmm. Let me see it. You're right. There *are* a couple of errors. Let's talk to the mechanic. . . . Excuse me, but could we review the bill with you be-fore we take the car?

Mechanic: Sure, are there any problems?

Marco: I think there are some extra items. For example, we told you that we would do our own oil change.

Mechanic: Oh, that's right, you did say that. I won't charge you for it. That's our mistake.

Adela: Also, what's the $10 cleaning charge?

Mechanic: Oh, that's our standard fee for cleaning up at the site of an accident.

Adela: Hmmm. Nothing was cleaned there that I remember.

Mechanic: OK, you're probably right. No glass was broken in the accident. I'll deduct that from your bill, too.

Marco:	And what about the $2 toll charge?
Mechanic:	We had to go over the Water Street bridge. And charges are round-trip.
Marco:	Oh, I see. OK, can you fix the total now?

**page 110 Getting a Car Loan
Conversation 1.**

Narrator:	Listen to the conversation between Stan and Ms. Bates.
Voice:	Good afternoon. This is Herndon Savings Bank. How can I direct your call?
Stan:	I'd like to find out about car loans.
Voice:	I'll connect you with Ms. Bates in the loan department. Hold the line, please.
Ms. Bates:	Alice Bates. May I help you?
Stan:	I want to find out what your car loan rates are.
Ms. Bates:	Are you interested in a new or used car?
Stan:	A used van, actually.
Ms. Bates:	A loan for a used van is 11.5 percent or 10.5 percent if you have an account with us. And you must put down at least 20 percent.
Stan:	Can I get the lower rate if I open an account now?
Ms. Bates:	Oh, yes. As long as you maintain a minimum balance of $400, we'll deduct your car payments automatically and record your payments on your monthly statement.
Stan:	Hmmm. That *would* be convenient. How long is the loan?
Ms. Bates:	We offer 12-, 24-, or 48-month car loans.
Stan:	Can you tell me what the monthly payments for a $4,000 loan would be for 48 months at 10.5 percent?
Ms. Bates:	I'll figure that for you. . . . Your payments would be $118.33 a month for 48 months.
Stan:	Is there a penalty for paying off the balance early?
Ms. Bates:	No, sir. You can pay off the loan at any time.

Conversation 2.

Narrator:	This conversation is introduced by a computerized phone message.
Operator:	Hello! You have reached the Metropolitan Credit Union computerized network. If you know your party's extension, and are calling from a touch-tone phone, dial it now. If you need mortgage information, press 1 now. If you need credit card information, press 2 now. If you need auto loan rates, press 3 now. If you need to speak to an operator, please stay on the line.
Voice:	Hello! You have reached the Metropolitan Credit Union's new- and used-auto rate line. For information about a new car, press 1 now. For information about used cars, press 2 now. Metropolitan used-car loan rates are as follows: For a 24-month loan, the rate is 8.9 percent; for a 48-month loan, the rate is 10.25 percent; for a 60-month loan, the rate is 10.45 percent. All rates have a flexible down payment. If you wish to speak to a loan officer, please press 1 now.
Mr. Wright:	Hello, this is Bill Wright. What can I do for you today?
Stan:	Can you tell me what the monthly payments for a $4,000 car loan would be for 48 months?
Mr. Wright:	One second, please. Let's see . . . That's 10.25 percent, so you would have 48 monthly payments of $117.50.
Stan:	Is there a penalty for paying off the balance?
Mr. Wright:	No, sir. You can pay off the loan at any time.

Conversation 3.

Narrator:	Listen to the conversation between Stan and Mr. Irwin.
Voice:	Simmons Trust. Good morning.
Stan:	Hello. Can you please connect me to the auto loan department?
Voice:	I'll connect you to Mr. Irwin.
Mr. Irwin:	Good morning. Mr. Irwin, Personal Loans.
Stan:	Good morning. I'm looking for a used car loan of $4,000. Could you please tell me what your present rates are?

Mr. Irwin:	Of course. Let me check. We offer a four-year loan at 11.5 percent with a 10 percent down payment. Monthly payments on $4,000 would be $121.67.
Stan:	Hmmm. Eleven and a half percent is pretty high. I have an account with your bank. Does that make any difference?
Mr. Irwin:	No, I'm afraid all auto loans are approved at the same rate.
Stan:	I think I'll shop around a bit.

UNIT 10
Under the Law

page 116 What Did You See?

Narrator:	Listen to the conversation between Quang, Diep, and the police officer.
Officer:	OK, so he got your wallet and your watch. Did the watch have any identifiable marks on it?
Quang:	Yes, it was engraved in Vietnamese on the back.
Officer:	OK. Now, try to tell me whatever you can about the mugger. What did he look like? Try to be specific. How tall was he? Was he fat or thin? What color were his skin, hair, and eyes?
Quang:	I couldn't tell his size or coloring, because he was behind me the whole time. But he felt like a weight lifter when he shoved me.
Diep:	He gave Quang a nasty cut. The medic used five stitches to close it up.
Officer:	That's awful! But, you know, Ms. Tran, your brother was lucky nothing more serious happened.
Quang:	I know, I know.
Officer:	What did the mugger say?
Quang:	I don't remember exactly. But I do remember he had a raspy voice, and I smelled cigarettes.
Officer:	That's a good clue. What was he wearing?
Quang:	He was behind me the whole time, so I didn't get a look at him. But when he ran off, I could hear the sound of heels. Like he was wearing cowboy boots.
Officer:	You'd think a mugger would wear sneakers, wouldn't you? Well, muggers aren't too smart, or they'd be in another line of work. You've been very observant, Mr. Tran.
Quang:	I was just so tired and hungry when I got off the bus, I wasn't paying attention. I might have avoided the whole incident.
Officer:	Sometimes you just can't avoid a mugging. At least you didn't panic. You never know what a mugger might do.
Diep:	Please! I don't even want to think about it! At least Quang knows that no amount of money is worth more than his life.

page 119 How Can I Be Sure?

Narrator:	Listen to the conversation between Joan and the Equal Employment Opportunity Commission (EEOC) officer, Ms. Hays.
Ms. Hays:	Sexual harassment on the job is illegal.
Joan:	Well, I'm not sure if what happened to me really qualifies.
Ms. Hays:	Let me explain what we mean by sexual harassment.
Joan:	That would help.
Ms. Hays:	Sexual harassment is any sexual attention that you don't want or don't agree to.
Joan:	How serious does it have to be?
Ms. Hays:	We consider all sexual harassment serious, including unwanted stares, sexual jokes, or pressure for dates or sex.
Joan:	Well, Dr. Landers did ask me out a couple of times. But mostly he puts his arm around my waist or on my shoulder, or he stands so close that I feel like I'm going to suffocate.
Ms. Hays:	Any unwanted touching, from hand-holding, hugging, or pinching, all the way to assault or rape, is illegal.
Joan:	Well, I'm worried because he's my supervisor. He has control over my job. I'm afraid that he might try to get me fired from the hospital.
Ms. Hays:	That's also illegal for him to do.
Joan:	I've just been feeling so tense about the whole thing. I'm having a hard time concentrating at work, and I'm afraid my work is suffering.

Ms. Hays: Sexual harassment is very hard on people. It often creates stress and fear in victims, who then want to quit their jobs. It lowers productivity, too.

Joan: Some of my friends say I should feel complimented by the attention, but I just feel cheap. I just feel very alone and at the end of my rope.

Ms. Hays: There's nothing complimentary about sexual harassment. You shouldn't feel alone, either. A majority of women in the workplace say they've been sexually harassed at one time or another.

Joan: All right then. I do think I have a legitimate complaint. Yes, I *am* going to file.

page 121 Know Your Rights

Narrator: Listen to the conversation between Marty and the police officer.

Officer: Are you Martin Evans?

Marty: Yeah. What's this all about?

Officer: I have a warrant for your arrest, Mr. Evans.

Marty: What? There must be some mistake.

Officer: Sara Evans is charging you with assault and battery.

Marty: She's what? You're kidding! She had an accident. She fell. I didn't . . .

Officer: Excuse me, Mr. Evans, but I want to read you your rights under the Miranda ruling.

Marty: This can't be happening.

Officer: I must warn you that you have the right to remain silent. Anything you say can be used against you in a court of law. You also have the right to hire a lawyer to defend you. If you can't afford a lawyer, the court will appoint one to represent you for free.

Marty: Oh, no.

UNIT 11
Can I Buy a House?

page 129 Talking to a Real Estate Agent

Narrator: Listen to the conversation between the real estate agent, Marsha, and Yolette and Al.

Marsha: It helps to know what you need and what you want in a home. And what your price range is.

Yolette: We can afford a house in the low- to mid-$80,000 range.

Marsha: OK. Now, would you consider a house that needs work, or do you prefer one that's in move-in condition?

Yolette: I'd really prefer a house that is in good condition to begin with.

Marsha: Are you willing to commute?

Al: Hmmm. I guess I'd consider a house a little further out, like in Manassas, but I'd really rather stay in Herndon. We both work here and don't want to waste lots of time traveling.

Marsha: OK. Now, how big a house do you need?

Al: Well, there's just the two of us now, but Yolette's parents may come to live with us some day. So we need two or three bedrooms, or at least room to expand.

Yolette: And I'd like a formal dining room. We entertain a lot, so we need a dining room.

Al: Yes, and we'd like a garage with a workshop for my tools and projects, or a finished basement.

Yolette: I'd like a big, sunny kitchen, too, so I can grow my own herbs and spices. And a nice, sunny yard, so I can grow flowers and vegetables in the summer.

Marsha: Good. You know what you want. Is there anything else? Do you like two-story houses or everything on one level?

Al: I think we'd prefer two stories, but we'd seriously think about a one-story house if the price was right.

Marsha: OK. I think I've got a good idea of what you're looking for. Let me show you some of the homes that are on the market now.

page 132 Thinking about a Move

Narrator: Listen to the conversation between Roberto, Stan, and Diep.

Roberto: Where's Yolette today?

Stan: It's the Jamisons' moving day. Did you forget?

Roberto: Oh, that's right! I'm so happy for them. I'm only sorry they moved to Manassas. I liked having them nearby.

Diep: Oh, it's not that far. There's a bus that goes right near their house, you know.

Roberto: Yes, of course, you're right. And it's a perfect house for them.

Stan: I hope I have half their luck. I've been looking for an apartment for months, but so far nothing's worked out. The really nice places are always just beyond my budget.

Diep: I'd like to find a bigger place, too. My brother Quang is living with us now, so the children have to double up with me. It's very tight, but I don't think I can afford a bigger place.

Roberto: Maybe you can get a housing grant, Diep.

Diep: What's that, Roberto?

Roberto: The county gives housing grants to working families that make below certain income limits.

Stan: Maybe I can get one, too?

Roberto: I really don't know, Stan. But maybe Diep could qualify because she has two children.

Diep: That just may be the answer. Thanks for the suggestion, Roberto. Soon we may all be looking in the real estate section.

Roberto: Well, I'm pretty settled where I am, but, you know, Marco has been talking about getting his own place now that he's working full-time. Eddy and Cruz never leave him alone. Have you ever thought of getting an apartment with a roommate, Stan?

Stan: Hmmm. You know, that's not a bad idea. Let me think it over and talk to Marco over the weekend.

page 136 Finding a Place
Ad 1.

Narrator: Listen to the conversation between Stan and a landlord.

Landlord: Oh yes, our four-room apartment is lovely. There are great views from the terrace and . . .

Stan: Excuse me, does four rooms mean it's a one- or two-bedroom apartment?

Landlord: This is a one-bedroom. There's a living room, an eat-in kitchen, a dining area, and a bedroom.

Stan: Do you have any two-bedrooms available?

Landlord: I'm afraid not.

Ad 2.

Narrator: Listen to the conversation between Marco and a landlord.

Landlord: It's a great apartment for two roommates. Very modern, with clean, wall-to-wall carpeting and a washer and dryer.

Marco: How much is the rent?

Landlord: With a two-year lease, the rent is $790.

Marco: Hmmm. Does it include all utilities?

Landlord: It includes heat and hot water, and the parking space, of course, but not electricity.

Marco: What if we don't want a two-year lease?

Landlord: I'll have to get back to you on that. Sometimes these things are negotiable.

Marco: OK, let me know. Here's my number. . . .

Ad 3.

Narrator: Listen to the conversation between Stan and a building manager.

Manager: Two young men? Hmmm. I'm not sure . . .

Stan: My friend has a full-time job, and I work and go to school part-time.

Manager: Well, I need a two-month security deposit.

Stan:	You mean two months' rent in advance?
Manager:	Yes. And an extra $250 deposit against damages if you take the apartment furnished.
Stan:	Furnished, hmmm. Does that include dishes or linens?
Manager:	No, only furniture. Very good stuff, too.
Stan:	I see. Well, I'll talk to my friend and get back to you.

Ad 4.

Narrator:	Listen to the conversation between Marco and a building manager.
Marco:	We need a two-bedroom apartment.
Manager:	Two-bedrooms start at $650, including utilities.
Marco:	I see. Does that include parking?
Manager:	Yes. That includes one parking space. The apartment itself is fully furnished in beautiful modern decor. And you can't beat the convenience of Vienna.
Marco:	What if we wanted an unfurnished apartment?
Manager:	We can do that, but we charge the same rent.
Marco:	Do you have a two-bedroom available now?
Manager:	We have one available at $700.
Marco:	I thought you said it was $650.
Manager:	They *start* at $650. Apartments on higher floors are more expensive. The only one available now is 7D, which is $700.
Stan:	I see. Well, it sounds great, but I'll have to talk to my friend about the price.
Manager:	Well, don't take too long. This apartment will be snapped up in no time.

Ad 5.

Narrator:	Listen to the conversation between Marco and a landlord.
Landlord:	That apartment used to be the superintendent's, but it's vacant now.
Marco:	It seems a bit expensive for a basement apartment. Does it include parking?
Landlord:	No. Parking's available, but it's extra.
Marco:	What if we helped take care of the building?
Landlord:	Hmmm. We could throw in the parking space then.
Marco:	What about reducing the rent?
Landlord:	I could take off, say, $50 a month, if you'd be available to answer emergency calls at night and put out the trash on Thursdays.
Marco:	What about free parking and reducing the rent to $500?
Landlord:	Hmmm. I'll have to meet you and your friend first, of course. Let me think about it.

Index of Functions

NOTE: The structures in boldface type are introduced in Level 3.

	Unit(s)
asking for/giving advice	10, 11
asking for/giving information	2, 3, 5
clarifying/verifying	prelim., 1, 5
comparing/contrasting	5, 11
complaining	3
correcting	3
dealing with numbers (budgets, costs)	3, 9, 11
describing (objects, events, problems, processes)	3, 4, 5, 7, 8, 9
expressing agreement/disagreement	8
expressing uncertainty/confusion	7
expressing embarrassment	7
expressing emotions	7, 10
expressing preferences	5, 11
expressing needs	2
expressing opinions	8
expressing surprise	10
giving/accepting apologies	7
giving/following oral and written directions	4, 5, 8
giving/getting personal information	prelim.
giving reasons/explanations	2, 9
hypothesizing	11
introducing oneself/others	prelim.
making small talk	1
persuading	8
predicting	7
reporting (events, findings)	2, 4, 5, 7, 10
requesting assistance	1
speaking emphatically	3
stating a position	8
turn taking	1

Index of Structures

NOTE: The structures in boldface type are introduced in Level 3. Simpler structures (simple present and past tenses, *yes/no* questions, articles, etc.) are generally not indexed.

	Unit(s)
adjectives: comparative, superlative	4, 5, 11
adjectives: descriptive	4, 5, 11
adverbs of frequency	3
ask + infinitive	11
conditionals: *If / then* statements	1, 2, 3, 7, 12
dependent clauses	6, 8, 9
future tense	1
imperatives	1, 4
intensifiers: *too, very*	10
modals: *can / can't*	2, 3, 12
modals: *could, should, would*	1, 3, 5, 8, 9, 12
modals: *may, must*	1, 4, 8, 12
passive voice	4, 10, 12
past participles	12
past tense	prelim., 3
past continuous tense	9
prepositional phrases	5
prepositions of place	prelim., 2, 5, 10
prepositions of time	prelim., 10
present participles	7, 12
present perfect continuous tense	12
present perfect tense	8, 10, 12
present tense	prelim.
pronouns: reflexive	4
questions: *How + far/long/often/many/much*	5, 6
questions: *Wh-*	prelim., 2, 5, 8, 9, 10, 12
questions: *What about . . . ? What if . . . ?*	7, 11
questions: *yes / no*	10
reported speech	2, 8
verbs: past tense in time clauses	6
verbs: two-word	6
when clauses	9, 10
while clauses	5, 9